D1555587

FOOD PRODUCT DEVELOPMENT

From Concept to the Marketplace

FOOD PRODUCT DEVELOPMENT

From Concept to the Marketplace

Edited by
Ernst Graf and Israel Sam Saguy

An **avi** Book
Published by Van Nostrand Reinhold
New York

An AVI Book
(AVI is an imprint of Van Nostrand Reinhold)

Copyright © 1991 by Van Nostrand Reinhold

Library of Congress Catalog Card Number 90-43406
ISBN 0-442-00185-1

Manufactured in the United States of America

Published by Van Nostrand Reinhold
115 Fifth Avenue
New York, New York 10003

Chapman and Hall
2-6 Boundary Row
London, SE1 8HN

Thomas Nelson Australia
102 Dodds Street
South Melbourne 3205
Victoria, Australia

Nelson Canada
1120 Birchmount Road
Scarborough, Ontario M1K 5G4, Canada

16 15 14 13 12 11 10 9 8 7 6 5 4 3 2 1

Library of Congress Cataloging-in-Publication Data

Food product development: from concept to the marketplace / [edited]
    by Ernst Graf and Israel Sam Saguy.
        p. cm.
        "An AVI book."
        Includes bibliographical references and index.
        ISBN 0-442-00185-1
        1. Food industry and trade—Management. 2. Food—
Marketing.
        3. New products. I. Graf, Ernst, 1953-   . II. Saguy, Israel,
1946-   .
        HD9000.5.F5964 1990
        664'.0068'5—dc20
                                                                90-43406
                                                                  CIP

Contributors

Abraham, David B.
Associate
A. T. Kearney, Inc.
222 South Riverside Plaza
Chicago, Illinois 60606

Amernick, Burton A.
Partner—Pollock, Vande Sande &
 Priddy
Patent and Trademark Attorneys
1990 M Street, Northwest
Suite 800
Washington, D.C. 20036

Bauman, Howard, Ph.D.
Food Industry Consultant
1433 Utica Avenue South Suite 70-4
St. Louis Park, Minnesota 55416

Best, Daniel
Senior Editor/Technology Analyst
Prepared Foods
8750 W. Bryn Mawr Avenue
Chicago, Illinois 60631

Clark, J. Peter, Ph.D.
President
Epstein Process Engineering, Inc.
600 West Fulton Street
Chicago, Illinois 60606

Ferguson, Kristin S.
Vice President of Marketing
Foodservice Division
Tyson Foods, Inc.
P.O. Box 2020
Springdale, Arizona 72765-2020

Godfrey, Patricia D., R.D.
Nutritionist
The Pillsbury Company
330 University Avenue S.E.
Minneapolis, Minnesota 55414

Goldberg, Ray A., Ph.D.
Moffett Professor of Agriculture and
 Business
Harvard Graduate School of Business
 Administration
Boston, Massachusetts 02163

Graf, Ernst, Ph.D.
Research Scientist
The Pillsbury Company
330 University Avenue S.E.
Minneapolis, Minnesota 55414

Harrington, Elizabeth
Vice President
A.T. Kearney, Inc.
222 South Riverside Plaza
Chicago, Illinois 60606

Hofmeister, Kurt R.
Director of Product Development
American Supplier Institute, Inc.
Six Parklane Boulevard, Suite 411
Dearborn, Michigan 48126

Jewson, Dwight, Ph.D.
CEO and President
Strategic Frameworking, Inc.
West Stockbridge, Massachusetts
 01266

Joglekar, Anand M., Ph.D.
Int'l Qual-Tech, Ltd.
2820 Fountain Lane North
Minneapolis, Minnesota 55447

Karel, Marcus, Ph.D.
State of New Jersey Professor of
  Food Science
Rutgers University
New Brunswick, New Jersey 08903-
  0231
Professor Emeritus of Chemical and
  Food Engineering
M.I.T.
Cambridge, Massachusetts 02139

Labuza, Theodore P., Ph.D.
Professor of Food Science and
  Technology
Department of Food Science and
  Nutrition
University of Minnesota
St. Paul, Minnesota 55108

Langguth, Susanne
Bund für Lebensmittelrecht und
  Lebensmittelkunde e.V.
Godesberger Allee 157
Bonn, Federal Republic of Germany

Leslie, Robert B., Ph.D.
Unilever Research
Colworth Laboratory
Sharnbrook
Bedford MK44 1LQ, England

May, Alfred T.
Int'l Qual-Tech, Ltd.
2820 Fountain Lane North
Minneapolis, Minnesota 55447

Morehouse, Jim
Vice President
A.T. Kearney, Inc.
222 South Riverside Plaza
Chicago, Illinois 60606

Moskowitz, Howard R., Ph.D.
Moskowitz/Jacobs Inc.
14 Madison Avenue
Valhalla, New York 10595

Paulus, Klaus, Ph.D.
NATEC Institut für naturwissen-
  schaftlichtechnische Dienste GmbH
Behringstrasse 154
2000 Hamburg 50
West Germany

Pellegrino, Robert
V.P. and General Manager
Fries & Fries
1199 Edison Drive
Cincinnati, Ohio 45216

Rossen, Jack L., Ph.D.
Center for Advanced Food
  Technology
Rutgers University, Cook College
P.O. Box 231
New Brunswick, New Jersey 08903

Russell, Margie
Technical Editor
Food Engineering
Chilton Way
Radnor, Pennsylvania 19089

Saguy, Israel Sam, Ph.D.
Associate Professor
Faculty of Agriculture
Department of Food Science and
   Technology
The Hebrew University
P.O. Box 12
Rehovot 76100 Israel

Schmidl, Mary K., Ph.D.
Director of Research
Sandoz Nutrition Corporation
Clinical Products Division
5320 West 23rd Street
Minneapolis, Minnesota 55112

Solberg, Myron, Ph.D.
Center for Advanced Food
   Technology
Rutgers University, Cook College
P.O. Box 231
New Brunswick, New Jersey 08903

Senior chapter authors are printed in bold

Contents

Preface

Numerous textbooks treat various aspects of food chemistry and engineering, yet little information is available on the process of industrial food research and development. Currently, no textbooks of academic courses cover the broad area of product development. This void keeps even the most qualified person from reaching an informed decision about a career in this field.

This book is intended to introduce the food industry novice to the diverse facets of the profession and to serve as a useful monograph for the expert by portraying the wide scope of R&D in an industry that is market-driven and highly vulnerable to demographic fluctuations. Food industry experts from diverse disciplines provide a broad overview of the numerous aspects of successful food research and development, from consumer trend analysis to commercialization. The book also highlights some of the activities and skill requirements that are unique to an industrial food research career.

We wish to express our sincere gratitude to all of the book's contributors, who have made its publication possible.

Ernst Graf and Israel Sam Saguy

FOOD PRODUCT DEVELOPMENT

From Concept to the Marketplace

Chapter 1

Designing New Products from a Market Perspective

Daniel Best

INTRODUCTION

The Second Industrial Revolution will change the process of new product development as profoundly as it has changed the modern manufacturing environment. Besieged by threats of foreign competition, financial restructurings, a revolution in manufacturing, logistics, and other project management techniques attuned to the demands of a changing work force, American industry underwent a period of acute self-examination during the late 1980s. With it came an awareness that corporate cultures developed in the post–World War II period were becoming obsolete, and that new structures by which new products could be designed, manufactured, and marketed must be developed. The 1990s will be marked by the implementation of new cultures.

In 1988, under contract to the Society of Manufacturing Engineers, A. T. Kearney Inc. surveyed over 7,500 top business executives and professionals for their insights into the manufacturing needs of industry as it prepares for the twenty-first century (Koska and Romano 1988). What emerged was a profile of engineering and manufacturing professionals distinguished not for their abilities as specialists, but rather for their ability to integrate and manage a wide spectrum of informational resources from the perspective of the overall objectives of the corporation. Key concepts expressed in the survey included ''matrix management'' and ''teamwork.''

Although the focus of the A. T. Kearney study was manufacturing, the conclusions of the survey are equally applicable to research and development. The descriptors affixed to A. T. Kearney's manufacturing engineer of the future apply equally to the product development scientist or engineer.

R&D management has changed in part as researchers have developed a better understanding of the process of innovation. Traditionally, ''innovation'' was managed as a sequential process, in which an idea originated by research or marketing provided the spark for prototype development, which, subsequently, was consumer-tested by marketing research, pilot-plant-tested by engineers, packaged by packaging scientists, marketed by the marketing department, and

The author expresses his profound gratitude to Ms. Lisa Nelson for the editorial support given to him during the preparation of this chapter.

maufactured by manufacturing engineers to criteria established by the quality control department.

Studies undertaken by a University of Minnesota Innovation Research Program suggested that this sequential approach did not provide an effective model for innovation (Schroeder et al. 1968, 521). Rather, said the authors of the Minnesota program review, innovation is the result of a "complicated multiple progression process of divergent, parallel, and convergent streams of activities." In sum, the authors viewed innovation and product development as cooperative, multidisciplinary processes that pool the talents and resources of diverse individuals and institutions. The challenge to manage that process remains.

During the 1980s, many food companies experimented with product development "teams" to manage the progression of a product or technology through its various stages of commercialization. All too often, however, these teams consisted of various specialists brought together under the auspices of a marketing manager who allocated job responsibilities according to specialization.

As the 1990s progress, these teams will likely consolidate into true cooperative units. R&D will be perceived less as an island of innovation and more as an equal partner in the new product management process extending from concept to market introduction and market share maintenance. To fit this scenario, product and technology development scientists and engineers will have to develop a better appreciation for the myriad decision-making variables that contribute to successful innovation. Key words for product development in the 1990s will be "quality management, integration, design, and organizational synergy." Corporations will compete on the basis of the quality of their products and the efficiency by which they manufacture, introduce, distribute, and market them. New product development will continue to provide the lifeblood of the food industry.

What does this mean for product developers? For one, the development teams of the 1990s will require scientists and engineers fully capable of communicating technical issues to nontechnical members of the team. Conversely, it will also demand that product developers be familiar with the marketing, financial, logistical, and manufacturing frameworks that gird their corporation's objectives. Finally, and more to the point of this chapter, product developers will have to know how to undertake projects from the customer's (i.e., the marketplace's) perspective.

DESIGNING PRODUCTS FOR A NEW ERA

Many companies still adhere to scattershot product development strategies (e.g., "It looks and tastes good, so let's consumer-test it and see if it flies"), but rising costs of new product introductions will discourage this approach. A decreased emphasis on extended consumer-testing puts the onus for success on product design strategies that take proactive views of the marketplace, corporate capabilities, and the strengths and flaws of specific product concepts. New product design demands a carefully choreographed "total concept" approach that goes beyond simply designing products that survive successive consumer-test hurdles.

Food companies in the 1990s will be less willing to fund marketing groups that switch new product objectives on their R&D partners in midstream, or product development scientists who focus upon expensive technological solutions to challenges when none is warranted by the marketplace.

Product design is a proactive process. Products should be fully conceptualized before actual product development is undertaken. This approach extends beyond identifying key consumer attributes of the product, such as taste, aroma, flavor, texture, appearance, and so on, to include addressing questions about how products should be manufactured, retailed, and marketed and many other issues that fall beyond the pale of purely technical issues.

A proactive approach to product design helps product development teams establish a consensus about project objectives and minimizes the risks of developmental blind alleys or communication gaps between marketing, R&D, manufacturing, finance, and any other project participants. If and when a project concept needs to be altered or redirected, that same consensus facilitates a smooth revision of the project objectives.

A number of project management techniques are applicable to the product design process. They range from PERT charts and fishbone cause-and-effect diagrams, first popularized by Kaoru Ishikawa, to Quality Function Deployment, or QFD, first outlined by Yoji Akao (King 1987). They all offer a systematic process by which the innumerable factors that enter into a design equation are identified, organized, prioritized, and acted upon. No matter which technique is eventually adopted, however, it is important to remember that project management techniques are not objectives in themselves; they represent management tactics, not strategies. The ultimate objective of any product development effort, no matter how it is executed, is to generate products that perform as well as they were designed to do.

NEW PRODUCTS AND CORPORATE HEALTH

The food industry was once America's sleepy commodity sector—safe, but lacking investor appeal. Why, after all, should there be opportunity in an industry that can grow only as fast as the 1% annual growth of the American consumer population? What growth there was could largely be attributed to the marketing wizardry of corporate giants such as Pillsbury, Procter & Gamble, Kellogg, and General Foods, which invested enormous sums in advertising to carve away minuscule market-share increments from well-established competitors.

The last decade provided a major evolution in this view of the industry.

Between 1983 and 1988, for example, the financial performance of food companies counted among Standard & Poor's 500 (S&P 500), a barometer of financial performance, exceeded that of the overall S&P 500 index. Between 1978 and 1988, the food industry generated the second-highest return to investors among the Fortune 500 (Anonymous 1989a). Food company stocks had become hot properties.

The megamerger mania of the era (which saw major consolidations, such R. J. Reynolds's 1985 merger with Nabisco Brands Inc. and Phillip Morris's 1988 purchase of Kraft Inc.) was no doubt a factor in this change, but there was another phenomenon at work: companies discovered the enormous returns that could be generated by adding value to commodity products in the form of convenience, nutrition, variety, economy, and consistent quality. Companies discovered that consumers would pay for value. The consequence has been an unparalleled period of new product development.

Rising disposable incomes, changing consumer lifestyles, an increased emphasis on health and nutrition, and increased exposure of consumers to ethnic foods all combined to put pressure on processors to offer something new. When processors discovered that consumers were willing to pay more for added-value attributes in their food products, it opened a floodgate of new product introductions in the marketplace. Sometimes, the results were nothing less than stunning. Consider the following:

• In 1975, a crisis in the cranberry industry prompted serious thinking about product diversification among executives at Ocean Spray Cranberries Inc., a Lakeville-Middleboro–based growers cooperative. By 1990, Ocean Spray's product portfolio included over 30 fruit juice products, many of them combinations of cranberry with different fruits. The coop successfully pioneered the use of aseptically packaged juice drink and concentrates; expanded into cranberry and cranberry/fruit combination sauces; and developed and promoted a market for cranberry ingredients in the foodservice and processing industries. These investments boosted Ocean Spray's sales from a plateau of $110 million in 1974 to approximately $900 million in 1989 (Anonymous 1989b).

• Poultry was largely a nonbranded commodity until Springdale, Arkansas–based Tyson Foods made a commitment to value addition. Tyson Foods took flight in the 1970s (Pehanich 1987). During this period, Tyson expanded from 9 product cateogories to 24 and introduced several value-added product concepts, including the breaded chicken patty, to the retail food industry. During the 1980s, Tyson pioneered products such as chicken-based frozen entrees, chicken-based "finger foods" ranging from "Flyers® Hot 'n Spicy Chicken Wings" to chicken corn dogs, preroasted and refrigerated whole chickens, and the Originals® line of marinated chicken breasts.

Interestingly, Tyson's product development investments during this period were never budgeted. Captained by Chairman and Chief Executive Officer Don Tyson, son of the company's founder, product developers were given the freedom to spend what was needed to execute product concepts of the quality to which the highest levels of management were formally committed. "By the time we start work on it, Don Tyson has already given it his blessing," one of Tyson's R&D executives said (Best 1987).

Combined with an aggressive acquisition strategy, Tyson's sales more than doubled, from $750 million in 1984 to close to $2.0 billion in 1988. During that period, the annual return to stockholders averaged between 25% and 30%, and Tyson's stock value increased over 22-fold (Anonymous 1988a). Good timing also played a role; consumer health concerns boosted per capita poultry consumption at the expense of beef during this period. Between 1980 and 1989, total annual poultry consumption increased from 43 pounds to 60 pounds per capita (on a boneless basis) while beef consumption declined from 72 pounds to 65 pounds per capita (Putnam 1990). Although increasing consumer demands for low-calorie and low-cholesterol meats contributed to increased poultry consumption, it is equally true that this trend was spurred by the efforts of major poultry processors such as Tyson Foods and Perdue Farms (of Salisbury, Maryland). Poultry product manufacturers were able to effectively leverage chicken's low-fat, low-cholesterol appeal by offering consumers a cornucopia of new, attractive, flavorful, and convenient poultry products.

These examples and others put into perspective the tremendous impact new product and process development has had on the food industry. They also reflect the evolution of the food industry's R&D structures, a process that continues today as companies seek newer, more efficient ways to exploit emerging technologies and marketplace opportunities. Whereas marketing, R&D, and manufacturing were once viewed as independent, sequential functions in the process of new product development, they have emerged in the 1990s as intricately bound, holistic "development teams" where the boundaries between technology and marketing have blurred. Science and technology in the food industry are increasingly defined by the demands, perceptions, and misperceptions of the marketplace.

A Rising Tide of New Products

Between 1984 and 1989, the annual number of new food product introductions increased 63%, from 5,617 to over 9,200, with approximately 17% of those products contributed by 1988's top 20 food companies (Anonymous 1990a; Anonymous 1989c). From 1988 to 1989 alone, the number of introductions jumped 12%.

Although the rewards of success are great, the costs of failure also are high. One rule of thumb predicts that only one product in ten ever make it as far as consumer-testing, and only 10% of those ever makes it to market. In 1989, it was estimated (Friedman 1989) that, ideally, it cost $54 million to introduce a new product into national distribution. For soft drinks, the cost could run as high as $100 million. This risk has been compounded by a recent trend among major corporations to forgo much of the traditional two-year battery of consumer tests in order to beat their competitors to the marketplace. The incentives for this appoach are illustrated by Procter & Gamble's 1983 introduction of dual-textured cookies. Carefully market-tested in Kansas City, this line of cookies had the wind knocked out of its 1984 national introduction by virtually simultaneous introductions of similar products by Keebler, Nabisco Brands, and Frito-Lay. All three competitors had foregone extensive market-testing in order to beat Procter & Gamble into the marketplace (Freeman 1987; Anonymous 1984).

The shifting balance of costs and benefits in new product development is forcing many traditionally consumer-test-driven food companies to reassess how they evaluate and react to new product opportunities.

The Battleground: What's At Stake?

Being able to react quickly to change, to recognize and optimally address consumer needs, and to manage technology effectively is the hallmark of companies that have successfully met their financial objectives. To a large degree, their financial success has rested upon the ability to elaborately choreograph their marketing, technology, and product development. No one of these pillars stands alone.

Barring exports, food consumption can grow only as fast as the population in absolute tonnage. Between 1988 and 1989, the U.S. population grew by an estimated 1%. By the year 2000, the rate will have slowed to 0.5% annual growth, according to the U.S. Bureau of Census. Furthermore, American consumers spend an estimated 11% of their disposable income on food, which, in constant dollars, translated into an average of only 2% growth between 1984 and 1987 (Anonymous 1989d).

The sheer volume of expenditures makes food processing (including foodservice) the largest manufacturing industry in the United States with estimated personal consumption expenditures of $339 billion for foods and beverages consumed at home and $165 billion for those consumed out of the home. (Hodgen, Janis, and Kenney 1988). Large as this number is, however, it does not include total industrial resources committed to food manufacturing.

U.S. Department of Commerce estimates overlook the tremendous impact of other food industry segments. A significant trend during the 1980s was the increasing number of R&D resources committed by food ingredient, packaging, and equipment manufacturers to food product and process development (Best 1988). Many of the decade's greatest advances in food technology came from starch, enzyme, food stabilizer, flavor, and emulsifier manufacturers that are classified as chemical industries. Susceptor materials, polyethylene tere-phthalate (PET) materials, and modified atmosphere and vacuum packaging developments from the chemical and packaging industries opened new horizons in product development.

One way to measure the value-addition provided by food processing technology is by measuring the value added to raw commodities as a consequence of food processing. This, in turn, provides a measure of the food processing industry's contribution to the gross national product

Professor John Connor, an extension economist specializing in food industry issues at Purdue University, calculated that in 1985 food manufacturing contributed $104 billion to the U.S. gross national product. This number mushrooms when the manufacturing contributions of peripheral industries (such as the food chemicals, packaging materials, and equipment industries) are included. In 1982, for example, Connor calculated that food processing made a $487 billion contribution to the U.S. gross national product, representing 16% of all economic activity (Connor 1989).

According to the *1989 U.S. Industrial Outlook* (Anonymous 1989e), in 1988 the meat industry represented the food industry's largest maufacturing sector, with $75 billion in shipments. It was followed by the dairy industry ($44 billion), then preserved fruits and vegetables ($41 billion). The numbers can be misleading, however, because the meat industry to date has been impeded by razor-thin commodity margins in the 5% to 10% range, while the relatively tiny $7.4 billion breakfast cereals industry commands manufacturers' profit margins approaching 50% (Connor 1989).

How Important Is R&D?

According to *Prepared Foods* magazine's 1990 annual R&D survey of 405 companies (Best 1990a), independent food processors invest about 3.7% of sales in R&D, whereas subsidiaries of larger companies invest an average of 2.3% of sales in R&D. These statistics vary considerably by company business category and size, however. The heaviest R&D investments were made by companies with at least 50% of their sales derived from high-margin prepared foods and specialty food products (average 4.7% of sales), whereas the lowest investors in R&D as a percent of sales were the confectionery (0.8%) and beverage (1.3%) industries.

By size category, small start-up companies (those with less than $1.0 million in sales) led the industry in R&D investments with an R&D commitment of 19.3% of sales—underscoring the important contributions they make to innovation in the food industry.

On an industry-wide basis, about 60% of food processors' R&D budgets is devoted to product and process development. These statistics reflect the critical role that new product and process development plays to ensure both the short- and long-term health of food processing companies.

- In the short term, new products generate consumer interest in new product categories and allow companies to capitalize quickly upon changing consumer trends. When the "Great Oat Rush" of 1988 and 1989 hit, fueled by a deluge of reports linking oat bran consumption to cholesterol reduction, companies quickly responded with an avalanche of oat-bran-containing products ranging from oat bran bakery products to pasta and even beverages. According to *Gorman's New Product News*, at least 44 new oat-bran-containing products were introduced in 1988, a number that jumped to 218 in 1989.

- Research and development investments lend companies flexibility in the form of a talent base and infrastructure that can be brought into play in times of crisis. For example, when self-styled consumer crusader Phillip Sokolof launched his October 1988 newspaper advertising campaign accusing food processors of "poisoning America" with highly saturated tropical oils in their products, food companies such as Quaker, Kellogg, Pillsbury, Keebler, and Sunshine Biscuits were able to introduce products reformulated without tropical oils within weeks of the Sokoloff campaign.

- R&D erects barriers to entry into new markets by competitors. The NutraSweet company's hold on U.S. aspartame production patents gave it the latitude needed to carve out a $900 million world marketshare for aspartame by 1990. Long-term investments in fat substitute technologies such as Nutra-Sweet's Simplesse® (microparticulated protein) and Procter & Gamble's Olestra® (sucrose polyester) fall into this category. Procter & Gamble's Pringle's® potato chip technology, which uniformly stacked potato chips in a canister to optimize product quality and handling costs, reflects a 20-year commitment to the marketplace before the product finally became profitable. Today, however, these chips have yet to generate competition.

- Investments in new product deveopment allow companies constantly to probe new marketplace opportunities. The 1976 introduction of surimi-based crab leg analogues by The Berelson Company, based in San Francisco, gave birth to the $300 million-plus U.S. surimi industry (Best 1989a). Rahway, New Jersey–based Tofutti Brands Inc. was founded upon a perceived need to provide kosher, nondairy ice cream analogues that conformed to the kosher requirements of the Northeastern Jewish population. In fact, the company mushroomed when it was also able to capitalize upon the dietary needs of an estimated 30 million lactose-intolerant consumers nationwide (Best 1990b).

- Investments in product and process development combine to squeeze new manufacturing efficiencies out of food production, rewarding companies on the bottom line. The 1980s saw a massive awakening to the manufacturing advantages inherent in the application of total quality management (TQM) and just-in-time (JIT) inventory management principles by major processors and suppliers. Coupled with advances in automation and information management, these developments will force companies to compete on wholly improved manufacturing efficiency levels. During the 1990s, food companies will likely invest heavily in logistics management technologies to integrate and cost-control the flow of basic manufacturing materials all the way to the supermarket shelf.

This latter trend has had and will continue to have a profound impact upon the relationship between food processors and their suppliers. Modern manufacturing demands weave ingredient, equipment, and packaging material suppliers and their food processor clients into interdependent webs of commitments defined by electronic information management capabilities. The time is not far off when every product purchased off a retail shelf or home-delivered will be instantly recorded and incorporated into the inventory management models of both the product's manufacturer and the suppliers of its components. These trends will narrow the field of suppliers given access to major processors and will heighten the technical and R&D service demands made upon them by their clients.

THE FIVE P'S OF MARKETING

The importance of new product development to the food industry reflects the fact that food processing is a consumer-driven industry. As such, it is highly susceptible to the vagaries of changing consumer demographics, tastes, fads, and mythologies. Product development in the food industry, whether at the manufacturer or the industry supplier level, is inextricably bound to the Promethean dictates of the consumer marketplace.

Marketing is much more than just advertising. Marketing refers to the entire process by which product opportunities are identified, designed, manufactured, and promoted to best fit the needs of consumers. Typically, marketing has been said to embody four P's: product, place, price, and promotion. To that list we can add one more: perspective.

Product

Product refers to a product's attributes as defined by the design objectives mentioned earlier. *All* product attributes need to be defined and prioritized in terms of their contribution to the success or failure of the product in the marketplace.

The process of identifying key product attributes may be as basic as defining what consumer needs are to be met by the product, or the inherent advantages that the product offers over its competitors. Or, it may involve quality nuances whose importance is difficult to measure individually in consumer tests, but which collectively have a great impact upon a product's quality perception.

These attributes could include, for example: the tendency of a drip coffee packet or an aseptic juice container to spill or splash when opened; the quality and the longevity of the butter aroma generated by a baked bread stick; the ease of disposal of a packaged dinner container; the crisp sound made by biting into an extruded snack; or the slightly cooked flavor imparted to an aseptic dairy product.

Such attributes should be defined from the perspective of *all* consumers and their lifestyles. For example, a squirt confectionery product marketed to children by a major corporation in the early 1980s failed when it became apparent that their parents did not appreciated the mess made by the product.

Increasingly, products also are designed to accommodate the needs of retailers; the use of time/temperature indicators on packages to help manage inventories, for example, can increase the likelihood that the products will be accepted by retailers.

In sum, product definition involves defining a product in terms of *what* the product is, *who* the consumers are, and *what* they want. Product attributes might include flavor, texture, nutritional qualities, appearance, serving size, package material and color, integrity, size of graphics, and so on; but at some point all product attributes must be prioritized according to the impact they are expected to have upon final product quality and acceptance. It is important for all product attributes at least to be addressed; and if, ultimately, they are not important, they can be eliminated during the process of prioritization. The price of omitting key consumer quality variables is great.

Place

Place refers to time and space. It goes beyond the basic marketing questions of who a product's customers are, where they are located, how they can be reached, or whether a product's market introduction is well timed.

At the most basic level, it is necessary to consider where a product rests on the grocery shelf. Do its colors and graphics stand out amid adjoining products? Is it the most convenient product on the shelf? The most versatile? Does it offer the best price for value? Does it have the simplest, most "natural sounding" ingredient statement with respect to its competitors? These questions all pertain to "market position," or the "unfair advantage" that a product has over its competitors.

A product's position on the supermarket shelf is critical in other ways. A controversial issue during the 1980's involved the retailing of low-acid, pasteurized tofu products in the ambient temperature conditions of the produce section. Their microbiological high-risk status demanded that they be refrigerated, yet it was questionable whether they would draw the same consumer interest if retailed in the refrigerated dairy case. One company, Los Angeles–

based Morinaga Foods, sought to exploit this niche by highlighting the quality and microbiological safety advantages of its aseptic tofu technology over other tofu products.

Other questions of time and place include how often a product is purchased and used by consumers. Is the product to be refrozen, will it be microwaved, or will it sit for hours on a steam table at an airport concession stand? Will the product generate leftovers that will be reheated? These questions all pertain to variables that define how consumers perceive product quality.

Product developers should be their own best critics, evaluating actual and potential competitive products and seeking to establish the "unfair advantage" their product provides over the competition. If these advantages cannot be properly articulated, perhaps the current product development efforts are misdirected. New products may generate superlative consumer test results until they are placed alongside competitive products. Consumers generally make only one decision to purchase a product, after all.

Often overlooked is the *potential* for competition. A product that makes a large and successful market debut will soon attract competitors who are in a position to undercut a new or potential market entry through price cuts, advertising, couponing, two-for-one sales, pressure on retailers, development of flanker products, or any of a number of strategies designed to emasculate a new product entry. One must ask, are the new product's attributes strong enough to withstand the assault?

One of the Campbell Soup Company's stated strategies during the 1980s was to explore the viability of innumerable flanker products in order to preempt *potential* competitors that could threaten its dominant marketshare in soups. The company had been shocked by the rapid success of a Japanese soup manufacturer (Nissin) and a Chinese manufacturer (Sanwa) in taking marketshare away from Campbell with the U.S. introduction of dry, Oriental-style noodle soups in single-serving packages (Messenger 1986). The solution to such competition is to ensure that points of difference between products remain well defined. One drawback to this approach is that its success or failure is very difficult to measure. How does one prove that a market entry has been preempted?

Successful products whose points of difference are attributable to patented or proprietary technologies have an added advantage: it takes time for competitors to respond, and timing is key in marketing. A product that has established itself as the benchmark in quality can be extremely difficult to shake from its position of dominance, as General Mills discovered in 1989 when it challenged the domination of the hot cereal market by Quaker Oats.

Timing is often overlooked by product developers in another way. Most companies read the same market data; so many develop similar product concepts in parallel, with success often depending on who can get their products to market first. Many good product opportunities have been lost when a competitor got wind of a company's product development activities and rushed its own prototype to market while the other company's marketing and R&D personnel argued over slight differences in the color or shape of their own prototypes.

Product "lifespan" needs to be considered. This is an admittedly nebulous marketing concept that seeks to describe the time it takes for products to be introduced, reach full market acceptance, and finally lose marketshare against competitors in terms of life-cycle curves. Many frozen novelty desserts introduced during the 1980s had very short lifespans, but for many companies the capital investments they were built upon were flexible enough to generate a constant stream of innovations. Consequently, many processors were able to realize a satisfactory profit stream from these products in a highly competitive marketplace (although many others could not). Fruit leather products, such as General Mills' Fruit Roll-Ups® and Sunkist's Fruit Wrinkles®, rapidly grew into a $300 million-plus category during the mid-1980s but depended upon a steady stream of new product variations to sustain the category.

Tofu and surimi are products that have very different lifespan profiles. Surimi was introduced in the United States with the Berelson Company's introduction of Sea Legs® crab analogues in 1976, at a time when crab was in very short supply. It slowly and methodically matured into a stable, estimated $300 million market that has had difficulty expanding (Best 1989a). Tofu originated as an ethnic food that became a cult product of the 1970s. It began entering the mainstream during the 1980s when attention to lactose intolerance and interest in low-calorie product alternatives was increasing (Best 1990b).

A product's success is not measured by its lifespan. Projected product lifespans are important only from the perspective of a project's financial objectives. Slow sales for a product with a long lifespan may be desirable if a company can justify and finance a major, long-term return on its investment (e.g., Procter & Gamble's Pringle's® potato chips). Conversely, a quick-in, quick-out product also may be justified if it generates a satisfactory return on investment. The major breakfast cereal companies were very successful in exploiting the children's cereal markets during the 1980s by simply changing the shapes, flavors, and colors of existing cereals and relaunching them on the coattails of favorite children's television or movie themes. The products were designed for minimal investments and very short lifespans. These issues have an impact on product development priorities. Products with short lifespans may have to be designed to be processed on existing equipment lines. They may also justify the use of lower-cost, lower-quality ingredients than products designed to generate repeat purchases and brand loyalty.

Timing also can help reposition old products. General Mill's Cheerios® cereal, which had reached market maturity, found new life during 1988 and 1989 when a high degree of adult consumer interest in oat bran enabled the company to highlight the solid oat pedigree of Cheerios®. The product was repositioned with minimal investment.

Price

Price cannot be separated from the elusive concept of "value." One way to view value is as the overall impact a product makes upon a consumer's quality of life. For example, value perceptions for middle- to upper-income consumers may be driven by quality perceptions (e.g., imported wines or cheeses) or convenience (microwavable dinners). For some of these products, low price may equate with low value. For mature consumers, value hierarchies may be dominated by serving sizes, nutritional profiles, and types of packaging. For these consumers, large serving sizes at a competitive price may be deemed wasteful. Lower-income consumers may affix higher values to lower prices. Consider this caveat, however: an industry expert once pointed out that one of the best markets for king crab legs was in low-income neighborhoods. Food is a relatively inexpensive way to upgrade lifestyles. For other consumers, eating situations may render mediocre-quality "filler foods" acceptable—even at high prices. Consider the purchases made by captive audiences at sports events, for example.

Too often product developers are constrained from developing products that fully meet consumer's criteria for acceptability because of ingredient, processing, and cost guidelines imposed by agents outside the product development process. The lesson of the Tyson Foods example cited early in the chapter is that there would have been no point in designing those products if project cost-constraints had not allowed the proper design of key, identified consumer value attributes into them. Cost is only one aspect of a product's value and, its importance can often be minimized by other product value attributes. If there is any lesson to be drawn from the marketing experience of the 1980s, it is that consumers will pay for value—given that a product does, in fact, connote quality (consider the prices of imported bottled waters, for example).

It is important that a product's value be firmly established from the perspective of its competition. Classical marketing would describe a product's market position in terms of two extremes: high-price, low-volume "premium" and low-price, high-volume (e.g., generic or private label) items. Ill-defined products that fall within these two extremes run the risk of being "stuck in the middle" of a market that is defined by products at both ends of the spectrum. Price should reflect a product's perceived value or competitive advantage.

Promotion

The meaning of the term "promotion" extends beyond the act of identifying the ideal promotional venues by which products may be marketed; it also involves the identification of concepts that lend themselves to promotion. It is in the latter area that R&D can make an essential contribution.

Promotion and advertising involve consumer perceptions of products, and product developers should remain intimately involved in the process of identifying key consumer "hooks" that lend themselves well to promotion. Products targeted toward children often rely upon shapes and colors (teddy-bear-shaped Nabisco Teddy Grahams® crackers, multicolored General Mills Trix® breakfast cereals, and Kraft–General Foods Jell-O® desserts to name a few). Product developers have the expertise to know what kinds of shapes can be engineered and which colors are available. Sound is a promotable attribute that can be engineered into snacks, such as Frito-Lay Doritos® or breakfast cereals such as Kellogg's Rice Krispies® ("snap-crackle-pop"), through judicious ingredient and process selection. Nonmelting properties were designed into Mars M&M® candies and have provided the hook for innumerable promotional compaigns.

Even small alterations in product design can have a major impact upon how a product is perceived in the marketplace. According to several market analysts at the time, Dairy Queen's first ice cream outlets in Japan lagged as Japanese propensities for smaller servings worked against the American tradition of equating large servings with generosity. To the Japanese, large servings were perceived as wasteful. The solution, in this case, was simple: sales expanded when portions dwindled. Nabisco expanded the market appeal of its Triscuit® crackers when it observed and subsequently promoted the crackers' ability to retain their crispy texture when microwaved with cheese. The addition of vitamin C to Kraft–General Foods Kool-Aid® and fruit snacks made them more palatable to parents.

In the area of health and nutrition, technical objectives dovetail nicely with promotional objectives. During the 1980s, major food processors competed heavily for adult markets on the basis of their products' promotable nutritional attributes. Kellogg, Kraft–General Foods, Quaker Oats, and General Mills strove to see which of their breakfast cereals could claim the highest contribution of U.S. Recommended Dietary Allowances (RDAs) for key nutrients per product serving, while Campbell Soup Company, ConAgra, H. J. Heinz, and Kraft–General Foods vied for the lowest caloric content on their frozen microwavable entree collections. In every case, considerable R&D input was required, in the form of palatable dietary fiber, mineral, or vitamin fortification technologies or low-calorie ingredient substitution technologies.

In the 1990s, good opportunities exist and will continue to exist for the poultry industry to promote its adoption of technologies to minimize *Salmonella*, *Campylobacter*, or *Listeria* contamination in its products (by using irradiation, for example). There are indications that "designer" foods adjusted to conform to the particular health needs of individuals or boosted with cancer-inhibiting nutrients may become a reality.

Even nonspecific auras of health and wholesomeness can be promoted. The "natural" foods industry managed to capitalize upon the wholesome connotations of "natural" products even when such value could not be documented. Similarly, the draw of "all-natural" ingredients provided a technological boon to the flavor industry even though no real social, nutritional, or medical benefits could be attributed to those ingredients.

Perspective

Consumer concerns over social issues tend to wax and ebb in tandem with the mediagenic value of those issues. The fifth aspect of product design deals with a variety of social, religious, political, and other issues that contribute to the tapestry of perceptions consumers have about their food supply. Product developers cannot afford to divorce these considerations from the design process. Pesticide residues, biodegradable packaging, vegetarianism and veganism, biotechnology, hormone use in animal husbandry, artificial versus natural flavors, monosodium glutamate, and even the "Chinese Restaurant Syndrome." Ephemeral as they may be, periodically these issues boil to the surface of public consciousness with major, even devastating, impacts upon the food industry.

Food processors are in the best position to provide products that address consumer conerns *if* these concerns can be anticipated. General Mills' oat-based Cheerios® breakfast cereal received a major boost during the oat bran fever of 1988–1989. Much of the research concerning oat bran's cholesterol-reducing properties had been available within the industry for years before being brought to the attention of the public. The Cheerios position was indeed fortuitous, but how many other cereal-based companies missed similar golden opportunities for lack of prescience?

Highly promotable product attributes of the 1990s might include the anticancer properties of ingredients, such as conjugated linoleic acid (CLA) from butterfat or omega-3 fatty acids from fish oils, or environmentally sensitive packaging. At the same time, anticipated changes in Food and Drug Administration (FDA) guidelines regulating health claims advertising should induce product development teams to devise new product attribute and marketing strategies to highlight the nutritional benefits of their products.

In general, societal concerns offer good opportunities to link technology with promotional objectives; in these contexts, technologies can be perceived in terms of the social benefits they provide. Morinaga Foods promoted its aseptically processed tofu technology on the basis of microbiological safety concerns associated with marketing traditional, pasteurized tofu at ambient temperatures. The legalistic tempest that swirled around biotechnology issues during the 1980s appeared to skirt the use of *Bacillus thuringiensis*, a microbial pesticide produced by biotechnology fermentation techniques that is harmless to humans and nonpest organisms. Irradiation offers solutions to problems of foodborne illness, in addition to cosmetic quality enhancements of produce. Regulated use of growth hormones in cattle production offers a safe alternative to black market use of growth promoters, as well as improving profit margins for growers. It was perspective that led certain food processors to experiment with environmentally acceptable packaging alternatives in anticipation of consumer and community boycotts of specific containers.

A final note on perspective: food manufacturing deals with the business and science of food production and consumption, so it is easy to overlook the fact that, historically, food production and consumption have been more closely linked to culture and religion than they have with commerce. For many consumers, the role food plays in their lives is steeped in tradition, reverence, and mythology. As with any other religious issue, sensitivity is warranted in dealing with such perceptions—as creators of some very successful food product advertising campaigns have discovered.

The religion and the mythology of food are among the many forces that drive food consumption in the marketplace. Product developers should be fully aware of how these forces impinge upon new product concepts in order to maximize the consumer appeal of their products.

DRIVING FORCES IN THE MARKETPLACE

Product and process developers, as interdependent contributors to the product development process, should be fully aware of the major consumer driving forces that will define the markets for their products. Some of these forces are discussed in the following paragraphs.

Demographics and Economics

The average age of the U.S. population is increasing rapidly, and this trend will likely have a profound impact on new food product development priorities.

During the 1960s and 1970s, the demographic surge that was labeled the "Youth Revolution" focused the attention of marketers upon the purchasing power of children and young adults. The 1980s recognized the specific needs and demographic purchasing power of young, single professionals ("Yuppies") through value addition, as well as families with two-adults. Food marketing during the 1990s and beyond will be increasingly defined by the overwhelming purchasing power of consumers aged 55 years or older.

The number of consumers aged 55 to 65 years and older is projected to grow by 18.5% between 1990 and 2000, while the number of American younger than 50 is projected to grow only by 3.5% (Ostroff 1989). This group will also be wealthy: according to the 1984 U.S. Census poll, consumers 55 years and older represented 21% of the total population but controlled 39% of total discretionary income (Best 1986). It is expected that these consumers will pay to get what they want.

What older consumers do want was suggested in a 1987 survey of over 1,500 consumers aged 50 to 74 years old conducted by Donnelly Marketing, a market research firm (Anonymous 1987). Asked what, if anything, they would like to change about products they currently purchased, 73% of the shoppers polled cited hard-to-open packages, followed by desires for improved product quality (29%), smaller packaging sizes (27%), reduced content of salt and preservatives (23%), and larger label print (12%).

Tastes also can change. Research pioneered by Dr. Susan Schiffman of Duke University during the 1980s suggested that, physiologically, taste preferences change as consumers age. Both sweet and salty perception thresholds increase with age (Best 1986). Consumers in this age group might prefer a greater flavor impact than consumers in lower age brackets.

Aging consumers are evolving their own very specialized eating niches that food companies should be able to exploit. For example, Nutrition Technology Corporation (Cincinnati, Ohio) was formed in 1982 specifically to develop food products that met the nutritional and sensory needs of the institutionalized elderly, a market it estimated could reach $1.0 billion in sales. Although its products were packed with nutritional value, the company took pains to engineer the sweetness, flavor, and textural profiles of its products to appeal to both elderly consumers *and* the younger purchasing agents of the institutions. The lesson is instructive: to maximize return on new product investments, many products will have to be designed to appeal to overlapping consumer age groups.

Although broad generalizations can be made about an aging population, food marketers and product developers should be aware that no one knows what form of particular eating preferences this will entail. This population surge will not be homogeneous. In fact, it is likely to fragment into a multiple of groups defined by their own eating and spending preferences. For example, a 1989 Rochester Institute of Technology survey titled "Lifestyles of Older Americans" proposed that the mature market can be split into six specific subgroups, each with its particular needs with respect to nutrition, food choices, convenience, ease of handling, and preparation. These subgroups were categorized as: self-reliants (25%); active retirees (20%); quiet introverts (19%); young and secures (13%); solitaires (13%) and family orienteds (10%). More identities will no doubt evolve.

Caution is warranted, however. Several surveys, including those undertaken by the Washington-based American Association of Retired Persons (AARP), underscore the sensitivity with which older consumers view their age and its attendant limitations. According to the AARP, older consumers are very likely to boycott products deemed to promote age stereotypes. The challenge is not to overtly design products targeted to older consumers, but rather to design products for wider market segments that *include* older consumers.

Other demographic trends also are worth noting:

• Although children and teenagers had a tremendous impact upon product development during the 1970s and 1980s (as expressed by the boom in snack foods consumption, for example), the population aged 17 to 22 years is projected to drop by 3 million by 1995. Presumably, future product development efforts will shy away from this category. That could be a mistake, however, as children and teenagers are likely to continue to wield tremendous purchase-decision-making power.

A 1989 survey of children's eating habits, for example, found that 32% of all children aged 12 to 14 prepared their own evening dinners, and over 40% of children aged 9 to 14 prepared their own snacks (Guber 1989). A 1987 survey determined that American children aged 4 to 12 annually spend $4.7 billion (in 1987 dollars), with many of those expenditures devoted to food purchases. Children in single-parent families or families where two parents work were more likely to prepare their own meals than children with a nonworking parent (Stipp 1988). If current trends toward smaller family sizes continue into the 1990s, and if projected labor shortages drive incomes upward as fewer workers enter the work force, it may well be that children will have more spending money to devote to food purchases.

Teenagers increasingly do the family shopping. In 1989, 50% of female teens and 30% of male teens did the family shopping on a weekly basis, reflecting the purchasing power they wield as a group (Anonymous 1990b).

For product developers, key decisions will have to be made about who the ultimate consumers of new products will be. Products appealing to children and teenagers may require flavor profiles very different from those of products designed to appeal to middle-aged adults. Packaging graphics and suitability for distribution venues (such as school vending machines) will have to be adapted accordingly. Although the ease of food preparation provided by the microwave oven makes it a convenient appliance for children to use, product developers also must include in their product designs safeguards against injury from hot susceptor material surfaces or from steam buildup in sealed bags.

• Higher immigration rates also are likely to occur during the next two decades due to a projected labor shortage. As with the large Southeast Asian, East Asian, and Latin American influxes of the 1970s and 1980s, these migrations will likely continue to evolve new American eating experiences. Product developers probably will find many new niche marketing opportunites to exploit, as American awareness of immigrant culinary trends grows.

• In the late childbearing years of the post–World War II baby boom population, there has been a "baby boomlet," which is likely to peak somewhere in the mid-1990s. The birth rate surged from 3.6 million in 1983 to 3.9 million in 1989, fueling the success of baby food companies such as Gerber, which saw sales surge from $448 million in 1986 to $660 million in 1989 (Otto 1990).

• Venues of consumption are another product design variable affected by socio-demographics and economics. The phenomenal rise of frozen, microwavable dinners during the 1980s is predicted to grow to a $2 billion industry, closely followed by a $700 million market for shelf-stable microwavable dinners, by the early 1990s (Scheringer and Otto 1990). This growth was propelled by the time savings these products offered consumers, as the purchasing influence of time-strapped two-income families grew in lockstep with the value affixed to the time savings offered by frozen convenience foods. During this period, portable refrigerated, shelf-stable and/or microwavable lunches also established their appeal in workplace environments and the automobile.

Whether time savings and convenience command as much importance for an aging population moving out of the prime child-bearing years and the workplace is still unresolved. It behooves product developers always to consider the particular circumstances surrounding the consumption of products.

What distribution systems will aging consumers prefer, and what are their product development requirements? How often will older consumers shop, and what will their refrigerated shelf-life requirements be? Frozen meals carried to the workplace may undergo considerable freeze/thaw cycling even if that was not originally expected of the product; so freeze/thaw textural stability and microbiological safety will have to be considered. What flavor, texture, and preparation attributes are likely to be considered important by immigrant labor populations? What products can be designed to best exploit the impulse-buying habits of teenagers doing the family grocery shopping? These are all examples of product development questions that will be shaped by the socio-demographic and socio-economic forces of the 1990s and beyond.

Health, Nutrition, and Safety

Nutrition sells. Health, nutrition, and food safety issues are major concerns of American consumers. Whether this phenomenon is attributable to an aging population, a strong media emphasis on nutritional issues, or improved nutritional education, the nutritional value of foods has become a very legitimate marketing issue.

According to a 1988 Frost & Sullivan report (Anonymous 1988b), over 80% of adults 64 years and older have a chronic health condition. Older consumers also tend to be better educated about nutritional issues than younger persons. Consequently, the Donnelly Marketing poll, referred to earlier (Anonymous 1987), found a very high level of concern about the nutritional qualities of foods among older consumers, where primary issues of concern included salt (88%), cholesterol (88%), calories (87%), and caffeine (68%).

Consumers do read labels. A 1989 National Food Processors Association survey (Anonymous 1990c) indicated that 79% of the 1,400 consumers polled "always" or "sometimes" read nutritional and/or ingredient statements on food labels before making a first-time purchase.

The impact that food labels can have upon American food purchasing habits was dramatically illustrated in a 1989 Federal Trade Commission report that investigated the effects of a 1984 breakfast cereal advertising campaign for Kellogg's All-Bran. The advertising highlighted a National Cancer Institute recommendation that increased dietary fiber consumption might reduce the risk of contracting some forms of cancer. (Ippolito and Mathios 1989). The study found that the ad campaign spurred persons in over 2 million households to begin consuming high fiber cereals, while the average weighted dietary fiber content of all breakfast cereals across the industry increased by 7%.

Calorie consciousness among consumers opened niche markets for products such as H. J. Heinz's Weight Watchers line of low-calorie products, which rapidly went mainstream. By 1989, according to the Atlantic-based Calorie Control Council, "two out of three American adults were consuming 'light' food products at least four times per week."

Consumer nutritional trends can rapidly be exploited by companies. A series of consumer publications touting the purported cholestrol-reducing properties of oat bran launched what was termed the "Great Oat Rush of 1988–1989" (Best 1989b). We have already noted the plethora of new products these developments generated.

Without question, there are gains to be had by designing products for maximum nutritional appeal to consumers. Dietary fiber ingredient choices could be dictated by consumer awareness of the source. Product designers may want to minimize the number of ingredients having "additive" perceptions on the food product's ingredient statement—a long-standing objective of the Campbell Soup Company and other major processors. Food product designers should remain fully cognizant and respectful of consumer ingredient and product safety concerns.

Several warnings are in order, however:

• While nutrition sells, nutrition *alone* does not sell. General Mills counted on a healthy, all-natural appeal when it first launched Nature Valley® Granola Bars into national markets in the late 1970s. Quaker Oats promptly relieved them of their marketshare, however, by coating granola bars in chocolate and rendering them into confectionery items—consumers could have their nutrition *and* their candy too.

Make sure a product looks, smells, and tastes good, and *then* worry about nutritional appeal.

• Nutritional issues can be ephemeral. There is a big gap between nutritional science and nutritional faddism. Nutritional trends not firmly established by scientific consensus run the risk of rapidly disappearing from the public consciousness. Product developers should evaluate their new product commitments in terms of the expected lifespan of a nutritional trend. The longevity of such a trend ultimately may have very little to do with science and very much to do with its ability to catch the public's imagination.

In addition, both product developers *and* marketers must remain aware of the risks attendant upon rushing to market with poorly substantiated claims *irrespective* of the legal liabilities involved. The 1988–1989 "Oat Rush" was accompanied by highly publicized introductions of products such as oat bran–containing licorice and oat bran–sprinkled potato chips. Both nutritional concepts and company reputations can become discredited in consumers' minds, regardless of the scientific validity of their claims.

• Finally, the legal environment for communicating nutritional information to consumers is, and is likely to remain, highly complicated. There is little competitive value in designing nutritional quality into products unless this quality can properly be communicated to consumers.

Be aware of the regulatory guidelines that constrain health and nutrition claims.

Technology

Technology is a tool; it is not an end in itself. Many new technology concepts have failed because product developers sought to adapt new product concepts to a particular technology rather than the other way around. Two good examples include the retort pouch, which was originally developed for military applications, and aseptic milk processing.

The trilaminate barrier pouch developed at the U.S. Army Natick RD&E Center for military "meal, ready-to-eat" (MRE) programs was developed to offer convenience in the field and a five-year shelf life under adverse storage conditions. In 1990, the food industry was still floundering in its search to find a profitable consumer application for this technology.

The aseptic milk processing technology was perfected in Europe to permit milk to be stored for extended periods at room temperatures. It found a home in Europe during the 1960s and 1970s, in part because refrigeration space was in short supply among consumers. American processors erred in assuming that these benefits would translate to the domestic marketplace.

For processors, the extended shelf life of milk offered cost savings in inventory and process management. Major investments in this technology by U.S. companies fizzled when dairy processors discovered that American consumers (a) liked their milk refrigerated, (b) preferred shopping for their milk on a weekly basis, and (c) disliked the slightly cooked flavor imparted to milk by aseptic processing. Furthermore, retailers were moving toward logistics management systems that valued products that were delivered and turned over on a daily basis.

The lesson drawn from these examples is that any new technology used in food processing must be evaluated in terms of its real and/or perceived consumer value, not just for its attendant benefits to processors or its technical elegance in the eyes of engineers. Successful application of technology in consumer markets demands a social perspective. Aseptic technology did find a very successful niche in portable juice drinks and juice concentrates. In this case, the technology dovetailed nicely with consumer demands for portable, convenient juice drinks that retained a high flavor quality. Even with milk, all was not lost: "semi-aseptic milk" is making a comeback of sorts as "extended shelf life" (ESL) milk. ESL milk is ultra-high-temperature (UHT)-processed to give a shelf life measured in weeks rather than days, and is sold refrigerated.

Most technologies adopted and applied by food companies remain "invisible" to consumers. Consumers buy a product off the shelf, consume it, and throw the package away, blissfully unaware of the packaging material, ingredient, processing, or analytical technologies embodied in it. Consequently, there is an urge among many suppliers and users of food technology to define their products only in terms of the benefits accruing to food manufacturers (such as cost savings, cosmetic improvements, increased shelf life, improved inventory management, etc.), while perceiving the consumer implications of the technology only in terms of end-product quality. This is a mistake.

The 1970s and 1980s saw several technological developments flounder. Although they were perceived to be invisible to consumers at the time, changing consumer awareness of health and environmental issues coupled with a powerful "consumer activist" movement served to bring these issues to the forefront of consumer consciousness. All of a sudden, the purveyors of these technologies were having to justify their products directly to consumers, a challenge they were unprepared to meet.

Major challenges facing the food industry in the latter part of the 1980s included irradiation and biotechnology. Although irradiation had long been used by the military to provide high-quality products with an extended shelf life, food industry efforts to introduce it into the public domain stalled because of the easy target that food irradiation provided consumer activist groups dedicated to the antinuclear movement. Unfortunately, the thrust of early marketing efforts on irradiation was directed to processors rather than consumers. Its benefits were defined in technical terms, whereas its real or perceived shortcomings were expressed emotionally. Irradiation's benefits were defined in terms of improved shelf life, a technical issue, when they could have been described in terms of improved microbiological safety, a consumer issue.

No existing technology's consumer image can be taken for granted. Daminozide, a federally approved growth promotant (tradename: Alar) used to improve the shelf appeal of apples, sparked a national scandal in 1989 when it was alleged by two consumer activist organizations to pose a health risk to consumers and, especially, to children. Highly publicized, the anti-Alar campaign was heavily criticized because of many of the assumptions made about Alar's health risks (Best 1989c).

The ensuing national review of Alar and other pesticides was often notably lacking in measured scientific debate on the relative risks and benefits to society of their use. From the public's viewpoint, the damage had been done. According to the International Apple Institute, the "Alar panic" was expected to cause an already beleaguered apple growing industry $100 million in lost income in the first year of the controversy. The Alar example demonstrates that even "invisible" technologies can rapidly appear in the public consciousness.

Other food technology concerns at the visible fringe of the consumer issue spectrum include: carcinogen formation from chlorinated water use in food processing; the use of synthetic colors and monosodium glutamate as food ingredients; highly centralized and automated processing of high-microbiological-risk products such as milk or poultry; controlled- or modified-atmosphere packaging of microbiologically unstable foods; and ozonation as a potential food preservation technology.

Technological efforts of the 1990s having the potential to stir controversy include the drive to develop food ingredient preservatives with innocuous label declarations and pest-resistant agricultural products.

Considerable work is being done to identify microorganisms that produce microbial growth inhibitors or biocides. In theory, these microorganisms or their by-products could be used to culture milk products and thereby contribute their preservative properties to the product. For example, nisin and subtilin are two ribosomally derived peptides with demonstrated bacteriocidal activity; yet there is also the risk that such ingredients might someday be viewed by the public as "unnatural" antibiotic additives if the social benefits of the technologies are not properly communicated.

Vegetables or fruit genetically selected or altered for enhanced pest resistance are currently being proposed as viable alternatives to chemical pesticide use in agriculture. Technologists should attempt to identify the variables to which the pest resistance of these new produce varieties can be attributed. Many vegetables and potatoes produce highly carcinogenic pesticides that can be far more dangerous to humans than the manufactured pesticides, including solanine (potatoes) and 8-methoxypsoralen (celery) (Ames and Gold 1989). A similar analogy may be drawn regarding biodegradable plastics. Manufacturers rushed to commercialize biodegradable plastic food packaging alternatives in the wake of public landfill concerns (Lingle 1990). Questions that were not properly addressed include (a) whether the biodegradation products were benign, (b) whether the packages would degrade under the dry, anaerobic conditions of many landfill sites. One starch manufacturer reputedly pushed the technology as a new market for its corn starches—the technology had become an end in itself.

It pays to review new product development from the greater social perspective presented by all of its component parts. Do not attempt a quick fix. Are there any ingredients, packaging, processing, or food safety attributes, or specifications that may someday focus either welcome or unwelcome public attention on a product? If there is a chance that a project will focus unwelcome attention on the product, the best solution may not be to abandon it (*all* products have some attendant risk, after all), but perhaps to take proactive action to ensure that the risks of controversy are minimized.

When the use of ethylene dibromide (EDB) as a grain fumigant came under public and regulatory scrutiny in the early-1980s, grain processors such as General Mills, Quaker Oats, and Kellog were prepared and well positioned to rapidly remove any trace of EDB residues from their product lines.

The social (ergo marketing) impact of technology also should be considered from the perspective of what is demanded of it. For example, the lifespan of foodservice contracts may not warrant attention to the longer-term social risk factor of a particular ingredient *unless* the ingredient itself has a long lifespan in the company's product line. For example, irradiated mushrooms used in a cream of mushroom soup may be limited to only a few products and thus easily eliminated or replaced if they become a social issue. On the other hand, brominated bread dough conditioners may be ubiquitous throughout a line of foodservice-designated bakery goods and consequently very difficult to replace with nonbrominated bread doughs that perform to specification if bromination ever becomes a social issue.

Manufacturing

Manufacturing considerations can play a major role in the public's perception of a product. The popular mythology that imbues traditionally processed foods with nearly divine qualities (everybody seems to have forgotten just how bad product quality was "back then") provides some marketers with a well-honed marketing advantage.

Ben & Jerry's Homemade (Waterbury, Vt.) built an ice cream business that mushroomed from $4 million in 1984 to $48 million in 1988 on the claim that its product was manufactured by using "traditional" techniques (Rogers 1989). Beer and bottled water manufacturers leverage consumer perceptions that bottled water is produced from pristine artesian sources when their water actually may be drawn from heavily industrialized locations, filtered, or pretreated in other ways. "Natural brewing" still defies definition. Large-scale bakers use equipment programmed to simulate the random errors of hand decorations on cakes and other baked goods for a "personal" touch. To the extent that products can offer personal touches, carefully selected flaws in product quality can actually represent marketing advantages for some of them (irregularly cut blocks of cheeses, for example).

Manufacturing technologies can leave products vulnerable. High-speed processing lines have been blamed for the high degree of *Salmonella* contamination in poultry (Key 1990). The manufacturing economies achievable by limiting a company's circle of suppliers or adopting just-in-time (JIT) inventory management structures may likewise restrict the freedom of movement of product development teams by limiting the number of ingredients or packaging materials available to them. Large-scale capital investments in specific manufacturing technologies may keep product development teams from seeking alternative manufacturing technologies for their products, even when market considerations warrant them.

FINAL CONSIDERATIONS

From a marketplace perspective, successful product design is highly complicated. It may require peeling back multiple layers of consumer, technological, manufacturing, and other variables before the product design is successfully positioned in the marketplace. The complexity of new product design offers the best argument for integrated team approaches to food product development, but planners should take care that the decentralized responsibility of a product development team does not inhibit its decisiveness.

The sheer number of new products introduced every year bears testimony to how quickly market niches are discovered and occupied. This environment offers very limited windows of opportunity to food manufacturers. Consequently, successful product development hinges upon a delicate balance between rushing a product to market and maximizing its potential in the development laboratory.

"There are lies, damn lies, and statistics," expounded Mark Twain. Statistics, consumer test results, and product design matrices represent numbers— only numbers—and not self-evident truths. The inherent difficulty of interpreting statistics leaves them vulnerable to misinterpretation and even manipulation.

Statistics can mislead in many ways. For example, no consumer tests are ever definitive. Consumer test confidence intervals often get overlooked as product developers prefer to draw conclusions from sample means. Consumer surveys tend toward a high degree of error because of the inherently high degree of variability between subjects in a population. Consequently, consumer test results should be approached with caution.

Errors can be introduced into consumer tests by omission—that is, by questions *not* asked of consumers. For example, questions about consumer likes or dislikes about a particular product may overlook how important those considerations are to making purchase decisions. Mean values of pooled test results may overlook the variability of responses between consumer subgroups or the hidden qualifiers that consumers attached to their responses.

Products may undergo a series of cost reductions and be triangle-tested to ensure their "equivalence" to prior formulations (within specified confidence limits). The pernicious erosion in product quality this can engender may not be apparent, as each successive change in product quality may be too subtle to detect by the limitations of available testing and analysis techniques. Compare the final reformulation to the original product, however, and the differences become very readily apparent.

Finally, all products have their weaknesses and strengths, and successful product design demands an intellectual integrity in assessing these product attributes. Many corporate cultures value a project-"championship" approach to product development, but this kind of approach can easily slip into self-delusion. A product's most ruthless critic should be its own developer; that is the surest way of minimizing the product's weaknesses and maximizing its strengths. Total concept approaches require critical examination of products from their total market perspective.

REFERENCES

Ames, B. and Gold, L. S. 1989. Pesticides, risk and applesauce, *Science*, April 25, 1989.
Anonymous. 1984. Proctor & Gamble Corp., Annual Report.
Anonymous. 1987. Insight into the Over-50 Market. Stamford, Conn.: Donnelly Marketing.
Anonymous. 1988a. Tyson Foods Inc., Annual Report.
Anonymous. 1988b. Mature Adult Packaged Foods. New York: Frost & Sullivan.
Anonymous. 1989a. The Fortune 500. *Fortune*, Apr. 24, 1989, 345.
Anonymous. 1989b. Ocean Spray Cranberries, Annual Report.
Anonymous. 1989c. *Gorman's New Product News* 24(12): 3.
Anonymous. 1989d. *Statistical Abstract of the United States: 1989*, 109th edition. Washington, D.C.: U.S. Department of Commerce, Bureau of Census.
Anonymous. 1989e. *1989 U.S. Industrial Outlook*. Washington, D.C.: U.S. Department of Commerce/International Trade Administration.
Anonymous. 1990a. *Gorman's New Product News* 25(12): 3.
Anonymous. 1990b. *The Lempert Report* 5(19): 2.
Anonymous. 1990c. Food Labeling and Nutrition: What Consumes Want. Washington, D.C.: Opinion Research Corporation.
Best, D. 1986. Redesigning foods for an aging population. *Prepared Foods* 155(11): 181.
Best, D. 1987. Tyson's R&D stresses the fundamentals. *Prepared Foods* 156(10): 56.
Best, D. 1988. Competing through R&D. *Prepared Foods* 157(12): 72.
Best, D. 1989a. Analogues restructure their market. *Prepared Foods* 158(11): 72.
Best, D. 1989b. A fiber is not a fiber is not . . . . *Prepared Foods* 158(3): 91.
Best, D. 1989c. Guilty until proven innocent. *Prepared Foods* 158(6): 58.
Best, D. 1990a. *The 2nd Annual Prepared Foods R&D Survey*, Chicago: Gorman Publishing Company, June, 1990.
Best, D. 1990b. Wherefore art thou Tofu? *Prepared Foods* 159(1): 81.

Connor, John. 1989. *Food Processing: An Industrial Powerhouse in Transition*. Lexington Books.: Lexington, Mass.

Freeman, L. 1987. The house that ivory built. *Advertising Age*, Aug. 20, 1987, 4.

Friedman, M. 1989. Hard questions, soft answers. *Gorman's New Product News* 25(6): 9.

Guber, S. 1989. Marketing to kids: It's elementary. *Prepared Foods* 158(9): 48.

Hodgen, D. A., Janis, W. V., and Kenney, C. F. 1988. U.S. industry highlights. In *U.S. Industrial Outlook, 1988*, p. 42-1. Washington, D.C.: U.S. Department of Commerce.

Ippolito, P. and Mathios, A. 1989. *Health Claims in Advertising and Labeling*. Washington, D.C.: Federal Trade Commission, Aug. 1989.

Key, J. 1990. Chicken consumption up, but so is salmonella; so where's health gain? *Chicago Tribune*, Feb. 4, 1990, N1.

King, Bob. 1987. Better Designs in Half the Time. Methuen, Mass: GOAL/QPC.

Koska, D. and Romano J. 1988. Countdown to the future: The manufacturing engineer in the 21st Century. Dearborn, Mich.: Society of Manufacturing Engineers.

Lingle, R. 1990. Biodegradable plastics: All sizzle and no steak? *Prepared Foods* 159(1): 144.

Messenger, R. 1986. Campbell's soups: The new generation. *Prepared Foods* 155(11): 76.

Ostroff, J. 1989. An aging market: How business can prosper. *American Demographics* 11(5): 26.

Otto, A. 1990. Who's in the high chair? *Prepared Foods* 159(1): 46.

Pehanich, P. 1987. Tyson Foods: Profile of a leader. *Prepared Foods* 156(10): 46.

Putnam, J. 1990. National Food Review: 1990 Yearbook Edition U.S. Department of Agriculture–Economic Research Service. 1990.

Rogers, P. 1989. Movers and shakers. *Dairy Foods* 90(4): 71.

Scheringer, J. and Otto, A. 1990. Freeze out for frozens? *Prepared Foods* 159(1): 55.

Schroeder, R., Van de Ven, A., Scudder, G., and Polley, D. 1968. Managing innovation and change processes: Findings from the Minnesota Innovation Research Program. *Agribusiness* 2(4): 501–523.

Stipp, H. 1988. Children as consumers. *American Demographics* 10(2): 27.

Chapter 2

Consumer Research

Dwight Jewson

OVERVIEW

The Changing Developmental Process

There was considerable new product introduction in the food industry during the 1980s (see Figure 2-1), but many forecasters predict that new products will have decreasing chances of success in the 1990s. As a consequence, line-extension-based development has accelerated dramatically, particularly as a percentage of overall new product development efforts. In this chapter, we will consider new product development as opposed to line extensions.

There is no single process for the development of new products. For some companies and some products, the process occurs over a period of years; for other companies and products, it can take as little as a few months. Moreover, the process of new product development is undergoing significant change. During the latter part of the 1970s and much of the 1980s, the process was highly structured and dependent on research at each stage. In the 1990s, the process is becoming much more fragmented, as some companies emphasize taking risks to get to market quickly.

Traditionally, there have been six key stages in the process of new product development:

1. Genesis
2. Preliminary evaluation
3. Early development
4. Advanced development
5. Introduction
6. In-market evaluation

Today, some companies are emphasizing shorter developmental timelines and ''getting to market'' more quickly. In these cases, the development process may be considerably changed, consisting of only four stages:

1. Genesis and evaluation
2. Early development
3. Introduction
4. In-market evaluation and advanced development

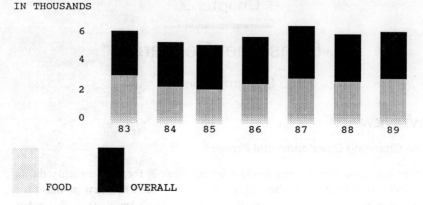

IN THOUSANDS

FOOD   OVERALL

Figure 2-1. New product introductions, 1983–89, overall and in food. Based on figures from: Marketing Intelligence Service, Ltd. Product Alert Progress. *Product Alert.*

The Role of Consumer Research

Not surprisingly, the role of consumer research in the new product development process is highly variable, and is currently under examination in many companies. Traditionally, consumer research was employed at all stages in the process. Today, in some cases, very little consumer research is utilized; instead, judgment and in-market experience are emphasized. In other cases, there is a significant emphasis on getting closer to the consumer. Regardless of the corporate orientation to consumer research, such research generally plays two roles:

1. Providing information to reduce risk and improve the odds of success.
2. Facilitating the new product introduction process.

The information role of consumer research is both developmental and evaluative. In its developmental aspect, it is concerned with:

1. Key consumer issues, needs, and benefits.
2. Key product features and attributes important to consumers.

As an evaluation aid, it considers questions such as:

1. Does the product address consumer issues, needs, and benefits?
2. Is the product different from other means by which consumers may address needs, get benefits, etc.?

The role that consumer research plays in the new product development process is important. In many companies, for instance, initial and subsequent qualitative steps represent actions that R&D, marketing, and advertising all can take in concert. This is important because new product development involves many different functions within a corporation, and consumer research often provides a mechanism through which the efforts of many people and functions can be coordinated.

Organizational Issues

New product development generally is a complex organizational task involving literally dozens of individuals from multiple disciplines. In food development, projects will frequently involve the following persons (titles will vary):

- V.P. Marketing
- Director (or V.P.) New Products
- Marketing research personnel
- R&D
- Research suppliers
- Marketing consultants

Increasingly (and importantly), manufacturing and sales personnel are involved in new product development as well.

Generally, the new product development process is one of the most complex organizational tasks that a corporation undertakes. Frequently, persons in different organizational functions have limited or almost no contact with one another; so a smooth-running new product development effort often is difficult to achieve. Different functions have different management criteria and structures, and personnel frequently change within a function. It is not at all uncommon for a new product development "team" to have a 50% or even higher turnover during the course of product development. Management of the organizational process is a critical, yet frequently overlooked, aspect of new product development. Steps that help to build teamwork and foster communication are important aspects of the endeavor, which can reduce frustration and wasted effort considerably.

The Idea

Genesis: Where Do Ideas Come From?

New products ideas generally emerge from these organizational functions:

- Marketing management, addressing business needs
- Research and development

Marketing Management

Marketing management personnel are involved in a continuous examination of changing consumer needs, developing market opportunities, and competitive developments. This examination frequently reveals tactical or strategic marketing directions that indicate new product development needs and opportunities.

Consumer research frequently is employed in this process to track consumer behavior, which summarizes purchasing patterns and trends, as well as consumer needs and issues. Strategic consumer research examines the role that a product category plays within the overall food life of the consumer and indicates areas of opportunity.

Research and Development

Depending on the capacities of an individual company, its R&D function may be engaged in primary research, which involves a technological development or breakthrough that suggests a new product; or it may be engaged in exploring "what is possible" within an area that has already been identified as important, or within an area that is of marketing interest to the company.

Thus, there are two functions, marketing management and R&D, attempting, not always smoothly, to coordinate their efforts for a single result. Marketing management frequently wishes to pursue development in areas where the technical issues are extraordinarily difficult. Conversely, R&D frequently is accused by marketing of suggesting ideas that, although technically feasible, do not meet consumer-based marketing needs.

Methods of Idea Development

There are a number of "formal" approaches to idea development. For example, Synectics, a Cambridge-based company founded by William J. J. Gordon in the 1950s, made the first attempt to provide a systematic process for focusing creativity.

Synectics offers a highly structured approach to idea development and generation. It utilizes a trained facilitator and a group that generally has no more than ten participants, traditionally drawn from various organizational functions, including marketing, R&D, and advertising, among others. Sessions generally are held off-site, away from day-to-day work distractions. They may vary from a few hours in length to an entire week. In "traditional" Synectics, the facilitator will work with one member of the group, a designated "client," utilizing a structured approach that begins with a listing of "wishes" or carefully phrased questions about "how to" accomplish a given objective. The Synectics Company has trained hundreds of facilitators in its methods, and conducting a

"Synectics" session has become a generic representation for a structured approach to idea generation.

Many individual practitioners and groups have modified the original Synectics approach or developed alternate approaches to idea generation. Common to many of these approaches is the use of a group of eight to ten participants. Frequently, these groups will include "experts" or participants from outside the organization who have been selected because their area of expertise may provide a fresh way of thinking about a given area of interest. The location of the session and the "props" utilized can be selected to foster innovative thinking. In one example, the participants in a children's cereal ideation were driven to a family resort where the session was held in a school bus filled with hundreds of best-selling children's toys.

Some methods of idea generation directly involve consumers in the process. Perhaps the best-known of these is the use of "supergroups" that employ consumers who have been trained in the creative process.

Idea Management: Development of a Pipeline

In many companies, development of a pipeline, or bank of new product ideas, is a priority. In these companies, the goal is to have a number of new product ideas ready for use. These ideas have been developed jointly by marketing and R&D, technically developed, and evaluated for marketing viability by marketing management. In some companies, this process involves quarterly idea generation sessions, which are two to three days in length.

Preliminary Evaluation

The preliminary evaluation of new product ideas generally is based on judgment, most often on the consensus of a new products team. In idea generation sessions, a ranking of ideas may be undertaken at the end of the session. Ideally, at this stage only ideas that clearly do *not* offer any marketing opportunity are eliminated. Ideas that are technically difficult are best retained for continued examination.

THE DEVELOPMENT OF THE IDEA

From Idea to Concept

Once an idea is conceived, it is important to quickly translate it into a concept that is intelligible to consumers. An initial concept statement is generally a paragraph long and clearly states:

- The product idea.
- Key product benefits.
- What is unique or different about the product.

The description may also include when the product is to be used and by whom it will be used. At this stage, concepts generally are presented without elaboration, imagery, or advertising verbiage. The task is simply to capture the basic idea.

The Role of Consumer Research in Concept Development: Methods and Approaches

Qualitative research can play an important role in the process of concept development. Generally, initial concepts are exposed to consumers in focus group interviews, mini-groups, triads, and in-depth personal interviews or "one-on-ones."

Focus group interviews are widely utilized in the United States as well as in other countries. In the United States, these interviews are the most commonly used form of qualitative (as opposed to quantitative) research. Groups generally are conducted with eight to ten consumers in research facilities where one-way mirrors allow direct viewing of the group and participation by new product development team members. Focus groups can possess a great deal of energy and are useful both for generative research, in which ideas are developed, and for preliminary evaluation, in which ideas are assessed with consumers.

Respondents for focus groups are prerecruited, usually by telephone, by using a screening questionnaire that can specify age, sex, attitudes, usage of certain products, or virtually any other requirements deemed appropriate for the development in question. Sessions generally last from one and one-half to two hours. Highly trained professional moderators are employed to conduct the group discussion. They frequently have considerable experience in new product development and expertise in research, development, and marketing.

Mini-groups are similar to focus group interviews but generally are conducted with only five or six respondents. They are particularly useful for talking with younger children (under age 12) who find a smaller group less threatening. Mini-group sessions generally last from one and one-half to two hours.

Triads are three-person interviews. They are generally of an hour or less in duration.

One-on-one interviews can be as brief as five minutes or can become in-depth interviews. Shorter interviews generally are used to assess the response to a new product or concept without the "group bias" that can develop in larger groups. They also allow responses from consumers with different characteristics, providing a cost-effective way to sample a number of different populations quickly.

In-depth interviews vary in length from 45 minutes to as much as three hours. These interviews generally are conducted by an interviewer with advanced psychological training and experience. They can be extremely useful in helping researchers to understand how a new product idea or concept fits into the overall life of the consumer. Such an interview might begin with a discussion of the consumer as a person and his or her general characteristics, concerns, attitudes, values, aspirations, and goals. It might proceed to an examination—in the case of a new food idea—of the consumer's food life, with respect to what is eaten, where it is eaten, and how it is prepared. The interview then might focus on the category in which the new product exists, with an examination of key issues and perceptions.

In developmental interviews, the discussion might be concerned with needs and gaps that a new product might address. In evaluative interviews, the discussion might center on the ability of the new product to meet key consumer needs, as well as focus on ways in which a new product or concept might increase consumer appeal.

Frequently, at the early stage of new product development, consumers will be exposed to a number of new product concepts in a single focus group session. A number of key questions are addressed:

1. Does the potential product meet a consumer need? Does it have a reason for being from a consumer point of view?
2. Does the potential product offer meaningful consumer benefits?
3. Is the potential product different from other products that consumers may use to meet a given need, including competing product- and non-product-based approaches to meeting the need?
4. What are the key product characteristics or attributes consumers seek in such a product?
5. What are key consumer "hot buttons" regarding the product? How can product benefits most effectively be communicated to consumers?
6. What are the key characteristics and the attributes that are important to consumers in such a product?
7. What are the general issues involved in the consumer's price/value considerations?

Generally, a minimum of two focus groups, and most often four to six, are conducted at the initial stage of new product development. Use of more than six groups generally is not warranted, unless extreme geographic differences exist, or different consumer groups need to be sampled.

A key strength of focus groups is that members of the new product development team can see consumers from behind a one-way mirror. Discussions after the focus groups are a valuable tool and can facilitate rapid concept development.

Depending on the new product development project, two or more rounds of focus groups may be conducted as concepts are refined or elaborated. The goal of the concept development process is to translate an initial idea into a clear, concise statement that readily communicates what the product is and what its benefits are. The following elements are generally essential to the development of such a statement:

- Name
- Consumer benefit
- Clear product description
- Support; reason for using the product
- Point of difference of the product

For example, the concept for a cereal might read:

Introducing new Nuggets, the high nutrition cereal that combines three grains—oat, barley, and wheat—with the vitamins, minerals, and fiber you need to start your day. Simply top with cream or milk, and enjoy. Nuggets can also be served warm, simply by heating in your microwave. New Nuggets, the healthy cereal that gives you the total and balanced nutrition you need.

The consumer response would likely point to several issues during concept development, but the key concern would be the possible absence of taste benefits, exacerbated by the perception that something high in nutrition will not taste good. In food products, great taste is generally a—if not the—key consumer benefit. The confusion of primary benefits, such as taste, with benefits that consumers often see as important yet secondary, such as nutrition or convenience, is a key issue in concept development.

A revised concept, which consumers might find more appealing, would incorporate a number of key sensory elements and focus on consumer concerns about taste:

Introducing new Nuggets, the delicious and nutty-tasting high nutrition cereal that combines the natural sweetness of crunchy oat, barley, and wheat with all the vitamins, minerals, and fiber you need to start your day. Simply top with cream or milk, and enjoy. Nuggets can also be served steaming hot, simply by heating in your microwave. With Nuggets, you can have both high nutrition and great taste. New Nuggets, the healthy cereal that really tastes great.

The Evaluation Process

Using both qualitative insights and judgment, the new product development team reaches a point at which it is satisfied that the concept effectively communicates what the new product is and what its key benefits are. Equally important, is the judgment of the team that the new product idea has sufficient consumer appeal to warrant its continued development. Here the role of consumer research shifts from development to evaluation.

The shift from development to evaluation is an important one. Generally, quantitative research methods will begin to be employed now, although the use of qualitative methods and judgment often continues to be an important part of the process. It is useful to separate the evaluation process into two phases: preliminary evaluation and volumetric estimation.

Preliminary quantitative evaluation utilizes various approaches, often called concept screening or concept testing. Exposure to prototype products may or may not be employed, depending on whether exposure to an actual product is essential to an understanding of concept appeal, and whether it is practically possible to include the product. Concept testing or screening also may be employed earlier in the development process, prior to qualitative concept development.

Typically, concept testing or screening will examine:

1. The absolute appeal of the new product concept. This is often called a monadic rating, in which the concept is not compared to other concepts or products; intrinsic concept appeal itself is measured.
2. The comparative appeal of the new product concept to other new product concepts and existing products. This comparative measure may be used to screen a number of potential ideas and select the most promising candidate(s), or it may assess the appeal of individual new product concepts relative to proven concepts or existing products. A control concept or concepts, known to be of either strong or weak consumer appeal, generally is included to measure the relative strength of the new product concept.

Frequently, major corporations have norms, or hurdle rates, for concept testing or screening, which set a minimum threshold for concept appeal. A concept scoring below that threshold will be either eliminated from further development or reviewed and redeveloped for greater appeal.

It is important to reemphasize that the development process is a fluid one. In some companies, concept testing or screening may precede qualitative concept development. Frequently, qualitative research is done after quantitative concept testing to strengthen or enhance promising ideas.

A final pre-market step in consumer research is volumetric estimation, which involves the use of quantitative concept testing within a mathematical model to predict the year-one in-market volume. Various models have been developed, all of which attempt to correlate consumer responses to new product concepts with consumer behavior in order to predict the sales potential or size of a new product opportunity.

One such model, developed by Burke Marketing Research, is called BASES. Here, concept testing is conducted among consumers via mall intercepts, and data are judged within a framework of product class averages as refined by managerial and research expertise. Another volumetric model, developed by Marketing and Research Counselors (M/A/R/C), is called ENTRO. We will consider volume estimation methods in more detail later in this chapter.

The speed with which the evaluation process takes place varies dramatically between products and companies. Today, there is considerable discussion of approaches that get to market quickly. Management judgment, R&D, advertising, and manufacturing may be actively involved in exploring technical developmental issues during the evaluation process or may not continue to be active after the go/no go decision is made. Generally, time and money will be closely monitored until a go decision is reached.

At this point, a number of activities involving consumer research generally occur simultaneously. They include advertising development, name development, packaging development, pricing, and product optimization.

Advertising Development

Advertising development can be divided into three phases:

1. Early development
2. Initial approaches
3. Advanced development

The process of concept development is the preliminary or early development stage of advertising development. In this phase, advertising is at the idea point; the advertising agency or the communications consultant may explore a wide variety of preliminary advertising ideas.

During the early phase, the level of commitment to a specific direction generally is low. Advertising agency account and creative personnel are in a generative mode, considering many communications issues and opportunities.

Simultaneously, other team members are focusing on the viability of the new product idea.

By the time of the second stage initial approaches, the advertising agency has identified as few as two or as many as ten potential directions for the advertising to take. If television advertising is being considered, the agency frequently will have translated these approaches into story boards, which combine initial copy efforts with artistic drawings. Story boards also may be animated with sound and action via videotape, and exposed as animatics.

These initial approaches generally will be revealed to consumers in focus groups or by other qualitative means discussed above. It is important to keep in mind that, from this point forward, the commitment of both marketing and the advertising agency to specific directions is increasingly evident.

Often, but not always, initial development is followed by quantitative testing that examines the relative appeal of alternative directions. Such testing will examine both the overall and the comparative appeal of an idea, as well as the clarity with which the main message is communicated.

In the third stage of advanced development, the agency generally has settled on a specific approach. This approach positions the product both in the marketplace and in the consumer's mind and thus is referred to as its positioning. If television is to be used, the agency often has committed to actual filming. At this point, considerable expenditures have been made, and commitment to a given direction is high.

Once a commercial is produced, it may or may not be quantitatively assessed before being aired on television.

Packaging Development

The role of consumer research in packaging development varies markedly. In some cases, consumers are not directly involved; in others, the range of qualitative and quantitative methods discussed above may be employed. The issue now is whether the packaging is a key marketing concern.

If, for instance, the package itself is intrinsic to the new product's concept, the packaging may be a central focus of the new product's development. This has been true for such recent introductions as Maxwell House Coffee in individual filter packs, or the innovation of aseptic packaging that has led to an increasing number of shelf-stable drinks and entrees. In another example, the package for Dial Corporation's shelf-stable microwavable Lunch Bucket was in R&D for five years as the central focus of new product development.

In concert with meeting functional criteria (i.e., the package contains and protects the product; the package is portable, storable, and easy to open) the package must communicate the product's brand and usage and must differentiate it from the competition. Consumer research also may consider the logo and its ability to convey the concept or positioning, as well as the consumer's ability to easily discern package or flavor designators. Packaging personality and imagery also must be considered and evaluated.

The package design may be consumer-tested. Frequently, however, such factors as long lead times for package development and speed to get into production force snap packaging decisions that allow little time for consumer research.

When there is sufficient time, the packaging may be evaluated qualitatively in the focus group interview, where consumers may consider the category of products, the competitive environment, and the package design's ability to generate impact and trial interest within that setting.

In another research format, a tachistoscope (T-scope) may be employed, which systematically exposes individual consumers to projected images of packaging designs and ascertains their ability to notice, discriminate, and retain packaging information. A package's impact is read by determining which alternative design communicates the appropriate information and imagery in the least amount of time.

Further packaging research may involve the use of in-store simulations to consider whether the package is easily visible in its competitive arena, or the use of semantic differential ratings to evaluate the communication of product attributes previously found to be important by management, agency, or consumer research.

Increasingly, emerging packaging issues must be addressed as well. These include informational issues, such as ingredient and nutritional labeling, and environmental concerns, such as the matter of overpackaging and solid waste management. In fact, some communities now are considering bans on such materials as styrofoam, plastic soda bottles, and disposable diapers.

Name Development

The development of product names is a gray area of consumer research. No hard or fast methods for name development or evaluation have been devised. Indeed, the process of name development frequently is contentious and problematic.

Consumer research, both qualitative and quantitative, can be used to set parameters for name development, outlining criteria and characteristics that may be relevant. Researchers can, for instance, suggest that the name may need to emphasize a key product benefit (e.g., low calorie products with the name Lean Cuisine). The name must also be easy to pronounce and to remember, have no negative associations, and fit the positioning of the product.

Primarily, names are generated either through a process of creative development or through linguistic processes used by name consultants. Creative development may be based on the technique of idea generation discussed above, or it may be done internally by creative personnel at an advertising agency.

Name consultants who use linguistic techniques can take a structured approach to discover how consumers use and understand language, as well as which sounds will best communicate name appeal.

Consumer research can be useful in name evaluation, although it is a complicated and involved process. Generally, research can reveal whether a name fulfills the criteria that were defined as essential for its success prior to its development, not whether the name is empirically "good" or "bad." This is particularly true if the name is a coined word, or when researchers are evaluating a new product name that may be common someday but is not yet a part of the consumer's vocabulary.

A particularly frustrating aspect of name development is the extent to which names have been previously trademarked. This author often has participated in name development projects in which many of the developed names were already trademarked and thus were not immediately available. In such a situation, the manufacturer may abandon the name altogether or try to buy its rights from the competitor, or, in the extreme case, buy the competitor!

Pricing

Pricing decisions frequently are dictated by product costs and objectives and competitive pricing levels.

From a consumer perspective, price sensitivity is highly variable. Consumers weigh and evaluate prices as they consider many factors: product uniqueness; competing or substitutable products; their perception of premium quality, superb value, and economy; the cash they have on hand; and their overall perception of product benefit or need. As a rule, the more innovative the product, the less capable consumers are of evaluating its price and value.

Consumers weigh the value of each product and make appropriate trade-offs. They may pay more for a product that they perceive to be of high quality or prestigious; in fact they may *want* to pay more of such a product. Convenience, brand imagery, and perceived taste benefits may all be worth a higher price. On the other hand, they may compromise some quality for a lower price or savings.

As a rule, qualitative research is not a reliable method for examining pricing issues. However, a qualitative framework for pricing can be determined by examining consumers' motivations to buy, attitudes, geographical considerations, and category perceptions. The psychology of pricing can be evaluated as well. For example, customers may respond more positively to purchasing a product for one dollar after buying it first at a regular price of four dollars than to obtaining two products for "just" five dollars.

Carefully constructed quantitative methods using a price elasticity curve as well as conjoint or trade-off procedures also can be useful.

To obtain a price elasticity curve, individual customers are exposed to a single price option determined to be within a range of current market pricing for comparable products. From their responses of interest or intent to buy, a price elasticity curve is developed, illustrating the optimum trade-off between the total number of units sold at a specific price and the revenue thus generated.

Using conjoint measurement, the manufacturer can analyze the variance of (order of) ranking data, determining the relative importance of attributes to consumers and how much they are willing to pay for them. For instance, a technological advancement in packaging may not be worth its additional cost to consumers, but they may be willing to pay for enhanced convenience attributes.

Critical to all pricing decisions is in-market experience, where price levels can be evaluated and adjusted to reflect such factors as the competitive environment, coupon and display alternatives, and promotional executions.

Product Optimization

At this point, the theoretical product becomes a prototype. R&D may independently or in conjunction with consumer research conduct a product-focused investigation to assess and determine the optimal levels of consumer acceptance in terms of necessary cost constraints and profitability expectations. Research methods at this stage include focus group interviews, in-home usage and evaluation, blind or branded testing, regression analysis, and perception ideal mapping, among others.

Focus group interviews may determine if the product satisfies the attributes requirements previously identified as salient, and may reveal product or positioning issues that must be addressed. Basic areas of concept testing are repeated—benefits, perceived usage, and purchase interest—as well as response to the product, which might include actual product tasting and response to appearance and smell.

A number of in-home usage techniques may be employed, which permit consumers to experience (sometimes comparing it with another product) the new product's packaging, preparation, and appeal (questions of whether it tastes good, who would eat it, etc.). Respondents may be product-category users, participants in concept development, or persons screened to fit other predetermined criteria. Data then are used to evaluate product fit with the concept, overall consumer acceptance, and future interest in the purchase.

Blind testing evaluates a product without support of any brand name or advertising, and is used to determine whether the test product is equal to or better than a benchmark or competing product. Branded testing evaluates the product's ability to fullfill its concept.

In regression analysis, another method of product optimization, consumers rate a number of individual product attributes from "excellent" to "poor," in addition to indicating how they like the product itself. Here researchers evaluate how each attribute contributes to the overall rating and determine which attributes emerge as most important to the consumer. If necessary, product reformulation may be undertaken and a second round of testing conducted. Results of the second test will be compared to those of the first to ensure that the product has indeed been improved.

In perception ideal mapping, consumers rate attributes for both the product being tested and an ideal product. The resulting gap between the product and its ideal measures both the degree to which and areas where the product needs to be improved.

Test Markets and Simulations

Test marketing, whether in simulation or not, is used as a predictive research tool for new product introductions. It uses mathematical models to project forecasts of sales and marketshare as well as to make recommendations for improvements in pricing, advertising, or promotion. It is at this point that the product is considered viable and ready to be introduced into an "authentic" setting to judge consumer interest in its purchase and repurchase, in preparation for a national introduction. The perceived risk of the introduction, the cost of marketing, and interest in speed may determine the method of research, which may entail a number of testing formats and methods of assessment.

Simulated test markets (STMs) were developed in the 1960s to measure, in a controlled setting, trial and repurchase intentions among target users and to estimate year-one volume. Simulation offers several advantages over in-market test marketing: lower cost (limited product needs, no distribution or media expenses), speed (an in-market test market may take a year to conduct versus six to twelve weeks for an STM), and security (competitors do not have access to the product).

The STM may expose consumers (often solicited at shopping malls) to the product among competing products in the controlled environment of a mock store setting. Prior to exposure, customers may be shown a number of commercials or shown story boards, including one for the new introduction within its competitive context. The consumers then are given funds or coupons to purchase products. Their decisions about whether or not to buy the new product provide a measure of the effectiveness of a number of marketing variables, including the introductory commercial, pricing, and packaging, thus helping to determine the most effective marketing mix for product entry. Those who try the product (as well as nontriers, who may be given the product) are followed up several weeks later in order to evaluate product appeal and interest in repurchasing along with various diagnostic measures.

Year-one volume estimates for the new product are made by combining the customer's intent to purchase, the customer's intent to repurchase, and the marketing plan, which factors in such data as advertising, consumer promotions, and anticipated distribution, as well as category purchase cycles and possible competitive pressure. Year-one volume for the product is obtained by multiplying the percent of consumers who will try the product by those who will repeat (after-use scores are employed to develop repeat scores). Volume estimates for STMs generally are accurate to approximately 20%, but accuracy is highly dependent on the marketing plan. If it is overly aggressive, the volume estimates will be too high; underestimations are possible if the marketing plan is lower than what may actually occur in the market.

Minimarket-testing, or controlled test marketing, is conducted by researchers who have arranged for specific stores in specific geographical markets to carry the new product. Display, promotion, and pricing—all facets of the introduction—are strictly controlled and contained. Consumers are not contacted directly before purchase; response to the new product may be evaluated through follow-up interviews later. Advantages of this approach over a full-fledged test market include speedier access to sales information, less competitive access to the product but the ability to observe the effect of competitive action, and lower overall cost. Drawbacks include the researchers' inability to judge the competitive response and the effect of advertising when the product has such limited availability.

A full-fledged test market is a significant investment, involving different stores in a minimum of two locations, and it may take up to a year, thus increasing the likelihood of competitive introductions. However, it affords the new product its first true test of market endurance within the competitive framework. The trade must be sold to carry the product, distribution requirements must be met, and full advertising support—similar to that proposed for national introduction—is employed. As a result, competitive responses can be evaluated, the threat of cannibalization (if it exists) observed, and consumer interest measured.

Unanticipated results—positive or negative—can be responded to expeditiously. For example, when Frito-Lay test-marketed its O'Grady's potato chip, a flavored variety sold better than predicted; so advertising quickly incorporated a flavor emphasis. When a diet variety of Pepsi's Slice performed much better than anticipated in a test market, supportive diet spots were quickly introduced.

The choice of where to test market is problematic. Arguments can be made both for test marketing in large communities with a broad demographic base and for centering the study in smaller, "average" communities. In either case, it is difficult to obtain a set of markets that truly represents the nation as a whole. Further difficulties in forecasting may arise from unrealistic "overattention" to the product, insufficient follow-up with consumers to measure essential repeat rates, or inadequate adjustments to the atypicality of the test market in relation to the national environment.

The assessment of in-market data may include observation studies, on-site interviewing of intercepted shoppers, surveys, consumer diaries, coupon redemption evaluation and customer follow-up, and UPC scanner data, as well as targetable cable television.

In the 1970s, Information Resources, Inc., devised two key and now widely used innovations in test marketing technology: InfoScan and BehaviorScan. In electronic test markets managed by Information Resources, Inc., InfoScan tracks product purchases by collecting point-of-scale information without customer awareness through the use of UPC scanner technology. BehaviorScan involves consumer panelists, who may be exposed to promotional variables through cable television targeting and on-set monitors, and then tracks individual purchasing with electronic in-store equipment. Trial and repeat levels, buying rate, loyalty, and a number of other important criteria become measurable. Thus potential product success can be optimized. A number of competing assessment models also are available, including ASSESSOR and ASSESSOR-FT, ERIM, and LITMUS II, among others.

A recent introduction by Proctor & Gamble illustrates how some manufacturers attempt to move "closer" to their consumers. In a Des Moines, Iowa, market, consumers call up their account at the register, and as products are scanned, a video display designed and installed by P&G illustrates savings or messages concerning individual products. An accumulating point system rewards customers for buying certain products; points can be traded in for merchandise such as a watch or a VCR. Every purchase thus is monitored, sales are increased for targeted products, and the retailer benefits from higher overall consumer traffic.

Qualitative research in the focus group format also may be employed during test marketing to evaluate consumer perceptions of the product and its ability to deliver key benefits, as well as to uncover issues and opportunities for product improvement and the enhancement of consumer satisfaction.

THE NEW PRODUCT LAUNCH

The decision to launch a new product involves marketing research, management judgment and experience, and the commitment of the people and the company involved. Only slightly more than half of all products that go to test market are eventually launched nationally. This is not surprising in view of today's market, where the rate of new product failure and the cost of introduction are high.

The decision to roll out the product on a regional basis only or to introduce it nationally after pretesting may be made on the relative strength of market forecasts, with the strongest results most likely to prompt national introduction. Smaller firms are most likely to begin introduction in specific cities; larger firms are more apt to choose regional roll-outs.

The use of in-market assessments may continue during roll-out, as marketing research focuses on consumer and competitive reaction to the new product and an evaluation of whether product sales can meet forecasts and expectations.

Focus group interviews may be employed among groups of consumers—triers, trier rejectors, and rejectors—to determine: the source of their first awareness of the product and advertising recall/effectiveness; product expectations; product trial and usage; and identification of benefits and concerns about the product. Current trends are to make responsive modifications as soon as possible.

ORGANIZATION ISSUES IN NEW PRODUCT DEVELOPMENT

Many obstacles to product development are found within the company structure. There is potential for friction not only between marketing and R&D, as discussed above, but as an inherent by-product of the existing management structure. New products may be managed by: market-oriented venture teams of experts (intrapreneurs), which change for each new project; new product departments, which are more permanent than the venture teams; new product committees, composed of top managers who tend to be conservative in their evaluation of proposals—and sometimes are regarded as adversarial to new concepts; and single-individual product planners.

The brand manager, who frequently is in charge of monitoring the performance of a particular product or line, interacts with all personnel involved in new product development, but wields his or her own influence through persuasion rather than authority.

There are many variations to the simplified structure described here, including recent managerial moves that encourage more flexible and market-responsive development; but the development of new products remains highly complex and multifaceted, and the failure of a new product sometimes can be directly attributed to a lack of organizational teamwork.

Within the organization's infrastructure, consumer research can play a vital integrating role. From idea to concept to prototype to product, consumer research is an objective tool that provides an eye and ear to the consumer, and gives the development managers a shared and focused frame of reference and integrating guidance.

BIBLIOGRAPHY

Anonymous. How to improve test marketing. *Research on Research: #21. A Report from Market Facts, Inc.*, Chicago.

Anonymous. Nov. 1984. New tools revolutionize new product testing. *Marketing and Media Decisions*, 76–66, 128–134.

Beck, Charles I. June 1988. Where will the new products of the 1990s come from? *Food Processing*, 35–41.

Birmingham, John. 1988. Dial's hearty office meal. *AdWeek's Marketing Week*, June 27, 1988, 20–23.

Dumaine, Brian. 1989. P&G rewrites the marketing rules. *Fortune*, Nov. 6, 1989, 34–48.

Fishken, David. Nov. 1983. Consumer-oriented product optimization. *Food Technology*, 49–52.

Giovanni, Maria. Nov. 1983. Response surface methodology and product optimization. *Food Technology*, 41–45, 83.

Honomichl, Jack J. 1986. *Honomichl on Marketing Research*. Lincolnwood, Ill.: NTC Business Books.

Kinnear, Thomas C. and Taylor, James R. 1983. *Marketing Research: An Applied Approach*. New York: McGraw-Hill Book Company.

Kotler, Philip. 1988. *Marketing Management: Analysis, Planning, Implementation, and Control*, 6th edition. Englewood Cliffs, N.J.: Prentice-Hall.

Lawrence, Jennifer. 1987. Testing juices up Slice's performance. *Advertising Age*, Aug. 24, 1987, S2–5.

Lehmann, Donald R. 1985. *Market Research and Analysis*. Homewood, Ill.: Richard D. Irwin.

Lilien, Gary L. and Kotler, Philip. 1983. *Marketing Decision Making: A Model-Building Approach*, 2nd edition. New York: Harper & Row.

Luck, David J., Wales, Hugh G., and Taylor, Donald A. 1987. *Marketing Research*, 6th edition. Englewood Cliffs, N.J.: Prentice-Hall.

Morich, Donald. Oct. 1989. Using tachistoscope, semantic differential and preference tests in package design assessment. *Quirk's Marketing Research Review*, 3(8): 31–46.

Park, Irene. June 1985. Taking sides on test marketing. *Marketing Communications*, 72–78.

Redington, Michael P. 1984. Case history: O'Grady's, definitely not just another chip off the block. Speech at 1984 New Products Conference, American Marketing Association, New York.

Rogers, Peter. May 1988. New product introductions. *The Manufacturing Confectioner*, 54–63.

Rosenfeld, Judith. June 1985. Speeding up test marketing. *Marketing Communications*, 67–70.

Schutz, Howard G. Nov. 1983. Multiple regression approach to optimization. *Food Technology*, 46–48, 62.

Shocker, Allan D. and Hall, William G. 1986. Pretest market models: A critical evaluation. *J. Prod. Innov. Manag*. 3: 86–107.

Tull, Donald S. and Hawkins, Del I. 1987. *Marketing Research: Measurement and Method*, 4th edition. New York: Macmillan.

Urban, Glen L. and Hauser, John R. 1980. *Design and Marketing of New Products*. Englewood Cliffs, N.J.: Prentice-Hall.

CONSUMER RESEARCH SERVICES

Adopter (Data Development Corporation): STM.

Adtel (Burke Marketing Services, acquired by SAMI, New York): electronic minimarket setup with television meters for commercial measurement, which also registers which family member is watching at what time, and wand scanners to track information about products not purchased in scanner stores.

ASSESSOR (Management Decisions Systems, acquired in mid-1980s by Information Resources, Inc.): STM with telephone follow-up.

ASSESSOR-FT (Management Decision System): ASSESSOR and Fastrac.

BASES I (Burke): concept volumetric simulation.

BASES II (Burke): in-home product testing with follow-up.

BASES III (Burke): test market interviewing, coupon monitoring to identify triers and nontriers, follow-up for triers.

BehaviorScan (Information Resources, Inc.): combines UPC scanner data for specific consumers and provides cable targeting.

ENTRO (Marketing and Research Counselors): volumetric simulation.

ERIM (A. C. Nielson): combines UPC scanner information retrieval for specific consumers and provides over-the-air broadcast rather than cable.

ESP or Simulator ESP (NDP Group): STM.

Fastrac (Information Resources, Inc.): a volumetric model, STM with home rather than mall interviews to control demographics.

InfoScan (Information Resources, Inc.): evaluates UPC scanner information in every store in specific markets.

LTM (YSW Group—Yankelovich, Skelly, and White, Inc., acquired by Saatchi and Saatchi): STM, annual monitor.

MAPPS (Maritz Market Research, Inc.): product planning and positioning.

MicroMarket (TeleResearch): STM.

National Purchase Dairy Panels (NPD): household panelists' report of purchases in preprinted diaries.

News (BBDO): pretest based on consumer survey data.

Quick Test Opinion Centers (Elrick and Lavidge, Inc.): shopping mall interviewing.

SAMSCAN (Selling Areas-Marketing Inc.—SAMI): minimarket.

Scan (Marketing Evaluations, Inc.): mail sample of brand opinion.

Speedmark (Robinson Associates): Simulated test marketing and predictive modeling.

Find (Find/SVP): quick information service.

TRAC (YSW Group—Yankelovich, Skelly, and White, Inc., acquired by Saatchi and Saatchi): forecasting models.

TRIM (TRIM Inc.): sales data from scanners.

Chapter 3

R&D Process

Ernst Graf and Israel Sam Saguy

INTRODUCTION

New products form the lifeblood of most food companies. An in-depth statistical analysis of historical data (*Business Week*, 1989, Special Issue: Innovation in America) demonstrated beyond any doubt that companies with the strongest performance in their markets are also the ones that invest the most in R&D. This conclusion is based on a very thorough evaluation of almost 900 companies in 40 industry groups and subgroups with yearly gross sales over $35 million and R&D expenditures of at least $1 million (or at least 1% of sales). There is a very high correlation between R&D spending and sales ($p > 99.9\%$) and profits ($p > 99.5\%$).

The composite food industry R&D spending in 1988 was 0.7% of gross sales or 10.1% of pretax profits; and even though the food industry spends less than 1% of its sales on R&D, this is a major investment considering the low profit margins of foods. A comparison of R&D expenditure as percent of gross sales for five different industrial categories is depicted in Figure 3-1. The data clearly show that the food industry is lagging behind most other industries quite significantly. As mergers and acquisitions alter the financial structure of many food companies, even this relatively small percentage is being reduced in an attempt to gain efficiency and competitive advantages. This downsizing of R&D to an expendable support function may be a symptom of the volatility of the food industry and its day-to-day survival nature. Only the future will tell if the American food industry can survive the fierce competition of the international arena.

Industrial research differs from most other corporate activities in that there may be no significant research achievements for long periods of time. Also, once discoveries have been made, it is very difficult to assess their monetary value. However, one major conclusion of the *Business Week* report is that R&D escalates sales and profits. Therefore, curtailing long-term research efforts and excluding R&D from long-range strategic planning activities will stifle a company's innovative spirit and pose a real threat to its survival.

Whereas academia focuses primarily on basic research, the American industrial scientist hardly ever enjoys the luxury of delving into a long-term basic research project. Food companies, with a few exceptions, spend most of their internal R&D dollars on product development and some on applied research, an approach that in some cases may be best described as "cook-and-look."

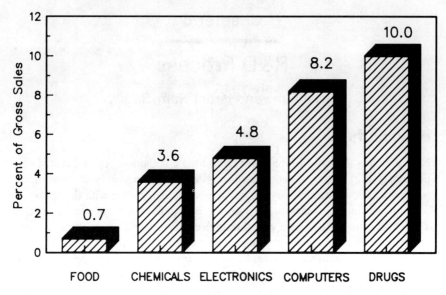

Figure 3-1. Industry composite R&D investments. Source: *Business Week*, Special Edition, 1989.

Most corporate research efforts are directed toward resolving problems that arise during product development. Oftentimes the distinction between applied research and product development is blurred, but it is in this gray zone that the average industrial food technologist spends at least 90% of his or her time. This chapter predominately covers this hazy area of applied research and product development.

Why does it take several years to develop a new food product? What kind of research does industry carry out? On what kinds of daily activities does an industrial food scientist spend most of his or her time? What are his or her functions and level of responsibility in the corporate organization? These are key questions that students contemplating a technical career in the food industry ask.

The current chapter addresses all of the above questions. Particular emphasis is placed on all the aspects of the industrial career that clearly differentiate it from an academic position. A detailed description of the various activities and the skills and abilities required during different project phases should be of special interest to anyone considering technical employment in the food industry.

The most striking difference between academic research and corporate food R&D is the existence of distinct phases during a commercial project. A single individual may carry out feasibility studies or a large multidisciplinary team may complete a commercialization project. These phases are marked by entirely different activities, requiring different sets of skills and abilities of the food technologist. This chapter will describe the exact nature of each project phase.

OVERVIEW OF PROJECT PHASES

An industrial project and academic research share certain characteristics:

- Enthusiasm
- Disillusionment
- Panic
- Search for the guilty
- Punishment of the innocent
- Praise and honors for nonparticipants

However, beyond these well-known principles, there are few similarities between basic research and corporate R&D.

Unlike academic research, most industrial projects have rather rigid time-tables and can be divided into distinct phases that are characterized by team size, types of activities, degree of upper management involvement, and talents needed. Based on many years of industrial food R&D experience, the authors have decided arbitrarily to divide the typical project into the following five phases and to discuss them in separate sections below:

1. Screening
2. Feasibility
3. Development
4. Commercialization
5. Maintenance

SCREENING

The initial phase of a project generally consists of evaluating a large number of ideas, comparing them to existing products, and presenting prototypes to R&D management and marketing. These efforts are often bootlegging projects carried out by a food technologist, a home economist, or an independent consultant and may last from a few days to several weeks. This phase is sometimes concluded with preliminary consumer testing and potential technology screening.

Idea Generation

Several years ago, Dr. Vernon Mattox, a retired biochemist from the Mayo Clinic in Rochester, Minnesota, was asked what discovery in the twentieth century had made the biggest impact on society. His answer was not Sputnik, penicillin, electricity, or even the Pillsbury microwave cake mix; it was the birth control pill. In contrast to a consumer product of such far-reaching socio-economic ramifications, most food inventions hardly influence society at all. Typically the food industry merely responds to changing consumer needs and therefore follows socio-economic, demographic, and nutritional trends. Most large companies even attempt to anticipate these changes by using sophisticated market research tools. Nevertheless, the resulting food products are consequences of current consumer needs and trends, rather than influences. This distinction, however, is not meant to downplay the importance the food industry has played in changing society.

Only a few projects are technology-driven. Instead, marketing usually approaches the R&D department and proposes broad concepts, which may include product ideas or simply quality attributes—for example, a low calorie snack; a convenient, single-serving breakfast item; a shelf-stable menu line; or a microwavable cookie batter for children. This situation does not prevent the food technologist from conceiving such ideas; in fact, numerous successful food products are known to have been the brainchild of R&D. But, again, most of these products are reactions to prevailing market trends rather than genuine inventions that will greatly influence societal patterns.

The next step is the creative brainstorming session, intended to generate a long list of concrete products and quality attributes. These "ideation" meetings (sometimes called Synectics; see Chapter 2) are often conducted by an outside moderator. By this method researchers collect literally hundreds of ideas without ever passing any value judgments. Participants are encouraged simply to say whatever comes to mind, however outlandish the idea may appear, with any judgmental evaluation by team members strongly discouraged. This process has the advantage of eliciting often unconventional thoughts, unleashing true creativity and imaginations that otherwise are often bridled by the scientific peer review system. After the meeting, the moderator or the responsible food scientist may group and categorize these ideas and attach priority ratings to them by some preselected criteria. The chosen product ideas then are ready to be developed into prototypes.

Prototype Development

Prototype development, employing common kitchen utensils and retail ingredients, often is a concerted effort between a food technologist and a home economist. Intuition, culinary knowledge, and artistic expression are the principal skills required during this project phase. Food chemistry, ingredient interactions, processing, and the question of feasibility largely are ignored at this stage. The main objective is to develop a physical rendition of the concept that can be shown to marketing and customers for review. Technical issues should be regarded as future challenges and should not be allowed to stifle any enthusiasm for a new product at this time.

Concurrent with prototype development, competitive product reviews sometimes are carried out to obtain a frame of reference. A wide range of food items similar to the prototype are purchased from local mom-and-pop stores and supermarkets, from out-of-state stores, and from abroad if that is deemed necessary. These products are prepared as suggested on the package and evaluated for quality, size, weight, package, cost, nutritional status, ingredients, convenience of preparation, and other consumer attributes peculiar to the product.

Technology Screening

The screening phase of a new product often concludes with a cursory analysis of the status of potential technologies available for the following: (1) achievement of the desired quality attributes, (2) processing, (3) packaging, (4) distribution, and (5) shelf-life stability. This usually is a paper-and-pencil exercise that relies heavily on past experience. The goal of such preliminary study is merely to recognize the key issues in the development of the product in order to estimate approximate resource needs and timetables, and to identify the best talents for the feasibility phase of the project.

Some crude prototypes, a competitive product review, and a preliminary technology assessment usually suffice to evoke an initial management and marketing response. In case of a positive reaction, the continued financial support for a project often hinges on the results of a limited consumer research study.

Consumer Feedback

The initial consumer reaction to a new product idea often is tested by using concept boards. A moderator shows a selected panel of 10 to 25 participants a series of posters containing numerous product descriptors and sometimes photographs of mock-ups. Using probing questions, the moderator solicits their opinions concerning a wide range of product attributes. As described in Chapter 2, concept testing can provide valuable qualitative feedback.

FEASIBILITY

Product ideas that survive the initial screening process are now scrutinized for their overall feasibility. Are the technologies needed for the product's manufacture available? What new processes will have to be developed? Are all the food ingredients approved? What are the shelf-life requirements? Can adequate microbiological safety be guaranteed? What distribution system will be used?

What are the technical risks involved in the development and commercialization of this product? How will the competition react to its market introduction? Is it financially feasible? Does it fit into the overall corporate product portfolio? Will it cannibalize any of the existing products? What is the marketing strategy?

Many of these feasibility issues are addressed herein in separate chapters on consumer research, marketing, manufacturing, and logistics. In this chapter, we focus on R&D-related activities, namely: (1) technology assessment, (2) manufacturing scenarios, (3) financial evaluation, and (4) risk analysis.

Technology Assessment

Technology assessment during the feasibility phase—unlike that of the screening phase— is an in-depth endeavor that lasts from two to four months. This assessment is aimed at delineating the entire process of manufacturing, packaging, and distributing the food product. It includes identifying the necessary equipment and often running preliminary pilot plant trials in the suppliers' facilities. Suppliers frequently are asked to participate in the technology assessment, particularly on the processing and packaging side. Ingredient suppliers also are consulted about the availability, or potential collaborative development, of special ingredients displaying unique properties required for the desired finished-food-product attributes.

Technology assessment usually is a joint effort between a food engineer and a product development scientist. However, these individuals lack the time during the short feasibility phase to develop any thorough understanding of the technologies required for the commercialization of the new product; so they solicit help from a wide range of resources. Not only do ingredient, equipment, and packaging suppliers become involved, but the team is likely to work with various in-house experts, librarians, equipment engineers, and consultants.

The initial step in any technological assessment and development project is to make a thorough literature search to determine the existing state of the art. Various databases for published information are available at a nominal cost and can be accessed by using a modem, a personal computer, and a software package such as DIALOG. The search should screen not only scientific and technological periodicals and reference books, but it should encompass the patent literature and technical bulletins of ingredients and equipment. Special attention should be focused on company research reports of previous pertinent R&D activities.

For the technology assessment, the food scientist often must rely heavily on the expert opinion of consultants. Most consultants to R&D are university professors or corporate retirees who typically have specialized knowledge in a narrow field that the R&D food scientist may lack. The consultant is likely to be invited to offer his or her advice in the form of a one-day meeting, and also may be asked to write a technical evaluation, to perform some experiments, to develop an engineering prototype, and to aid in the overall technology assessment process by means of a number of different collaborative projects (discussed in detail in a later chapter on industry–university relationships).

In addition to the possibility of obtaining expert technical advice, several other considerations may inspire the food scientist to invite a consultant for a one-day visit during the technology assessment phase:

- *Independence:* Outsiders have nothing personal to gain or lose from their recommendation, and thus can offer a neutral perspective.
- *Impartiality:* Because of their independence, consultatns may serve as arbiters between opposing corporate factions. Although these groups are reluctant to make any concessions to each other, they may accept an impartial outsider's view.
- *Creativity:* Broad experience with many food companies enables the consultant to utilize a vast experience base to solve a specific problem.
- *Focus:* Free from corporate administrative responsibilities, consultants often can respond more quickly than in-house personnel to requests for technical information.
- *Cachet:* Consultants may assume the role of a guru in stressful situations. Their approval of key technical decisions—especially unpopular or scientifically novel ideas—adds credibility to a given course of action and usually increases the psychological comfort level of R&D management personnel, who are technically remote from the project yet may bear overall accountability for it.

The end product of all the above technology assessment efforts is a brief technical summary. The first and most important statement in this document is an overall recommendation concerning R&D's ability to deliver the necessary breakthroughs or tools to produce and distribute the prototype developed during screening. This recommendation—containing the necessary qualifiers—is an informed judgment call based on information from the various sources.

The rest of the technology assessment document describes the recommended technologies and forms the basis for subsequent product development efforts.

Manufacturing Scenarios

An extension of the technology assessment is the creation of various manufacturing scenarios. Key personnel from R&D, corporate engineering, and operations perform various paper-and-pencil exercises to address the critical issues surrounding the production of the new product.

It usually is necessary first to decide where the food will be manufactured.

There are four obvious choices: (1) modify a processing line or install a new line in an existing plant; (2) build a new plant; (3) acquire a competitive business and utilize its facilities; and (4) use a co-packer, at least during the initial product introduction. Each option has both benefits and disadvantages, discussed in a later chapter on engineering and manufacturing. Usually product design criteria and marketing strategies dictate one of the above choices. For example, a product of immense technical complexity and concomitant patent leverage may preclude the services of a co-packer, whereas it may be desirable to use a co-packer to produce a standard salsa intended merely to complement a Mexican line of products in food service.

Related to the above manufacturing scenarios are questions concerning the location and the size of the production facility. Should the product be manufactured in a single plant? In intermediate-size production facilities near distribution centers? Or in many small commissaries? The selection of the geographical location takes into consideration the labor market, distribution routes, predicted consumer density, market volume, ingredient availability, ethnic and demographic regionalities, and many other factors.

A third aspect of the manufacturing decision is a floor plan of the plant and the physical layout of the processing line. Are the proposed process criteria identified during the R&D technology assessment compatible with the existing equipment and available floor space? Will a novel equipment design require special development? How many line operators will be needed to run the plant? Is the line outfitted with state-of-the-art equipment for cleaning, sanitation, safety, and statistical process control?

A detailed manufacturing plan taking all of the above variables into consideration forms an integral part of the feasibility study. It perceives potential manufacturing risks, it helps to generate a product development and commercialization timetable by identifying long-lead-time equipment, and it enables the team to make a financial forecast of manufacturing costs based on capital and labor. It also allows for a parallel team approach to attack potential bottlenecks or difficult tasks. These team efforts greatly reduce the overall development time.

Financial Evaluation

No feasibility study is complete without a preliminary financial evaluation of the projected product cost, return on invested capital, pretax profit margins, and other economic and accounting parameters. Most of the product cost to the food processor is estimated from the following expense items:

- Ingredients
- Packaging

- Plant labor
- Manufacturing
- Distribution
- Equipment
- Capital depreciation
- Advertising
- Supermarket slotting allowances
- R&D support
- General overhead, such as accounting, consumer complaint office, and other corporate functions

This list clearly shows that a complete financial feasibility evaluation comprises information provided by a broad range of corporate disciplines, including R&D, engineering, operations, accounting, and marketing. The assembly of a multifunctional team during the projects's infancy is essential to the fruition and success of the new product. (The importance of early communication among various disciplines is elaborated on in a later chapter on logistics.)

The net result of the above accounting exercise is then used by the project director during the risk analysis and preparation of a final recommendation to the general manager or board of directors.

Risk Analysis

The feasibility study often concludes with a brief risk analysis. The project director evaluates the technology assessment, manufacturing scenarios, proposed development timetables, consumers and market research results, financial projections, and other pertinent information. A final document is drafted that contains all the results and recommendations. Numerous projects are terminated at this stage for a variety of technical, economic, or marketing reasons without the involvement of senior management. Positive recommendations, however, are presented to a capital appropriation committee, the general manager, the board of directors, or some other high-level executive cabinet in order to obtain their sanction and financial support for the next and most important phase, development.

DEVELOPMENT

The majority of retail food products require from one to five years of development, whereas many foodservice products—such as new corn breadsticks in a fast food restaurant—can be developed in just a few weeks or months. A short timetable results for a product with short self-life specifications, little consumer and distribution abuse, little variability in its preparation by the end-user, few packaging needs, access to rapid and extensive consumer research testing, and an easy market introduction.

Development phase efforts typically are carried out by large, multidisciplinary teams. This strategy has been coined a "total systems approach," and its significance is discussed in detail in the later chapter on logistics. Within R&D—depending on the scope and complexity of the project—several engineers and food scientists and their technicians may collaborate, complementing each other's skills. Furthermore, external resources from many segments of the organization are utilized in the development phase of a new product. For example, a home economist from consumer service optimizes the sensory product attributes and carries out large consumer-abuse studies to increase product tolerance to the oven type, the heating temperature, freezer and refrigerator temperatures, recipe variations, other ingredients, and additional stresses. Further resources include individuals from consumer research, marketing, engineering, operations, quality assurance, and statistics, as well as nutritionists, microbiologists, patent attorneys, and regulatory affairs personnel. Most of these experts are from other departments in the company, but many are from outside, such as technical consultants, advertising agency representatives, consumer test moderators, and others.

Unlike academic researchers, corporate food scientists must meet strict timetables, work in large teams, interact with a number of nontechnical functions, and have very little personal freedom in their daily and long-term activities. Their efforts directly impact overall project success, and any deviation from a proposed deadline may affect a number of other business functions. Therefore, the corporate food scientist often lacks the luxury of investigating a topic as thoroughly as his or her academic counterpart does. Sometimes the corporate scientist must assume calculated risks and make a recommendation on the basis of a limited amount of information. Compared to academic investigators, the corporate food scientist is expected to display a greater degree of personal and professional versatility in dealing with various business issues.

Technical Plan

At the outset of the development phase, the R&D project leader—with input from team members—writes a comprehensive technical plan that has the following objectives:

- To delineate the best possible research plan to accomplish the development and manufacture of the new food product.
- To identify personnel needs, such as technicians, scientists, engineers, taste panels, statisticians, and external consultants.
- To request any extraordinary instrumentation, equipment and facilities required throughout the development course.

- To develop a budget plan and allocate resources for travel, trials, ingredients, personnel, and capital.
- To set up a tentative timetable that indicates major milestones, such as consumer tests and various decision crossroads. This timetable is shared with other business functions and is incorporated into a marketing master plan. Such timetables are not etched in stone but are subject to periodic review, as they merely serve to coordinate and synchronize the myriad of activities occurring during the development phase.

Similar technical plans also are written for product maintenance projects, such as the updating of unit operations, ingredient conversions to stay abreast of current health trends, or the technical resolution of long-term consumer problems. Such a technical plan is analogous to a thesis proposal or an academic grant proposal that briefly summarizes a problem, provides some historical background, and discusses approaches, potential recommendations, and benefits of a proposed study. Therefore, technical plans are not just tedious management requests; they facilitate a valuable mental process whereby a food scientist can become thoroughly familiar with a scientific problem and design the technical plan and experimentation to resolve it.

Formulation

The heart of any new product is its ingredient composition. The initial formulation usually is carried out during the screening and feasibility phases. With the commencement of the development phase, the product recipe is refined by a home economist or a skilled chef to create an artistic blending of the product's flavor, texture, and visual appearance.

The basic recipe now is transferred to the food scientist for reduction to a product formula. This conversion entails several steps:

1. *Scientific translation:* The recipe is translated into a formula containing reproducible numeric units. Each ingredient, including such foods as a clove of garlic, must be expressed on a weight percent basis, even when present in low concentrations, such as a dash of salt.
2. *Sourcing:* Ingredients are selected to meet the following criteria:
   a. *Quality:* The quality most appropriate to the product should be specified. Statistical process control charts normally are required to comply with recent JIT (just-in-time) manufacturing procedures and quality standards.
   b. *Variability:* The ingredient of choice should display the least possible variability in color, flavor, moisture content, and behavior in the finished food product, as expressed by a set of performance specifications.

   c. *Cost:* Ingredients with similar attributes sometimes vary widely in cost. The chef or home economist may not be aware of alternate ingredients, but the food scientist must find the least expensive substitute that meets all the quality criteria specified in the initial recipe.

   d. *Processability:* Ingredients must tolerate the process; that is, small variabilities in ingredient delivery or process unit operations should not affect the performance of the ingredient in question. For example, a slight increase in baking time or temperature may cause noticeable discoloration of a naturally occuring dye, whereas an artificial substitute might be unaffected by process variability. Also, the ingredient should be able to be handled easily by plant equipment and personnel; for example, the addition of 200 eggs to a large dough mixer could be accomplished much more readily by the substitution of dry egg solids or liquid eggs.

   e. *Shelf-life:* The ingredients must display enough storage stability to permit adequate warehousing and distribution time—including storage time in the consumer's home—for both raw materials and the finished food product. For example, many naturally occurring flavors are much more susceptible to oxidative deterioration than their synthetic counterparts.

   f. *Safety:* Each ingredient must meet strict company requirements concerning its chemical, physical, and microbiological safety. Prior to ingredient procurement, the company mandates that the supplier must sign a legal guarantee assuring the safety standards. Also, safe handling practices must be assured for each ingredient. For example, a concentrated jalapeno pepper oleoresin may pose a significant health hazard to the line operator, whereas a dry extract would be much safer.

   g. *Availablility:* Large quantities of the ingredients must be in continuous supply. This may require some ingredient substitution in the initial recipe. For example, an exotic spice might not always be available in the United States because of political unrest in the country of origin, but a spice extract would be available in guaranteed abundance throughout the year.

3. *Product shelf life:* The product has to be reformulated to impart the necessary shelf-life stability. Sometimes this can be achieved simply by replacing an ingredient present in the intial recipe by a similar ingredient of lower molecular weight to reduce water activity. Generally, however, the prolongation of product shelf life presents the biggest challenge to the food scientist. For example, the home economist may formulate a high-quality flour tortilla that is preservative-free, moist, and tender to the bite, and can be filled with meat and condiments and rolled without tearing. Yet all of these quality attributes vanish after just a few days of shelf life,

possibly because of microbial growth and starch retrogradation. Only by selecting the appropriate range for the water-to-glycerol ratio and by optimizing extrusion, sheeting, and baking parameters can a tortilla be manufactured that maintains the above organoleptic traits during extended refrigerated storage. (Shelf-life methods will be discussed below.)

4. *Process:* A basic process for large-scale manufacture has to be developed from the basic recipe, as discussed in the next chapter on food engineering. This process design often introduces ingredients not listed in the original recipe. These ingredients, called processing aids, are used at very low levels and include chemical agents such as potassium sorbate, cysteine, and calcium chloride in dough products. The former two ingredients are employed to reduce the necessry mix time, thus decreasing the energy requirement, whereas the addition of calcium chloride controls the proofing rate. Similarly, many refrigerated canned dough products are sprayed with a fine mist of oil as a release aid to prevent adjacent products from sticking to each other. Processing aids usually do not have to be mentioned on the ingredient declaration at their very low usage levels.

5. *Regulatory compliance:* The original home economist's or food scientist's recipe often must be reformulated to comply with local, state, and federal food regulatory agencies. The product must consist of all GRAS (Generally Recognized As Safe) ingredients that are sanctioned by the FDA for use in that particular food, it must meet the standard of identity, and it may require mineral and vitamin enrichment. The complexity increases if the food contains any meat components. Most large food companies employ a staff with at least one regulatory expert, who assures conformity to government rules for both food composition and labeling on the package, such as the ingredient declaration, weight, nutritional information, and any health claims. (See Chapter 6.)

In addition to meeting legislative food guidelines imposed by the government, food scientists may have further formulation constraints forced upon them by the marketing department. Food advertising aimed at the affluent health-conscious consumer of the late 1980s and the 1990s has incorporated numerous health claims, such as the heart seal, no cholesterol, no tropical oils, no saturated animal fats, reduced calories ("light" products), low salt, no preservatives, no artificial flavors or coloring agents, and so on. Furthermore, many products require the kosher seal, and—with the aging baby boom generation—many future food products may be labeled for use by narrow segments of the population with special nutritional needs.

Not all formulation efforts, however, are mere translations of the original recipe to a formula that meets the above criteria. At times there may be a need for the reformulation of a standard food product to incorporate special features, such as food with a high nutrient and calorie density for polar expeditions, dehydrated food for military personnel, or shelf-stable food for NASA space programs. At other times, the prototype may consist of a mere vision that requires some technological breakthroughs for its preparation—such as the microwavable sundae containing hot fudge on a brownie and cold ice cream, whose successful formulation was the result of several years of focused R&D efforts and of a broad knowledge base in microwave technology. Most such long-term projects lead to strong technical insulation in the form of patent protection and trade secrets.

Food Engineering

The involvement of food engineering in product development is a complex task that requires solid technical competence. This topic is covered in a separate chapter on engineering and manufacturing. Here we simply wish to focus on the design of new equipment and the need for pilot plant experimentation as a part of scale-up.

Equipment Design

Designing new processing equipment can be one of the most challenging and rewarding activities of a food engineer. However, only rarely is the food engineer provided with such an opportunity, as food companies rely heavily on the special skills of engineering firms and equipment manufacturers for the design of most new equipment.

New equipment projects can be divided into three main categories: (1) modification of existing equipment, usually carried out by the plant engineer; (2) addition of new production capacity to meet growing sales or to replace a co-packer, in projects that usually adopt existing equipment with only minor design changes; (3) development of a novel commercial process based on laboratory research—and even here most of the basic unit operations and equipment modules will utilize established designs.

The designer of a new piece of equipment has to consider many constraints that limit the number of alternatives. Such constraints are the physical nature of the process, processing versatility, self-cleaning and CIP (cleaning-in-place) options, government regulations, material availability, and economics. The cost has to be taken into consideration for scaling the size of the equipment. Despite apparent savings with increasing equipment size, most recent manufacturing trends lean toward designing smaller yet more flexible processing lines.

Another major constraint needs mentioning: the time available for completion of a design is in many cases the primary factor limiting the number of alternate designs. As indicated above, because of these time constraints and the complexity involved in novel equipment design, the food industry only rarely designs its own equipment. Some proprietary modifications and patented processes are common, but in most cases the vendor is the major resource for equipment design.

Identification and Resolution of Scale-up Issues

The ultimate purpose of all pilot plant and small-scale lab production is crystallized in the proverb "Commit your blunders on a small scale, and make your profit on a large scale." Experience has shown that small-scale experiments in the laboratory will not be of much use for large-scale production; so to optimize quality and to develop a cost-effective production line, pilot plant experimentation should be conducted. These tests provide the basis for scale-up, identify possible quality problems, show critical control points and process capability, establish production standards, and so on.

The main objective of a pilot plant is two-fold. First, it must provide design data; engineering methods, which may include modeling techniques, experimental design, dimensional analysis, and so on, are utilized to collect the appropriate information. Second, it must produce small quantities of the new product for various consumer tests.

Product/Process/Packaging Interactions

A fair number of the development efforts are concentrated on understanding the various interactions shown in Figure 3-2. The most common and best understood interactions are product–product and ingredient interactions. For an in-depth discussion of various ingredient interactions, the reader is referred to a standard food science textbook, such as *Food Chemistry* (Fennema 1985), as the topic does not fall within the scope of this book. Typical examples include: the effect of salt in altering the perception of sweetness of sucrose; moisture transfer between a pizza crust and the sauce, causing bottom sogginess; the effect of calcium on the leavening rate of an SAPP (sodium acid pyrophosphate)–soda system; the synergistic antioxidant effects of BHA and BHT; and so on. Most of the time these interactions can be predicted in a new food system, and formulation changes can be designed to prevent the interactions or at least to mitigate possible deleterious effects. Invariably, however, novel ingredient interactions will manifest themselves during product development. These effects often are poorly understood and can be discerned only through tedious experimental design studies. The disentanglement of synergistic or inhibitory ingredient interactions and their clear separation from primary product, process, or packaging effects on various product attributes usually takes months of inves-

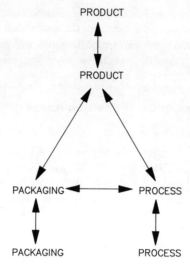

Figure 3-2. Product, process, and packaging interactions.

tigation. Because of the complexity of most foods, many suspected interactions can never be statistically validated under normal experimental conditions, and the results only provide directions.

Another important interaction is the reciprocal relationship between ingredient functionality and processing conditions. Food engineers focus most of their development efforts on understanding such mutual influences. Like ingredient interactions, intricate process–process interactions cause many unexpected results and greatly affect ingredient functionality. For example, the tenderness of corn tacos is affected—among other variables—by the masa granulation, the residence time in a belt oven, and the subsequent frying time. These convoluted relationships necessitate the involvement of a statistician, both in the design of experiments and in computer-aided analysis and interpretation of the data. The results often consist of response surfaces that ultimately help the product–process optimization.

A third realm of interaction is the effect of packaging on processing and ingredient functionality, and vice versa. Most packaging–processing interactions have been studied for decades and are well understood. Some examples of these types of interactions are: (1) shrink-wrapping of foodstuffs, which requires approximately 40% shrinkage of the packaging material from the original dimensions; (2) aseptic processing, which requires packaging materials that will ensure aseptic conditions; (3) EVAL (ethylene vinyl alcohol), which loses its barrier properties when it absorbs moisture and therefore is not suitable in processes such as steam sterilization; (4) polyester packages, which become friable at low temperatures and cannot be used by the frozen food industry; and (5) pressure and/or vacuum stability, another process/packaging factor that determines the suitability of the package for typical process conditions such as sterilization.

Packaging–product interactions, however, are an area of intense current research. Until recently, the primary function of packaging materials was to hold the food and shield it against airborne contaminants, but there now is a strong trend to change the passive package into an active component of the food. With the advent of novel technologies, such as microwave cooking, CAP/MAP, and others discussed in a separate chapter, interactive packaging is expected to: direct heat to specific parts of the food in the microwave oven; serve as a temperature barrier during microwave cooking, remaining cool outside; vent steam at a certain pressure; change color at a preselected heat input; dissolve and be edible; remove oxygen, generate carbon dioxide, or maintain a modified atmosphere; cool or heat a beverage when a tab on an aluminum can is pulled; do much more. These expectations about the package increase the degree of ingredient–packaging interactions exponentially, as the package becomes an integral part of the food. For example, a high level of fat on the surface of a food accelerates the heat transfer from an aluminum susceptor pad to the food, thereby affecting the degree of packaging-aided crisping, whereas the geometry of the package alters the effect of salt on the uniformity of dielectric heating.

The optimization of a food takes into account all of the interactions shown in Figure 3-2, as well as the factors described in the above formulation section. Food quality evaluations are carried out by both chemical and organoleptic testing procedures. (Moskovitz describes a number of techniques for optimizing food quality in Chapter 8 of this book.) All laboratory results are verified by conducting qualitative and quantitative consumer tests throughout the development phase. (The criteria for selecting the most suitable consumer test were described by in Chapter 2.) However, despite the availability of these analytical results, the food scientist retains the privilege and the obligation to use his or her own judgment and on occasion to question the validity of a consumer response.

The above discussion of intricate ingredient, processing, and packaging interactions makes apparent that the optimization of a truly new product requires a high level of experimental sophistication and an enormous team effort backed by top management support.

Shelf-Life Studies

Shelf life may be defined as the length of time that a product is acceptable and meets consumer expectations regarding its quality. The shelf life of a food product is vital to its success in the marketplace, and is an extremely important attribute for any new product. Product shelf life depends on: (1) the environmental conditions that the product is exposed to during distribution, in the store and the consumer's home; and (2) how much of the product's initial quality can be lost before its final quality will no longer be acceptable to the consumer.

The shelf life of a food product is affected by many factors and parameters, which can be categorized as follows: (1) microbial spoilage; (2) chemical reactions pertinent to the mode of failure of the specific product; (3) changes occurring during processing; (4) protective barrier properties of the package; and (5) environmental conditions during distribution and storage. Some of the major modes of deterioration include microbial spoilage, unacceptable losses in nutrient value, and undesirable changes in flavor, color, and texture.

Normally, before the shelf life of a new product can be considered during its development, a crucial issue must be resolved: the question of the product's microbiological stability. It is essential to understand and eliminate all possible safety hazards that might arise from the growth of food pathogens during product distribution and storage, such as *Salmonella*, *Staphylococcus aureus*, *Listeria monocytogenes*, *Clostridium perfringens*, and *Clostridium botulinum.* Then, other microbial product failures, due to molds, yeasts, and nonpathogenic bacteria, have to be addressed. Lowering of water activity and pH, modification of the headspace gas composition, thermal treatment, and inclusion of additives in the formula are common ways to overcome some of the microbial problems. Determining standard plate counts for the product, when held under typical storage conditions, is the usual means of monitoring its microbiological shelf-life stability. Products also should be subjected to distribution and storage temperature extremes simulating possible abuse conditions, to study their deleterious effects on product safety. For example, several freeze/thaw cycles may generate severe irreversible changes in frozen products, leading to microbial growth and potential health hazards.

To initiate shelf-life studies, the product development scientist needs to make an educated guess regarding the mode of deterioration that limits the shelf life of the product. To accomplish this task, several resources should be utilized: (1) in-house information on similar products; (2) published scientific literature (e.g., Labuza and Schmidl 1985; Labuza 1982; Saguy and Karel 1987); (3) commercial data on competitive products; and (4) ingredient information provided by suppliers.

After the mode of failure is determined, a shelf-life study can be set up. A common approach used to evaluate the product throughout its shelf life is based on the sensory assessment of a "quality factor." By definition, the shelf life ends when samples stored under controlled conditions are perceived to be unacceptable by a trained sensory panel or a selected group of consumers. The use of an expert panel normally is preferred. Care must be taken to see that the panel truly represents the average consumer palate. For example, the employees of a bakery may be desensitized to certain flavors in sweet rolls and should be excluded from participating in a panel evaluating novel bakery products.

In some products, the food scientist can analytically determine an index of deterioration (ID) throughout the shelf life, that is, a chemical or physical property that corresponds to the sensory quality of the product. Examples include moisture, water activity, peroxide value, headspace oxygen content, redox potential, malondialdehyde, compressibility, trimethylamine in decomposing fish, water-holding capacity, loss of ascorbic acid, and others. Therefore, shelf-life-related changes in the ID correlate with quality loss. Whenever possible, it is advantageous to complement sensory evaluation of the quality factor with at least one ID measurement. ID evaluation generally can be carried out with better accuracy than sensory assessments and also lend themselves to kinetic modeling.

The kinetic approach best describes the changes occurring in the stored product, and thus is a very reliable assessment for the simulation of possible distribution scenarios. The quantitative analysis of quality changes requires that the ID be expressed as a function of processing and storage conditions in a manner that allows simulation of those changes. In other words, shelf-life prediction needs a mathematical model that expresses the effects of environmental and formulation factors on the ID. This kinetic model is often nonlinear and coupled and contains partial differential equations. Usually the model calculates temperature effects by using the Arrhenius equation and ingredient concentration effects using zero-, first-, or second-order reaction kinetics.

During product development, preliminary shelf-life results often are needed before the end of the actual shelf life, which in some cases may be as long as 12 to 24 months. A rapid method is required periodically to evaluate the effects of various formulation and processing variables on the shelf-life stability of the product being developed. To accomplish this task, various accelerated shelf-life tests (ASLTs) have been devised. To perform ASLTs correctly, it is best to measure at least one ID and employ a kinetic model. The basic assumptions and tenets of ASLTs were described in detail by Labuza (1982).

ASLTs typically are conducted at elevated temperatures. Because most reaction rates increase exponentially with temperature, raising the temperature by 10°C causes an increase in quality loss by a factor of 2 to 6. This simplified factor, called the Q_{10}, depends on the food being evaluated, the mode of failure, and the temperature range. The value of the Q_{10} needs to be determined experimentally for each food. If the mode of deterioration is known, this factor also can be estimated from the literature in order to predict the effects of best and worst possible storage conditions on the shelf-life stability of a new food product.

Typical storage temperatures for ASLT studies are summarized in Table 3-1.

Table 3-1. Typical ASLT storage temperatures.

Food category	Control temperature (°C)	ASLT temperature range (°C)
Frozen	−40	−15 to −5
Refrigerated	2	5 to 15
Shelf-stable	22	30 to 45

The product is stored at three to four different temperatures within the specified range in order to calculate the Q_{10} factor. Each temperature is maintained constant within 1 °C, and the ASLT temperature range usually is raised only slightly above the control temperature in order to avoid changes in the product failure mode. Because of glass transitions in the food, nonlinear Arrhenius kinetics and concomitant changes in the mode of deterioration recently were observed, even in frozen foods stored at temperatures below −10°C (Levine and Slade 1986).

Besides elevated temperatures, additional ASLT conditions have been employed occasionally. Other accelerating factors include elevated humidity, high oxygen tension in the headspace, and cycling temperature fluctuations. However, the complexity of these factors requires special mathematical data manipulation and makes their application quite cumbersome.

Both standard and accelerated shelf-life testing requires careful methodology. A number of choices concerning the test conditions must be made before one starts the study:

- Appropriate quality factor or index of deterioration
- Storage temperature(s)
- Additional ASLT conditions
- Control and number of replicates
- Total storage time
- Number of variables
- Kinetic model

Because of the complexity of many shelf-life studies, it is advisable to employ an experienced statistician to help with both the design of the test and the final data analysis. For example, a fractional factorial design may be necessary in order to maintain a manageable number of data points without compromising the validity of a mathematical model based on the test results. Shelf-life testing also requires the cooperation of the analytical chemistry department, sensory personnel, and additional external resources, depending on the product.

Shelf-life tests hardly ever are carried out just once. The first study often discloses additional modes of product failure, leading to refinements in the subsequent test. Also, if the data indicate that the quality of the new product turns unacceptable before the end of the shelf life, then further product development is needed, involving reformulation, process optimization, the gas composition of the headspace, and the packaging design. In some products the test results even may demonstrate that the target shelf life is not attainable. Then the question of whether to launch the new product with a shorter shelf life or to abandon the entire project is a marketing decision.

Tolerance Testing

The term tolerance describes the allowable range of deviation from a standard. Although a food product has a target formula, the ingredient delivery systems in the plant are not precise or accurate enough always to hit the target for each ingredient. Instead, there is a range for each ingredient, which depends on the type of equipment used. In order for the engineering department to specify the appropriate scales and delivery equipment, the R&D team must define the acceptable range for each ingredient through laborious experimentation. The food scientist deliberately increases and decreases the percentage of an ingredient from the standard formula and then measures various responses; and from these results, the scientist determines the acceptable ingredient variability. Most of the time, ingredient interactions necessitate a large experimental design to define the range for the entire food composition. This information then is compiled in a document called the process development criteria (see below), to be submitted to corporate engineering.

Besides ingredient tolerance, the R&D team also measures processing tolerance. Several variables may require testing at each unit operation. When the product is to be baked, for example, researchers must determine the acceptable operating range of oven temperatures for each pass. During the development phase, operating windows must be defined in order to specify the processing and packaging equipment. Also, tolerance testing is necessary to develop statistical process control charts for plant operators to use. (Some of these manufacturing aspects will be discussed in Chapter 4.)

The purpose of these tolerance experiments is not only to design the equipment but also to intentionally build tolerance into a formula and a process. Ideally, R&D engineers a food product whose most important quality attributes are affected only slightly by variables that are known to be difficult to control. Mathematically, researchers attempt to minimize the slope between an ingredient or a processing variable and the response, such as an organoleptic measurement. Tolerance testing helps researchers to recognize such shallow response areas and thereby to develop a product of superior quality for the consumer.

Finally, the new product is tested for consumer abuse tolerance. A home economist keeps different variables under various stressful storage conditions, prepares them without adding certain requested ingredients, cooks them in a range of microwave ovens, overcooks them in a conventional oven, and subjects them to additional product-specific abuses. Again, this process helps researchers to select the most tolerant food formulation.

Documentation

Detailed documentation of all R&D results usually concludes the development phase. Both engineers and scientists contribute to this important endeavor. The terminology for the different documents may vary from one company to another, but their objectives and contents are very general. The following documents are written at the end of the development phase:

- *Testing procedures (TP):* Any new method—chemical, sensory, or physical, such as baking performance—developed for testing incoming ingredients or the product during different stages of its manufacture requires the write-up of a formal TP that has its own TP number. This decreases the testing variability among quality assurance (QA) technicians and QA laboratories from different plants, increases the consistency over several years, and facilitates computerized data acquisition and manipulation.
- *Ingredient specifications (IS):* Each ingredient is characterized by a separate IS containing an IS number. The IS lists the visual and performance attributes required from that ingredient, the testing procedures used for measuring these attributes, shelf-life requirements, and any other relevant information. Sometimes the same ingredient may be purchased under two different ISs if used in different products, as the criticalities of quality attributes, the testing procedures, and the quality grade may vary in different applications. Ingredient specifications are written for the benefit of suppliers, procurement, plant QA, and R&D. They also allow accounting to easily track the total ingredient costs by plant, product, or ingredient category.
- *Product specifications (PS):* Each product is described by a complete product specification. PSs are used primarily by plant personnel, as they detail the entire process of food manufacture, including formulation, process specifications for each unit operation, preparation of preblends and subassemblies of items such as a sauce to be used in a menu, hazard analysis critical control points (HACCP) information, statistical process control charts, QA sampling procedures, chemical and microbiological testing procedures, finished product performance criteria, and processing line sanitation schedules. The writing of a PS is a concerted effort of project scientists, engineers, and a corporate QA manager. Product specifications also are helpful for new R&D personnel attempting to learn about the product during a later maintenance project.
- *Capital appropriation request (CAR):* A capital appropriation request gen-

erally is submitted to the board of directors as soon as possible, or at least 6 months before the commercialization phase begins. It succinctly states the business proposition, a competitive market profile analysis, a summary of the technologies involved and how they leverage the new product, and a ledger of the commercialization and product roll-out expenses. A CAR often exceeds several million dollars because it covers all the processing equipment and facilities, such as revamping or expanding an existing plant or construction of a new building.

- *Process design criteria (PDC):* The project engineer, with assistance from the food scientist, writes the PDC document approximately 6 to 12 months before commercialization, depending on the equipment lead time. Its sole objective is to translate all of the knowledge gained during the product development phase into process design criteria, that is, detailed specifications for each unit operation. For example, specifications for a baking step include oven temperature, residence time, type of heating, air flow, number of passes, temperature gradient across different passes, belt material, and many others. It also may specify the type of statistical process control equipment built into the oven, such as a scale or microwave analyzer to continuously monitor the total product moisture loss. The PDC is a vehicle for transferring all this information from R&D to corporate engineering, which (1) designs the process equipment based on the PDC, (2) orders or builds the equipment, (3) installs it in the plant, and (4) carries out the shakedown before R&D starts the commercialization phase of the project.

- *Technology transfer document (TTD):* The technology transfer is a summary of all R&D results, both positive and negative. This historical document—similar to a Ph.D. dissertation—describes the background of the project and then takes the reader along the entire development journey in a chronological sequence. The rationale for writing a TTD is primarily to distill results scattered over 10 to 50 notebooks into a single organized report that serves a teaching purpose for any new team member and helps expand the company's technology base.

- *Patents:* Most novel technologies are safeguarded against competition by patent protection rather than being kept trade secrets. Although the patent attorney drafts this legal document, the food scientist or engineer is responsible for submitting the technical research report that forms the basis of both the specification and the claims. Therefore, the scientist bears overall accountability for the patent's contents, breadth, and scientific clarity. Usually a close collaboration exists between the attorney and the technical liaison until the patent is filed.

- *Publication:* In rare circumstances, food scientists and engineers are permitted to publish some of their development findings in refereed scientific journals. The divulgence of such information usually requires a vice president's approval, which is granted only if publication will not jeopardize any trade secrets or business opportunities. Examples of publishable findings include: (1) very broad concepts that are already known in some form; (2) patents that have been issued and therefore are common knowledge; and (3) patents that are filed in Europe, as these applications become public domain within 18 months of the priority filing date regardless of issuance or rejection.

Unlike academic reports, most corporate documents written by one scientist are countersigned at least once by a peer or a superior, assigned a docket number, microfilmed, and distributed to relevant departments, with one copy archived in a central repository, usually the library. These rigorous record-keeping procedures are necessary to assure efficient technology transfer between different departments, to maintain some documentation uniformity throughout the various technical areas, to facilitate future project revival efforts after a project has become extinct or dormant for a period of time, and to litigate any potential patent infringement cases.

COMMERCIALIZATION

After the new product has been developed to the satisfaction of both R&D and marketing, it is ready for commercialization. Depending on process complexity, this stage may last anywhere from a few weeks to 12 months. The commercialization phase is characterized by highly intense activities and by daily communication between different business segments of the corporate organization, including R&D, engineering, operations, marketing, market research, and plant personnel. Commercialization is a gratifying career experience for the food scientist and the engineer, as it marks the culmination or fruition of a long-term research effort; but, it also may impose much stress on R&D personnel due to possible extensive travel and living away from home for extended periods of time. Both personal and technical conflict situations may arise that require immediate resolution; deadlines need to be met; teamwork becomes more important than ever before; and new issues must be addressed on a daily basis, leaving little time for systematic planning and designing of experiments.

Of all the miscellaneous R&D activities occurring during the commercialization phase, plant start-up occupies the largest fraction and involves the most R&D personnel.

Start-up

Start-up can be defined as R&D's plant involvement from the time the first piece of new equipment enters the facility until the entire process is handed over to the plant manager for production. It can be separated into two distinct phases, equipment shakedown and process optimization.

Equipment Shakedown

Civil engineering of a plant expansion or the construction of a new facility usually is concurrent with the latter part of the development phase. The site is expected to be available for equipment installation by the time that commercialization begins.

Plant start-up begins with the installation of the new equipment. Corporate engineering assumes accountability for setting up the equipment and testing the circuitry, gears, and overall operability. The vendor may participate in this process to aid in any troubleshooting. Occasionally R&D also conducts a small trial on the equipment to confirm the requested process specifications.

Equipment shakedown rarely offers any unexpected surprises or R&D hurdles and can be completed in approximately two to eight weeks, depending on the size and complexity of the new processing line.

Process Optimization

After the equipment is installed and its processing capability has been determined, R&D begins a full-fledged scale-up of the pilot plant process. Many unit operations contain well-known calculated scale-up factors and lend themselves to a predictable scale-up, but other pieces of equipment introduce poorly understood processing variables that completely alter key quality attributes of the new product. These latter unit operations account for extended start-ups and even for delays in product roll-out.

In cases of scale-up difficulties, the various product and processing interactions described above mandate a lengthy reoptimization. Because a full-sized processing line contains many more processing variables than a small pilot plant process, product optimization during start-up requires large statistical factorial design studies. The execution of these experiments is similar to that of pilot plant studies, in that it usually takes a large team to run the line and collect the copious processing data. The ultimate goal of all the start-up experimentation is to consistently emulate the quality and shelf-life stability of the gold standard—that is, the new food product that has undergone ample consumer testing and been approved by R&D and marketing at the end of the development phase.

A frictionless successful plant start-up is the dream of every R&D project team, and several books and industrial classes have been dedicated to achieving this goal (e.g., a thorough course entitled ''How to Successfully Transfer Products and Processes from R&D into Manufacturing,'' developed and taught by the American Management Association in its on-site seminar division in New

York). In summary, most experts agree that a smooth start-up requires, among other factors, a solid product knowledge base acquired during the development phase, R&D leadership by an experienced scientist or food engineer, and personnel continuity throughout the entire project. However, despite following all of the expert advice on effective technology transfer, plant start-ups often tend to obey the following five Murphy's laws:

1. In any field of endeavor, anything that can go wrong, will go wrong.
2. Left to themselves, things always go from bad to worse.
3. If there is a possibility of several things going wrong, the one that will go wrong is the one that will do the most damage.
4. Nature always sides with the hidden flaw.
5. If everything seems to be going well, you have obviously overlooked something.

Confirmatory Shelf-Life Study

Scale-up not only affects the processability and quality of a new food product, but if often alters its shelf-life stability. Depending on the mode of failure and the food scientist's approach to inhibiting the chemical reaction(s) leading to deterioration, scale-up may increase or decrease shelf life. Because of difficulty in predicting its precise effect on food stability, a confirmatory shelf-life study is carried out. The method of choice is a standard test—instead of an ASLT—under both ideal and realistic storage conditions, such as fluctuating temperatures or freeze/thaw cycles. Ideally the products to be tested are produced by the plant under typical steady-state manufacturing conditions. This way the test confirms acceptable product quality throughout the shelf life of realistic food, not hand-picked showcase samples.

Quality Approval

To remove any bias or arbitrariness from quality judgments of scaled-up products, the final production samples often are tested against gold standards in a home use test that provides data on food quality, packaging, serving directions, and any potential handling issues. This test may contain additional cells to evaluate the effects of miscellaneous variables. As soon as the R&D team is convinced it has achieved the highest possible quality and feels ready to start to ship, a meeting is set up with marketing to obtain final product approval. In some organizations, the blessing of the general manager or even the chief executive officer also may be required prior to a major product launch.

Keylines

Toward the end of development or at the beginning of commercialization, the food scientist is responsible for providing label information to set up printing keylines for the package. The following information usually is included:

- Standard of identity (product name).
- Ingredient declaration.
- Net weight. These calculations are based on statistical process capability and must follow a set of complex ''risk of violation'' rules.
- Expiration dates and storage information.
- Serving suggestions.
- Company name and address.
- Licenses.
- Nutritional labeling.
- Health claims and consumer education. For instance, some Kellogg cereal boxes inform the reader of the health benefits of regular exercise and of a diet rich in fiber and low in cholesterol and saturated fats.
- Safety instructions. Examples include tips on how to open the package or how long to leave the product in the microwave oven after cooking before removing it.
- Quality pledges.
- UPC symbol for laser scanning at the cash register in retail stores.

Complex federal and state laws and regulations necessitate the involvement of a regulatory professional in the development of the label information. Laws specify the print size, height-to-width ratio of the nutritional panel, contrasting color for the print and the background, and many other details. For example, there are rules that determine when to use a common or usual name for a product description, when to use a descriptive name, and when to use a fanciful name (e.g., for products whose identity is obvious). Although many of the labeling laws are ambiguous, their interpretation should follow some commonsense principle, as expressed in the following quotation from Taylor Quinn, former director of compliance of the U.S. Food and Drug Adminstration:

If it walks like a duck,
and it talks like a duck,
then call it a duck.

Much of the label information is contributed by a variety of corporate functions, but the food scientist bears overall accountability for initiating and coordinating the collection of the individual pieces and for checking the accuracy of the contents.

Store Audits

Shortly after product introduction in a limited test market or a full-fledged national roll-out, store audits are conducted in a few selected cities. Hundreds of products are purchased in representative stores and analyzed on site for product quality, package integrity, temperature, headspace composition, and other attributes unique to the particular food item. The help of an experienced statistician often is requested, both to plan the test design and to analyze and interpret the results.

Store audits are an attempt to determine the effects of actual distribution and store conditions on the final product quality seen by the consumer. Therefore, a store audit may be considered an extensive final shelf-life study with real-life variables superimposed on it, such as temperature and humidity fluctuations, rough handling, and low atmospheric pressure during transcontinental ground transportation across the Rocky Mountains. Store audits often are complemented by specific distribution tests, such as monitoring the core temperature of a foodstuff from the time it leaves the plant until it reaches the retail shelf. Several new technologies, such as Lifeline, are so advanced that the product's complete temperature history can be recorded.

During the commercialization phase, many other short-term projects in addition to those listed above require immediate attention. Many of these issues, however, are addressed on an emergency basis, and their thorough resolution must wait until the next and last phase of the project—product maintenance.

MAINTENANCE

Most major food product lines require continuous R&D support throughout the product lifetime. The extent of R&D involvement varies with the type of product, the season, focal consumer health issues, and many other product-specific factors; but a team of one food scientist and one process engineer usually manages to address all the key issues. Toward the end of a product cycle, this support often diminishes to one food scientist or process engineer, who may attend to additional project responsibilities.

Product maintenance requires both R&D experience and technical breadth. The food scientist must demonstrate the ability to work independently, handle multiple assignments, use various resources, and cultivate positive collaborative relationships with plant personnel. This person must establish priorities, dividing his or her time between troubleshooting or putting out fires in plants and developing a deeper technical understanding of the product and the process.

A fair amount of effort is spent on problem solving in plants. The QA manager may have recurring problems with an ingredient that is out of specification, the processing line may not run smoothly during a flour crop changeover, or the consumer response office may report a high mold complaint rate following conversion of an artificial spice flavor to a natural spice blend. Most such issues require some experimentation at the plant, followed by occasional R&D work at headquarters. With any subsequent ingredient and processing changes the specifications need to be updated. The tedious assignment of maintaining a current specification system usually becomes the responsibility of the R&D food scientist.

On rare occasions the food scientist becomes immersed in projects created by consumer advocate groups. Although many of these issues are controversial and may not warrant product bans, consumer perception often weighs more heavily than absolute truth, and the food processor must respond rapidly in order not to lose any marketshare. Recent examples include ethylene dibromide (EDB) fumigation of flour and Alar (daminozide) treatment of apples. Similarly, the food manufacturer often feels compelled by consumer demand to go along with popularized health dogmas despite ongoing scientific disputes and lack of conclusive human nutritional studies. For instance, during the late 1980s tropical oils were the culprit in the etiology of cardiovascular disease in humans, and soluble oat brans came to their rescue.

The development of a deeper technical understanding during the maintenance phase may lead to some long-term research projects involving industrial–academic collaborations. Such projects have dealt with the staling of cereal products, the toughening of breadlike products in the microwave oven, olive discoloration of peas and beans, and crystal formation in cheese, ice cream, doughs, and other foodstuffs. These projects simulate university research in that they provide the investigator with some academic leeway and allow for genuine creativity by removing the initial processing and time constraints that are associated with all other R&D phases.

Although many of the above maintenance problems may occur only with occasional products, most foodstuffs require maintenance related to product quality improvement and greater profit yields.

Product Quality Improvement

Most large food companies maintain a professional consumer response staff. They receive questions, comments, suggestions, and complaints from consumers by mail and via toll-free 800-number calls. The function of consumer response personnel is threefold:

- *Customer satisfaction:* Because the negative purchasing impact of every dissatisfied customer may outweigh the positive impact of happy customers by a factor of 10 to 50, each consumer response is dealt with individually. Questions are answered by phone or by a personal letter, suggestions are forwarded to R&D for technical consideration, and faulty products are replaced to regain the customer's confidence in the expected food quality.

- *Consumer trend analysis:* Consumer responses are tabulated and categorized for each product. Computerized analyses of these results may reveal consumer trends, such as a high level of dissatisfaction with excessive packaging material, that can be translated into new product ideas that meet a real consumer need and may gain a competitive advantage.
- *Product quality improvement:* Consumer complaints are a powerful tool for the early identification of defects in the product design and of additional modes of failure that were not recognized during the product development phase. The absolute level of customer dissatisfaction and consequent cost to the company are rather difficult to estimate from the complaint rate, as the multiplier between complaint and complainable incidence is generally unknown. However, customer complaints do permit assessment of the relative magnitude of each design fault, which, in turn, aids in the setting of R&D priorities and the allotment of necessary resources.

Quality improvement projects not only result from customer complaints, but they also can be suggested by the trade, distributors, and internal departments, such as the sales force, plant personnel, or R&D. Because of their familiarity with the product, these people often recognize various means for improving overall product quality that were not obvious to the original product development team.

Typically, R&D projects dealing with quality improvement focus on the following:

- *Flavor:* A number of flavor houses may be solicited to participate in a flavor project to improve the quality of the presently added flavor(s).
- *Ingredient sourcing:* Once the new product has succeeded in the initial test market, substantial R&D efforts may be devoted to sourcing ingredients of improved overall quality. For example, fisheries may be inspected all around the globe in order to obtain fish caught on vessels containing the most stringent quality control criteria because initial processing and storage conditions are the major determinant of future shelf-life quality and value to the consumer.
- *Reformulation:* Products often are reformulated during the maintenance phase to improve the nutritional quality or various organoleptic attributes, such as texture. For example, animal fats may be replaced with unsaturated vegetable oils to follow the most recent health guidelines of the American Heart Association. A seemingly simple ingredient substitution such as this would require extensive R&D involvement to assure consumer acceptance

of the product, to confirm and optimize the processability of the reformulated product, and to test it for shelf-life stability.

- *Processing:* Increasing statistical process control often reduces the variability of product attributes, thereby improving product consistency and overall quality. An increase in product quality also can be achieved by optimizing individual unit operations, such as replacing a batch mixer with a continuous mixing operation.
- *Packaging:* During the lifetime of a product packaging material, the design and the equipment may be upgraded several times, both to better protect the food and to align its image with current packaging trends. This includes the addition of antitampering devices, resealability, microwavability, and many other safety and convenience features.
- *Physical characteristics:* Food products often require physical adaptation to meet novel needs created by broad demographic and social changes in Western societies. Examples include a single-serve option and serving instructions that can safely be followed by children.

Most of these quality improvement projects are completed within a few months, but some—such as the development of a new process—may require several years of applied research and development. Such intense R&D efforts usually are supported only when they also lead to future cost savings, as described next.

Profit Improvement

The primary goal during product development and initial product introduction is to attain the highest possible quality and to gain consumer acceptance. As the repeat purchases hold up and the new product grows into a viable business, increasing the profit margins will assure its long-term survival in the competitive marketplace. R&D can impact the manufacturing cost of the new product by three means: formulation, process, and packaging improvements.

Formulation

Cost savings may be realized by using both less expensive and smaller amounts of ingredients, and by reducing the cost of handling them. Improvements may include:

- *Alternate ingredients:* During initial ingredient selection the food scientist often opts for a Cadillac, in terms of the quality and the quantity of non-commodity ingredients, to assure the highest quality. With expanding knowledge of the product, however, the scientist may identify a less expensive ingredient alternate that still meets all the performance criteria, such as the substitution of one gum with another, or the replacement of a whole spice with an artificial oleoresin. Similarly, product experience gained during the maintenance phase may allow a decrease in the level of an expensive ingredient with no sacrifice of the quality or the shelf-life of the product.

- *Ingredient consolidation:* Reducing the total number of ingredients and suppliers used by a food processor results in large cost savings due to increased manufacturing efficiency, improved vendor support, better inventory control, and decreased paperwork. However, in some cases where a supplier has held a monopoly through patent protection, it may be advantageous to source an alternate supplier. This usually provides the company with a great deal of procurement leverage, which usually results in a substantial price reduction.
- *Product standardization:* As in ingredient consolidation, cost savings may be captured by standardizing the formula, product weight, and package for a multiple product line, because of greater manufacturing efficiency and improved supplier contracts.

Process

Cost savings may result from a number of different process improvements:

- Improving the process efficiency may lower the amount of on-line ingredient and finished product waste (shrinkage).
- Improving the process efficiency may result in less downtime for the plant.
- The development of a continuous process as a replacement for a batch procedure may increase quality consistency and possibly decrease labor intensity.
- Tight statistical process control lowers variation in the final product weight. This decrease in manufacturing variability reduces the amount of product that needs to be given away because, as defined by U.S. "risk of violation" rules, the difference between the declared weight and the target weight is proportional to the standard deviation in weight.

Packaging

Large cost savings may be realized by decreasing the gas barrier properties of a particular packaging film, by reducing the physical strength of a food package, by changing the design, or by improving the efficiency of a packaging line in the plant. As in the case of ingredient selection, the packaging engineer often overdesigns the package and its functional components and then slowly eases off, depending on the market results.

SKILL REQUIREMENT

Figure 3-3 presents an overview of the five project phases, as discussed in detail throughout the present chapter. From the various activities and skill requirements depicted in this summary, it becomes apparent that a suitable match

ACTIVITIES	PROJECT PHASE	SKILL REQUIREMENTS
Idea Generation Competitive Product Review Prototype Development Technology Screening Consumer Feedback Managerial Support Business Interactions	SCREENING	Creativity Salesmanship Culinary Skills Sensory Skills Vision Technology Awareness Independence
Technology Assessment Packaging Evaluation Manufacturing Scenarios Financial Evaluation Consumer Tests Risk Analysis	FEASIBILITY	Experimentation Ingredient Interactions Technology Awareness Product/Process Interactions Planning and Organization Ability to Set Priorities Effective Oral Communication
Technical Plan Formulation Shelf-Life Product Safety Food Engineering Plant Trials Documentation	DEVELOPMENT	Technical Depth Experimental Designs Interaction with Resources Planning and Organization Contact with Businees Team Team Player Written Communication Skills
Start-up Keylines/Specifications Confirmatory Shelf-Life Quality Approval Store Audits	COMMERCIALIZATION	Problem Solving Quick Thinker In-Depth Product Knowledge Interpersonal Skills Stress/Conflict Management Team Player Corporate Function Knowledge
Ingredient Substitution Plant Problem Solving Technical Understanding Update Specifications Response to Consumer Issues Product Quality Improvement Profit Improvement	MAINTENANCE	Problem Solving Technical Breadth Ability to Set Priorities Plant Communication Skills Use of Resources Independence Multiple Assignments

Figure 3-3. Summary of project phases.

between the product phase and the R&D scientist depends on the person's career goals, experience level, and technical background. Although no strict educational prerequisites exist for industrial food R&D positions, many large food corporations recruit primarily B.S. engineers and M.S. food scientists at the exempt level. Table 3-2 shows the degree distribution, broken down by title and function, in the U.S. food industry. The information in Table 3-2 buttresses our contention that the food industry is consumer-driven and rather "low tech" as compared to the chemical or the pharmaceutical industry.

The following summary gives typical criteria for assigning food scientists to each of the five project phases:

- *Screening:* An experienced food scientist with strong culinary and artistic talents is best suited to this phase. The individual must feel comfortable with a loose corporate structure and display a high degree of creativity. Screening does not require strong technical competence but a thorough market/consumer awareness and a broad knowledge of technology availability.
- *Feasibility:* This phase usually is tackled by both a food scientist and a processing engineer, one of whom should be experienced. A successful feasibility study relies heavily on technical breadth rather than depth. The engineer and the food scientist must be thoroughly acquainted with up-to-date ingredient, processing, and packaging technologies. At the same time, they possess a working knowledge of fundamentals of food chemistry, ingredient interactions, and product/process interactions and have the ability to design and execute effective experimentation.
- *Development:* Under the guidance of an experienced food scientist or processing engineer, this is the ideal training phase for any food industry novice. It contains elements resembling academic experimentation, yet allows the new hire to become familiar with the typical corporate team approach to solving multidisciplinary problems. The new food scientist or engineer has the opportunity to become acquainted with the various business functions and learn their corporate accountabilities (e.g., marketing, market research, consumer service, corporate engineering, operations, analytical chemistry, patent attorneys, and statisticians). The development phase also provides some limited exposure to plants and to the industrial specification and documentation system.
- *Commercialization:* Successful commercialization absolutely demands an experienced scientist or engineer at the helm of the R&D team. This individual must exhibit in-depth knowledge of the product, its ingredient interactions, and product/process/packaging interactions and be familiar with the product's development history, to be able to react quickly and proficiently to crisis situations. General commercialization experience also is

Table 3-2.   Title by education.

Job title	High school or less	Some college	B.S.	M.S.	Ph.D.
President	10.6%	28.7%	41.5%	14.9%	4.3%
V.P./manufacturing	5.8	17.3	48.1	25.0	3.8
V.P./R&D	0.0	5.3	10.5	42.1	36.8
Plant manager	12.7	28.9	44.4	14.1	0.0
Production manager	12.5	23.8	53.8	8.8	0.0
Engineering manager	3.8	21.5	53.1	21.5	0.0
Process engineer	0.7	13.0	69.9	15.8	0.0
Packaging manager	15.0	30.0	40.0	15.0	0.0
Technical director	0.0	2.5	47.5	23.8	26.2
QC manager	1.4	16.1	61.5	17.5	3.5
Food scientist	0.0	8.2	54.4	25.7	11.7
Sanitation manager	14.3	42.9	36.7	6.1	0.0
Distribution manager	15.6	31.2	40.6	12.5	0.0

Percentages may not add up to 100 because of incomplete or duplicate answers.
SOURCE: *Food Engineering* 1989 Salary Survey.

crucial for the scientist to deal effectively with both technical and inter-personal conflicts, which invariably arise during plant start-ups.

- *Maintenance:* This phase is well suited for either an experienced food scientist or a new hire, provided that the assignment is clearly stated. Because maintenance projects run the gamut from problem solving in the plant to conducting long-term research, it is difficult to generalize about skill and knowledge requirements. Most maintenance projects, however, are intended to resolve an issue within a well-defined time frame; so the scientist or engineer involved in these short-term projects is expected to display technical breadth, independence, and the ability to handle multiple assignments, and to converse effectively with people in various functions and at different intellectual levels. Excellent oral communication skills play a major role in building productive relationships between R&D and the plants.

Despite personal preferences for certain project phases, it is imperative that the well-rounded food professional be subjected to the entire project cycle at least once. A full appreciation of all aspects of product development leads to the broad experience base that is essential to a successful career in industrial food R&D. However, after the scientist has had some initial exposure to the complete product development cycle, his or her interests, skills, and career goals are closely matched with project needs, generally to the benefits of both the individual and the corporation.

OUTLOOK

The preceding sections depict a highly complex, lengthy, and time-consuming R&D process for a typical U.S. corporation that requires multidisciplinary teamwork and efforts. Obviously, certain logical questions should be raised: How much is the estimated cost? How long will it take? Is the process cost-effective? Is the expense justified? Are there better and shorter ways? Even though there are no optimal, straightforward answers that can be generally utilized and implemented in the food industry, it is possible to highlight some possible ways of improving the product development process and to make some recommendations, which are based on the authors' personal preferences and experience. However, each and every company clearly must find its own unique "yellow brick road."

The first and perhaps foremost issues are the time frame and the cost of new product development. To assess the cost of a complex process such as product development, one has to consider the number of successes as compared to the number of failures. This ratio may be calculated by the success probability, which will be addressed shortly.

The estimated development cost for a single product through each of the various phases of development, based on some published data (Urban and Hause) and on the authors' own judgment, is outlined in Table 3-3. These data depict a simplified assessment for large, medium, and small companies.

Table 3-3 shows the cost for medium and small companies to be significantly lower than that for a large company during screening, feasibility, and development. The commercialization cost, however, is similar in all three cases. The most striking fact is that the overall probability of success (defined as the product of all the probabilities of success during each project phase) significantly diminishes with decreasing company size, from 1.1 to 0.27 to 0.06, respectively. The higher probability of success has a price tag paid by the larger firms. It is also apparent that smaller companies overall spend more money to introduce a new product, as reflected in the total project costs in Table 3-3. Hence, because most small companies have a small or nonexistent budget buffer, correct budget appropriation and control are extremely important. Big companies can "live" with several failures, but a small company works under the threat of losing a "one-time" opportunity. Therefore, risk assessment becomes critical.

It is particularly striking that for a small company and/or an entrepreneur venture company, the probability of success is very low, estimated to be below 0.1%. In other words, less than one successful introduction per 999 failures is expected! This failure rate, however, is strongly dependent on the definition of screening.

The average time required for developing a new product is estimated as 28, 24, and 15 months for large, medium, and small companies, respectively. This time frame is much too slow and should be altered (a topic that will be addressed shortly).

From the data presented in Table 3-3, it also is quite obvious that for a large corporation the time frame for a typical product development cycle and the cost involved are excessive. An article in *Business Week* (Byrne 1989) addressed this issue under the heading. "Is Your Company Too Big?" Some of the article's points were as follows:

- Big companies failed to pioneer in many of the decade's most important technological innovations.
- Despite the "bigger-is-better" notion, propagated by recent takeovers and acquisitions, the global marketplace requires attributes seldom associated with bigness. It demands speed, agility, and the ability to improvise and customize.
- Only in some cases does the economy of scale still apply.
- The 500 largest corporations alone account for nearly 30% of the U.S. gross national product, and they employ 80% of the scientists and engineers who work in the industry. The food industry is no exception.

Table 3-3. Typical development cost, duration, and probability of success for a new food product (adopted from Urban and Hauser, 1980).

Stage	Large Company			Medium Company			Small Company		
	Probability (%)	Cost ($000's)	Time (months)	Probability (%)	Cost ($000's)	Time (months)	Probability (%)	Cost ($000's)	Time (months)
Screening	5	50	1	3	25	1	3	5	1
Feasibility	50	250	3	30	100	1	10	20	1
Development	50	1,000	12	40	550	10	30	350	5
Commercialization	85	5,000	12	75	5,000	12	70	5,000	8
Total R&D Process	1.1	6,300	28	0.27	5,675	24	0.06	5,375	15
Total Project		9,000			10,000			12,000	

- People in organizations spend too much time justifying why they should not do something rather than working to meet new goals or objectives.

However, size is hardly the issue. The crucial question here is how to optimize new food product development. In a recent talk, Dr. James R. Behnke, Senior Vice President of Technology, Grand Metropolitan Food Sector (Behnke 1989), addressed this topic. His main conclusion concerned the need for "excellerating"—a term coined by Behnke to denote a combination of excellence and acceleration. Excellerating, which dictates a total new mind-set and operating process for R&D, includes six critical elements:

1. *Business strategy:* Everything boils down to having a clear and concise business strategy. The strategy should provide direction for working on the right things versus working on things right.
2. *Think big, act small:* It is necessary to combine the simplicity and agility of a small company with the resources of a large company. This approach may be described as regional and niche marketing built upon earlier successes with realistic predicted volumes and timetables versus national marketing with forced timetables and unrealistic volume expectations that "make the numbers work."
3. *Fail small, fail early:* It is important to start with the consumer and the marketplace. Only when consumer expectations are met can a company invest the time and resources needed to get it "right." Mini-market tests utilizing small-scale production are essential. The consumer should be an integral and intimate part of the development process. Numerous small start-ups aimed at small markets constantly must be made.
4. *Risk taking:* Traditionally, the food industry has rewarded risk aversion, not calculated risk taking. The "shoot the messenger" syndrome is quite common. Companies are paralyzed with piles of useless data and very little useful information. Management should implement controlled risk taking and simultaneously encourage creativity. Management also must develop the right environment to allow innovation to flourish, and must create an atmosphere of entrepreneurship so that people will feel comfortable and empowered to take calculated risks. Management should support failure by actively rewarding mistakes and efforts that were well thought out, executed with alacrity, and thoroughly learned from.
5. *Promoting more—not less—competition:* Companies should learn from their competitors, in the United States and internationally.
6. *Venture teams:* Product development requires a new approach and mind-set. The formation of venture teams provides a sense of urgency, personal ownership, and a common objective for all team members. Champions who can drive and lead these venture teams are essential. Decentralization

and the formation of independent business units play a major role in creating ownership and personal commitment.

This vision of excelleration provides some clear direction and leadership for new product development in an era of fierce international competition.

Another noteworthy contribution to the shaping of industrial food R&D for the 1990s and beyond is a concept developed by Philip L. Smith (1988), who served as the General Foods CEO until 1988. He established seven principles that link research, marketing, and business strategy:

1. *Corporate vision:* The linkage between research, business strategy, and marketing must begin with an overall corporate vision founded on a mission and key values. The vision should be clear, succinct, and exciting, and at the same time should leave wide latitude for the pursuit of new opportunities.
2. *Research direction as a two-way process:* Direction for research is both a top-down and a bottom-up process. This will guarantee both short- and long-term research and market involvement.
3. *Forced interaction:* Interaction between research, business planning, and marketing must be forced. This forced interaction tends to lower the corporate propensity to secrecy. Progress is more important than secrecy; hence, external acquisition of technology should be considered.
4. *Technical intensity:* Different businesses and technologies have inherently different levels of technical intensity and complexity.
5. *Looking outside:* Companies should look beyond their own walls for new ideas. No company has exclusive possession of the best talent and creativity. It is essential for any big company to survey small research firms, universities, and the marketplace, in the United States and internationally.
6. *Budget flexibility:* R&D should be operated with a disciplined budget, yet there has to be enough flexibility to permit some amount of scientific dabbling.
7. *Periodic check on research spending:* It is crucial to check on the compliance of research expenditures with the company's strategic direction.

In conclusion, the authors would like to reemphasize the role of the consumer. The R&D scientist should create a consumer-obsessed revolution (Peters 1987). It is necessary routinely to look at the smallest nuance of the tiniest program through the consumer's eyes, that is, as the consumer—not the R&D scientist—perceives it!

To survive competitively in the 1990s and beyond, companies must accelerate the product development process. Three essential requirements are needed: the ability to ensure the production of consistently high-quality products, the ability to make cost-effective products, and the flexibility to respond rapidly to marketplace changes. Currently, most product development processes cannot meet these challenges. To reach these goals, innovation in both technology and business strategy is essential. The best use of technology results not from the unbridled acquisition of leading edge equipment, but from innovative and disciplined management and from a thorough technical understanding of processes and technology. Basic scientific understanding is paramount to achieving excellence in both R&D and in the marketplace.

REFERENCES

Behnke J. R. 1989. Private communication.

Business Week. 1989. Innovation in America. Special Bonus Issue.

Byrne, J. A. 1989. Is your company too big? *Business Week*, Mar. 27, 1989, no. 3097: 84–94.

Fennema, O. R. 1985. *Food Chemistry*, 2nd edition. New York: Marcel Dekker.

Labuza, T. P. 1982. *Open Shelf-Life Dating of Foods*. Westport, Conn. Food and Nutrition Press.

Labuza, T. P. and Schmidl, M. K. 1985. Accelerated shelf-life testing of foods. *Food Technology* 9: 57–64, 134.

Levine, H. and Slade, L. 1986. A polymer physico-chemical approach to the study of commercial starch hydrolysis products (SHPs). *Carbohydrate Polymer* 6: 213.

Peters, T. 1987. *Thriving on Chaos*. New York: Knopf.

Saguy, I. and Karel, M. 1987. Index of deterioration and simulation of quality losses. In *Objective Methods in Food Quality Assessment*, ed. J. G. Kapsalis, pp. 233–260. Boca Baton, Fla. CRC Press.

Smith, P. L. 1988. Tighten the linkage between research, business strategy and marketing. *Research Technology Management* 31 (2): 6–8.

Urban, G. L. and Hauser J. R. 1980. *Design and Marketing of New Products*. Englewood Cliffs, N.J.: Prentice Hall.

Chapter 4

Engineering and Manufacturing

J. Peter Clark, Ph.D.

INTRODUCTION

Engineering has been described as the science concerned with putting scientific knowledge to practical uses. In the context of food product development, the science involved is food science, and the practical uses are commercially viable food products. For a new food product to become a successful article of commerce requires that it be manufactured efficiently, economically, and safely. As described elsewhere in this book, new food products are developed in kitchens and at laboratory benches to satisfy an identified consumer need. Engineers are needed to translate a small-scale formulation and process into a commercial-scale manufacturing operation, to design an appropriate facility, and to keep such a facility operating efficiently.

In most food companies, the operation of manufacturing facilities to satisfy customer orders is the responsibility of an operations or manufacturing department. Continuous improvement in the economic viability of a product requires the application in manufacturing of a number of scientific, engineering, and management skills.

This chapter will describe the key roles played by process, project, and manufacturing engineers in the transition of a food product from concept to market.

ENGINEERING DEFINED

A wide range of engineering disciplines have been accorded professional recognition, including: aeronautical, civil, chemical, electrical, mechanical, structural, nuclear, metallurgical, industrial, agricultural, and sanitary engineering. For each of these disciplines, there are accredited academic programs in many colleges and universities, awarding bachelor's, master's, and doctor's degrees. Most engineering academic programs include a common core of courses in mathematics, physics, chemistry, mechanics, statics, dynamics, thermodynamics, material science, fluid flow, and heat transfer, as well as many courses specific to the particular discipline. Engineering curricula are noted for their rigor and heavy reliance on laboratory courses. Most institutions require more than 120 semester hours or 180 quarter hours of coursework for a bachelor's degree, and students are increasingly taking more than four years to complete the program.

Cooperative education programs, in which students alternate study and work experiences, are common for engineering students. Such a program usually extends the time needed to receive a bachelor's degree to at least five years.

Master's and Ph.D. degrees in engineering usually require the performance of advanced research and the writing of a thesis, although coursework-only programs are available for a master's degree at some universities. Undergraduate programs are accredited by the Accreditation Board for Engineering and Technology (ABET) with the cooperation of the various national professional societies.

Food engineering is a relatively newly recognized discipline within engineering, with a small number of academic departments. Food engineering degrees can be obtained at the University of Illinois, Michigan State University, Purdue University, and the University of Colorado (where the department is called Food and Biochemical Engineering). In most cases, these degrees are granted by departments of agricultural engineering with the cooperation of departments of food science and technology and chemical engineering. Thus, although the practice of engineering in the food industry might be called food engineering, most practitioners are in fact trained in one of the more conventional engineering fields.

Probably the engineering field most directly applicable to the food industry is chemical engineering; the food, pharmaceutical, and bio-engineering division of the American Institute of Chemical Engineers is one of the largest divisions of that professional society. Other engineering fields in which employees of food companies commonly have studied include mechanical, electrical, and industrial engineering. Relatively few of these people had the opportunity to study food science or biological sciences in college; instead, they must learn the specifics of the food industry on the job or in postgraduate training. Likewise, the food scientists responsible for product development typically have little education in the engineering disciplines and so must learn the consequences of their decisions on subsequent steps in the development process through experience and by interaction with their engineering colleagues.

PRODUCT DEVELOPMENT SEQUENCE

Normally there is a fairly well-defined progression of stages in the development of a new food product from concept through demonstration to design, construction, and manufacturing. The individual stages often are performed by separate departments or organizations so that the transition from one stage to the next is accompanied by a "handoff." It is at the interface between organizations and disciplines that most problems arise, because of difficulties in communication and intrinsic differences in approaches.

Learning how to manage the entire sequence of critical stages smoothly is one of the great challenges of corporate management. Different companies have reached different solutions, and these solutions have changed over time, even within the same corporation.

Within a corporate structure, there typically are vice presidents of marketing, technology, manufacturing, finance, and administration. (Even these positions may be further consolidated or divided, but they are the major distinct elements of most organizations.) Engineering may fall within technology, or within manufacturing, or it may be split between the two. Product development in a technical sense almost always is within technology, but usually there is a major component of marketing that also is concerned with new product development. Some companies have experimented with having product development scientists report to marketing, but this approach usually is unsatisfactory because of the communications difficulties that can arise. On the other hand, it is seen as a means of ensuring the responsiveness of laboratory scientists.

Some of the best results in product development occur when multidisciplinary teams are formed early in the life of a project so that transitions from stage to stage become changes in activities without major changes in personnel. This arrangement obviously requires personnel who are flexible, versatile, and adaptable.

Where different personnel assume responsibilities at different development stages, excellent documentation and procedures are required. In addition, it is helpful for all parties to understand the nature of activities at all stages. One purpose of this book is to promote such understanding.

ENGINEERING CHALLENGES IN PRODUCT DEVELOPMENT

The fundamental and universal engineering challenge in food product development is scale-up, as typical concept development is performed on kitchen or laboratory equipment in small batches, by hand, with a typical focus on achieving desirable qualities. Quantitative data rarely are collected. Most consumer food products are characterized by relatively low unit values, rather high production volumes, and a wide variety of manufacturing challenges. Many food products sell for less than one dollar per unit (a single package or container), and most consumer food products are packaged in quantities of less than one pound (or its equivalent). Packaging rates can range from about 100 units per minute (for dry materials such as breakfast cereal or potato chips) to over 1,000 units per minute (for soft drink or beer cans).

Food products mostly are made from natural materials, which are subject to variations in physical properties, often are solids, and undergo difficult-to-predict physical, chemical, and biological reactions.

Existing and familiar food processes are difficult to describe by conventional physical and chemical laws because of the variability and nonideality of the materials, and new processes are even more difficult challenges for the typical engineering approach of mathematical modeling and prediction. Nonetheless, the same techniques found useful in other process industries can be applied with some success to food products. Valentas, Levine, and Clark (1990) present an extensive description of process scale-up in the food industry.

Scale-up and demonstration typically must be performed empirically, that is, by trial and error with successively larger-scale equipment. The efficient way to proceed is step by step or stage by stage, rather than by attempting to integrate all the possible operations at once.

ENGINEERING ROLE IN A TYPICAL FOOD PROCESS

Figure 4-1 shows a block flow diagram that could apply to many food processes.

Referring to Figure 4-1, one can examine each of the typical steps in a food process and illustrate them with some specific examples. This section will address some scale-up issues that might arise.

Food products usually contain a variety of ingredients; relatively few have only one or two, and many have several dozen. These ingredients may be commercially available in a useful form, or they may require extensive processing from agricultural commodities to reach a useful condition. For example, wheat flour is a commerically available ingredient for baking that is ready for use as received. On the other hand, corn kernels that will be used in breakfast cereal, pet foods, and snack foods usually must be broken, at least, and they may be steeped in water and ground before use. Meats may require dicing, vegetables

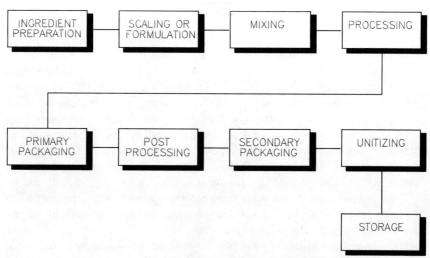

Figure 4-1. Generic block flow diagram for a food process.

could require peeling, dry powders might need to be suspended in liquids, and fats might have to be melted. Each of these operations becomes a process in its own right, which eventually will require the design, selection, and operation of equipment.

Ingredients in a form suitable for use must be weighed, metered, or dispensed in some reliable and accurate manner to yield a complete formula. Typically, in the early stages of development, small batches of a recipe or formula are made; for commercial purposes, much larger batches or continuous formulation is required. The transition from small batches to large-volume continuous or semicontinuous formulation is one of the more dramatic and fundamental changes that can occur in processing.

Techniques for weighing and measuring also can change dramatically. In the laboratory or kitchen, individual and small-scale weighing is the normal practice. In commercial practice, automatic scales for solids and meters of various types for liquids usually are used. In automatic weighing, it is critical that solids be capable of controlled and reliable flow. Many solids that are important to the food industry have tendencies to stick, flood, and cake, all of which complicate the engineer's challenge.

At some point, almost all food products undergo a mixing operation. This may involve the mixing of dry solids with other solids, the mixing of solids into liquids, the mixing of liquids with each other, the mixing of oils and aqueous solutions, and the incorporation of gases into liquids. The viscosity (or "thickness") can range from thin, as in juices and soft drinks, to very thick and pasty, as in bread doughs. There may be suspended solids that have a tendency to settle, as in sauces and soups. The suspended particles may be fragile, such as meat cubes, and the incorporation of gas (such as air) may be desirable or not. All of these considerations contribute to the selection of an appropriate mixing technique. Typically, in the kitchen or laboratory, mixing may be done by hand in a small bowl or with a kitchen appliance. In the manufacturing facility, mixing, of necessity, will be on a much larger scale and will use mechanisms with operating principles that are completely different from the small-scale ones. Practically the only way to establish that a commercial mixer is satisfactory is to try it at close to the required scale. At the very least, geometrically similar equipment should be used as early in the development process as possible.

When additional operations such as heating and cooling are combined with the mixing operation, scale-up becomes even more complex. Mixing times should be determined by experimentation and by the measurement of an acceptable statistical variation in composition from place to place in the mixer as a function of time. It often may happen that mixing long enough to achieve uniformity will lead to unacceptable degradation of the mixture's components. Thus compromises must be made, and some variability in composition easily may occur.

After mixing there often is a processing step, such as forming, extruding, baking, cooking, frying, fermentation, or any one of many others that might be appropriate. These operations may be performed on the whole mass of the mixture or on some subdivision of it. For example, in baking, a mixer full of dough, which may weigh 1,000 pounds, will be divided into many individual loaves that are proofed and baked in pans. A mixer load of cookie or cracker dough will be divided into tens of thousands of individual pieces that will be baked. A mixer load of soup may need no further processing before being put into cans.

Packaging is a critical element in almost all processed foods (see Chapter 5). The primary packaging step may be putting the product into a can, jar, bottle, flexible pouch, bag, or some other type of wrapping. The primary package usually is hermetically sealed, which means it excludes permeation of gases, air, and water vapor. A hermetic seal also can provide evidence of tampering, which is an increasing consumer concern. Rates of packaging, as previously mentioned, vary widely, but they usually are high in comparison to many other manufacturing operations. Multiple packaging lines often are necessary to achieve required production rates, to provide redundancy and reliability, and to accommodate various package sizes. Packaging in the laboratory usually is done in small numbers and by hand. Identifying reliable automatic equipment to accomplish the required task is a major engineering challenge.

After the primary packaging, many food products are processed further to extend their shelf life or otherwise modify their properties. For example, canned products are sterilized by heating, ice cream is hardened by cooling, frozen foods are frozen, and some foods simply are held to allow flavors and textures to develop properly. Adaptation of the post-processing step(s) from a typical small-scale batch operation in the laboratory to large-scale, often continuous, commercial operations is another major engineering challenge.

Secondary packaging may involve placing containers in shipping cases or trays, but on a commercial scale it also includes labeling, coding, case coding, and cartoning prior to case packing in some instances. Secondary packaging may not even be considered in detail in the early development stages, but it requires some early consideration to permit case development to satisfy shipping requirements. Any proposed new shipping case must be subjected to vibration and drop tests to demonstrate that there will be no breakage (and leakage of liquids) during normal shipping and handling. These tests require the manufacture of several pallet loads of typical product in primary and secondary packaging. This must be done by hand or in cooperation with outside sources before final decisions can be made on case design and case packing equipment.

Likewise, decisions must be made regarding the configuration, size, and methodology of unitizing large quantities of cases for efficient storage and handling. A very common procedure is to stack cases of food products on standard wooden pallets to achieve a final weight of 1,000 to 2,000 pounds. The stack often is wrapped with stretchable plastic film to keep the cases from falling off. Alternate methods include the use of slip-sheets (large corrugated cardboard panels on which cases are stacked in place of pallets). Slip-sheet–mounted units need special equipment in order to be handled, but they eliminate the nuisance of dealing with wooden pallets. Pallets can be either one-way or returnable. For certain kinds of storage facilities such as highly automated warehouses with stacker cranes, there may be captive or slave pallets of special design to accommodate the mechanism. These pallets never leave the warehouse.

Some food products may not be unitized because they are not intended to be stored for long times in a warehouse. Fresh dairy and bakery foods typically are placed in special trays or baskets for ease of handling on direct store delivery (DSD) trucks. Issues of unitizing and storage rarely are considered by food product developers but are of great concern to facilities design engineers.

ENGINEERING ROLE IN A TYPICAL FOOD PRODUCT DEVELOPMENT PROJECT

Figure 4-2 shows some of the stages in a typical food product development project, along with engineering's typical involvement. Engineers are infrequently involved in the identification of a need or an opportunity, but they should have some role, even in the concept development stage. As concepts are tested and revised, the engineering team should be looking ahead to the potential problems of the test market and national production. For example, the engineers might make early estimates of the cost of ultimate production in order to test the financial viability of a concept. They might also assist in the production of small quantities of product in pilot plants for use in focus groups and home use tests. Because of long lead times for certain processing equipment and tight schedules, it often is necessary to be quite creative to manufacture sufficient quantities for the test market. A typical test market will represent a small percentage of the anticipated national market but is usually more than an ordinary pilot plant can accommodate. At this stage in a typical development project, some outside assistance may be obtained.

There may be several sources of assistance:

1. Consultants, including consulting engineering firms that specialize in the food industry, may offer some help. Directories of such firms are published annually by such trade magazines as *Food Engineering*, *Food Processing*, and *Processed and Prepared Foods*.
2. Equipment vendors often have pilot facilities to demonstrate their specialized equipment, which they can make available to potential customers.
3. Universities, government laboratories, and specialized industrial laboratories may be available for testing and even small quantity production.
4. Ingredient and packaging material suppliers can provide technical assis-

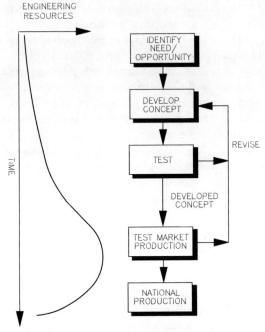

Figure 4-2. Typical steps in food product development and engineering involvement.

tance and some specialized facilities. For example, the suppliers of containers used for thermal processing (cans, jars, and retort pouches) routinely assist in developing safe thermal processes for new products.

An important option that engineers should investigate when anticipating the production of test-market quantities and even small-scale national production is the use of co-packers or co-manufacturers, lists of whom can be found in the directories mentioned above. These firms will manufacture or package food products for other companies with any designated label; so many of these manufacturers are barely known to the public because they themselves have few, if any, branded products. On the other hand, many manufacturers of well-known branded foods will also manufacture products for other companies under the right circumstances. Thus variety of arrangements is nearly limitless and must be negotiated in each case. Typically, engineers, manufacturing employees, and purchasing personnel work as a team to identify co-manufacturing candidates, to evaluate their capabilities, to work with them to achieve satisfactory results, and to negotiate mutually agreeable terms.

Co-packing may be a useful technique because it can reduce capital expenditure by using existing facilities and equipment, can accelerate schedules, can draw upon relevant expertise, and can provide a useful learning experience. On the other hand, there is at least the perception that quality control will be more difficult with co-packing, there is a risk of exposing proprietary information, there may be some compromise of desired manufacturing techniques, and operating costs may be relatively high because the co-packer obviously will expect to earn a profit on any assets deployed. These negative features must be considered and neutralized as much as they can be for co-manufacturing to be an acceptable approach.

A common alternative for test-market production is to construct a small manufacturing line in an existing facility using as much of the existing equipment and facilities as possible. The use of an existing operating facility often means that existing services and utilities can be used, reducing capital exposure and the time before operation. Location of this production in an existing facility may mean convenient access to existing storage and distribution facilities as well. Existing corporate experience and management skills also may be applied. Finding available space, obtaining the cooperation of operating people who have their own priorities, and installing a new line without interfering with existing operations are all typical engineering challenges when this approach is used.

Rarely, a company will decide to construct a new facility from scratch for test-market production. By comparison to the other approaches mentioned, this usually requires the highest cost and takes the longest time, but it stands a better chance of achieving the optimal design and preserving the greatest confidentiality. This approach presents all the challenges of constructing a national facility except for the scale.

Whether large or small, the construction of a new facility, the expansion of an existing facility, or the renovation of a facility in a major way introduces a number of new elements. The principal new element is the building itself. Food companies may have chemical, mechanical, electrical, and industrial engineers on staff or may be accustomed to using persons from such disciplines in process development and scale-up, but relatively few food companies have architects on their staff.

Architects are responsible for designing and supervising the construction of buildings. They usually are hired as consultants and may be associated with the same firms that can provide process engineering consulting services, or they may be associated with contractors and construction managers, or they may be associated with both. In any event, the food process development engineer or manager must help to define building space, volume, and configuration requirements for the proposed new process. The architect will point out such support requirements as offices, team rooms, toilets and lockers, mechanical rooms for boilers and compressors, storage for raw material and finished goods, corridors, loading docks, building code requirements, fire safety regulations, and environmental constraints.

It is necessary to identify the site, which is a major exercise in its own right, including such issues as access to raw materials, access to markets, access to transportation, labor supply, convenience to headquarters, zoning, construction labor costs, and land costs. Once appropriate locations are identified, specific sites must be evaluated for cost, constructibility, environmental issues, and possible expansion. Site selection can be such a long process that large companies typically have options on or have purchased attractive sites in several parts of the country against future needs. State and local development authorities usually are very helpful in identifying candidate properties because they usually are eager to attract taxpaying and job-creating investment.

A site needs to be identified early in a facility design exercise because so much of the design is site-specific. Setbacks, seismic codes, utility access, highway access, and drainage are just a few of the issues that dictate a building's location, design, and configuration. In planning a new facility for a test market and especially for the national production scale, the food company process or project engineer must manage a multidisciplinary team of professional people, many of whom are consultants. At the same time, the engineer must maintain good communications with the product development elements of the company to identify changing requirements and to report possible problems and opportunities.

Through all of this, the engineer must remember that he or she is designing a food plant.

ADDITIONAL CONSIDERATIONS FOR MANUFACTURING FACILITIES

Early in a product development project, it is important for engineering and manufacturing to identify any unique ingredients or materials and to confirm that adequate quantities of these constituents will be commercially available. It may be that a large-scale facility will have to be self-sufficient in supplying special materials that are unique to a given product. Thus, for example, although cocoa, chocolate liquor, and cocoa butter are all commercially available, large confectioners generally start with cocoa beans and produce these materials for their own use. One consequence is that there may be surplus by-products, such as cocoa, that must be sold to make the entire project viable. Another example is the corn used for snack foods. Ground corn meal is commercially available, but many snack food manufacturers purchase whole corn and grind it themselves.

Likewise it is important to identify any unique processing equipment and to determine commercial sources for it. In the development process, equipment often is built from scratch, or existing equipment is heavily modified. On a commercial scale, it may be impractical to build sufficient quantities or capacities internally. In this case, the equipment must be carefully specified and out-side manufacturers identified and employed to provide the requirements in the correct time frame.

The selection of consultants must be done carefully to ensure that consider-ations unique to food processing are observed. All food plants must be designed for sanitation, maintenance, and economical operation. In addition, there are specific government requirements of the U.S. Department of Agriculture (USDA) and the Food and Drug Administration (FDA) that dictate certain design features and even the preparation of certain specific documents, with which only architects experienced in the food industry are familiar. Imholte (1984) is a good reference on sanitary design.

MANUFACTURING

The most critical issue in current food manufacturing, once a product is suc-cessfully introduced and a facility is successfully designed and built, is the continuing need to improve the product's quality while reducing its manufac-turing costs. The key to such continuous improvement is to have adequate and timely information about the product. To achieve its objectives, the organiza-tion must be designed to respond to the information correctly and rapidly.

Organizations in modern food plants have changed profoundly from tradi-tional, multilayer, autocratic forms to a flatter, somewhat more democratic, team approach. This transition has been achieved in part because fewer people are needed in a highly automated plant; but it also is a result of the recognition that when people are consulted and their ideas are solicited, they can help to improve operations. The use of a team approach usually means that the team members have an identification with a line or product, they are cross-trained so that they experience variety in their working life, the work rules and assign-ments are less restrictive than in a traditional approach, and a certain amount of organization and discipline is delegated to the workers themselves.

If the members of a team are to do their job and to achieve continuous improvement, they must be provided with timely and useful information. The dramatic advances in electronic information processing and computer use that have occurred in recent years have given manufacturers the tools needed to provide and process such information. The computers currently used for infor-mation processing at different points in a corporation, factory, or process usu-ally are incompatible with one another; so information available at one level of the enterprise normally is not available elsewhere. The concept of computer integrated manufacturing (CIM) addresses this obstacle to providing timely and useful information at every level (Clark and Balsman 1990).

Figure 4-3 shows the integration pyramid often used to illustrate the chal-lenge. At the lowest level, process control, the information available is for a

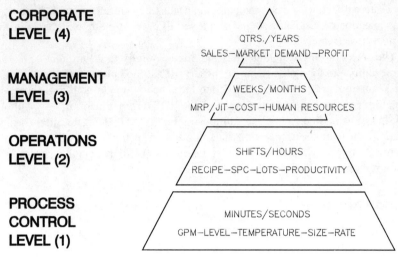

CORPORATE LEVEL (4)

MANAGEMENT LEVEL (3)

OPERATIONS LEVEL (2)

PROCESS CONTROL LEVEL (1)

QTRS./YEARS
SALES—MARKET DEMAND—PROFIT

WEEKS/MONTHS
MRP/JIT—COST—HUMAN RESOURCES

SHIFTS/HOURS
RECIPE—SPC—LOTS—PRODUCTIVITY

MINUTES/SECONDS
GPM—LEVEL—TEMPERATURE—SIZE—RATE

Figure 4-3. The levels of computer integration.

short time scale of minutes or seconds and concerns counts, rates, and process conditions. Often this information is used to control valves or machine settings in order to maintain desired conditions. However, this information, especially rates, also can generate data that are meaningful to other levels of the business.

The operations level may refer to an entire line or to a department. It focuses on a longer time span of multiple hours or shifts and is concerned with production of larger quantities such as multiple pallet loads, calculation of the yield of raw materials, and provision of recipes for various products. At this level, statistics can be collected for use in statistical process control (SPC). A typical calculation might compare a count of pallets obtained from a counter or a data entry with the integrated results of instantaneous rate data provided in level one, to identify potential losses in yield.

Level three, the management level, refers to the entire facility and deals with a time scale of weeks or months. It is concerned with the cost of goods, the scheduling of human resources, the provision of adequate raw materials, and the maintenance of low inventories. The management level typically would provide a production schedule to the next level down and would receive production results.

Level four, the corporate level, has a longer time scale of quarters or years. It typically represents the headquarters of a multifacility corporation and is concerned with sales, market demand, and enterprise profits.

Each level of the pyramid as displayed here may correspond to one or more physical computers and multiple software programs that digest data and produce reports. For example, at level one the hardware may be programmable logic controllers (PLCs). At level two, there may be the equivalent of personal computers or small work stations. At level three, there may be a minicomputer, and at level four there might be the so-called mainframe computer. Each of these devices might be provided by a different vendor. In an ideal arrangement, there would be no need to record and reenter data; rather the information would flow automatically from its point of origin up to the next level over appropriate communication media such as copper cable or fiber optics. For such information to flow, the protocols of communication must be standardized, and often there must be translators resident in each level to provide a link to the adjacent levels.

The trend in food manufacturing (and in other manufacturing as well) is to develop data exchange protocols that are compatible with multiple vendors, and high-powered software programs that can be tailored to specific applications.

A completely integrated food manufacturing facility in the sense just described is not yet known, but all modern food facilities are attempting to achieve this ideal.

SUMMARY

Engineering and manufacturing play key roles in the movement of a food product from concept to marketplace. These roles are usually, but not always, played by people with engineering educations; food scientists and people with extensive practical experience can and often do contribute as well. It is important that the engineering aspects of food manufacturing be considered early in the development process because the solution of scale-up and automation problems can be expensive and time-consuming. Outside resources from consultants and suppliers often can be used to successfully address engineering and manufacturing challenges. Once the plant is designed and constructed, the great challenge in food manufacturing is the clever use of information technology to achieve continuous improvement in quality and economics.

REFERENCES

Valentas, K. J., Levine, L., and Clark, J. P. 1990. *Food Processing Operations and Scale-up.* New York: Marcel Dekker, Inc.

Clark, J. P. and Balsman, W. F. 1990. *Computer Integrated Manufacturing in the Food Industry, Engineering and Food* ed. W. E. L. Spiess and W. Schubert 781–789. London–New York: Elsevier Applied Science Publishers.

Imholte, T. J. 1984, *Engineering for Food Safety and Sanitation.* Crystal, Minn: Technical Institute for Food Safety.

Chapter 5

Food Packaging Meets the Challenge

Margie Russell

INTRODUCTION TO THE PACKAGING INDUSTRY

One sector of the food industry has become a giant. It is bigger than Goliath in the land of David or Gulliver in the land of the Lilliputians. This giant is the food packaging industry.

Packaging has become high tech; it is no longer just a box or a bag that gets a product into a supermarket and then home onto a consumer's shelf. But no matter how advanced a science packaging has become, its primary objective still is to protect the product; and today the package has become an essential part of the food product.

This enormous growth has been due to a number of significant factors that have contributed to packaging's emergence as an industrial giant. Technology advances definitely have played a part, for without many of these developments—such as plastic soda and ketchup bottles and microwave containers—none of these new products and packages would have been available.

Improvements in raw materials also have occurred, and many packages that were on shelves several years ago have been replaced by better, lighter-weight, and cleaner containers. Clarity has always been a vital criterion for packaging, and advances and improvements constantly are being developed to give consumers crystal-clear containers. In addition, changes in food formulations have contributed to packaging's growth because new food products require new packages. The responsibility for food formulation falls solely on the processor, but the processor must communicate with packagers and resin suppliers in order to plan the package.

Changes and improvements in liddings and adhesives also have contributed to the industry's growth because new packages, especially those made for the microwave, use easy-to-open peel-off lids, and without those liddings such packages would not be possible.

Even in the wake of changes and company mergers and acquisitions, the packaging industry continues to advance. Several giants have merged (e.g., Carnaud and Metal Box plc), and a significant number of other companies have formed joint ventures in order to tap each other's markets and technologies. Many industry analysts think that such mergers and ventures will hinder and reduce R&D efforts in the packaging area, but it is probably still too early to verify this idea.

Unquestionably, the packaging industry is a vital area. Anyone involved in the food industry participates in packaging at one time or another, and many changes have occurred in the industry because of consumer requests. This chapter will provide an overview of this growing industry, addressing such topics as rigid containers, plastic containers, flexible packaging, specialty packages, the solid waste issue, and future trends in the industry.

RIGID CONTAINERS

The casual observer might note that metal cans and glass jars have been around for quite some time. Indeed, they have, and they most likely will be available for a long time to come. However, the rigid container market no longer exclusively includes metal cans and glass containers, as plastic bottles entered this arena several years ago. This section takes a look at these markets.

Although it has been attacked by plastic on all sides, the metal can market appears to be holding its own in fighting for a share of the container industry. In fact, the steel can is enjoying a resurgence because steel cans remain an option for packagers when prices of other types of containers rise. Steel manufacturing has vastly improved over the last few years too; so the consumer now receives a better, lighter-weight can. And, more important, cost reductions in steel cans have never led to a reduction in performance.

According to the U.S. Department of Commerce, the metal can market experienced continued growth in 1988, with total product shipments reaching 112 billion units (Copperthite (1988). Shipments were expected to reach 116 billion units in 1989, an increase of 3.7% from 1988; and at such rates, the Department of Commerce projected that the industry would grow at an average annual rate of 3%, measured in constant dollars, during the 1988–93 period. This growth figure is affected by demands in the major end-use markets for metal cans: beer, soft drinks, and food packaging.

An increase in soft drink consumption will provide one of the main growth end-use markets for metal cans. Consumption increases will be due to the diet-conscious consumer, who will drive up sales of diet sodas significantly. In an interesting strategy by the beverage companies, soda is being marketed as a breakfast beverage as well. Also, lite beer consumption is predicted to increase as part of the diet trend.

Juice and food packaging—other end-use markets of metal cans—will increase by providing convenience products to consumers. Can packagers will be emphasizing the single-serve trend as well as providing products for the health-conscious—low fat, low salt, low cholesterol products.

Aluminum showed excellent growth over the last decade and is expected to grow moderately during the 1990s. The main end-use markets for aluminum are beverages (which will continue to rise in consumption), juices, and some baby foods. The aluminum sector's growth will also be spurred when the market finally reaps the benefits of its recycling efforts over the past few years. Interestingly, plastics do not threaten the aluminum market as much as steel does because plastics serve many multipurpose markets that aluminum does not reach (Anonymous, *Food Engineering*, 1989a).

Aluminum beverage can shipments had reached an estimated 79 billion units in 1988. The Department of Commerce reported that aluminum would continue to dominate the soft drink and beer markets although can stock and pricing problems would cause some erosion; the agency predicted that steel would provide 10% of the shipments of soft drink cans in 1989.

Unlike the metal market, the glass container sector has been struggling somewhat as a packaging choice. The Department of Commerce reported that in 1988 shipments of glass containers fell for the second year in a row to 276 million gross units, with shipments for 1989 projected to fall 1% to 273 million gross units. This industry was expected to grow at an average constant dollar rate of only 1% annually during the 1989–93 period.

Overall, the end-use markets for glass will become more concentrated because of declines in the general packaging sector. Glass packaging in specific end-use markets probably will be limited to products that require a container with the traditional properties of glass: image, product visibility, and moisture and oxygen barriers. Industry sources and manufacturers claim that some products will remain in glass for a long time. For example, mayonnaise historically has always been packed in glass. Several companies have studied the possibility of a conversion to plastic for mayonnaise products but decided that plastic would not do the job.

Baby food and juice products also retain glass as the container of choice by a wide margin. Glass is a cost-effective container in that industry. A changeover to plastic might mean substantial losses because many plastic containers cost twice as much as identical glass ones.

Plastic bottles are the newer members of the rigid container market and have shown the greatest growth in this sector. Since the advent of plastics, nothing else has invaded the packaging industry with quite as much vengeance.

Plastic bottle shipments in 1988 rose 8% to 38 billion units, according to the Department of Commerce, and in 1989 shipments were expected to rise 7.6% to 41 billion units. High density polyethylene (HDPE) made up 65% of resins consumed and polyethylene terephthalate (PET) accounted for 25%.

General packaging is the largest single end-use of plastic containers, whereas beverage use accounts for 33% and food for 21%.

Tight resin supplies and price increases in this sector have existed since 1988, when several facility explosions occurred in the United States. This situation affected the market's growth rate, along with a slowing in technology advances (container conversions from metal/glass to plastic having already taken place) and concerns voiced about the solid waste issue.

The Department of Commerce also projected that shipments of bottles for carbonated soft drinks and other beverages would reach 10.2 and 4.4 billion units, respectively, in 1989. These products will fuel this market's growth and are the largest food applications for rigid plastic containers.

THE INVASION OF PLASTIC

The biggest player in the packaging industry is plastic. Since the proliferation of plastics in the 1960s, this versatile material has invaded every segment of the industry and literally caused a packaging revolution. Indeed, this same material took soup out of cans and ketchup out of glass bottles.

However, there is not just a single plastic material; there is an array of plastic materials that can be used for food packaging applications. Several common examples are polyethylene terephthalate (PET), HDPE, LDPE, oriented poly-propylene (OPP), polyvinyl chloride (PVC), polypropylene, polyvinylidene chloride (PVDC), ethylene vinyl alcohol (EVOH), and nylon. This list is by no means exhaustive; it represents a few of the many plastic materials available, a subject far too vast to cover in this chapter.

Although plastics provide a new dimension for food packagers, their short-comings in several areas (shelf life, heat resistance, and oxygen and water permeabilities) have limited their usefulness in food packaging in the past. However, with improvements in the plastics known as barrier polymers, many plastic packages now rival glass and metal in the excellent shelf life and barrier properties that they have always provided food packagers. It is the purpose of this section to concentrate on these complex materials, which have drastically revolutionized packaging opportunities.

Barrier polymers usually are classified as materials that protect a product through the end of its shelf life. Specifically, for food packaging, the material must provide a strong barrier against oxygen and prevent the migration of sub-stances between the package and the product. Barriers may be enhanced through modifiers or additives, resulting in a superior protective layer that might not have been possible without the additive or surface modification (Russell, *Food Engineering*, 1989b).

The importance of the advances of barrier plastics is so great that if packages were ever changed to have shorter shelf lives, massive changes in lifestyles would ensue. The consumer is so accustomed to buying products that will remain safe and stable and taste good for a somewhat extended period of time that daily trips to the grocery store or market are now just distant memories.

Currently, a number of different types of barriers are used in food packaging, with special barrier materials for certain applications. For example, the high nitrile resins (HNRs) are generically those resins that contain the cyano func-tional group, also called the nitrile group. (This resin family is known as the Barex group, manufactured and marketed by BP Chemicals International,

Cleveland, Ohio.) HNRs are used extensively in packaging for their gas barrier and chemical resistance properties. This unique combination produces an outstanding flavor/odor barrier and gives excellent aroma retention (*Food Engineering*, 1989e).

For economic reasons, HNRs are not used where commodity resins, such as polyolefins, are performing well. HNRs typically find applications where other plastics cannot economically provide the combination of properties required, or where designers wish to replace traditional materials such as glass or metals. A few of the food products currently packaged in HNRs include: processed meat, cheeses, bakery products, sauces, peanut butter, cooking oil, bouillon concentrates, fresh pasta, and herbs and spices.

An improvement in moisture barrier properties cannot yet be achieved in a "pure" HNR, but such improvement is possible by coextruding or laminating it with a polyolefin, which is the basis for several fresh pasta packages. The resin's ability to contain carbon dioxide, used in the modified atmosphere within the package, and to exclude oxygen makes it ideal for this application.

Nylon barrier materials are chosen for packaging applications because of their functional contributions. They offer clarity, toughness over a broad range of temperatures, thermoformability, and resistance to fats and aromas. In most applications, they are used as films, as single components in multilayer structures. Nylons are characterized by repeating amide groups ($-CONH-$) in their main polymer chain.

The majority of packages using nylon-based films are found in such applications as cheese, bacon (vacuum-packed), hot dogs, and other processed meats. In these types of packages, the interior often is flushed with carbon dioxide which removes trace oxygen and significantly extends the shelf life of the product. Some typical applications are fish, fresh meat, and poultry. A recent development using nylon was seen in the production of a "canless" canned ham; here the product was vacuum-packed and cooked in the package.

One of the most popular barrier materials used today, and probably the one that started the packaging revolution, is ethylene vinyl alcohol copolymer (EVOH). EVOH resins are copolymers of ethylene and vinyl alcohol. The most popular forms now in use are the Eval EVOH resins, manufactured by the Eval Company of America, a joint venture between Kuraray Co. Ltd. of Japan and Quantum Chemical Corporation, USI Division in the United States. These resins are produced by copolymerizing ethylene and vinyl acetate and then hydrolyzing the vinyl acetate to vinyl alchohol. The resulting polymer offers a superior barrier to gases, odors, and aromas. Often, EVOH can be used with a variety of other polymers such as polypropylene and polyethylene to form various kinds of plastic packages.

On a historical note, EVOH was part of the excitement of the packaging revolution in 1983, when the introduction of the first multilayer rigid plastic bottle took the industry by storm. The "Gamma" bottle was produced by American National Can, and its layers consisted of polypropylene–a regrind layer–tie layer (an adhesive layer)–EVOH–tie–polypropylene. At that time, Wishbone barbecue sauce was packed in this bottle, soon to be followed by Heinz Ketchup. The reason this particular package was considered a break-through in plastic packaging was that the material withstood processing tem-peratures of 90°C and provided a shelf life of one year.

As developments with plastics continued, EVOH was used as the barrier material in several more packages in 1985, most notably in single-serve ther-moformed containers of applesauce and in the first retort application, American National Can's Omni container. The package withstood severe retort conditions of 275°F for 30 to 45 minutes and was used by Hormel for its line of single-serve entrees.

The Hormel line started the convenience trend, as these containers offered single-service and microwavability, something a metal can could never offer. And continuing this trend in 1986, The Dial Corporation introduced its Lunch Bucket line, which is a retort product in a bowl-shaped container, replacing the old style can-shaped container. (See Figure 5-1.)

EVOH again made history when in 1987 various juice products were pack-aged for the first time in 64-ounce plastic bottles. EVOH is used in these struc-tures as a barrier to oxygen and to prevent flavor scalping. Two famous-name juices were introduced in these bottles: Tropicana and Minute Maid (see Figure 5-2). And thanks to EVOH and other plastics, more products familiar to most American households recently received new packages very different from their originals: Kraft Inc.'s Cheez Whiz in the Zap-A-Pak (see Figure 5-3) and Del Monte's line of Vegetable Classics (see Figure 5-4).

Finally, the oldest, and still the most widely used, barrier material in pack-aging is polyvinylidene chloride (PVDC). Vinylidene chloride (VDC) is co-

Figure 5-1. Lunch Bucket container.

Figure 5-2. Minute Maid Orange Juice container.

Figure 5-3. Cheez Whiz containers.

Figure 5-4. Del Monte Vegetable Classics container.

polymerized with various other monomers to form thermoplastic resins; all commercial VDC resins consist of at least 50% vinylidene chloride. The barrier and strength properties of VDC copolymers depend on the chemical compositions of the molecules and their orientation. A high VDC content imparts high barrier properties and gas resistance.

PVDC is an excellent barrier material in packaging because of its low permeabilities to gases and liquids and its resistance to foodstuffs and chemicals. The largest producer of PVDC is the Dow Chemical Company, which markets PVDC under the name Saran. Dow Chemical estimates that over 220 million pounds of PVDC (resin and latex) were used across the globe in 1988. This figure compares to about 30 to 35 million pounds of estimated EVOH consumption. This level of consumption represents an overall marketshare of 86 to 88% for PVDC. Even though the EVOH growth rate may be higher than that of PVDC, the older material still has tremendous value in current and future markets.

A significant amount of Saran (including latex and solvent coating resins) is used in fresh red meat, processed meat, and cheese markets. The barrier property of PVDC is unaffected by the high relative humidities that are typical in meat and cheese packaging and the temperature of storage.

Saran in the form of a coating on polyester, cellophane, and polypropylene sees many applications in the snack food and processed meat and cheese markets. The benefit of having a barrier layer at the food/package interface as a seal layer and flavor barrier is gaining recognition in the industry.

In addition, Saran is being used in retort and aseptic processing applications for products such as soups, entrees, juices, and puddings. Since Saran's barrier properties are insensitive to relative humidity, it is an ideal barrier for use in shelf-stable packaging requiring one year or more of shelf life.

As good as barrier polymers are, however, they have a few distinct disadvantages. EVOH is produced mainly through coextrusion, which may cause price fluctuations, and PVDC presents problems in scrap reuse. The principal disadvantage of these polymers, though, is their reaction to water and humidity. It has been reported that several polymers are moisture-sensitive, especially in applications of high heat. Water and oxygen often permeate package layers and are absorbed by the barrier layer, causing more gas permeability and a shorter shelf life for the product. Studies have shown that the absorbed water in the barrier layer is permanently retained.

Generally, at higher temperatures the oxygen and water permeabilities of many polymers greatly increase, and the quality of food products drops significantly. The higher the temperature, the higher the activation energies of those polymers, so that the permeability rates rise.

The plastic packages that provide such superior barrier protection to food products are complex structures. But, one might ask, are these packages getting overlayered, and have they become too complex? Yes and no; there is no simple answer. Packages definitely have become more complex, but the real issue with packaging is whether the package provides the benefits sought. On their part, manufacturers are always looking for a simple package, but many of these packages are multilayered, and clearly do not qualify as simple designs.

There is always a trade-off between long shelf life and complicated packaging and a shorter shelf life and less complicated packaging. On the whole, no packaging producer wants to put more layers in a package than are necessary. A packaging producer will never develop a package that is *too* complicated to manufacture.

The greatest constraint to making complicated packages is money. The functions of packaging have changed dramatically over the years, there are a number of ways to put a package together, and materials and their costs keep changing. Thus the industry is dealing with very sensitive products and processes; and although there may appear to be a degree of overpackaging going on, layers are never added for profit.

How many layers, then are needed? Is it possible to get adequate barrier protection by using 5 layers as opposed to 15? Yes, it is, in the majority of cases; and, on the average, it is possible to obtain adequate protection with fewer layers when the package has superior barrier materials. For example, take a look at two comparable packages, one using average barrier materials and one using superior materials. The material used in the first structure might be poly-ethylene terepthalate (PET), which cannot be called a high-barrier material. PET often is used as a barrier and as a structural component, but it is not a good and economical barrier for many products (e.g., mayonnaise) because the container thickness may reach 30 mil, where a mil equals 0.001 inch. The result is a container that costs a lot of money and takes a long time to make and to fill. A high-barrier material such as PVDC or EVOH at 1 mil thickness would be more economical and work more effectively than PET. More layers may mean a package that is more complicated and sophisticated, but this does not necessarily mean that the package is better.

The industry may have reached a point of diminishing returns now with barriers and plastics packaging, and users must assess whether gains are really worth their costs. Industry processors and packagers agree that it would be "ideal" to return to a monolayer structure, but right now there is no monolayer structure available that would give a superior barrier for a plastic package. To go back to a monolayer structure for plastics, a very sophisticated and effective resin must be developed—a development that appears to be a fair distance down the road.

A product that now is creating a stir in the industry, and which contrasts with traditional barrier materials, is a line of silica-coated films. In spite of the attention these films are commanding, the theory behind them is not new (the idea being about 20 years old); but the technology cannot yet be applied cost-effectively in production operations. Nevertheless, there are numerous advantages to silica-coated polyester: an excellent moisture, gas, and flavor barrier; a barrier unaffected by relative humidity; clarity; microwave transparency; material that is retortable, unaffected by normal cooking temperatures, and safe for food contact; and oriented films that can be used in the coating process.

Silica is the common name for silicon dioxide, a chemical derived from sand, the primary component of glass—glass being an amorphorus mixture of inorganic oxides in a random physical network that is about three-fourths silica. A variation of silica or pure quartz is needed as the material in a silica coating.

Surface coating of silica on polyester film imparts gas and moisture barrier properties equivalent to those of PVDC or EVOH under ideal conditions. The oxygen permeability of silica-coated PET does not change with moisture content as EVOH does. The moisture permeability of silica-coated PET is the same as that of vacuum metallized PET or of PVDC, and better than that of EVOH.

The deposition of silica on film is very difficult, however, requiring a technology that is not yet totally developed, the use of an electron beam. Neither silica nor any of its variations can melt or evaporate, so it must be brought into a total sublimation state. Sufficient energy must be imparted to discharge surface silica molecules directly from the solid into the vapor state, a very time-consuming and extremely costly process (*Food Engineering*, 1988d).

The only identified commercial packaging application of silica-coated film has taken place in Japan, where the product is retorted tomato or cream pasta sauces in stand-up pouches. The base material is a 12-micron or 0.0005-inch-gauge polyester film manufactured by Toyobo and vacuum-coated by Toyo Ink with silicon oxide. The silica-coated film then is shipped to Toppan Printing for laminating. Printing is done on a separate web of polyester, and the silica coating is in the middle of the lamination. This lamination is used to fabricate three-piece stand-up pouches; the pouches are filled by Ajinomoto on Japanese Toppan machines with 140 grams of pasta sauce products. After filling, the sealed pouches are retorted in water, lying down at 120°C for 30 minutes. The shelf life of Ajinomoto's Rumic brand product is approximately one year at ambient temperature.

FLEXIBLE PACKAGING

Flexible packaging usually designates any type of package that is "movable." Flexible packages are not rigid containers like metal cans or glass jars. They have several different shapes, depending on machinery and market considerations: round, square, or oblong bags, pouches, sacks, and overwraps.

Probably the largest-growing area in packaging is the flexible segment. Many observers think that flexible packaging—aseptics, retort pouches, dual-oven-able, paper—will eventually replace other packaging alternatives. The reasons for this are many: flexible packaging can replace rigid containers; it is cost-effective; semirigid containers may be developed as alternatives to rigid and contemporary flexible containers; and flexible packaging is energy-efficient. Less energy is required to make and recycle some forms of flexible packages than to make and recycle aluminum. (Russell, *Food Engineering*, 1988c).

There is no greater diversity in the flexible packaging sector than in film production for the snack food industry. Snack food packaging must unequivocally meet the demands of the product: oxygen and light barrier properties, moisture protection, compatability with machinery, and the ability to provide a good "billboard" for the product.

A continuing trend in snack film production is that of replacing paper substrates with oriented polypropylene (OPP). OPP is a polypropylene-based resin that is mechanically stretched in directions that are at right angles to each other. Once this biaxial orientation has taken place, the film shows an improvement in strength, moisture barrier, and temperature resistance.

Currently, six types of snack food film structures are used for vertical form/fill/seal packaging of salted snacks: cellophane/cellophane, cellophane/coated

OPP, OPP/coated glassine, OPP/HDPE, and two forms of OPP/metallized OPP. For the forms of the last structure, two levels of metallization are used: the 4% light transmission level introduced about 10 years ago, and the less than 2% level, now the industry standard (*Food Engineering*, 1989d).

Metallizing is a process used to improve the barrier properties of clear products (films). The films are specially treated to enhance metal adhesion and then plated with a thin coating of metal, usually aluminum. This layer of metal is generally 30 nanometers (nm) thick and provides barrier properties for packages that are difficult to obtain by using other methods. Metallized films greatly enhance moisture and gas barrier properties; the metal also keeps out light, which causes rancidity in most snack products.

In general, approximately 60 to 70% of the flexible packaging in snacks is OPP, encompassing three main markets: clear, metallized, and opaque. Metallized OPP is the fastest-growing plastic snack film today, where wide usage is seen in the microwave popcorn segment of the snack food market.

Susceptor Films

Although the subject is mentioned several times in this chapter, it would be impossible to cover the entire microwave industry in so short a space. However, an area that merits particular attention in this discussion of flexible packaging is the use of susceptors/receptors in microwave applications.

Vacuum-deposited aluminum is the most commonly used metal in microwave receptor films because of its ease of manufacture. Sputtered metals also can be used, and various alloys can be vacuum-deposited or sputtered onto polyester films to create receptors.

Technologies now exist whereby a receptor film can be placed on the bottom or the top of a paperboard dual-ovenable container, thereby adding a crisping and browning feature to the package. Receptor/susceptor films (the terms are used interchangeably) convert microwave radiation to the conductive heat required to crisp and/or brown the surface of a food product. Microwave radiation heats food by agitating molecules in the food, and it agitates molecules in the vacuum-deposited or sputtered metal to create conductive heat as well. Dense metal materials reflect microwave radiation, but receptor films absorb it. (*Food Engineering*, 1988b).

The construction of a receptor package depends on the application; the most important variables are type of metal and level of deposition. In fact, these films generated much interest in early 1989 when their safety was questioned by the Food and Drug Administration. The materials used in susceptors have not been approved for use at the elevated temperatures reached in many of these applications, but the films still are being marketed as the FDA has not reached a conclusive opinion on the mechanisms.

The Realm of Aseptic Packaging

There is no real mystery about aseptic packaging. It is complicated, the processing and the packaging are dependent on one another, and it must be done correctly the first time. There is just no second chance with aseptic processing, and there is no test to see that it has been done right.

Aseptic processing is the continuous sterilization of a food product, the sterilization of the container, and the filling and sealing of that container in a sterile atmosphere. A loss of sterility in any area affects the sterility of the final product.

Aseptically processed food is processed by using high-temperature, short-time methods. In most cases aseptic packaging involves the use of specially treated paperboard layered with plastic film and aluminum foil. Such a package has many advantages over conventional containers because it requires no refrigeration, has a fairly long shelf life, and is compact, convenient, and easy to store.

The first retail aseptic package in the United States was the Tetra Brik container from Tetra Pak. The introduction of this container into the U.S. market was delayed for some time—the container and process having already become popular in Europe—because the FDA would not give clearance for the use of hydrogen peroxide as a sterilant in the process. Then, in 1981, clearance was granted for the use of hydrogen peroxide as a sterilant for polyethylene, a major constituent of the package.

The now-familiar Tetra Brik container consists of five to seven plies. Typical construction of the brikpak includes polyethylene, paper, aluminum foil, and printing. Tetra Pak machines, and other similar machines now on the market, are form/fill/seal units that sterilize packaging material with hydrogen peroxide and heat. Rolls are continually fed into a vertical machine that then sterilizes, forms, fills, and seals the container. In the United States, these machines usually are used for the production of milk and fruit juices.

A new twist on aseptic technology appeared in the industry in 1985–86, when several applesauce manufacturers produced their product in single-serve thermoformed containers. The use of preformed containers in an aseptic system can create problems because the containers must be kept sterilized throughout the entire filling process. One such system currently being used is the Mead Packaging/Rampart Packaging Crosscheck system, which can process a number of products such as juices and applesauce. In this system, the sterilization medium often is hot citric acid.

In addition to the Crosscheck system, there are a few other systems awaiting FDA approval for the aseptic processing and packaging of low-acid foods. Undoubtedly, this development will affect an expanding market because aseptically packaged foods grew at a steady rate of 12 to 13% in 1989, with the trend expected to continue into the 1990s. Examples of aseptic products are seen in Figures 5-5 (applesauce) and 5-6 (pudding).

Figure 5-5. Seneca Applesauce containers.

Figure 5-6. Hunt's Snack Pack pudding.

SPECIALTY PACKAGES

The packaging industry's next big breakthrough may let the shopper keep fresh broccoli, cauliflower, or poultry in the refrigerator in a fresh, "just-packaged" condition for weeks before use. Controlled atmosphere packaging (CAP) and modified atmosphere packaging (MAP) represent the latest technological advances in the industry, and a few of these packages have already reached retail markets.

CAP is a preservation method for those food products that continue to respire after being picked, such as fresh fruits and vegetables. In this system, a precise combination of gases in the environment surrounding the food product maintains the product throughout its shelf life. To apply CAP technology, all packaging materials must have the correct porosity or barrier in order to regulate the continuously changing package headspace, which results from the respiration of the product combining with the gas mix in the headspace. In addition, these packaging materials must ensure that anaerobic conditions causing toxic bacteria (e.g., *Clostridium botulinum*) do not develop in the package.

On the other hand, MAP usually involves prepared foods—foods that are precooked or processed. In this instance, packaging materials must provide high barriers to mositure and oxygen and maintain the special gas mix inside the headspace. The modified atmosphere inside these packages slows the respiration and reproduction rate of the bacteria that are on the surface of all food products and cause spoilage over time. By slowing the reproduction of these bacteria, spoilage is retarded, and the shelf life of the product is extended.

A principal driving force behind the CAP/MAP technology is the consumer demand for fresh, refrigerated foods without preservatives. Many such products can go from the refrigerator to the microwave to the table in a matter of minutes. A study by Kline & Company, Inc., packaging industry consultants of Fairfield, New Jersey, projects that the CAP/MAP sector will require 11 billion packages in 1993. According to Kline, barrier bag master packs, containing individual packages similar in appearance to the traditional tray with film overwrap, will account for about 55% of the packages in five years. The master pack will retain the CAP or MAP atmosphere until opened in the back room of the retail store. Thermoformed or preformed individual trays sealed with anti-fog-treated lidding will account for slightly over 25% of these packages in 1993. Pallet shrouds for full pallet loads and individual film bags containing up to 15 pounds of fresh product will account for the remaining packages.

The poultry industry will be the primary user of CAP/MAP technology in 1993, accounting for over 75% of all the packaging units. Fresh pork and beef products will be packed in CAP/MAP packages, with each accounting for less than 5% of all packaging units. Other areas of expected use include selected fruits and vegetables, fresh pasta, specialty bakery products, and prepared foods.

As expected, there are several special processing requirements for packaging products under a controlled or modified atmosphere. In controlled atmosphere packaging, the permeability characteristics of the container must match the respiration characteristics of the product. The gas transmission of packages is a complex phenomenon, with transmission complicated by changes in the atmosphere arising from product-induced changes.

A successful controlled atmosphere package that is used for produce must reduce the respiration rate but maintain aerobic conditions. Fruits and vegetables continue living after harvest, using oxygen to metabolize carbohydrate reserves and generate carbon dioxide and water in the process. The goal of controlled atmosphere packaging is to extend shelf life by reducing the aerobic respiration rate while avoiding anaerobic processes that affect taste, texture, and aroma. Generally, the faster the respiration rate, the faster produce ages.

When produce is placed in a closed container, its respiration diminishes oxygen and elevates carbon dioxide concentrations. This occurs whether or not the container has been flushed with a mixture of oxygen, carbon dioxide, or nitrogen. The extent to which the produce modifies its atmosphere depends on its respiration rate, which varies widely among produce types. Many factors affect respiration rates in produce, including physical damage, stage of maturity, contamination by microbes or insects, and the storage temperature. Storage temperatures are vital in keeping produce. Researchers have found, for example, that the respiration rate of many types of produce doubles for every 10°C rise in temperature.

Controlled atmosphere packaging also must accommodate the respiration characteristics of a wide range of produce. Not all produce items respire at the same rate, and each item has an optimum oxygen and carbon dioxide content for extending its shelf life. This means that different products require different film permeabilities to establish the proper atmosphere for quality retention.

Some commercially available packaging films have oxygen permeabilities ranging from 0.05 to 5,000 cc/mil/100 sq. in./24 hrs/@ 73°F/@ 50%RH. Films at the high end of this range are known as low barrier films, as they have a limited permeability and allow some gas exchange between the package interior and the external atmosphere. A single film has limitations, however, because the package size for a particular item is determined by the surface area needed to attain the optimum atmosphere inside the package. Such films usually are not satisfactory for a wide range of packaging sizes and shapes for retail use.

To date, there are very few CAP applications for produce; one patented system for the controlled atmosphere packaging of produce is available in limited test markets. The FreshHold system from Hercules, Inc. extends the refrigerated shelf life of produce by 50 to 200%. The first packer to apply the system was Fresh Western Market, Inc., of Salinas, California, which began using the system in August 1989.

The goal of the Hercules program was to develop a packaging system that could accommodate a wide range of products. The first item packaged in the

FreshHold system was broccoli florets, a rapidly-respiring produce item. The FreshHold system consists of a clear impermeable rigid or flexible container with an active (breathable) membrane label placed over vent holes in the container. The container need not be a barrier container, but its permeability must be accounted for in determining the permeability of the active label. Containers typically are made of polyvinyl chloride, but they can be made of other materials such as polypropylene. The lidstock is Mylar.

The active label is made of a polyolefin film with its permeability tailored to high, medium, and low ranges or respiration. The company claims that the size and permeability of the active label can be varied so that it can be matched to the respiration characteristics of any produce type. The permeability of the label film can be adjusted via a proprietary manufacturing process. The package's active label enables control of the atmosphere in the container within defined optimum limits of oxygen and carbon dioxide.

In modified atmosphere packaging applications, on the other hand, it is crucial to start with a very low initial bacterial load on the food product. This is a necessity for extending shelf life because the objective of MAP is to slow the growth of organisms on the food. In short, the fewer bacteria to control initially, the longer the product's shelf life. As with the requirements of controlled atmosphere packaging applications, temperature control is very important: any fluctuations in temperature create unfavorable conditions on the package.

Packaging machinery in MAP applications is very important to the success of this market. The machinery must provide the required line speeds and efficiency, create the proper package shape, and accurately deliver the necessary gases to the headspace of the package. Two types of machines normally are used: form/fill/seal machines and fill/seal machines.

Form/fill/seal (f/f/s) machines form tray packages from rigid materials such as high barrier coextrusions of polystyrene and EVOH. Some common units are those from Multivac, Tiromat, and Mahaffey and Harder. In most manufacturing settings, a forming web (rigid barrier sheet) is unwound into the machine. Holes are punched in this material before forming, and these holes later are used to evacuate air from the headspace and replace it with the gas mix. The rigid sheet is formed into the desired package shape. Filling occurs next, with speeds determined by the product and requirements of the package.

In addition, these machines can be customized to thermoform lidstock for the product. Lidstocks usually are flexible materials that can be formed or used flat on the package. The next step in the MAP process is sealing the lidstock to the tray and introducing the modified atmosphere into the headspace. This is accomplished in a sealed chamber on the machine; it is evacuated, and the modified atmosphere is flushed through the holes that were made in the rigid web. The packaging materials then are sealed together by using a combination of time, temperature, and pressure.

Fill/seal machines, on the other hand, use rigid trays that are formed by a packaging supplier. The process of sealing and placing the atmosphere in the package is similar to that of f/f/s machinery. These machines are chosen if the product prevents obtaining efficient line speeds on an f/f/s unit. Fill/seal machines also are available from Mahaffey and Harder.

As expected in MAP applications, the packaging materials used in the process are critical to its success. Consider, for example, the requirements of materials for effective MAP applications in the three most popular product areas: cooked poultry, meat snacks, and pasta (*Food Engineering*, 1989f). In these applications, two types of packages normally are used:

1. Package A:
   - *Film top web:* oriented polyester, PVDC coating, printing ink, adhesive layer, heat seal film with anti-fog.
   - *Rigid bottom web:* high barrier heat seal film (EVOH barrier), adhesive layer, heavy caliper foam PS sheet (pigmented).
2. Package B:
   - *Film top web:* formable polyester, PVDC coating, adhesive layer, heat seal film with anti-fog.
   - *Rigid bottom web:* high barrier heat seal film (EVOH barrier), adhesive layer, heavy caliper HIPS sheet (pigmented).

In prepackaged cooked poultry, both of these packages (A and B) can be used successfully because they maintain the original cooked flavor/nutrition quality while providing the consumer with the convenience of reheating in the package. One design has a barrier foam polystyrene lamination for the tray portion (package A), and the other uses a high impact polystyrene (HIPS) barrier lamination tray material (package B). The tray structures are the key to consumer acceptance of these package concepts. Although the barrier properties of these structures are critical, the tray also performs well during reheating in the microwave.

In package B, the HIPS is a key to achieving high production speeds on form/fill/seal thermoforming equipment. Special density selection of both the HIPS resin and the barrier sealant is essential in order to meet the microwave requirements necessary for reheating cooked poultry products. If additional heat resistance of either the foam polystyrene of the HIPS sheet is desired, a PPO-PS resin (polyphenyl oxide–polystyrene blend belonging to GE Plastics) can be added to the sheet formulation to increase the heat distortion temperature.

Although the top film structures have comparable barrier and sealant property requirements, package A does not have a thermoforming requirement for the polyester film; hence, an oriented grade is used. Package B uses thermoforming to enhance product appearance and compensates for product size variation without altering the tray height. Both package concepts require anti-fog sealants because the MAP system requires a nonfogging film to provide good product visibility.

One good example of a poultry application currently on the market is the Perdue Done It! fresh cooked poultry product (see Figure 5-7). This package represents a joint development effort: barrier laminated expanded polystyrene (EPS) foam tray by Amoco Foam Products Company, barrier films for tray and lidstock by Du Pont, f/f/s equipment by Multivac, film conversion by Plicon, Curwood, and Printpack, and product development and packaging specifications by Perdue Farms (*Food Engineering*, 1988a).

This package doubles refrigerated product shelf life from two to four weeks, as compared to the conventional PVC-overwrapped EPS foam tray. High impact polystyrene (HIPS) laminated to both sides of the EPS sheet adds rigidity, preventing sidewall cave-in as carbon dioxide in the package atmosphere is solubilized into moisture on food product surfaces. Lidstock for this package is a multilayer barrier polyester with an anti-fog feature; and the gas mixture for the modified atmosphere includes carbon dioxide (to inhibit bacterial and fungal growth) and nitrogen (used as an inert filler). The Perdue product line in the modified atmosphere package includes breast cutlets, nuggets, wings, thighs, drumsticks, and roasted boneless breast in three different package sizes.

Typical structures for MAP meat snacks use similar film structures to that of

Figure 5-7. Perdue Done It! chicken package.

package A. Tray materials typically are either Barex (nitrile resin belonging to BP Chemicals International) laminations or high-barrier HIPS structures. The lidding material has two key functions: it provides anti-fog properties and an easy-peel opening, whether applied as the rigid web or as the lidding sealant.

For meat snack applications, both rigid rollstock and preformed tray packaging systems are used, based on market size, product sizes, or weight variations. Rollstock operations typically are geared to high volumes requiring only tray depth changes to create new product size/weight variations. High protection from both oxygen and moisture is required, as the storage life is four to six weeks under refrigerated conditions.

A major MAP growth market is fresh pasta. In this market, total product visibility is required. Typical structures for the lidding again are similar to package A. However, most processors do not require anti-fog lidding films, believing that excessive fogging indicates that the package has been temperature-abused.

The rigid tray material typically has been a polyvinyl chloride (PVC) sheet that is PVDC-coated or laminated with PVDC adhesive to a polyolefin sealant. The oxygen barrier properties of the PVDC coating generally are two or three times better than those of the PVDC adhesive. Copolyester sheet has excellent forming properties, but it is more difficult to cut and more costly than either PVC or Barex structures. Consumers may prefer an easy-opening package, but package security and barrier properties that assure product freshness are the critical concerns.

When evaluating gas mixtures for different product applications, one should remember that only carbon dioxide has an inhibitory effect on microbiological growth in food products. Its benefits usually are seen at a 25 to 30% concentration in the package atmosphere, and more effective microbial control is obtained at a 40% or greater concentration. When striving for these carbon dioxide levels in the atmosphere, one must recall that moist products tend to absorb carbon dioxide, and most films have a carbon dioxide permeation rate four to five times greater than that of oxygen. Thus, to obtain a residual level of 40% carbon dioxide over a four- to six-week package storage period, the initial package atmosphere concentration may need to be 60% carbon dioxide or more.

As good as it may be, or as high tech as it may appear, the technology of CAP/MAP is not without problems. The main trouble with this technology is that toxicity in the product can occur before spoilage because using CAP/MAP techniques limits the growth of spoilage flora but does not necessarily limit the growth of pathogens. The major hazard with this type of packaging (usually MAP) is growth and toxin production by the fatal *Clostridium botulinum* organism.

Proteolytic strains of *C. botulinum* grow best at 35°C (95°F), and some nonproteolytics can produce toxin at refrigeration temperatures. When MAP is used, the temperature must be precisely controlled and kept below 3°C because refrigeration will not prevent growth and toxin formation of nonproteolytic *C. botulinum* strains.

Unfortunately, the inherent technology of MAP also gets it into trouble. When foods with sufficient moisture content (which allows bacterial growth) are placed in an environment that discourages the growth of aerobic spoilage organisms but supports the growth of anaerobes, the product may taste fine but could be toxic. In MAP/vacuum-packaged foods where aerobic growth is curtailed, extended shelf life can provide time for the *C. botulinum* toxin to be produced. Longer storage times at fluctuating temperatures add to an existing problem.

Studies have been conducted on this problem, but currently the Food and Drug Administration has no policies governing MAP at the commercial level. However, there is no substitute for excellent santitation practices and temperature monitoring during processing and packaging. Shelf-life dates, too, should be closely watched and not grossly exceeded (beyond the processor's suggested date) at the retail level.

THE SOLID WASTE ISSUE

Not long ago, it was possible just to talk packaging for packaging's sake. Unfortunately, that is no longer the case. Now, anyone who talks packaging must also discuss solid waste, the inevitable result of a society producing too much trash. The idea of "throwing it away" is rapidly becoming ancient history. There is no longer an "away" for solid waste.

How did the country get into this mess? There are several reasons and many opinions: too many people generating too much trash, an emphasis on being a throw-away society, poor waste management, and no recovery or recycling efforts. The nation must face a cold, hard fact and must effectively deal with it: the United States is running out of places to put solid waste, and something must be done about the deteriorating situation now.

The United States generated approximately 160 million tons of solid waste in 1988. Put another way, each American contributes 3.6 pounds/day or 1,300 pounds/year of trash to the solid waste stream. If this rate continues as expected, the nation will generate 190 million tons by the year 2000 (*Food Engineering*, 1989c). As disposers are running out of places to put solid waste, the answer to this problem is no longer the use of landfills. Experts have predicted that more than one-third of the nation's landfills will be full within the next few years.

The most extensive and recent study on the solid waste issue was completed by Franklin Associates, Ltd., of Kansas City, Kansas, in 1988. This study, *Characteristics of Municipal Solid Waste in the United States*, examined gross discards of several solid waste materials; as listed below (percentages equal weight percent of the total group shown):

Paperboard: 41%
Glass: 8.2%
Metal: 8.7%
Plastics: 6.5%
Rubber, textiles, wood: 8.1%
Food wastes: 7.9%
Yard wastes: 17.9%
Miscellaneous inorganic wastes: 1.6%

In general terms, all packaging represents approximately 34% by weight of the entire municipal solid waste stream. However, plastics always receive the most criticism regarding disposability because of their *volume*. Plastics account for only 7% by weight of the solid waste stream but account for 20 to 25% by volume—they weigh less but take up more space than any other packaging material.

The United States took a stand on the solid waste issue when the Environmental Protection Agency's (EPA) Office of Solid Waste created a Task Force late in 1988, and early in 1989 issued a report on the waste crisis, outlining goals and recommendations for action by EPA, state and local governments, and industry and private citizens. According to EPA, depending on the region and waste type, problems in managing municipal solid waste will vary. But, in dealing with an increasing amount of solid waste each year, the agency reports that some efforts and trends are common in several areas.

As landfill space begins to be premium real estate, efforts to site new areas, recycling centers, and incineration sites are meeting mounting opposition. This opposition stems from concerns about environmental or health risks from contaminated ground and surface waters and toxic ash from waste combustion and air emissions, and from resistance to such factors as noise, odors, and anxiety over property values, leading to the NIMBY syndrome (Not In My Back Yard).

Although recycling and reuse of waste materials are publicly acceptable methods for managing municipal solid waste, the existing waste management infrastructure often discourages effective recycling efforts. However, a workable plan may be found in integrated waste management, a term that refers to the complementary use of a variety of waste management practices to safely and effectively handle the municipal solid waste stream with the least adverse impact on human health and the environment.

An integrated waste management system will contain some or all of these components:

- Source reduction (including reuse of products)
- Recycling of materials (including composting)

- Waste combustion (with energy recovery)
- Landfilling

In integrated waste management, all the elements work together to form a complete system for the proper management of municipal waste. Waste stream constituents are matched to the management practices that are best suited to those particular constituents, in order to reduce toxics, reduce quantity, and safely extract any useful energy or material from the waste prior to final disposal.

To most effectively reduce waste management problems at the national level, EPA recommends the use of a hierarchy. This hierarchy begins with source reduction and reuse, in order to reduce both the toxic constituents in products and the generation of large quantities of waste. Source reduction may occur through the design and manufacture of products and packaging that have minimum toxic content, use a minimum volume of material, and/or have a longer useful life.

The second rung in the hierarchy is recycling of materials, including composting of food and yard waste. Recycling is near the top of the hierarchy because it prevents potentially useful materials from being combusted or landfilled, thereby preserving waste disposal capacity.

Although lower than source reduction and recycling in the hierarchy of management options, waste combustion is useful in reducing the bulk of municipal waste and can provide the added benefit of energy production. Landfilling also is lower in the hierarchy but is essential to handle wastes such as nonrecyclables and the noncombustibles such as demolition waste and construction debris.

Everyone has a role in making integrated waste management work. In 1988, EPA set a national goal of 25% source reduction and recycling (up from the then-current 10%) by 1992. To reach the 25% source reduction and recycling goal, the remainder of the waste must be handled by combustion and landfills. On-line and already permitted combustors will handle about 20% of the waste stream. The remainder (about 55%) is projected for landfills.

In dealing with the solid waste issue, the packaging industry suffers from a lack of credibility. Attacked by consumer groups and environmentalists who in turn have lobbied state legislators, the industry has found itself blindsided on this issue. The packaging industry now must defend itself against an onslaught of misinformation and distortions. However, it could have prevented some of these attacks if it had initiated actions much earlier, say in early 1988, by starting educational programs and recycling efforts. Moreover, a recent consumer poll revealed that a company's stand on solid waste and recycling issues will affect consumer purchases—one-half of the customers polled will change brands if the company does not take a "favorable" solid waste stand.

One good example of industry involvement did occur before bills were passed by anxious legislators in 1988 and 1989. The Society of the Plastics Industry (SPI) began a program of assigning numbers on containers in order to designate which types of materials were present in the containers, thereby aiding recycling efforts. An example of the designation is shown in Figure 5-8. In addition, at the end of 1989, SPI announced that 17 states had passed coding laws following the society's system for grading plastic containers. These laws are expected to affect approximately 53% of the U.S. population. Florida was the first state, with the law taking effect in July 1990. The following states were to follow suit in 1991: Texas, Massachusetts, Wisconsin, Illinois, Ohio, Missouri, Colorado, North Carolina, South Carolina, Minnesota, Louisiana, and Maine. In 1992, this law will go into effect in California, Indiana, Michigan, and Iowa. The society estimates that almost 50% of all plastic bottles now sold have been coded or are in the process of being coded.

To the industry's dismay, this one good program initiation did not prevent a legislative landslide from occurring in 1989. The first and most famous ban happened in Suffolk County, New York, when legislators placed a ban on grocery bags and fast food containers composed of polystyrene. Minneapolis/St. Paul, Minnesota and the state of Wisconsin were also nervous about throwaway nondairy food containers and planned to impose bans by the end of 1990. But possibly the most damaging piece of legislation was brought before the state legislature in Maine. Along with a ban on various throw-away containers, the state may decide to ban aseptic-type (brikpak) containers and other multiple layer packages. The reasoning behind the proposed ban is the widely held belief that commingled waste represents a tremendous hazard to the environment and that all such containers should be banned.

The packaging industry also took the initiative in 1989 with the manufacture and sale of several recycled products. For example, Procter & Gamble now recycles milk jugs into detergent containers. Approximately 20 to 30% recycled

Figure 5-8. An example of the Society of the Plastics Industry's symbol for packaging material designation. Source: Society of the Plastics Industry.

HDPE from dairy containers is used in bottles of Tide and Downy. The now-famous Spic and Span bottle is manufactured from nearly 100% recycled PET soda bottles.

Interestingly, in some other industries many companies are changing the formulations of products—concentrating the product to create a smaller package, a good example of source reduction. Products undergoing such reformulation include Downy and Pepto Bismol.

In addition to recycling, several processors and packagers have changed packaging materials because of the solid waste issue. Some companies are changing to all-aluminum cans as opposed to steel, as steel lacks an easy-open end, and aluminum gives higher recycling rates. Some companies have eliminated the use of heavy metals in their labels, and some have switched from polystyrene trays to molded pulp trays.

A final concern affecting the industry and its dealings with the solid waste issue is that of biodegradability, which the public has perceived to be nature's way of handling the trash dilemma. Yet, the public does not understand that biodegradability and biodegradable packaging films are a myth. "Nature's way" does not have the slightest chance of working in a modern-day landfill.

Biodegradable films break down into more simple chemical compounds when attacked by microbes, and the act of biodegradation works best in the presence of water and air. If water and air are present in a landfill, biodegradable materials eventually will degrade into water vapor and carbon dioxide, leaving behind mineral and inorganic contents; but today's landfills are an unnatural environment. Modern landfills literally entomb solid waste in order to contain odors and gases, allowing no oxygen or water into the system. The result is that solid wastes are recovered from landfills, years after their burial, in virtually the same condition in which they were put into the site. Recent landfill "digs" have uncovered unbelievable evidence: ten-year-old carrots in perfect shape, readable newspapers, and intact steaks.

The packaging industry also entered the melee of biodegradability when it introduced degradable films, used primarily for bags and sacks, composed of 60% polyethylene and 40% cornstarch, extruded into a masterbatch. The theory behind this production is that microbes will attack and break down the starch molecules in a landfill. There is no evidence, however, of how long this process could take. The addition of the masterbatch ultimately will increase the cost of resins used in the manufacture of these bags, a cost the industry may not want to pay. (See the graph of resin cost increases with the addition of degradable masterbatches, Figure 5-9.) The case for biodegradability is quite weak when all these factors are taken into consideration. And, more important, many industry watchers believe that degradability hinders plastic recycling efforts.

Certainly, the solid waste issue impacts the packaging industry in many ways; but, in addition to the steps already taken by the industry, there are still other

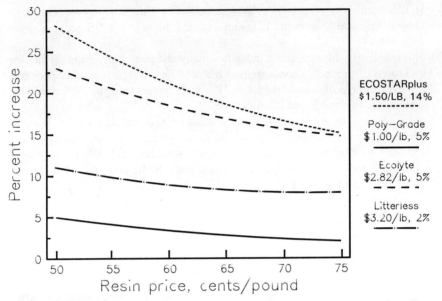

Figure 5-9. Resin cost increase with the addition of degradable masterbatches from film extrusion. Source: Kline & Company, Inc., Fairfield, New Jersey.

ways to improve packaging's self-image. Packaging professionals should make sure solid waste issues reach the top level of management in their companies. They should advocate consumer education programs and attend legislative hearings, getting directly involved with laws that might affect packaging. They should also keep informed of industry developments in this area; for example, several joint ventures forming recycling efforts have come to light (e.g., The Dow Chemical Company and wTe Corporation). Still, all packaging professionals should remember food packaging's main goal: food product safety and quality. This goal overshadows any other purpose or use of food packaging.

FUTURE TRENDS AND CONCLUSION

The changes and the revolutions in the packaging industry in the last decade have been remarkable. Who would have expected to have ketchup in plastic bottles, complete entrees in plastic packages sitting on a shelf with no refrigeration, and poultry products that stay fresh up to four weeks under refrigeration? Thanks to packagers who slaved over the designs of new containers, processing companies who worked with the packagers to get the formulations correct, and consumers who demanded changes in food products, these changes did occur. The packaging industry, has come from orphan to star status in a few short years.

What is next for the industry? There probably will not be so many dramatic changes like the ones of the last decade. The rate of change will slow because major conversions from one material to another already have taken place. This does not mean, however, that there will be no changes in packaging; they just will occur more slowly.

There will continue to be material improvements (e.g., lighter weight, cleaner cans, better and clearer plastic products). Resin suppliers are always seeking to improve their raw materials, which eventually will be used in plastic packages. For example, barrier resins will be improved so that more of these materials can be used in severe processing situations such as hot filling and retorting. To illustrate this point, a dramatic improvement recently occurred with the introduction of Johnson Controls' heat-set polyester terephthalate bottle for use in hot filling 64-ounce Ocean Spray cranberry juices. This bottle, an award winner, provides strength and durability in a process where regular PET bottles would collapse and melt under vacuum and hot filling. Also, it represents another conversion from glass to plastic, a purchase option most consumers favor.

In addition, packages that are "active" in nature may be available soon. Still under development and wrapped in secrecy, these packages may respond to food products and adjust the environment to preserve the contents. Continuous interaction is the basis of these packages, as the mechanisms that change the environment are built into the packaging materials.

Furthermore, the industry still will be affected by market influences. The convenience push will continue unabated as the number of single-person households increases, as well as the population of elderly individuals. The microwave influx into many more American households will continue too, influencing the demand for more microwavable products. In addition, consumers will continue to demand fresher foods with no added preservatives, as the push for "natural, healthy foods" continues. The result will be more challenges for the packaging industry, to produce an adequate supply of economical packages that will maintain freshness and be convenient to use while giving the barrier protection that the product requires.

The biggest challenge the industry will face still will be the solid waste issue. The industry will need to produce packages that provide all the requirements that its many markets demand without creating mounds of trash. This is a tough challenge indeed, but with proper planning, consumer education, and recycling, the packaging industry should meet the challenge. And, as mentioned earlier, it is the industry's responsibility to initiate solid waste handling policies, rather than to leave them to misinformed citizens and nervous legislators, but without losing sight of packaging's main goal: food safety and quality.

The packaging industry is a rapidly growing industrial sector destined only to get bigger. Learn the acronyms and the applications! A world of opportunity awaits practitioners in this dynamic area.

REFERENCES

Brown, W. E. 1986. Vinylidene chloride copolymers. In *The Wiley Encyclopedia of Packaging Technology*, ed. Marilyn Bakker, pp. 692–696. New York: John Wiley and Sons.

Copperthite, Kimberly G. 1988. Cans and containers. In *The U.S. Industrial Outlook, 1989*, pp. 7/1–7/6. Washington, D.C.: U.S. Department of Commerce.

Food Engineering. 1988a. Perdue Done It! with the EPS foam MAP. 60(4): 65–66.

Food Engineering. 1988b. Designing microwave packaging with receptor films. 60(10): 50–51.

Food Engineering. 1988d. Achieving barrier properties through silica coating. 60(12): 41–44.

Food Engineering. 1989c. Government agency sets action agenda for solid waste. 61(6): 68–70.

Food Engineering. 1989d. Barrier packaging is vital in preserving salted snacks. 61(8): 55–56.

Food Engineering. 1989e. Products receive excellent protection with nitrile resins. 61(10): 59–60.

Food Engineering. 1989f. The impact of materials and gas on chilled foods. 61(10): 62–63.

Hasenauer, Randal J. 1986. Film, oriented polypropylene. In *The Wiley Encyclopedia of Packaging Technology*, ed. Marilyn Bakker, pp. 320–325. New York: John Wiley and Sons.

Russell, M. 1988c. The packaging boom continues. *Food Engineering* 60(10): 63–73.

Russell, M. 1989a. Facing an uphill battle. *Food Engineering* 61(1): 93–98.

Russell, M. 1989b. Barrier plastics. *Food Engineering* 61(5): 89–104.

Sacharow, Stanley and Brody, Aaron L. 1987. *Packaging: An Introduction*. Duluth: Harcourt Brace Jovanovich.

Schroeder, Karen. 1989. New barrier structures for CAP/MAP packaging. In *Proceedings of the Tenth International Coextrusion Conference*. Princeton, N.J.: Schotland Business Research, Inc., Sept. 1989.

Szemplenski, T. E. 1986. Aseptic packaging. In *The Wiley Encyclopedia of Packaging Technology*, ed. Marilyn Bakker, pp. 20–23. New York: John Wiley and Sons.

Tubridy, M. F. and J. P. Sibilia. 1986. Nylon. In *The Wiley Encyclopedia of Packaging Technology*, ed. Marilyn Bakker, pp. 477–482. New York: John Wiley and Sons.

Varriano-Marston, Elizabeth. 1989. A unique breathable packaging system for produce. In *Proceedings of Pack Alimentaire '89*. Princeton, N.J.: Schotland Business Research, Inc., June 1989.

Chapter 6

Safety and Regulatory Aspects

Howard E. Bauman, Ph.D.

CURRENT SAFETY OF FOOD

Food production is an area of commerce that affects all consumers every day. Most of the food consumed by the public is manufactured in processing plants, produced in restaurants of all types, and served by caterers or deli-type operations; and these entities bear the burden of responsibility for producing safe foods. Government food regulatory agencies are responsible for monitoring the industries to ensure compliance with their regulations and a safe food supply. Many factors are affecting the ability of these entities to guarantee a safe food supply. Moreover, the food industry has moved rapidly toward global production and distribution of food, which is resulting in ever increasing amounts of food products moving in world commerce.

Today's consumers are becoming more aware of the potential hazards of food and will be more vocal in the future in demanding safe food. Currently consumers' perceptions of hazards differ from what experts believe to be reality, as the consumers' perceptions are based primarily on publicity that has overemphasized the hazards in certain areas such as food additives and pesticides.

Unfortunately, the news media have been relatively silent about microbiological hazards, which cause more problems in our society than any other food issue. Information will have to be developed and disseminated to consumers and the media in an understandable and believable form to correct these perceptions, and to help the public focus on and become educated about the real hazards. Currently the "boy who cried wolf" is winning.

The U.S. food supply is safe compared to the food supply worldwide. The food industry and the government agencies have done an excellent job to date, considering the tools they have had available. How long the food supply can maintain that reputation depends on the ability of the food industry, in cooperation with government entities, to develop, utilize, and publicize new techniques to ensure its safety under current and future conditions of food production and preparation.

During the past two decades, many changes have taken place in the manufacture of food. Foods now are being produced at high speeds and may be shipped directly to supermarket warehouses in a matter of hours or a few days. These products are available to the consumer within a very short time in the retail market. This speed has made it likely that classical food safety test results on finished products may not be available from the quality control laboratories before the food is consumed—especially for perishable refrigerated foods with a limited shelf life.

Other changes have been and are continuing to be made in formulations of food products, the processes used, and the distribution systems. This problem is magnified by the lack of education of some participants in the food chain, including the consumer, on the dangers inherent in improper cooking, handling, and storage of foods, especially those involving some of the newer food product innovations. There is also a lack of consistent control of critical elements of the food distribution system. Temperatures are not consistently controlled to guarantee proper handling of the products in the distribution systems, including transport temperatures and those of in-store refrigeration units and home refrigerators.

This area is critical because pathogenic bacteria not previously considered sources of concern with refrigerated food now are more prevalent. Many of these bacteria, such as *Campylobacter jejunei*, *Listeria monocytogenes*, and *Yersinia enterocolitica*, will grow at normal refrigeration temperatures. This is a serious issue with foods that have been pasteurized or partially cooked and sold refrigerated. If they become recontaminated with these pathogens, harmless competing spoilage organisms will not be able to grow in preference to the pathogens. Further, the development of foods using controlled or modified atmospheres, which allow the foods to be kept fresh-looking and -tasting for longer periods of time under refrigeration, may add substantially to this risk. The extended time may allow the slow-growing pathogens to increase to substantial numbers before the food is eaten. Because of the large quantities of a food that may be produced in one day, it is now possible simultaneously to infect and/or cause illness from pathogens or microbial toxins in larger segments of the population than was possible a few years ago.

The regulatory agencies, because of budget constraints and or diversion of funds to other areas of concern, are increasingly handicapped in their ability to inspect a food production facility frequently enough to ensure safe operation and consistent compliance with the food laws and regulations. They are further affected by the fact that there is a continuing increase in the quantities and types of imported foods, many with unknown practices of production and control, which puts an additional burden on the regulatory agencies.

The quantity of imports, especially perishable items, has reached a point where only a small fraction of these products can be tested by the regulatory agencies prior to entry into the U.S. food system. Most testing procedures are costly and time-consuming, and it is further recognized that end-product testing cannot reliably assure that a food is safe. Only small fractions of any particular lot of food can be tested under practical conditions, and because of the heterogeneity of most foods, problems will be missed. These changes in the food supply system are straining the capacity of the regulatory agencies to ensure that all manufactured and imported food is safe.

It is obvious that in order to assure a safe food supply the current control systems of both the regulatory agencies and the food industry must be changed. If it is impossible to inspect safety into a system, then an organized effort must be made to prevent the food from becoming unsafe during its production and subsequent distribution. The food industry and the regulators must reassess the current mechanisms of control and develop and install new techniques and procedures that not only will assure safe food, but also will level the playing field of criteria, controls, and procedures for domestic, imported, and exported products. All foods, regardless of source, should be treated equally. Responsible food manufacturers want to produce safe food, and the agencies want to monitor the food appropriately, but science and changes in foods and their production systems have created new problems that must be solved on a cooperative basis.

CURRENT REGULATORY CONTROL

Thousands of laws and regulations currently in effect in the United States are designed to control the food and allied industries in the preparation and manufacture of safe food and food components. The intent of this chapter is not to deal with the details of the laws and regulations, but rather, from a practical point of view, to discuss the various agencies involved in food safety and their responsibilities. The details of the regulations are available from the various jurisdictions. This section gives a brief description of the various agencies that regulate food and processes and their responsibilities.

Cities and Counties

Cities and counties have designated government entities with their own criteria and regulations relating to food safety, for the most part located within the public health agencies. These entities are primarily involved in food hygiene and the sanitation of facilities that produce or handle food at the retail level, where there is direct contact with the ultimate consumer of the food. They interact mainly with retail stores, restaurants, caterers, and institutions under their jurisdiction. The local health officers also may serve a larger function, as they are in an ideal situation to identify health issues related to a food that might also be in distribution elsewhere in the country. Their efforts can lead to prompt notification of state and federal agencies of the possibility that a particular problem may be widespread.

States

All 50 states have regulatory organizations, which mirror in many ways the federal organizations that are responsible for safe food. In the states, the reporting relationship may differ from the federal agencies in that those responsible for safe food may be located in either the state's department of agriculture, its department of health, or its department of consumer affairs.

Many states have adopted by reference the regulations of the federal Food and Drug Administration and by and large operate within those regulations. The states primarily are concerned with intrastate food production and manufacturing facilities. However, one state, California, through the passage of Proposition 65 has begun to impinge on the federal jurisdiction over food products as well as nonfood products moving in interstate commerce through the use of labeling requirements that differ from those of the federal agencies.

The states can play a large role whenever there is a food safety issue by working with other states and the federal agencies in solving and controlling the problem. Because of the widespread and rapid deployment of food throughout the United States, it is essential that all regulatory agencies work together in a cooperative manner. The Association of Food and Drug Officials has been working diligently toward uniformity and cooperation.

Federal Agencies

The federal government is concerned with imported and domestic foods that move in interstate commerce. The Department of Agriculture, because of its unique control over all meat and poultry products, has intrastate control as well. The federal agencies also regulate food ingredients and other components used in the manufacture of food that may become part of a food either directly or indirectly. Areas covered may range from sources such as packaging materials or exposure to substances during production or manufacturing to boiler water additives, sanitizers, and pesticides, to name a few. These agencies also are concerned with the suitability of modes of distribution, storage, and handling of foods that may contribute to a hazard.

Their jurisdiction also includes those areas where food is served in interstate travel, such as in restaurants on interstate highways, in airplanes, on passenger trains, and in cruise vessels. They have taken the position that ingredients that have moved in interstate commerce that are subsequently used in foods produced and sold intrastate are subject to their jurisdiction. Several agencies in the federal system impinge on the regulation of food.

The Food and Drug Administration (FDA)

The Food and Drug Administration is an agency of The Department of Health and Human Services responsible for all foods for humans or animals that move in interstate commerce with the exception of meat and poultry products. The agency is responsible for regulation and approval of food additives, packaging materials, or any other materials that will be or may come in contact with food, whose components may reasonably be expected to migrate to food. FDA also is responsible for housewares that may be used in the preparation of food or come in contact with it, and it also has jurisdiction over cosmetics, drugs, and medical devices.

The Food and Drug Administration does not have the authority to preapprove food formulation and labeling and does not have a continuous inspection system in food production plants. FDA relies on visits to plants by inspectors to verify whether they are operating within the laws and regulations of the agency. The inspectors also sample product on the market to verify label claims, and conduct tests on products that may indicate the presence of hazards.

Food Safety Inspection Services (FSIS)

FSIS is an agency of The Department of Agriculture that is responsible for the safety and wholesomeness of meat and poultry products produced and sold in the United States or imported from other countries. Meat and poultry products produced in retail stores in the United States, however, are exempt from its jurisdiction. FSIS utilizes the food and food component approval lists of FDA in approving ingredients, additives, packaging materials, or other components of food and food production that reasonably may be expected to become a component of food, directly or indirectly. FSIS has authority for the preapproval of buildings, grounds, production systems, equipment, formulations, and labeling of foods under its jurisdiction. This agency differs from FDA in that FSIS does have continuous inspection of plants. Recently there has been a move toward less than continuous inspection of some of the plants under FSIS jurisdiction. Current indications are that FSIS will be moving toward a preventive system of control of food safety.

Environmental Protection Agency

The Environmental Protection Agency is responsible for approving and establishing tolerances for pesticides used on crops, in manufacturing plants, or in home use in the United States. By inference EPA also controls pesticide use on crops that are imported into the United States, either as a commodity or in finished products.

This control is accomplished through published permissible tolerances. The agency also is responsible for the approval of sanitizers that may be used in food plants and in the home. The enforcement of the tolerances is left to the jurisdiction of the regulatory agencies responsible for the users of the materials.

Consumer Product Safety Commission (CPSC)

Both CPSC and FDA are responsible for the safety of premiums that may be offered in conjunction with food. FDA also has jurisdiction over housewares that may come in contact with food, whether related to commercial food or used in the home. FDA is concerned with premiums from an ingestible safety standpoint (e.g., lead in paint on drinking glasses or lead in pottery that may be used for cooking), whereas CPSC is concerned with the safety of premiums as they relate to flammability, part size, or any other hazards related to the age of the expected user.

National Marine Fisheries Service (NMFS)

The National Marine Fisheries Service is unique among agencies, in that it will furnish an inspection service that is voluntary and is paid for by the facilities that use it. The NMFS recently embarked on a program of developing a Hazard Analysis Critical Control Point (HACCP) system of control for cooked ready-to-eat refrigerated shrimp and crab meat. This action was mandated by the U.S. Congress. NMFS is working with the affected industries and has model programs in place in a number of facilities (National Marine Fisheries Service 1989).

CURRENT PROCESSOR COMPLIANCE

Undoubtedly, some food companies, particularly smaller organizations with little expert legal or technical assistance, are not aware of all the organizations that regulate the foods they produce. Further, many do not have a comprehensive view or understanding of the food laws and regulations under which they operate. In some instances they may not have the technical expertise to recognize that they may have a food that represents a hazard. The larger companies have the expertise, but may not necessarily deploy their efforts adequately with regard to food safety issues.

Food safety issues and problems start further back in the food chain and peripheral areas than most people realize. Food production is a complicated system.

If one traces the components of even a simple food, it becomes apparent that many companies may be involved with it, including some not directly in the food area that may impinge dramatically upon it. For example, package manufacturers who have only produced packages for nonfood items may enter the food field because of a package innovation. Unfortunately, such package convertors, not having been involved in the food area previously, generally are not familiar with food laws. Therefore they do not know that there are regulations governing the package and its ingredients if it comes in contact with food or may become a component of food. The transportation system also may have detrimental effects if the food transports also are used for hauling hazardous waste and chemicals.

There is also a problem throughout the chain of suppliers in relying only on letters of guarantee of compliance with regulations. Many suppliers do not know the composition of the ingredient or packaging material they are supplying; they simply have been assured by their suppliers that it is in compliance. Unless the user demands composition information on food and package ingredients, the possibility exists that unsafe packages and improper components or ingredients—in the eyes of the law—may enter the food chain. In the future, it should be impossible for a food manufacturer to use packaging or food components of unknown composition. Proprietary information is no excuse for not having this information because confidential arrangements can be made to obtain composition data.

In the food process itself, as mentioned earlier in this chapter, there are many problems concerning the ability of control systems to keep up with the requirements that are necessary for the production of safe food. Most current quality control systems are based on after-the-fact detection of problems that may have occurred in the food production system, rather than a control system designed to prevent hazards from developing. It is impossible to inspect safety into a product. Hazards must be prevented.

A PREVENTIVE FOOD SAFETY SYSTEM (BAUMAN 1974 AND 1990)

A preventive systems approach to food safety control does exist. It is known as the Hazard Analysis Critical Control Point system (HACCP). This system was developed for the production of food to be used in spacecraft through a combined effort of the National Aeronautics and Space Administration (NASA) and the U.S. Army Natick Laboratories. The system has been modified and applied to commercial food production for a number of years with great success. The story of how it came about is interesting and illustrates that necessity is indeed the mother of at least some problem-solving innovations.

In the latter part of 1959, a contract was written to produce food for the first manned space flight. The specifications for the food were unusual in that it had to be bite-sized and coated with an edible coating so it could be eaten without crumbling. No one at that time knew what effect particulates in the space capsule would have, especially as related to asphyxiation of the astronaut. In addition, it was necessary for the food product to withstand a gravity force of nine. It was possible to meet these criteria, but one other was much more difficult: the requirement that the food be as close to 100% safe as was possible. This proved to be particularly onerous. It was discovered that if the accepted methods of quality control testing were used, it was necessary to destroy most of a batch of food in order to conduct all the tests deemed necessary to approach this degree of assurance. In spite of this, statistical analysis showed that even this amount of destructive testing was not sufficient to achieve the level of assurance desired. For instance, in order to detect with 99% assurance a defect level of 5 spoiled cans of food per 1000 cans, it would be necessary to test at least 920 cans. It became obvious that the current methods of quality control and testing of foods, after the fact, were not adequate, and this brought into question the use of these methods in food plants to control food safety. Obviously, food companies were not conducting high levels of testing in their laboratories.

It was concluded that a new system for food safety control was necessary. It became obvious that the only way to approach 100% safety would be to develop a preventive system of control to ensure that pathogens, toxins, viruses, harmful chemicals, or other safety defects were not in the finished food product. The thought was good, but its development and execution were another matter. How does one go about designing a preventive system? One clue to the answer was NASA's requirement for documentation of all ingredients and their sources. NASA also required in-depth information on the plant producing the product and the personnel involved. All tests run and data derived were documented. This requirement applied to suppliers as well. The difference from normal plant documentation was that this information was not kept in bits and pieces in different areas, but rather was assembled in one place. It was found that this assembled information allowed for the first time a comprehensive overview of the total production of a product, including the field or water that the ingredients came from, the production systems, the distribution systems, and the use and abuse the food might receive during production as well as in the space capsule. This approach allowed the research team to think of food production as a system rather than a series of isolated events.

A suitable method still was needed for predetermining the potential hazards that might exist in a system. The zero defects program of NASA was considered, but this effort was directed mainly at hardware. Nondestructive tests such as ultrasound and X ray were used, but these types of tests were not the answer for most problems in food testing. In looking further, the team learned of a technique used by the U.S. Army Natick Laboratories called the modes of failure analysis. It did have possibilities, and after review and modification, the modes of failure method was adopted. This technique proved to be the key to being able to perform a hazard analysis on a food product from raw material to final consumption. Once a hazard analysis was completed, it then was possible to select those points in the food production chain that would most likely contribute to a hazard. Thus was born the Hazard Analysis Critical Control Point system of food control.

The systems used initially were elaborate, including the production of food in what essentially was a clean room. The real effort was in trying to reduce the system so that it would be cost-effective and could be used as a standard practice in food plants. Experimentation was conducted on the system in food plants for several years, and in 1971 the procedure was presented at a food protection conference in Denver, Colorado. The first official government regulatory agency use of the HACCP approach was in the development of the low-acid canned food regulation by FDA. The above-mentioned level of testing needed to detect low levels of canned food spoilage spurred the efforts in this area.

As discussed in the following paragraphs, some basic moves must be made before it is possible to embark on a HACCP program, whether in industry or in government.

A Cultural Change Is Necessary

Top management and high level government officials must unequivocally take the position that they will strive for safe food, and that all employees should conduct themselves in a fashion that will carry out this objective. A three-way partnership must be developed in industry, between the plant manager, the quality assurance manager, and the line personnel in the plant. This holds true in government as well, where the partnership likely would consist of regional directors, supervisors, and inspectors. A three-way partnership is important because the plant manager/regional directors and the quality assurance manager/supervisors cannot be involved in all areas continuously. It must be recognized that people working on the line/inspectors also must be involved in the effort because many of them, through experience, almost instinctively know when something is not right in the process. Cooperation between industry and government is essential for proper installation and monitoring of the HACCP program.

It is necessary to train all people in the HACCP system. If people understand the rationale behind the criteria that have been established, then they will more likely work with the program and not against it. Both industry and government must follow through on their commitment. They cannot allow safety rules to be negotiated. The people in the plant and inspectors are very astute; if they observe or become aware of any compromise on safety, they will soon ignore the program. Thus it is critical that ground rules and criteria be established, especially those criteria used for determining whether a product—when a critical control point has been exceeded—can be released. These ground rules must be developed cooperatively as well.

A HACCP review committee should be established in each company and in the government agencies, with multidisciplinary representation ranging from microbiologists, engineers, quality assurance personnel, and operations personnel to product scientists and so on. The committee's composition may vary, depending on the particular product or process that is under review. It should be a standing committee within the organization. The chairman of the group as well as a few additional members, such as microbiologists, chemists, and so on, should be permanent to maintain its continuity and uniformity.

A Ten-Point Safety Program

The fundamentals of getting organized for food safety are listed in a ten-point product safety program. This listing describes the areas that must be covered in a HACCP program but not how to do it. Other programs undoubtedly will be developed as HACCP becomes more widely used; however, this program is illustrative of a system that works. The ten points are as follows:

1. *Specifications.* Specifications, as used in this program, means complete descriptions and requirements for ingredients, including accessories such as packaging materials. Specifications for a product must be so complete that anyone could use the document to produce the identical product.

2. *Safety analysis.* This is the hazard analysis that determines the critical control points in the food system used to produce a particular product. It must be carefully done and reviewed adequately so that all persons involved are confident that the potential hazards have been identified. This effort must be conducted by people trained in the technique of hazard analysis. It must be kept in mind that HACCP monitoring is for critical defects, and 100% monitoring must be carried out where feasible. If it is not possible, then appropriate statistical testing must be used. Any decision criteria developed must reflect the level of monitoring possible.

3. *Purchasing requirements.* All ingredients, equipment, packaging, and so on, should have rigid specifications and be purchased only from approved suppliers. A HACCP program does not permit the use of low-cost bidders unless all bidders have been approved to supply the particular product. This helps assure that the product will be produced as designed. Suppliers' plants should adhere to the same safety control practices as the purchasing company when they are producing the item for the purchaser.

4. *Good manufacturing practices (GMP).* The HACCP system incorporates GMPs because they deal with known safety issues such as hygiene, sanitation, good housekeeping, and so on.

5. *Physical systems hazard control (PSHCs).* This is a schematic of the actual flow of the product in production and delineates the equipment used, the piping, the interrelationship of accessory equipment (e.g., storage tanks, etc.). It also shows all of the CCPs (critical control points) located in the production system. This is a critical document and must be approved by the HACCP review committee. Changes in the system cannot be made without the approval of the review committee and without a new hazard analysis if needed.

6. *Recall system*. Products should be coded and invoices handled in such a way that all products can be traced through the distribution system. The lots of ingredients used in any production code should be recorded. This will allow an exact recall effort if an ingredient is the reason for the recall. Recalls or detainment will be only as effective as the recorded data will allow. A good recording system coupled with HACCP monitoring generally will result in only a few hours of production being involved. Lot sizes should be limited to relatively short periods of production time to facilitate narrowing the production time frame of any suspect product.

7. *Contract manufacturing*. Contract manufacturers must adhere to the same requirements that the contracting company requires of its own plants.

8. *Facility auditing*. Facilities must be audited on a periodic basis to ensure that they are operating according to company standards. They must assure that all of the critical control points are being monitored as required, with all deviations recorded as well as the disposition of any product implicated in a deviation. The verification records for the HACCP system also are reviewed.

9. *Customer complaints*. This area, often relegated to a consumer response group, must be monitored by the chairman of the review committee and the quality assurance managers of the affected business on a regular basis. Complaints very often are an early warning that something may be wrong with a product.

10. *Incident reporting*. All deviations from normal operations must be reported according to a prearranged plan to specific people responsible for assessing the situation and reacting appropriately. Incidents may range from a plant inspection by the government to a deviation in a critical control point. It is not always possible for plant personnel to appreciate the enormity of such problems. Reporting of incidents also allows the review committee to have an overall view of how well the operations are functioning, depending on the incident rate.

Principles of HACCP

Also important to the proper structuring of a HACCP system are the seven principles of HACCP as developed by the National Advisory Committee for Microbiological Criteria for Foods (NACMSF 1990), sponsored by the Food Safety Inspection Service of The Department of Agriculture and the Food and Drug Administration of Health and Human Services. The principles include the following:

1. Assessment of hazards associated with growing, harvesting, raw materials and ingredients, processing, manufacturing, distribution, marketing, and preparation and consumption of the food.

2. Determination of critical control points (CCPs) required to control the identified hazards.
3. Establishment of the conditions that must be met at each identified hazard.
4. Establishment of procedures to monitor CCPs.
5. Establishment of corrective action to be taken when there is a deviation identified by the monitoring of a CCP.
6. Establishment of effective record-keeping systems that document the control of CCPs and corrective action taken in response to deviations.
7. Establishment of procedures for verification that the HACCP system is working correctly.

It appears likely that the HACCP system will be mandated in the United States as the preferred system of food safety control. There is also a move in the World Health Organization to introduce and recommend HACCP worldwide. It would be wise for companies to become familiar with the HACCP system and begin installation of the program in their organizations. The best approach is to start by assessing the products being produced and to establish priorities based on the highest degree of hazard. This is necessary because companies with many plants and lines may take several years to complete the task.

REFERENCES

Bauman, Howard. 1974. The HACCP concept and microbiological hazard categories. *Food Technology* 28(9): 269–274.

Bauman, Howard. 1990. HACCP. Concept, development and application. *Food Technology* 44(5): 156–158.

National Advisory Committee for Microbiological Criteria for Foods. 1990. Unpublished deliberations. U.S. Department of Agriculture/Food and Drug Administration/U.S. Department of Commerce/U.S. Army Natick Laboratories.

National Marine Fisheries Service (NMFS). 1989. *Plan of Operations—Model Seafood Surveillance Project*. Washington, D.C.: National Marine Fisheries Service, Office of Trade and Industry Services.

RECOMMENDED READING

Food Processors Institute. 1977. *Control of Critical Points in Food Processing. A Systems Approach*. Washington, D.C.: The Bosley Corporation.

International Commission on Microbiological Specifications for Foods. 1986. *Microorganisms in Foods 2. Sampling for Microbiological Analysis: Principles and Specific Applications*, 2nd edition. Toronto, Canada: University of Toronto Press.

National Academy of Sciences (NAS). 1985. *Meat and Poultry Inspection: The Scientific Basis for the Nation's Program*. Washington, D.C.: National Academy Press.

National Academy of Sciences (NAS). 1985. *An Evaluation of Microbiological Criteria for Foods and Food Ingredients*. Washington, D.C.: National Academy Press.

Chapter 7

Logistics: The Missing Ingredient in New Product Development

James E. Morehouse,

Elizabeth Harrington, and David B. Abraham

INTRODUCTION

The truck pulled away from the dock, loaded with a shipment of the new product. As promised, the development of the product had taken only 12 months. Credit for the speed of development went to a multifunctional design team, which included employees from the marketing, sales, manufacturing, and R&D departments. This mix of personnel brought expertise from multiple functions to the design process. All parties agreed that the team caught many potential problems while they were still in their infancy, which is a major improvement compared to past product development efforts. All were confident that a winning product was on the way.

The new product arose as an extension of another recently introduced product; coating the existing snack in chocolate had seemed a logical development. As part of a growing market segment, the chocolate coating would appeal to a younger consumer. The package was redesigned to target this market, and a catchy new name was developed.

The chocolate coating created new distribution requirements for the product. Although it would remain in the dry section of the store, temperature-controlled shipping would be required due to the low melting point of the chocolate. Therefore, the product could not be shipped with its predecessor unless both were shipped temperature-controlled.

Advertising was begun in the test-market regions, and aggressive promotions encouraged customers to order the new product. The company eagerly paid slotting allowances in the test markets. Inventories built as manufacturing refined the process. All agreed that this was the smoothest product development effort in years. Expectation of success rose with promising results from preliminary focus groups.

During test marketing and roll-out, store buyers were kept aware of the special transportation requirements of the product. Predictably, these requirements created problems for the trade. The buyers responsible for these snacks typically were not responsible for products with temperature-control requirements. In addition, typical buyers of temperature-controlled product did not order product from this area of the store. As a result, the product often either did not get ordered, or it was shipped without proper temperature control. Lagging sales and high damage claims eventually required that the product be reformulated.

Why did this problem arise? The engineers guaranteed that they had attained the perfect melting point, balancing shelf stability, material costs, and ease of manufacturing—but they did not adequately consider the impact of logistics on the product.

In this example, transportation requirements impacted the way the customer ordered the product. These requirements should have been studied extensively during product development; but, as in most new product development teams, the logistics expertise of the team was inadequate. Eventually, the impact of the transportation requirements surfaced. In order to correct the problem, the product had to be reformulated with a higher melting point. This change reduced the temperature-control requirement, allowing the product to be ordered and shipped in a manner that was natural for retailers. However, the original problems could have been avoided with additional logistics involvement during product development.

DEFINING LOGISTICS

Logistics encompasses the process of procurement, transportation, and storage of goods from their source to the customer. Figure 7-1 diagrams the wide range of activities that require logistics management. Logistics involves purchasing, transportation, materials management, order management, and information management. Effective logistics requires integrated planning, control, and execution of all logistics-related activities. In addition, managing logistics requires

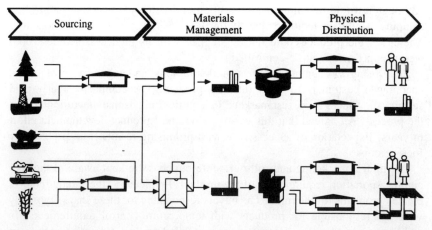

Figure 7-1. What is logistics? Copyright 1989, A. T. Kearney, Inc. All rights reserved.

looking beyond the boundaries of one's own organization. Effective logistics management can be achieved only as suppliers work cooperatively with vendors and customers to minimize logistics costs throughout the entire supply chain.

The problem of the melted chocolate resulted from a common attitude toward logistics. Arrangements for warehousing space were made through logistics personnel, but little reason was seen for logistics involvement in the product design process. Designers asked a few questions about packaging and cycle times, but many questions were not asked. The results almost proved disastrous.

Despite the relatively high visibility and awareness of distribution issues in the food industry, logistics personnel rarely are involved in the product design process. Product design teams, which have gained widespread acceptance in the industry, fail to include adequate logistics representation. Food processors report that in 1988, logistics costs accounted for 9.1% of their net sales.

Cost-effective logistics can make or break a food product. As the above case demonstrates, getting logistics involved early in the design process provides a usually untapped source of advice that can be critical for success.

NEW PRODUCT SUCCESS: THE IMPACT OF LOGISTICS

Many aspects of product design and roll-out impact logistics effectiveness. Likewise, effective logistics impacts a product in many ways. Logistics involvement must begin early in the development process and continue throughout the process.

Packaging

Package design requires logistics involvement during the product design phase. Packaging is the dominant attention getter in the food store, and therefore, it is designed to appeal to the target market. Hence, packaging receives a great deal of attention during product design. Packaging, in turn, has a major impact on logistics, particularly when the "display package" directly impacts the performance of the protective or shipping package.

Several years ago, a major consumer product manufacturer decided to change the packaging on its best-selling product. Bottles were changed from glass to plastic, as reductions in material costs, package weight, and waste due to breakage provided a cost justification for the change. Extensive tests indicated that consumers would accept the new packaging. As soon as the switch was made however, damage problems appeared in the warehouse. It quickly was discovered that the new product could be stacked only three pallets high instead of four. Instantly, warehouse space requirements grew by 33%.

The impact of packaging on logistics stretches far beyond warehousing costs. Packaging also should be designed with transportation costs in mind. Truck trailers conform to standard sizes. Cartons can be sized to maximize cube utilization during shipping. This task is easily accomplished, but the right people need to be involved. If cube utilization is not studied during package design, companies will find themselves paying to "ship air" (not use the full cubic capacity of a truck).

In addition, pallet configuration designs need to consider package and carton size and strength. If cartons are not designed to fit on standard pallets, extra cost will be incurred from excess damage due to carton overhang, or from poor cube utilization due to inefficient stacking patterns needed to fit the product on a pallet with overhang.

The impact of package and carton design is a major contributor to a long-term logistics success or failure. New product packaging designed without the input of logistics will result in long-term inefficiency.

Where to Manufacture, Store, and Test Market

The eventual physical distribution network also should be considered during product development. A physical distribution network involves the location of manufacturing facilities, warehouses, and the customer base; and the distances between these points have a major impact on logistics costs. Therefore, site selection for manufacturing facilities, warehouses, and test markets should take into account the eventual transportation distances and corresponding transportation costs.

Choosing a manufacturing facility is a complex and critical decision; but whether the product is manufactured by a co-packer or in-house, transportation distances should be kept in mind. Where will the product be stored? Where will demand come from over the long term? Minimizing transportation costs may spell the difference between success and failure. Although effective rate negotiation may pay substantial dividends, the best way to save transportation dollars is to optimize mileage.

Integrating logistics into site selection for production, warehousing, and test marketing will add value to a new product through reduced cost and improved service.

Transportation Methods

Transportation issues involve more than just mileage. Transportation methods should minimize damage, ensure freshness, and provide the service the customer wants. Many product characteristics should influence transportation methods.

Certain food products experience high damage rates. Several years ago, a large fast-food chain introduced a new waffle-style ice cream cone to complement traditional sugar cones. It was assumed that breakage rates during shipment for the waffle cones would be equal to breakage for the sugar cones, but the waffle cones were soon found to be substantially more brittle that the sugar cones. The additional damage made the waffle cone an unprofitable product.

It later was discovered that the manufacturer actually had provided the fast-food company with expected damage rates. Optimistically, the fast-food company management considered their own damage experience with sugar cones to be more accurate than the manufacturer's estimates even though they had never before handled waffle cones. Given the potential for damage, the company should have selected a safer means of transportation. A true understanding of the impact of transportation requires an understanding of product handling characteristics.

Inventory Location and Customer Service Strategies

The strategy most frequently applied in the distribution of new products is to locate finished goods inventory close to each target market. Because service is critical early in a product's life cycle, inventory is pushed into the field in the belief that order cycle times can be reduced. The idea that excess inventory can provide superior service is valid, but the trade-off between total cost and service must be better understood to provide the best service at the lowest possible cost.

Pushing inventory into the field increases overall inventory levels by increasing safety stock. The extra handling required to accept inventory into market-area warehouses also adds extra cost to the system, as does the requirement for two transportation movements instead of one. Given the wide range of options available for contract transportation services, producers should consider the option of centralized inventory during product roll-out. By centralizing inventory and investing in superior transportation, a company may find its customer service to be equivalent or even superior to scenarios with distributed inventory.

A number of benefits accrue from centralizing inventory. Primarily, centralized inventory reduces the likelihood of stockouts, which often occur when inventory is positioned incorrectly. On many occasions, stockouts occur in one region while excess inventory sits idle in another. If sales are good in the East, but slow in the Southwest, decentralized inventories present major problems. Once the inventory is out in the field, redistribution is extremely costly. This problem can be reduced by centralizing inventories.

Centralizing inventory also reduces overall inventory levels, as safety stock no longer has to be maintained in multiple locations to buffer demand uncertainty. Centralized inventories may not work in all cases, but manufacturers should not blindly follow the traditional thinking that new products require distributed inventories. With currently available transportation services, good service is attainable from a centralized location despite the fact that distances to the customer are greater than with market-area warehouses. Often the additional cost of using premium-quality transportation is offset by savings in warehousing and inventory carrying costs.

Forecasting, Production Planning, and Inventory Control

Forecasting new product demand poses interesting challenges for all food manufacturers. The consensus seems to be that even with the best research and most sophisticated test marketing, it is essentially impossible to forecast demand accurately. However, considering the risks involved, the importance of forecasting is paramount during new product roll-out. If manufacturers understate demand, stockouts kill their battle for shelf space. If they overstate demand, they risk filling a warehouse with worthless inventory. Although it may be difficult to predict the future, some of the answers regarding forecasting lie in the recent past.

Forecasting accuracy can be improved by shortening the forecasting time cycle to take advantage of the most up-to-date information. Instead of forecasting for weeks or months, it is possible to forecast by the day or hour. The inventory should be closely monitored. The key to short-cycle forecasting is accurate and timely scanner data. Companies that receive and apply up-to-date sales information will have a major advantage. With scanner data becoming more current and more readily available, the opportunities to improve forecasting are growing. Manufacturers who can monitor their product from the point of sale will be able to react and adjust their production plans to quickly changing conditions. As a result, they will increase their effectiveness in managing their inventories.

Manufacturer/Supplier Relations

By sharing information with suppliers, manufacturers greatly improve their ability to introduce new products. In order to encourage sharing of point-of-sale data, manufacturers may want to provide incentives for their customers. Possible incentives include allowing customers to specify a desired stacking pattern or a unit-load height. Alternatively, customers may ask manufacturers to apply barcode labels used by their inventory tracking system. Some customers may want unit loads composed of a mixture of products. It is important to find out which services are important to the individual customers. Providing special services makes a manufacturer a customer favorite, enhancing the manufacturer's ability to establish critical relationships.

Grocery retailers and wholesalers indicate that of customers who provide scanner data to manufacturers, 61% provide the data for one of two reasons:

- The manufacturer's size of profit contribution.
- Specialized service or preferred supplier status.

Thus, the majority of customers provide such information only to their "preferred suppliers." Who are the key customers? How does one become a "preferred supplier" for these customers? Manufacturers should find ways to provide incentives that will encourage key customers to work closely with them.

These suggestions about providing differentiated customer service do not apply just to the seller; buyers also will provide special services to their best suppliers. Scanner data represent only the tip of the iceberg. In the future, the sharing of information will provide a look at customer inventory—a privilege well worth seeking. In addition, slotting allowances may be reduced, or special merchandising support may be provided for key suppliers. Partnerships formed with the intent of reducing costs throughout the logistics system require a great deal of trust. Companies able to forge such partnerships with their key customers gain a valuable competitive advantage.

The Importance of Flexibility

New products pose different management challenges from those of mature products. The sales, manufacturing, distribution, marketing, and promotional data that have accumulated for a mature product make surprises relatively unlikely. However, new product launches are guaranteed to provide surprises. Demand forecasts can be inaccurate. Production problems can crop up without warning. The balance between supply and demand can be disrupted at any time. Considering the risk involved with new products, managing their logistics requires a great deal of planning and flexibility.

Flexibility is not simply a function of reacting to surprises; it must be built into the logistics system. If one co-packer cannot handle demand, the company must be ready to bring another on-line. If sluggish demand results in large stockpiles of inventory, then production schedules may need to be altered in order to cut production; and then there is the problem of being stuck with a large stockpile of materials. Perhaps inventory will have to be repositioned closer to the customer; or maybe the inventory should be centralized to neutralize the impact of regional demand fluctuations.

Logistics flexibility must be planned for during in the product development process. It is important to understand that mistakes will be made. The critical factor is not simply the ability to avoid mistakes, but rather the flexibility to react to changing conditions before surprises grow into problems. If a company's logistics system is not designed with flexibility in mind, efforts to react to changing conditions most likely will lead to chaos.

From packaging to transportation planning, site selection to forecasting, and production planning to customer service, logistics must be involved in product design. The integration of logistics into the design process will result in superior products and smoother roll-outs.

NEW PRODUCTS AS LOGISTICS TRIGGER POINTS

Over the years, there has been a trend in the evolution of companies and their logistics function that A. T. Kearney characterizes by classifying the management characteristics of a company into four stages. Each of these stages encompasses a set of common attributes that define a manner of thinking about and managing a business. On occasion, a new product will serve as the catalyst for progression from one stage to the next.

Stages of Logistics Excellence

A basic description of each of the four stages of logistics development follows. Figure 7-2 provides a graphical representation of these stages.

• Stage I companies manage their business one day at a time. Long-term planning is overwhelmed by the need to devote resources to fighting fires.

• Stage II companies discover budgets as a means of evaluating business functions. Each functional area commits itself to performing its independent function within its budgeted cost. The focus of a stage II company is typically on cost containment managed period by period.

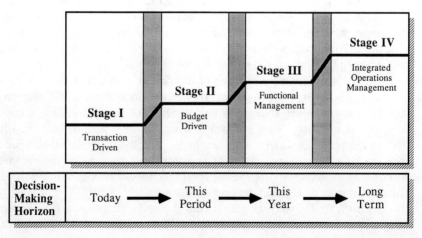

Figure 7-2. Stages of logistics evolution. Copyright 1989, A. T. Kearney, Inc. All rights reserved.

- Stage III companies come to understand critical trade-offs. Rather than simply focus on reducing costs, the stage III company balances cost and service. Within a function, efforts are coordinated to achieve a desired strategy. Functional strategies are planned on a year-by-year basis.
- Stage IV companies coordinate across their functions to manage their business in an integrated fashion. Cost and profit center management are eliminated in order to optimize overall profitability. Functional boundaries are blurred, and interdepartmental communication is improved. Functional excellence becomes subservient to the excellence of the entire business, and long-term strategies are developed and employed.

In this scheme, opportunities to progress from one stage to the next are known as "trigger points." These points must be identified and exploited in order to maximize business success. Regardless of the source of an opportunity, successful companies capitalize on the trigger points more effectively than their competition does. It has been found that companies are capable of improving just one stage at a time. Attempts to progress more rapidly create more change than the organization can absorb, usually resulting in failure to achieve the desired objectives.

New Products as Trigger Points for Change

Sometimes a new product opportunity will serve as the trigger point for positive change.

L'Eggs Pantyhose serves as a textbook example of how innovative distribution methods can change a business. By delivering directly to stores, providing merchandising labor in the store, and retaining ownership of inventory until it is sold, L'Eggs instantly became a retailer's dream supplier. This strategy completely modified L'Eggs logistics operation and changed the structure of the panty hose business.

Frito-Lay provides another example of competitive advantage attained through innovative distribution methods. Frito-Lay has a distinct quality advantage because of product freshness, which stems from its store door delivery system.

Alternatively, logistics trigger points may result from the opportunity to enter a new distribution channel. Gatorade provides an excellent example of how a change of distribution strategy may facilitate entry into new markets. Gatorade originally was sold through the traditional grocery channel, but the decision was made to redirect sales to convenience stores in order to move the product closer to the places where people exercise. Sales skyrocketed.

In the near future, new distribution systems will be developed to take advantage of the growing demand for fresh products. The difficulty of distributing short-shelf-life products on a national level traditionally has resulted in generic or regionally branded fresh products; but improved food engineering technology has made nationally branded fresh products feasible. Because fresh foods operate with significantly higher profit margins than shelf-stable and frozen foods, the manufacturer who captures this market can expect healthy returns. Its attractive margins justify high-cost, high-value-added logistics. The ability to get high-value fresh product on the shelf with consistent quality at a reasonable cost will require logistics excellence and innovation. Although efforts so far have not been overly successful, national food companies soon will use new distribution methods to take advantage of this emerging market.

The range of logistics breakthroughs that may result from new products is numerous. A new product may serve as a trigger for major adjustments to a distribution network. Alternatively, a new product may inspire the development of new information systems that change the way that inventory is managed and orders are received. Innovative packaging may inspire the development of new material handling technology.

Properly managed, new product ideas serve as a catalyst for logistics innovations that can be applied across an organization. Companies that apply what they learn during new product development to their day-to-day business will remain a step ahead of their competitors.

New Product Development as Catalyst for Excellence

As today's most progressive companies attempt to tackle stage IV issues, new product development will serve as a key indicator of their likelihood of success. By nature, new product development pulls business functions together in a coordinated effort. For this reason, integrated decision making during new product development will demonstrate the potential benefit of integrating business decisions across functional boundaries.

Companies that realize the benefits of functional integration during new product development will be increasingly likely to integrate across the functions for daily operation and strategic decision making. Integrated decision making is still a goal for the future, but tomorrow's pioneers in that area are integrating for new product development today.

CONCLUSION: STRATEGIC LOGISTICS FOR COMPETITIVE ADVANTAGE

Three factors are the keys to "strategic logistics" for new products:

• First of all, strategic logistics requires getting logistics expertise involved early in the product design process. Such early involvement will help to reduce surprises during product development, but, more important, early logistics involvement will result in superior products.

• A second key to strategic logistics is pushing logistics responsibility to a higher level in the organization. The growing importance of logistics in busi-

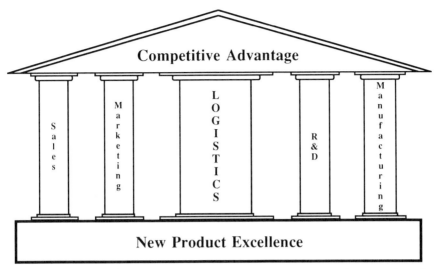

Figure 7-3. Strategic logistics is critical to achieving competitive advantage through new product excellence.

ness requires increased visibility of logistics issues at the highest company level (see Figure 7-3).

• A final key to strategic logistics is the formation of logistics partnerships with key customers. The improved relations stemming from these partnerships will reduce barriers facing new product introduction (e.g., slotting allowances). As these partnerships evolve, inventory, cycle times, and cost will shrink throughout the entire distribution system. The extra value such partners provide for one another will guarantee long-term success for both parties.

Strategic new product logistics will make a company the preferred supplier of its customers. Its superior image and position as a preferred supplier will help the company to dominate its chosen markets and distribution channels, and thus give it a long-term competitive advantage.

RECOMMENDED READING

Anonymous. 1989. How logistics fits in. *Distribution*, Apr. 1989, 28.

Anonymous. 1989. Logistics: A trendy management tool. *The New York Times*, Dec. 24, 1989, Sec. 3, 12.

Anonymous. 1989. Suppliers: Manage your customers. *Harvard Business Review*, Nov. 1989, 40.

Bowersox, Donald J., Closs, David J., and Helferich, Omar K. 1986. *Logistical Management*, 3rd edition. New York: Macmillan (an introductory logistics textbook).

Chapter 8

Optimizing Consumer Product Acceptance and Perceived Sensory Quality

Howard R. Moskowitz, Ph.D.

THE IMPORTANCE OF CONSUMER ACCEPTANCE

Much has been written on food quality, often from the point of view of objective physical and chemical sciences. Researchers in food science and cognate disciplines conceive of food as a collection of physical and chemical properties, obeying laws whose discovery lies in the purview of "objective" science. Despite their research, it remains for the consumer to decide about food quality, to judge whether or not a food is acceptable, and to decide if the product will be consumed.

This chapter deals with the assessment of those subjective characteristics known as "food quality." It shows how the researcher can measure what the consumer calls "quality" from a variety of points of view, and how the product developer can both determine the key dimensions that promote perception of "quality" and engineer a product to possess those dimensions so that it will be selected and eaten.

This chapter blends theory and practice. It takes its subject matter and approach from psychology (especially psychophysics, the science of sensory perception), from marketing research (which deals with consumer behavior), from statistics (which sets up and analyzes experiments), and from sensory evaluation (which deals with the descriptors of food attributes). The reader is encouraged to apply the techniques discussed herein to other food products beyond those discussed here. The approaches are meant to be general, and the examples are designed to illustrate and educate. The chapter presents an approach, a technology, and a philosophy of research rather than a set of cut-and-dried methods.

MEASURING ACCEPTANCE AND SENSORY CHARACTERISTICS

Free Responses versus Scales

Investigators measure acceptance by a variety of methods. In the business world, one often measures acceptance by the number of complaints about a product. If the manufacturer provides an 800 (toll-free) number for complaints, then one can monitor acceptance by the complaints that consumers call in, and by the types of complaints that they evidence. This is the anthropological approach—one does not put the panelist in an artificial situation by forcing the panelist to use a scale, but rather watches behavior and counts (or otherwise measures) natural hedonic responses. The amount eaten of a product also can be used by measure acceptance: place a set of products out in front of consumers in a naturalistic setting and measure the amount of each product consumed. This approach also assesses the overall acceptance of each sample, and allows the researcher to measure relative acceptance by weight of product consumed. Finally, as is sometimes done in the military to assess menu acceptance, one can weigh the amount of product left over after a meal. ''Plate waste'' is a powerful measure because it directly quantifies the acceptance of each of the items in a meal, under the most typical of eating situations.

Procedures such as those described above are coming into vogue as alternative methods for measuring acceptance. These traditional methods, which were among the first to be used both in human acceptance studies and in animal feeding (to show animal food preferences because animals do not use scales), are becoming increasingly popular as advanced methods for measuring acceptance. They are not restricted by the ability of panelists to understand scales, but simply look at behavior.

Paired Comparison Methods

Historically, the first well-accepted method for measuring acceptance consisted of paired comparisons. Here the panelist is required to choose between two samples, in terms of which is better. (In other psychological tests, the panelists might be asked to choose which of the two stimuli is stronger, or more intense on a specific attribute.)

The paired comparison data generate a matrix of ''wins'' versus ''losses'' that can be analyzed by various statistical means, such as Thurstone's methods (Thurstone 1927). The paired comparison analysis generates scale values. Stimuli that are preferred by a small margin (e.g., stimulus A is preferred 48% of the time, and stimulus B is preferred 52% of the time) will lie close together, whereas stimuli that are preferred by a great margin (e.g., stimulus Q is preferred 70% of the time over stimulus R) will lie far apart on the scale.

Paired comparison procedures are a favorite of marketing researchers, who usually investigate two products in a commercially oriented ''product test'' to determine which is the preferred sample. The results of the paired comparison test are used to select one of the stimuli as preferred, either for continued development or for launch into the marketplace.

Paired comparison procedures are useful in assessing relative preference for a limited set of stimuli. However, they do not provide benchmarks in terms of absolute acceptance. The discovery that 60% of the panelists prefer sample X over sample Y does not indicate whether both are acceptable, both are unacceptable, and so on. (We presume that the greater the difference is in percent preference, the larger the difference is on the underlying liking scale that the Thurstonian methods would develop from the paired comparison data. We do not know, however, the actual degree of acceptance).

Acceptance Scales

Most researchers, and by now many consumers, are familiar with the scales commonly used to measure product acceptance. Over the past decades researchers have published numerous scales to quantify how good a food tastes. These scales range from the simplistic classification of like versus dislike (or like versus dislike versus neutral) all the way to more complicated scales, having different scale points. Sometimes researchers present consumers with a scale (e.g., 1–9), with each point accompanied by a descriptor. At other times the researchers present the consumers with a scale anchored only at the top and the bottom. Table 8-1 gives verbal descriptors for some hedonic scales.

From time to time, disagreements break out about the proper (or at least most sensitive) scale to use to measure acceptance. Some researchers believe that one must always choose words or phrases to accompany the scale points, whereas others are satisfied simply to anchor the scale at the ends. (There is no clear evidence favoring either side.) The issue of the number of scale points used to measure acceptance always raises the hackles of researchers, who are polarized around this topic. Some researchers aver that the consumer can accurately rate products only on a limited number of scale points (e.g., fewer than seven),

Table 8-1.   Verbal descriptors for hedonic scales.

Scale points	Descriptors
2	Dislike, unfamiliar
3	Acceptable, dislike, not tried
3	Like a lot, dislike, do not know
4	Well-liked, indifferent, disliked, seldom if ever used
5	Like very much, like moderately, neutral, dislike moderately, dislike very much
6	Very good, good, moderate, tolerate, dislike, never tried
5	Very good, good, moderate, dislike, tolerate
5	Very good, good, moderate, tolerate, dislike
9	Like extremely, like very much, like moderately, like slightly, neither like nor dislike, dislike slightly, dislike moderately, dislike very much, dislike extremely

Source: Meiselman (1978).

whereas others opt for a larger but manageable scale with each point clearly named (e.g., the nine-point hedonic scale favored by the Quartermaster Corps in Chicago and later at the U.S. Natick Laboratories). Still others, basing their argument on the findings of psychophysics, prefer to use a wide scale anchored at both ends, or even an open-ended scale with presumed ratio properties (Engen 1964; Moskowitz 1981b). Finally, disagreement exists about whether it is useful to have a third region—neutral (neither like nor dislike)—in the scale, or whether the panelist should be forced to categorize the product as liked or disliked (and then scale the sample).

Results from Studies—Simple Stimuli

The scientific literature contains some valuable information on the scaling of likes and dislikes, with data primarily limited to simple ("model") systems (e.g., pure chemicals dissolved in a solvent). Much of the literature pertains to taste and smell stimuli, primarily because in the chemical senses hedonics (likes and dislikes) play an important role. Furthermore, one can change the concentration of a taste or an odor stimulus quite easily when the stimulus is a simple chemical or a chemical mixture.

The key results are as follows (Moskowitz 1981b):

1. When a panelist is confronted with a taste or a smell stimulus (simple chemical or flavor mixture), the hedonic response often emerges first, before the panelist describes the product as weak or strong, or defines its character; that is, people react instinctively with a "like" or "dislike" statement. In analyzing the different dimensions that people use to describe products, Yoshida (1964) reported that the hedonic dimension almost invariably emerged first.

2. Hedonics follow a different rule from that of sensory intensity if the stimulus is pleasant. Sensory intensity (viz., perceived sensory magnitude) correlates highly with physical intensity. For instance, increasing the concentration of sugar in a water solution results in judgments that the sample tastes sweeter (Moskowitz 1971). This comes as no surprise. However, if instructed to judge the degree of liking, the panelist will report that the sample first tastes better as the concentration is increased, but soon a concentration is reached at which liking peaks. Beyond that, any further increases in concentration not only fail to increase liking, which has peaked, but begin to decrease it (Moskowitz et al. 1974). The stimulus actually can taste very unpleasant at high concentration. The general form of the relation follows an inverted U-shaped curve. First noticed more than a century ago by the German psychologist Wilhelm Wundt (see Beebe-Center 1932), this inverted U curve has become the basis for the current optimization of products (where the goal is to find that combination of ingredients generating the optimum level, without overstepping the limits and plunging off the side of the acceptance curve or acceptance surface).

Applications to Actual Foods — Grading

Acceptance testing is too important in the "real world" for the testers to wait for academically acceptable, appropriate procedures to be developed. Despite the appearance of procedures in the scientific literature, backed up by the appropriate statistical arguments, methods, and algorithms, practitioners in the food industry have used one or another scaling procedure for a hundred years or more, if only to get a crude measure of whether or not a product meets standards for shipment to stores and then on to consumers.

The earliest procedures consisted simply of grading samples on a simple, easy-to-understand scale. Oftentimes the experts would do the grading. Although they did not rate acceptability in terms of consumers, the experts would assign a product a grade in one of several categories (specific to each food). Products falling into an inferior grade would be rejected, and might be "reworked" (viz., reprocessed) or even simply sold as animal feed. It should come as no surprise that each industry had its own sets of grading procedures, developed specifically for the products in that industry, and that the grading remained in the domain of professionals with extensive knowledge. Although not meant to be a consumer acceptance procedure (but rather a method for categorizing products into different classes) the grading procedure essentially served as a measure of expected consumer acceptance. Whether, in fact, the grades that experts rejected were those that a consumer might reject was unclear, however.

With increased interest of the food industry in consumer responses during World War II, researchers began to focus on consumer needs and wants. A natural outgrowth of this effort was the military's attempts to create a standardized scale for food acceptance. The 1940s witnessed the publication of a variety of monographs dealing with the measurement of food acceptance, culminating in the adoption of a standard scale, called the Hedonic Scale (Peryam and Pilgrim 1957). This scale, shown as a nine-point scale in Table 8-1, had been developed by the Quartermaster Corps in Chicago and found widespread use as a measurement tool to quantify responses to simple chemical stimuli in scientific experiments (Moskowitz 1981b), foods being tested for palatability (Moskowitz and Sidel 1971), and even surveys for military food preference (Meiselman et al. 1971).

Developing Normative Scale Data for Product Acceptance

In the increasingly competitive food industry, manufacturers attempt to provide the best-tasting foods possible, within cost and other externally imposed constraints. Acceptance scales find their greatest use here as indices of future product acceptance.

The U.S. government began the trend with the use of the nine-point hedonic scale as a measuring tool by which to accept or reject different submissions by vendors for the military food program. Sensory evaluation, first in Chicago and then at Natick, was routinely used to process the submissions, with an in-house taste panel of untrained consumers that evaluated them. Submissions were accepted that met specific criteria, which equaled or exceeded a defined score on the hedonic scale.

Similar procedures exist in company after company in the commercial sector, whose employees must make daily decisions to change ingredients, to modify processes, to accept submissions from vendors of raw materials, and so on. Each company develops its own set of norms, based upon its favorite acceptance scale. The key to this approach is that the scale used is historic, with norms attached to it. Whether it be a nine-point hedonic scale, a six-point scale, a 0–100 scale, or whatever, the scale user knows what region on the scale defines an acceptable product for the product category.

In addition to evaluating alternatives to current products (differing only in minor ways), a company can monitor the acceptance of competitors' products by an ongoing quality control audit. The acceptance scale is the critical factor here. It is consumer-driven, as it is the consumer out in the field who is the manufacturer's target audience. The consumer understands the scale and uses the scale to rate the manufacturer's product, along with the products offered by competitors. The test can be performed "blind" (i.e., without identifying the manufacturer or the brand) or "branded." Table 8-2 compares blind, branded, and "image" ratings of acceptance for instant coffees, made by a large panel of coffee consumers (Moskowitz 1985). The panelists used a 0–100 scale to assess liking, with 0 defined as "definitely not buy the product" and 100 defined as "definitely buy the product." Note the wide range of acceptance levels on this scale, and the strong effect that identifying the product and the manufacturer plays in affecting acceptance. (The same consumers evaluated both blind and branded products, to ensure comparability.)

Frequency and Acceptance Measures

We have been dealing here almost entirely with scales of liking, which have different descriptors and different numbering systems. There are other types of acceptance measures beyond such scales. These measures yield additional and different information.

The most important scalar measures beyond simple liking consist of measures of frequency of eating. Researchers recognize that a product that a person likes very much may not necessarily be a product that the person will consume very often or in great quantities. Rather, consumers may like certain foods very much but may consume them infrequently, perhaps because those foods are too

Table 8-2. Comparison of blind and branded ratings of coffees on purchase intent (0–100).

	Blind	Branded	Image (name only)	Impact of brand (branded–blind)
Maxwell House	37	59	63	22
Folgers	42	56	62	14
Taster's Choice (Regular)	39	54	57	15
Nescafé (Regular)	37	41	40	4
Maxim	29	46	47	17
Sunrise	38	35	37	−3
Yuban	40	42	44	2
Kava	27	25	34	−2
High Point	39	43	40	4
Sanka	36	49	49	13
Taster's Choice (Decaffeinated)	42	52	52	10
Nescafé (Decaffeinated)	45	43	40	−2
Brim	40	50	48	10

Source: Moskowitz (1985).

satiating physiologically (which limits the amount that one could eat), or because they may rapidly tire of those products.

Measuring frequency in the simplest format requires a question about the number of times during a fixed interval (e.g., one week, one month) that a consumer would eat a food. Although there are issues of validity (viz., can the consumer accurately gauge frequency?), the frequency question can differentiate between items that are highly liked and frequently consumed and other items that are equally liked but consumed less frequently. Table 8-3 shows some results from a study of food preferences of military men. The panelists (soldiers, filling out a food acceptance questionnaire) rated both the degree of liking and the frequency (times per month) that they would like to eat the product (Meiselman et al. 1971). The two scales are not correlated highly—products that are highly liked may be consumed more or less frequently.

Historically, the frequency scale was presaged by other attempts to get at frequency, or at least dimensions beyond simply liking. Schutz (1965) proposed the FACT scale, which presumed to integrate both frequency of consumption and liking into a single scale. The FACT scale never received the acceptance that it should have, perhaps because it was not clear that a single scale could, in fact, combine liking and frequency. The two well may be slightly correlated, but they may tap different aspects of behavior. Schutz's FACT Scale is as follows:

Table 8-3. Nine-point hedonic scale versus desired frequency of eating.

Item	Liking	Frequency/month
1 Hamburger	6.95	9.25
2 Pizza	6.82	4.64
3 Lobster Newburg	5.44	3.16
4 Ham	6.79	4.05
5 Chicken	7.26	6.40
6 Pot roast	6.79	3.85
7 French fried potatoes	7.28	10.36
8 Mashed potatoes	6.75	8.54
9 Boston baked beans	5.52	3.75
10 Rice	5.46	4.19
11 Fritters	5.25	2.06
12 Sweet Potatoes	6.90	7.99
13 Creamed corn	6.13	6.62
14 Carrots	5.40	4.51
15 Brussels sprouts	3.96	1.51
16 Broccoli	4.51	2.22
17 Peas	5.57	3.91
18 Yellow squash	3.88	1.34
19 Banana salad	5.04	2.70
20 Mixed fruit salad	5.70	4.86
21 Waldorf salad	4.08	1.86
22 Coleslaw	5.25	4.89
23 Lettuce tomato salad	6.28	1.74
24 Tossed green salad	6.56	11.14
25 Sugar cookie	5.24	4.75
26 Chocolate pudding	6.25	5.15
27 Devil's food cake	6.29	4.14
28 Cherry pie	6.26	5.50
29 Ice cream	7.32	9.60
30 Strawberry gelatin	5.64	3.46
31 White bread	7.18	16.87
32 Milk	8.03	22.00

Source: Meiselman *et al.* (1971)

Eat every opportunity
Eat very often
Frequently eat
Eat now and then
Eat if available
Don't like—Eat on occasion
Hardly every eat
Eat if no other choice
Eat if forced

A more comprehensive approach to frequency as an alternative measure of acceptance has been proposed and utilized by Balintfy and his colleagues, based upon an ''operations research'' approach. According to Balintfy et al. (1974, 1975), acceptance of a food is a function of two variables: innate acceptance of the food, and the time since the food was last eaten. Any food can increase in acceptance (up to its basic limit, unique for each food) if one does not consume the food for a very long time. In contrast, the same food can drop in acceptance by being consumed repetitively. This concept Balintfy labeled the ''Time Preference Curve,'' and he derived the curve mathematically, as shown schematically in Figure 8-1. Depending upon the frequency of serving, acceptance will vary. The concept of time preference is a valuable organizing principle because it accounts for the fact that some foods never lose their basic acceptance (e.g., bread, salad) even though they are consumed daily, whereas other foods (primarily meats, such as steak) may lose their acceptance when served too often.

Parenthetically, it is instructive to note that Balintfy developed the concept of time preference to assist in computerized menu planning, where the aim was to serve a food at the optimal frequency to maintain its baseline acceptance, rather that to overserve the food (and diminish its acceptance). Balintfy's model allows the menu planner to select the optimum serving frequencies of many foods in a menu, in order to ensure that the cumulated or sum of hedonic values of all of the items will remain as high as possible. (This maximization ensures that the maximum number of consumers will be satisfied.)

TESTING PRODUCTS IN AN APPLIED SETTING FOR CONSUMER MARKETING

How does a product developer or marketing researcher test products? Among whom does he or she test? What happens in the test? Who are the respondents—

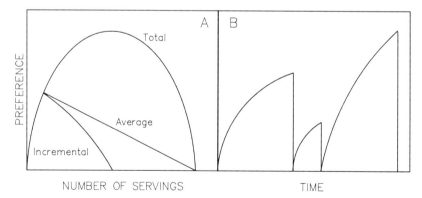

Figure 8-1. Relation between serving frequency, total preference, average preference, and incremental preference (panel A). Preference for meat loaf served on four occasions (days 1, 7, 10 and 20) during a 30-day cycle. Source: Balintfy et al., 1975.

consumers, experts, local conveniently available individuals? These questions are the "nuts and bolts" of product testing. Product development to satisfy consumer requirements can be only as good as the test that is implemented. This section provides an overview of how commercial sector research is done, the different steps, the types of panels, the types of designs, the questions, and the limits one has to impose on interpreting the data.

Basic scientists test stimuli in laboratory situations, exerting a great deal of control over the stimuli and the test conditions. This is not the case with marketing researchers and sensory analysts, who deal with real foods under pressure of time and cost, to get the right (viz. "profit-oriented") answers. In response to real-world pressures to provide direction to product developers and marketers, those charged with the task of testing products have developed protocols or test procedures appropriate to different stages (e.g., from very early stage development "at the bench," to initial/middle stage consumer testing, to final "confirmatory" market testing).

Benchtop Screening

This is a formal name given to the quite informal process of a product developer's giving prototypes to colleagues, his or her spouse, and neighbors to solicit their reactions to the sample. There is no quantification of responses; however, the product developer often gets a sense of whether development is heading in the correct direction, or whether the development track needs to be modified because the product misses the target.

Focus Group Discussions

The researcher gathers 6 to 12 consumers together for a discussion of the product, usually lasting one to two hours (Sokoloff 1988). The consumers sit around a table, and the moderator leads the discussion using a prepared "guide" (consisting of a list of topics). The panelists may have tried the product at home prior to the discussion (and then have gathered to discuss their reactions), or they may try the product at the session for the first time, and discuss their reactions during the session, in a structured interchange. Panelists interact with each other and with the moderator. Usually the guidance and feedback obtained in this fashion are "qualitative" and indicate general directions, instead of being quantitative or number-based. Panelists may fill out a questionnaire during the discussion, which usually is used to "warm up" the panelists so that they are more verbal and "attuned to the product." Rarely does the researcher tabulate the data from the questionnaire for serious analysis. The discussion may focus on the product itself, its sensory characteristics, positive and negative attributes, and so forth. Often the interviewer/moderator also will present the panelists with a concept and ask them to discuss whether or not the product delivers what the concept promises. Emerging from the discussions (there are usually several such focus groups in a project) is a report provided to the product developer. Often the product developer, sensory analyst, marketing researcher, and marketer sit behind a one-way mirror in the focus group facility, to learn first hand how the panelists react. (The audience can hear the reactions, which are simultaneously recorded, and can observe the facial and body expressions of the participants.)

Research Guidance Testing

Done within the purview of R&D, research guidance testing consists of testing one or several (or even many) products with a group of consumers, usually in the local area near the R&D facility. The consumers represent the ultimate user group. Their purpose is not to make a final statement about the product, but simply to contribute their reactions as a development aid. The research guidance tests are run early in the development process and sometimes throughout the process, so that the developer can learn how consumers react to the prototype product. Guidance tests can be run at home with the panelist picking up product at the research office, or they can be run in a supervised central location facility. The tests can be short or long, depending upon the research requirements. Overall, one thinks of the research guidance panel as "developmental," comprising a critical aspect of the early-stage research process. The information obtained in the guidance tests usually remains in the purview of the product developer or sensory analyst, and is not necessarily shared with the marketing department. Often the goals are technical—to assess how consumers react to specific formula changes or process variations. The tests can be designed to help the developer make judgments about which product to choose for later full-scale tests, or they can help the developer learn about the characteristics of the product as consumers perceive them.

Full-Scale Confirmatory Tests

These tests focus on the response of many consumers to one or two "final-stage" products. The tests are confirmatory because they are used to confirm (or disconfirm) the judgment of the product developers. Presumably, by the time the research has reached the confirmatory stage, the product being developed or modified should have passed earlier screens. The product should exhibit increased acceptance over the current product (for product improvement or new product development), or it should maintain parity acceptance (versus the current product, for a cost reduction or for an ingredient substitution problem). Confirmatory tests usually are run by the marketing research department rather than by R&D, and are implemented among a broad sample of consumers, geo-graphically dispersed, who represent different users of the available brands. The information obtained is primarily preference (versus the competition) or achievement of a satisfactory absolute score. The diagnostics, or sensory attri-butes, may probe the different aspects of the product. Diagnostics are used to explicate why the product performed the way it did, but the researcher tests so few products in the confirmatory test that the diagnostics are not used to "guide further development." Only in the case of a disaster, where a new product seriously fails to demonstrate the needed acceptance level or preference score, does the product developer seriously consider the diagnostics, and then only in limited fashion in recognition of the fact that the research tested only one or two products.

Quite often in full-scale confirmatory tests the investigator uses a concept to create expectations about a product, and then measures the degree to which the product fulfills what the concept promises. This is the "concept product test." With a large base of consumers it becomes practical to test a number of alter-native prototypes against a concept, with each individual consumer evaluating only one of the prototypes. The confirmatory test then allows the researcher to select the specific prototype that is most acceptable and also lives up to the concept.

WHAT DRIVES OVERALL QUALITY AND ACCEPTANCE

Part of the researcher's job, whether in food science, marketing research, or even basic research, is to discover what characteristics drive acceptance. We know how to measure acceptance by any of a variety of techniques discussed previously. But what exactly is it about a food that makes one food acceptable and another unacceptable?

There are a number of factors that drive acceptance and play a key role in the product development cycle:

1. The attitudinal importance of attributes is a factor (both sensory and non-sensory attributes play roles).
2. Sensory attributes themselves exert different levels of importance, depending upon the product, the panelist, and the sensory attribute level.
3. Individuals differ in what they find important—sensory segmentation exists; thus there are clearly identifiable groups of consumers in the pop-ulation evidencing different patterns of likes and dislikes.
4. Body state (satiety versus hunger) may influence acceptance.
5. The context of consumption and expectations influences acceptance.

This section deals with the first three factors in detail, providing a scientific background as well as illustrating the practical import of the findings for food product development and quality assurance.

Attitudinal Importance

In their own minds, consumers have a hierarchy of what is important to them; and it is up to the investigator to uncover this hierarchy. We are dealing here with attitudes rather than reactions to an actual product. The test methods used to reveal the hierarchy must be appropriate to attitude measurement.

The easiest method (but not necessarily the most productive or least bias-prone) consists of asking the consumer to rank various attributes in terms of importance. The attributes can be divided into "sensory-based" (e.g., sweetness, crunchiness, color) for a product (viz., a cereal) and "acceptance-, image-, and delivery-based" (e.g., good taste, good texture, good nutrition, fair price, attractive packaging, etc.). It will be seen that:

- Consumers have little or no problem understanding the task of describing which characteristics are most important versus which are least important.
- Consumers can easily rank or rate the acceptance, image, and delivery characteristics in terms of importance.
- Consumers have a much harder time rating the importance of sensory attributes than rating the importance of liking or image. How does one rate "the importance of sweetness" in a beverage? This is an ambiguous question. Does one talk about the importance of being "on target"? Without further explicating the sensory attribute, the investigator cannot really instruct the panelist to scale importance.

Another, perhaps more direct, method for measuring annoyance consists of instructing panelists to rate "annoyance" for specific product defects. Panelists are given a scale such as an anchored 0–100 scale (0 denotes not at all annoyed; 100 denotes extremely annoyed). The investigator then presents the panelist with a variety of problems, which may be sensory problems (e.g., the product tasted too bitter; the product was too dry), image problems (e.g., the product was not sufficiently nutritious), package problems (the package was too difficult to open), and so forth. For each defect, the panelist rates expected annoyance (Moskowitz and Jacobs 1986).

Annoyance scaling is easy for panelists. Annoyance is a concrete term, and presenting a panelist with concrete problems makes his or her job easier. Table 8-4 shows the results of some of these annoyance ratings for chocolate puddings. "Too much" often differs from "too little," indicating an asymmetry of attribute importance.

Table 8-4. Annoyance ratings, chocolate puddings.

Appearance

Too light	59
Too dark	38

Aroma

Aroma too weak	58
Aroma too strong	50

Flavor/taste

Chocolate flavor too weak	76
Chocolate flavor too strong	57
Overall flavor too weak	78
Overall flavor too strong	56
Not sweet enough	58
Too sweet	71
Sweetness took too long to appear	60
Sweetness appeared too fast	45
Sweetness does not last long enough	50
Sweetness lasted too long	58
Not tart/sour enough	23
Too tart/sour	74
Not bitter enough	27
Too bitter	79
Aftertaste was not strong enough	39
Aftertaste was too strong	74
Aftertaste was not bitter enough	26
Aftertaste was too bitter	84

Texture/mouthfeel

Not creamy enough	69
Too creamy	30
Too thin/watery	88
Too thick	48
Too gritty/grainy	87
Too smooth	19
Not lumpy enough	18
Too lumpy	85

Image/usage

Did not taste enough like homemade	60
Did not taste natural enough	72
Not taste fresh enough	83
Not heavy enough	54
Too heavy	54
Too high in calories	74
Not nutritious enough	68
Not healthy enough	77
Not appropriate for children	83
Not appropriate for adults	81

How Sensory Attributes Drive Liking

Sensory research on likes and dislikes, of both simple stimuli (e.g., sugar in water, odorants dissolved in a solvent) and actual foods (e.g., beverages), reveals that as sensory intensity increases, liking first increases, then peaks, and then drops, as shown in Figure 8-2. The relation appears schematically as an inverted U curve (Wundt, as cited in Beebe-Center 1932). The specific parameters of the curve (e.g., the steepness of the curve, the point at which liking reaches its optimum, whether the curve is symmetric, and so on) are considered as research projects (e.g., Moskowitz 1981b, Moskowitz et al., 1974).

On a more practical level, the organizing principle presented by the inverted U curve for liking can be applied to foods. For a specific food, assuming that the panelists have rated several variations of the product, one can plot sensory intensity on the abscissa versus liking on the ordinate (Moskowitz 1981a). If the stimuli comprise simple, one-dimensional variations, it should be possible to see fairly smooth curves (e.g., sweetened coffee, a result of adding sucrose to coffee, with overall sweetness on the abscissa versus liking on the ordinate).

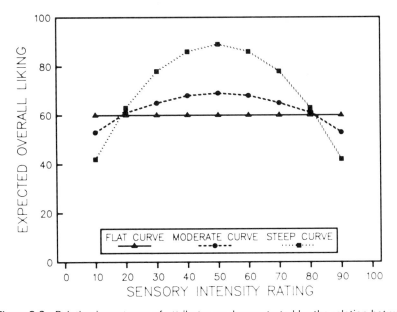

Figure 8-2. Relative importance of attributes as demonstrated by the relation between sensory intensity (abscissa) and estimated liking (ordinate). The steeper the curve is, the more important the attribute. Importance is measured both by the steepness of the curve and by the area under the curve (subtended by the curve). Flat curves denote relatively unimportant attributes because overall liking does not change dramatically with changes in attribute level.

If the stimuli comprise more complex products, such as different in-market items, then the same types of curves will emerge, but there will be scatter around the curve of best fit. Still, as Figure 8-2 shows, one can get an idea of which attributes are important drivers of liking and which are not. Flat curves correspond to unimportant attributes; although panelists can perceive differences in a product's sensory attributes, a relatively flat liking curve suggests that there is little change in expected liking with changes in sensory intensity.

Figure 8-3 shows curves for four attributes of a carbonated beverage. The area under the curve (subtended by the curve) can be used as a quantitative measure of attribute importance.

Individual Differences in Liking—Sensory Segmentation

Scientists are accustomed to searching for organizing general principles; thus psychophysicists interested in the mechanics of sensory perception search for general laws of perception and find them. The acceptance of foods, however, is pervaded by individual differences, which appear consistently from study to study, invalidating any general single rule that attempts to relate acceptance to sensory magnitude. Despite the reliability of an inverted U-shaped curve, if one

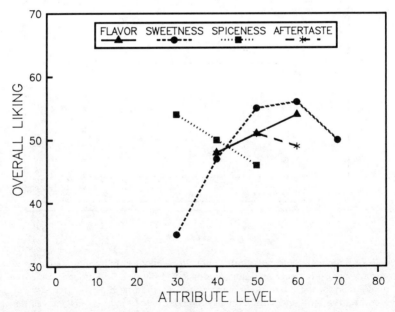

Figure 8-3. Relation between sensory attribute level and overall liking, for a carbonated beverage for different attributes.

samples responses from enough panelists, it becomes apparent that this "reliable" curve is the average of many different-shaped curves. Individuals show different patterns of liking versus sensory attributes, and different sensory levels at which liking is maximized. Pervasive individual differences appear with simple model systems, such as sugar solutions in water, as well as in more complex foods, such as coffee, juices, sauces, pies, and so on.

From a practical point of view, these pervasive individual differences in liking may represent opportunities in the marketplace for the creation and marketing of niche products. Instead of considering that the market consists of individuals with similar tastes (who are differentiated on other, non-food-related characteristics, such as income, brand bought most often, etc.), Moskowitz (1986) suggested that manufacturers take advantage of individual differences in order to segment the marketplace by consumer preferences. According to his hypothesis, the continuum of individual differences may be divided by a clustering method that looks for groups of individuals showing similar preference patterns. There should be a limited number of these clusters in the population, and the researcher should be able to uncover them and to classify individuals as belonging to a cluster by straightforward test procedures.

The following algorithm was recommended by Moskowitz (1985) and used in a large number of commercial studies:

Algorithm for sensory segmentation:

1. Develop profile of product X attribute on sensory attributes only.
2. For each panelist, relate that panelist's liking ratings to the ratings of a sensory attribute. The panelist's liking rating is the dependent variable. Use a quadratic equation:

$$\text{Liking} = A + B(\text{Sensory}) + C(\text{Sensory}^2)$$

3. Each panelist generates a unique level (for each attribute) at which the panelist's liking rating peaks. Determine the "optimal sensory level" for each panelist for each attribute. [Note that the optimal sensory levels are expressed on a common sensory scale, determined in Step 1, above.]
4. The database for segmentation comprises a matrix of columns (sensory attribute) by rows (panelist).
5. Factor-analyze the columns, to reduce redundancy. Save the factor scores corresponding to each row.
6. Cluster the rows (viz., panelists), using the factor scores.
7. The clusters correspond to panelists with similar "optimal sensory levels"—viz., sensory segments.

The goal is to cluster together individuals showing the same sensory optimal levels—viz., individuals whose peak liking occurs with similar sensory profiles.

The algorithm does not consider the actual degree of liking, but just the pattern of liking.

In its simplest form, the sensory segmentation approach divides group data as shown in Figure 8-4. Depending upon the degree of segmentation desired (and the population size), one can go more deeply into the population than this, dividing it into three or four clusters or segments. Only a sufficiently large base size of consumers is required to ensure that the segmentation is valid. With too few consumers, segmentation beyond two groups often can produce solutions or clusters having relatively few individuals in them. Confidence that this is a real segment (rather than noise or variability in the data) would be diminished with small base sizes in a cluster.

As an example of segmentation, consider the results shown in Tables 8-5a and 8-5b for a fruit-flavored carbonated beverage. Interest was focused on reactions to the beverage from a large number of consumers, tested in four different regions. The consumers evaluated 16 beverages each (from a total of 29 prototypes), and rated sensory characteristics as well as liking. Following the algorithm just described, the researcher uncovered three major segments, defined as low impact, fruit juice oriented, and carbonated soda oriented. Because the study was done in four different markets, one can ask questions about the segments themselves and about the segment distribution across countries. Table

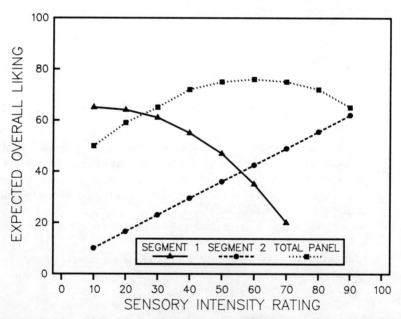

Figure 8-4. How a single curve relating overall liking to sensory attribute level can result from the combination of responses from different segments.

Table 8-5a.   Average optimal sensory levels (by total panel and by sensory segment).

Base size =	Total 827	Segment A 185	Segment B 203	Segment C 439
Aroma	65	58	65	68
Color	59	58	54	62
Carbonated	57	54	41	66
Sweet	59	60	59	59
Juicy	69	46	77	75
Fruit flavor	71	49	77	77
Tart	48	42	44	52
Thick/syrupy	56	47	56	61
Aftertaste	57	52	57	59

Segment A = Low impact (want very little of an attribute).
Segment B = Juicy, high fruit flavor (fruit juice oriented).
Segment C = Tart, carbonated (carbonated soda oriented).

Table 8-5b.   Distribution (by market) of the sensory segments.

Market	Total	Seg/A	Seg/B	Seg/C
North-Europe	100%	10%	35%	55%
South-Europe	100%	6%	10%	84%
Mid-East	100%	63%	18%	19%
Asia	100%	12%	35%	53%

8-5a shows the definition of the segments, and Table 8-5b shows the distribution of segments by region.

Implications of Sensory Segmentation for Product Improvement

Traditionally, marketers required to improve current products and/or to increase marketshare, obtain responses from an entire panel of consumers, and set their target as satisfying as many as possible. It once was thought (albeit perhaps naively and incorrectly) that failure to improve a product dramatically must be the fault of the product developer, who simply did not know what to do physically to the product to boost the liking rating for the total panel. For example, with products such as soups, coffees, and so on, marketers looked far and wide for new ingredients and processes, more often than not ending up with only marginal improvements over their current products despite the high investment costs of product development.

Sensory segmentation suggests that there may be limits to the acceptance enjoyed by any product, when there exist in the population segments showing radically different taste preferences. Whereas one segment may truly enjoy certain sensory characteristics of the product, and thus "uprate" the product, the complementary segment may find that same "product improvement" to be a strong negative, and will downrate the new prototype. The result certainly is a product improvement for the first group, but the average effect from the two segments brings down acceptance to parity scores with the current product. The acceptance range for a product usually is shorter for the total panel than for some (or all) of the segments.

Strategically, it makes sense for the marketer to develop products for the segments rather than to develop the products for the entire panel of consumers, as it is with the segments that one can hope to create an entry that will enjoy high acceptance and repeated purchases. Trying to satisfy the full population may be too difficult and even impossible. Identifying a segment and then satisfying it with a formulation will be easier, as Table 8-5b suggests, because for each segment several, and often many, prototypes enjoy high acceptance. Furthermore, by testing prototypes along with in-market products, the product developer and marketer can determine which segment already is satisfied with entries in the market, and which segment (possibly smaller in size) has not been satisfied. It is the latter segment that represents the real market opportunity for an improved product.

CONSUMER-GUIDED QUALITY IMPROVEMENT AND TOTAL QUALITY ASSURANCE

In recent years, with the increasingly competitive nature of the food industry, interest in the commercial sector has turned from maximizing profits by minimizing cost to maximizing profit by providing to the consumer products of demonstrably high quality, and maintaining this quality on a consistent basis.

Sensory analysis and product testing have exerted a great influence on quality improvement and maintenance over the years, especially with regard to the aesthetic characteristics of appearance, aroma, flavor, and texture. It has been the sensory characteristics, as registered by a panel, that have given product development and quality assurance feedback that they have achieved a target, and that they are maintaining the target.

This section presents an approach that can be used to develop and maintain product quality, given the available technology of statistics and consumer research. The past ten years have seen the growth of new approaches using sensory and consumer inputs, coupled with experimental design. The combination of sensory data and statistics has gone far beyond simple statistical analyses that tell the user whether two products do or do not differ significantly. Today, by judicious use of statistical modeling (explained below) the product developer can be guided by consumer inputs to create improved products that are of equal or lower cost compared to those of current competitors.

The technical aspects of this approach deal with the following questions:

1. *Experimental design:* What is it, and how does a product developer and sensory analyst or marketing researcher use it?
2. *The test:* How does one lay out and run the experiment?
3. *Modeling:* How can one develop models relating physical or process changes to acceptance and sensory characteristics?
4. *On-line quality estimation:* How can the R&D laboratory or production integrate physical probes (i.e., instrumental measures) into the database?
5. *Quality assurance:* How can the data be used to maintain quality, beyond simply optimizing it, on an ongoing, batch-by-batch basis?

Experimental Design

The term experimental design refers to a class of statistical methods that allow the investigator to create (for subsequent evaluation) varying combinations of ingredients or process variables, with the property that these variables are independent of each other (viz., statistically uncorrelated). A plethora of different experimental designs can be used (Cornell 1981). If one's interest is focused on the effects of many variables, such as assessing process variations where several dozen alternative settings can be made, then screening designs are appropriate (Plackett and Burman 1946). Such other designs as linear (main effects) designs, factorial designs, and central composite designs allow the investigator to assess the effect of changing ingredients while recognizing that (1) there are interactions among the ingredients, and (2) the relation between ingredient (or process) levels and the criterion response (e.g., liking) is a curve rather than a straight line.

To illustrate the approach, let us consider data from a study of a fish sausage. The experiment comprised different formulation levels of four key ingredients: fish, water, fat, and flavoring. Table 8-6 shows the experimental design (which is a central composite, half "replicate" design). The ingredients shown in Table 8-6 are relative values.

Running the Evaluation

Usually experimental designs and product evaluations are run as part of the research guidance function, as this study was. The panel comprised 50 adult women.

The panelists were recruited to participate for a four-hour session, during which time each panelist evaluated 11 of the 17 samples, in a randomized order. Panelists rated each sample on a variety of attributes, using a fixed 0–100 scale (see Table 8-7 for the attributes). Panelists find the 0–100 scale easy to use.

The attributes tap a wide variety of different characteristics, including sensory, acceptance, and often image perceptions. In addition to the product eval-

Table 8-6. Experimental design (four variables).

Prod	Fish	Water	Fat	Flavor
101	3	3	3	3
102	3	3	1	1
103	3	1	3	1
104	3	1	1	3
105	1	3	3	1
106	1	3	1	3
107	1	1	3	3
108	1	1	1	1
109	3	2	2	2
110	1	2	2	2
111	2	3	2	2
112	2	1	2	2
113	2	2	3	2
114	2	2	1	2
115	2	2	2	3
116	2	2	2	1
117	2	2	2	2

Note: Numbers for formulation = relative indices only.

uations assigned by the consumer panelists, two more sources of data were available:

1. Instrumental measures (i.e., "probes") of textural and chemical product integrity, obtained from instruments that measured the physical characteristics of the fish, at production (on a batch-by-batch basis).
2. Cost of goods, estimated by totaling the costs of the ingredients.

All of these data were available for the 17 prototypes that R&D developed.

Table 8-7. Attributes used in the study (Table 8-6).

Liking (provided by consumers):	Sensory (provided by consumers):
—Overall	—Thickness
—Appearance	—Darkness
—Aroma	—Aroma Intensity
—Flavor	—Flavor Intensity
—Aftertaste	—Spiciness
—Texture	—Fish Taste
	—Saltiness
	—Aftertaste
Instrumental (provided by R&D and production):	—Moistness
—Probe 1	—Chewiness
—Probe 2	—Juiciness
—Probe 3	—Greasiness
—Probe 4	—Firmness
—Probe 5	

Modeling the Data by Equations

Experimental designs allow the investigator to create simple yet powerful models relating independent variables (here formula and/or processing conditions) to responses. Usually these models comprise simple linear or quadratic equations, with interactions (represented by multiplicative cross terms between pairs of predictors). The equations are written as follows:

$$\text{Rating} = A + B(X) + C(X^2) + D(Y) + E(Y^2) \ldots$$

where X, Y = independent variables; rating = attribute rating or measurement by an objective instrument; A, B . . . = coefficients and additive constants estimated by a least-squares program, with the property that they create numerical predictions of the ratings that are as close as possible to the actual observed data.

Using the Equations

The equations developed for the product are mathematical expressions that summarize how the independent variables relate to and predict the dependent variable. Each dependent variable, whether sensory rating, liking, cost of goods, or objective measurement from an instrument (quality control panel rating, expert panel rating if available), can be represented by its own equation. The equations allow a variety of end uses:

1. *Prediction:* What is the likely attribute profile corresponding to a specific combination of ingredients or processing conditions? Because the equation uses values of the independent variables as inputs, the investigator can readily solve the equation for any specified values of the independent variables.

2. *Estimation of the maximum:* What combination of the independent variables generates the highest possible rating on an attribute, given the requirement that the investigator remain within the upper and lower limits of each independent variable? Statisticians have developed algorithms to search through the various combinations of independent variables to find the specific combination that maximizes the rating. The procedure used here is known as a "hill-climbing technique."

Table 8-8 shows the optimization (column labeled "None").

3. *Constrained optimization of the product:* What combination of independent variables generates the highest possible rating on an attribute, with the constraint that other variables (e.g., other attribute ratings or physical measures) must at the same time lie within bounds that the investigator sets? An example might be the optimization of overall liking, with the constraint that the cost of goods of the product must be between 0 (the lowest level) and X (where X is the highest level, and is set by the investigator). The optimum or maximally acceptable product may demand a very high cost. The cost constraint will force

Table 8-8.   Optimal formulations for fish (with specified constraints).

Constraint	None	Cost <340	Cost <280	Fishy = 50	Fishy = 60
Formulation					
Fish	2.23	2.38	2.44	1.05	2.39
Water	1.00	1.87	3.00	2.27	1.00
Fat	2.70	2.81	3.00	2.92	2.42
Flavoring	3.00	2.97	3.00	1.54	3.00
Cost	405	340	279	527	398
Liking					
Overall	56	55	54	43	56
Appearance	49	46	49	41	49
Aroma	43	46	46	48	43
Flavor	59	57	58	43	58
Aftertaste	52	51	51	40	52
Texture	52	53	51	43	53
Sensory					
Thick	55	52	50	46	57
Dark	38	42	37	34	42
Moist	62	65	70	48	65
Aroma	50	51	48	43	52
Flavor	59	59	59	54	59
Spicy	49	48	48	41	50
Fishy	59	57	55	50	60
Salty	55	54	56	46	56
Aftertaste	51	50	53	48	52
Chewy	55	51	49	41	55
Juicy	55	60	65	47	57
Greasy	44	46	53	43	45
Firm	59	50	49	43	60
Instrumental measures					
Instr1	12	12	11	10	12
Instr2	1173	1180	1179	703	1188
Instr3	190	155	110	950	226
Instr4	60	66	62	58	65
Instr5	36	26	29	15	36

the formulation to achieve a lower than maximal acceptance so that the constraint can be satisfied. The logic applied to constraints applies to other attributes, singly or simultaneously, with the attributes being physical measures, sensory measures, acceptance of the product by several groups simultaneously, and the like. Table 8-8 shows the optimization for cost and sensory constraints applied to the model. Occasionally the constraints are too severe, and no product within the range of variables tested can satisfy them.

4. *Products whose profiles match a predesignated (goal) profile:* We have been dealing up to now with maximization problems, where the goal was to find a combination of independent variables that in concert generated an attribute rating as high as possible. It is possible to change the focus entirely, by considering the following problem: What combination of independent variables generates a profile that is as close as possible (in some absolute or percentage sense) to a predesignated profile? Table 8-9 shows examples of such "profile" fitting, with a variety of goals and with different weights attached to each goal. Depending upon the weight (or the criticality of reaching the goal), the formulation will vary. The goals may be set by consumers (e.g., who evaluate competitive products) or by instruments (i.e., attached to the production line).

Sensitivity Analysis

We are used to thinking that optimization and model building provide the researcher with a "point" corresponding to the best product. In reality, the point may be the highest point on a broad plane of almost equally acceptable formulations, differing from each other only by minuscule amounts. Optimization locates only the precise top of the mountain. Even when the top is a relatively flat plane, the optimizer will land at that one "highest" point. To better understand the nature of the optimum (viz., the topography around the optimum, which shows sensitivity to changes), one can run a sensitivity analysis. Such an analysis allows the investigator to hold all the independent variables constant at a predesignated value and to vary one of the independent variables in small increments, from low to high, within the range tested. The ratings for the dependent variables corresponding to this incrementing action reveal the sensitivity curve. Table 8-10 gives an example for one variable (flavoring), using all of the attributes (including sensory, liking, cost, and instrumental measures). By consulting tables such as this, the investigator quickly understands how formula variables "drive" ratings.

The Current Status and Future of Optimization in Total Product Quality

Sensory researchers have begun to use optimization procedures and experimental designs to get a better understanding of the relation between physical variables and sensory/acceptance reactions (including perceived quality). Although not a fundamental tool of sensory analysis, experimental design has become more widely accepted as a key statistical tool. Instead of limiting themselves to describing reactions or computing statistical differences between samples on sensory or dimensions ratings, sensory analysts, along with product developers, have begun to use sensory ratings as dependent variables in the mathematical models. The models allow the researcher to predict the likely

Table 8-9.   Results from matching a goal (set by consumer ratings).

Goal from weights:	Consumer (1), equal goal weights	Consumer (2), equal goal weights	Consumer (3), unequal goal weights
Formulation			
Fish	1.70	1.00	1.00
Water	3.00	2.10	1.00
Fat	2.10	1.00	1.30
Flavoring	1.10	1.50	1.00

	Est	Goal	Est	Goal	Est	Goal	Weight
Cost	450		683		693		
Liking							
Overall	43		38		38		
Appear- ance	54		37		43		
Aroma	48		46		44		
Flavor	43		37		38		
Aftertaste	41		35		36		
Texture	42		43		39		
Sensory							
Thick	55	60	45	40	50	40	1
Dark	40	40	49	60	43	60	1
Moist	60	60	50	50	49	50	1
Aroma	47		52	50	50	50	1
Flavor	60	50	55	40	53	40	5
Spicy	49	38	41	50	43	50	5
Fishy	55	60	50		52		
Salty	58	60	45		48		
Aftertaste	58	60	49		51		
Chewy	40		48		48		
Juicy	55		42		41		
Greasy	49		39		38		
Firm	48		53		55		
Instrumental							
Instr1	12		13		13		
Instr2	637		720		595		
Instr3	1074		1169		1193		
Instr4	56		63		58		
Instr5	31		16		27		

consumer (or expert panel) reaction to known formula and process changes, and permits the product developer to ascertain, quite quickly, the formula region corresponding to the optimum product, and the region of formulation that needs the most control and monitoring.

Table 8-10. Example of sensitivity analysis.

Varying flavoring*	1	2	2.33	2.67	3
Cost	442	451	454	457	460
Liking					
Overall	43	49	51	52	54
Appearance	51	48	48	48	49
Aroma	48	47	47	47	46
Flavor	43	49	51	53	55
Aftertaste	41	45	47	49	51
Texture	44	51	52	53	54
Sensory					
Thick	57	56	56	55	55
Dark	47	49	47	45	41
Moist	60	58	59	61	63
Aroma	51	50	50	51	53
Flavor	59	61	62	62	62
Spicy	48	48	49	50	51
Fishy	56	58	58	59	59
Salty	55	54	55	56	58
Aftertaste	54	54	53	53	52
Chewy	43	48	49	49	49
Juicy	54	52	53	55	58
Greasy	45	44	44	44	44
Firm	48	56	56	55	53
Instrumental					
Instr1	13	12	13	13	13
Instr2	629	878	984	1101	1230
Instr3	1038	908	747	528	250
Instr4	62	65	65	65	64
Instr5	28	27	27	28	30

*Holding fish, water, fat constant.

DEVELOPING A CONSUMER-DRIVEN QUALITY ASSURANCE SYSTEM

The traditional use of optimization is to develop new products or to reformulate current products in order to achieve a single objective—maximal acceptance (either within cost constraints or within sensory limits). Product modeling and optimization can have, and are beginning to play, a key role in product quality assurance because they indicate where changes in formulations lead to changes in sensory acceptance.

The quality assurance program presented in this section looks at plant-to-plant variations to see which specific characteristics may be driving quality changes (as measured by consumer acceptance). It is also designed to maintain quality at the plant level by programming PCs to act as consumers when provided with data from batch runs.

Basics of the Quality Program

The program consists of these building blocks:

1. *Stimuli:* systematically varied stimuli, along with actual products pulled from various plants and various runs.
2. *Panelists and other sources of data:* consumer ratings, expert panel ratings, quality control panel ratings, and instrumental measures obtained for the same set of test products, and subsequent data (viz., from production batches) obtained from one of these data sources (e.g., instrumental measures of the batch production run).
3. *Modeling:* standard response surface modeling of the systematically varied products.
4. *Hardware:* PCs, either manually used by R&D or quality control personnel or attached to analog measuring instruments, which monitor processes during production.

Premises of the Quality Program

The basic premise of the system is that changes in the product's sensory characteristics (e.g., from plant-to-plant variations) can be correlated with acceptance to determine which specific sensory characteristics are key to driving liking. (Not all sensory characteristics that change in production batches are equally serious.)

Furthermore, given the model relating input variables (ingredients, process) to consumer acceptance and to instrumental measures of the product, the investigator can use the model to estimate the likely input values (viz., ingredient levels, process levels) corresponding to the instrumental profile of each batch. Once this input profile is estimated, the model then estimates the likely consumer reaction to the batch.

The Stimuli

As in standard multiple-product tests, the stimuli comprise a variety of products of the same type. R&D systematically varies the product by following an experimental design that allows the exploration of a wide number of alternative ingredient and processing variables. The design can cover many variables (screening design) or may consider a few variables in depth.

Test Procedures

The test procedures follow the conventional approaches discussed above. Both consumers and company employees participate. Consumers rate the products on consumer characteristics and acceptance. Company employees (whether in-house expert panelists or plant panelists, or both) can participate as well. Finally, the researcher uses instrumental probes (or the expert panel or the plant panel) that can be applied to the product, either when the product is in the process of production or afterward. These instrumental, expert panel, and plant panel ratings will serve as "goals" in optimization.

Database and Modeling

The database comprises the formulations or process settings, consumer ratings, expert panel ratings (or quality control panel ratings), and instrumental measures. These data are integrated into one interactive database, as shown previously. The models used for the database are the equations, which may be either linear, quadratic, or more complex equations (depending upon the expected relation between independent variables and dependent measures).

Using the Database to Control Quality

The database allows the researcher to control quality in two ways:

1. *Control of input (production factors):* Sensitivity analysis shows the expected consumer liking changes for known changes in each of the independent variables. The investigator can assess the expected effect on liking of many variables, and thus can discover the critical range for each independent variable (beyond which acceptance decreases).

Key variables to control at the production level are those wherein departure from a target level could point to large changes in liking. Table 8-10 shows flavoring level to be one of the key physical variables that must be monitored; in contrast, fat and water make little difference. Production needs to monitor these two variables less intensively.

2. *Monitoring batch quality:* Given data from instruments, or from a quality control panel, obtained for each batch or the day's production, one can use the data to estimate the likely input combination (ingredient, process) that would have generated this profile. Once the input profile is estimated, it becomes a straightforward matter to compute the likely consumer rating corresponding to that input. Consequently, given any profile of ratings, whether from instruments or experts, it becomes possible to accept or reject the batch because one can estimate the consumer reaction that would be assigned to the product. Table 8-9 showed such an analysis for a variety of sensory profiles of products.

AN OVERVIEW

Sensory analysis and product testing provide the product developer and the marketer with an emerging technology to achieve and control quality. Consumer inputs at the early stage of development can highlight sensory characteristics that signal quality. Consumer reactions to prototype products, whether these products are varied systematically or are simply prototypes, allow the product developer to keep on course with the development and make sure that the product is acceptable.

A consumer-guided quality system is a reality when one generates an integrated and interactive database. First, the integrated database shows how sensitive consumer acceptance is to changes in each independent (viz., input) variable. Sensitivity analysis helps quality assurance by identifying those key ingredient and processing variables that affect acceptance most strongly. Second, by relating independent variables under the control of the product to consumer ratings, expert panel ratings, and instrumental ratings, it becomes possible to estimate likely consumer reactions from ratings assigned by quality control panelists or from readings secured from instrumental probes at the production level. Thus, each batch of product can be measured instrumentally (or subjectively) and assigned an estimate of likely consumer acceptance and product sensory integrity.

Over the next decade, with refinements in product testing and the emergence of statistics into the mainstream of product development (especially modeling and optimization), particularly in view of the increasing importance of quality as a differentiating factor in foods, we may expect to see even greater advances. Total product quality is truly the next horizon for the food industry. It becomes clearer with each passing year that sensory analysis and product testing will play a major role in this emerging trend.

REFERENCES

Balintfy, J. L., Duffy, W. J., and Sinha, P. 1974. Modeling food preferences over time. *Operations Research* 22: 711–727.

Balintfy, J. L., Sinha, P., Moskowitz, H. R., and Rogozenski, J. G. 1975. The time dependence of food preferences. *Food Product Development*, November 9 (9): 32–36 and 96.

Beebe-Center, J. G. 1932. *The Psychology of Pleasantness and Unpleasantness*. New York: Van Nostrand Reinhold.

Cornell, J. A. 1981. *Experiments with Mixtures*. New York: John Wiley, Interscience.

Engen, T. 1964. Psychophysical scaling of odor intensity and quality. *Annals of the New York Academy of Sciences* 116: 504–516.

Meiselman, H. L. 1978. Scales for measuring food preference. In *Encyclopedia of Food Science*, ed. M. S. Petersen and A. H. Johnson), pp. 675–678. Westport, Conn.: Avi.

Meiselman, H. L., Van Horne, W., Hasenzahl, B., and Wehrly, T. 1971. The 1971 Fort Lewis food preference survey. U.S. Army Natick Laboratories, Technical Report TR-93-PR.

Moskowitz, H. R. 1971. The sweetness and pleasantness of sugars. *American Journal of Psychology* 84: 387–405.

Moskowitz, H. R. 1981a. Relative importance of perceptual factors to consumer acceptance: Linear versus quadratic analysis. *Journal of Food Science* 46: 244–248.

Moskowitz, H. R. 1981b. Sensory intensity versus hedonic functions: Classical psychophysical approaches. *Journal of Food Quality* 5: 109–138.

Moskowitz, H. R. 1985. *New Directions for Product Testing and Sensory Analysis of Foods.* Westport, Conn.: Food and Nutrition Press.

Moskowitz, H. R. 1986. Sensory segmentation of fragrance preferences. *Journal of the Society of Cosmetic Chemistry* 37: 233–247.

Moskowitz, H. R. and Jacobs, B. E. 1986. The relative importance of sensory attributes for food acceptance. *Acta Alimentaria* 15: 29–38.

Moskowitz, H. R., Kluter, R. A., Westerling, J., and Jacobs, H. L. 1974. Sugar sweetness and pleasantness: Evidence for different psychological laws. *Science* 184: 583–585.

Moskowitz, H. R. and Sidel, J. L. 1971. Magnitude and hedonic scales of food acceptability. *Journal of Food Science* 36: 677–680.

Peryam, D. R. and Pilgrim, F. J. 1957. Hedonic scale method of measuring food preferences. *Food Technology* 11: 9–14.

Plackett, R. L. and Burman, J. D. 1946. The design of optimum multifactorial experiments. *Biometrika* 33: 305–325.

Schutz, H. G. 1965. A food action rating scale for measuring food acceptance. *Journal of Food Science* 30: 365–374.

Sokoloff, H. 1988. Qualitative methods for language development. In *Applied Sensory Analysis of Foods*, Vol. 1, ed. H. R. Moskowitz, pp. 3–19. Boca Raton, Fla.: CRC Press.

Thurstone, L. L. 1927. A law of comparative judgment. *Psychological Review* 34: 273–286.

Yoshida, M. 1964. Studies in the psychometric classification of odor. *Japanese Psychological Research* 6: 111, 124–155.

Chapter 9

Quality Function Deployment: Market Success through Customer-Driven Products

Kurt R. Hofmeister

WHY QFD?

Bring products to market that satisfy your customers. It seems so obvious, so intuitive, so easy. "Isn't that what companies do?" proclaim newly hired college graduate trainees. The supervisor, with an understanding smile, explains: "Product development is a very complex process. Each department is specialized—market research, research and development, engineering, manufacturing, production, quality control, finance, purchasing, sales, and marketing. Coordinating these activities is incredibly difficult. At the same time, we have federal and state regulations, as well as cost controls to contend with. Product development people are too busy fixing the problems with products already in the marketplace. There is constant turnover in the work force: promotions, retirements, transfers. There are difficult trade-off decisions to make, and new manufacturing technologies. Then there is . . . ." The list goes on.

Product development clearly is an extremely complex process, but there is an effective way to approach it. Quality Function Deployment (QFD), a planning tool, is being utilized by the automotive, consumer products, electronics, computer software, service, defense, health care, and food industries to aid in the management of this process and to bring better products to market.

QFD originated in 1972 at Mitsubishi's Kobe shipyard in Japan. It was here that the first of the QFD matrices was developed. "Toyota and its suppliers then [in 1977] developed it in numerous ways" (Hauser and Clausing 1988). QFD was brought to the United States in 1983 and primarily focused on automotive applications. Since then, QFD has spread to nearly every industry.

QFD is a disciplined, yet flexible approach to product development. Its use will help an organization to:

- Gain an understanding of customer wants and needs.
- Recognize and incorporate company and regulated requirements.
- Develop product requirements to ensure that customer wants are being addressed.
- Evaluate the competition from a technical as well as a customer viewpoint.

- Establish long- and short-term priorities.
- Document the work as a knowledge base for the future.
- Formalize the communication process.
- Institutionalize continuous improvement.

The success of QFD is dependent on the use of a cross-functional interdisciplinary team working early in the product development cycle—an up-front commitment of resources and talented people. By way of example, the two companies depicted in Figure 9-1 provide products in the same industry, yet there are significant differences between them. The vertical axis in the figure represents number of product changes versus product development timing. The proactive company has fewer overall changes than the reactive company, but more significant is the timing of the changes. For the proactive company, changes occur early in the program timing, before the product design is frozen. Such changes are less expensive because they are made on paper, permitting the company to prevent problems instead of reacting to them. Conversely, the reactive company does not flush out preventable problems and will make an increasing number of changes as time passes because the problems inevitably will surface through testing and in other ways. After production start-up, new problems are found, leading to further changes. The reactive process feeds on itself, forcing a company to pull resources that should be applied to up-front programs to fix problems as they occur, so that the company becomes more reactive than ever. Worse yet, most companies reward and provide incentives for such fire-fighting behavior. After all, it is easy to see and recognize people

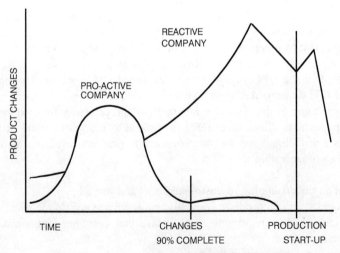

Figure 9-1. Product change comparison (ASI 1987).

who fix problems, but it is difficult for organizations to reward teamwork and people who prevent problems.

Companies must move from a reactive to a proactive position to survive in today's competitive world. Quality function deployment is an up-front planning method that, when properly nurtured and supported by corporate cultural changes, can help make the transformation happen.

THE QFD METHOD

Introduction

"The QFD method begins with a kind of conceptual map" (Hauser and Clausing 1988). This map consists of various types of matrices that are linked together. The first matrix is often referred to as the "House of Quality" because of the roof-like structure at its top; this chart is formally known as a product planning matrix. An example of a product planning matrix for a chocolate cake mix is shown in Figure 9-2.

The chart is complex-looking at first glance, as it contains a great deal of information. Fortunately, once one is familiar with a few simple conventions, it becomes second nature to read and understand the chart. The "house" can be divided into various rooms and segments. We shall now tour the various rooms, to gain an understanding of them and how they fit together.

Voice of the Customer (WHATs)

The first room of the house of quality is known as the WHATs. This is a list of customer requirements, which often is referred to as the "Voice of the Customer." These items usually are vague, general, and difficult to implement directly. Market research is one source of information for the WHATs. Some teams obtain customer wants and needs through the simple art of listening to customers and watching them use a product. Often the most powerful customer wants are never verbalized, but are observed. These wants are collected, organized, and consolidated by the QFD team. The customer for the chocolate cake mix QFD example is defined as the customer who buys and bakes the cake. Some customer wants for this example are listed in Figure 9-3.

Other Wants

There are other wants to consider besides those of the end-user consumer. Federal regulations, executive and company wants, and retailer wants all should be included. Such wants are brought into QFD and are placed in a room entitled "Important Control Items." They are kept separate from consumer wants to

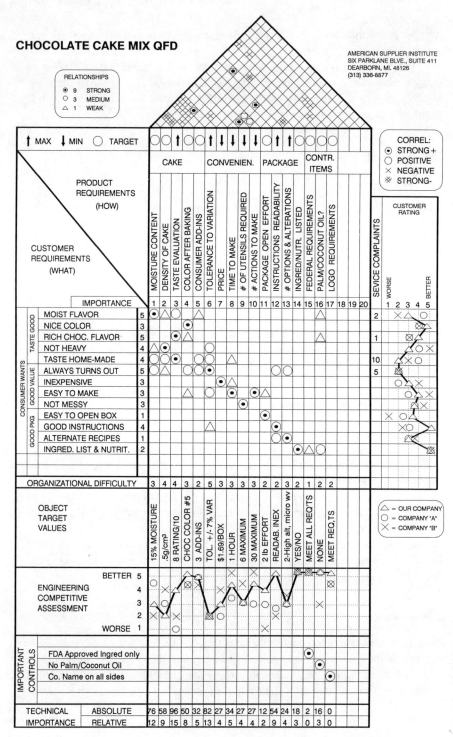

Figure 9-2. Product planning matrix for chocolate cake mix (ASI 1987).

WHAT

Moist Flavor
Rich Chocolate Flavor
Not Heavy
Inexpensive
Easy to Make
Not Messy
Easy to Open Box
Ingredients Listed

Figure 9-3. Voice of the customer (WHATs) (ASI 1987).

ensure that the consumer's voice is left intact and not diluted or confused with internal requirements.

Federal requirements and company requirements for the chocolate cake mix QFD might include: use of FDA-approved ingredients only, no palm/coconut oil, company name on all package sides. These wants usually are musts, and planners should be careful that they are not inadvertently forgotten!

Product Requirements (HOWs)

Once the list of WHATs is developed, each will require further definition. The list is refined into the next level of detail by listing one or more HOWs for each WHAT. The HOWs for the product planning matrix, known as product requirements, are measurable characteristics that describe the product in the language of the engineer. It is important to note that the HOWs represent "how to measure," not "how to accomplish." Product requirements should *not* be a list of ingredients or process parameters, as such a list would lock in and needlessly constrain the design and manufacturing people. In the chocolate cake mix QFD example, the customer want "Easy to Make" might be translated into the product requirements "Time to Make" and "Number of Actions to Make" (Figure 9-4).

Complex Interactions

Unfortunately this process is complicated by the fact that some of the HOWs affect more than one WHAT, as shown in Figure 9-5, and can even adversely affect one another. Attempts to trace the relationships of WHATs and HOWs can become quite confusing.

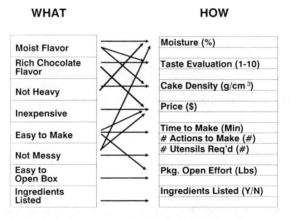

Figure 9-4. Product requirements (HOWs) (ASI 1987).

WHAT   **HOW**

Moist Flavor	Moisture (%)
Rich Chocolate Flavor	Taste Evaluation (1-10)
Not Heavy	Cake Density (g/cm³)
Inexpensive	Price ($)
Easy to Make	Time to Make (Min) # Actions to Make (#) # Utensils Req'd (#)
Not Messy	
Easy to Open Box	Pkg. Open Effort (Lbs)
Ingredients Listed	Ingredients Listed (Y/N)

Figure 9-5. Complex interactions (ASI 1987).

Relationship Matrix

One way to reduce this confusion is to turn the HOW list perpendicular to the WHATs and then define their RELATIONSHIPS in the created matrix. The RELATIONSHIPS are depicted by placing symbols at the intersections of the WHATs and HOWs that are related. The strength of the relationship can be shown as well, through the commonly used symbols illustrated in Figure 9-6. This method permits very complex interrelationships to be documented and facilitates interpretation. Figure 9-7 shows the relationships for a portion of the chocolate cake mix QFD study.

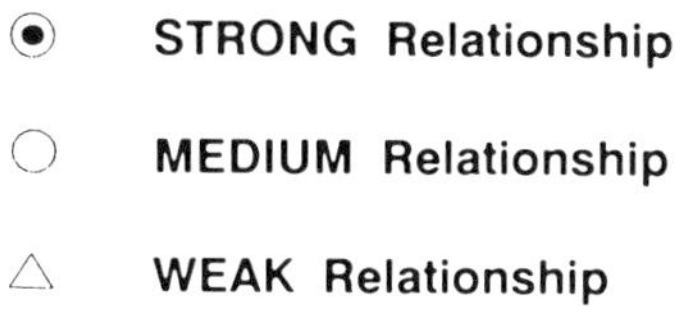

⊙   STRONG Relationship

○   MEDIUM Relationship

△   WEAK Relationship

Figure 9-6. Relationship matrix symbols.

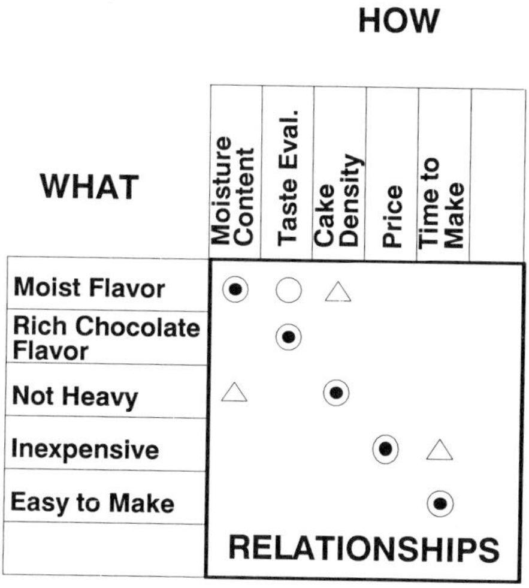

HOW

Figure 9-7. Relationship matrix (ASI 1987).

This process also permits planners to cross-check their thinking. A blank or weak row indicates that the company has no measure or product requirement in place to address the customer want. Likewise, a blank or weak column is an indicator of an inappropriate requirement or a missing customer want.

Objective Target Values (HOW MUCH)

The fourth key element of any QFD chart is the HOW MUCH section, which includes the measurements for the HOWs. These target values should represent how good it is necessary to be to satisfy the customer, and not necessarily current performance levels. The customer want of ''Moist Flavor'' was translated into a ''Moisture Content'' product requirement, and has a specified target value (HOW MUCH) of 15% moisture (Figure 9-8).

The HOW MUCHs, then, provide specific objectives that drive the subsequent product design and afford a means of objectively assessing progress, thus minimizing ''opinion-eering.''

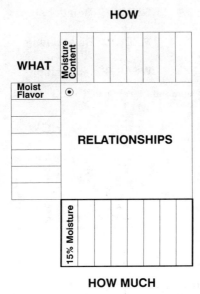

Figure 9-8. Objective target values (HOW MUCH) (ASI 1987).

Correlation Matrix (ROOF)

There are several useful extensions to the basic QFD charts, which greatly enhance their usefulness. They are used as required, according to the content and purpose of each particular project.

The correlation matrix is a triangular table, often attached to the HOWs, establishing the correlation between individual HOWs. The purpose of this roof-like structure (see Figure 9-9) is to identify areas where trade-off decisions and research and development may be required. As in the relationship matrix, symbols such as these shown in Figure 9-10 are used to describe the types of relationships.

Positive correlations are those in which one HOW supports another HOW. They are important because resource efficiencies may be gained by not duplicating efforts to attain the same result. In addition, if one takes an action that adversely affects one HOW, it will have a degrading effect on the other.

Negative correlations are those in which one HOW adversely affects the achievement of another HOW. These conflicts are extremely important, as they represent conditions in which a trade-off decision may be required.

The first step in resolving a negative correlation is to check the target values (HOW MUCH) for the affected HOWs. Are they mutually achievable objectives? If not, a trade-off decision may be required by adjusting the HOW

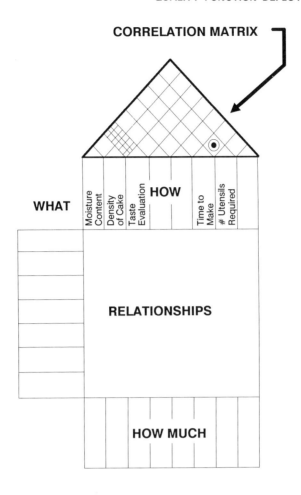

Figure 9-9. Correlation matrix (ROOF) (ASI 1987).

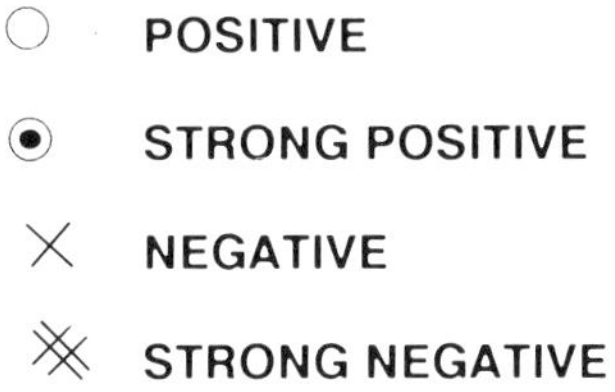

○ POSITIVE

⊙ STRONG POSITIVE

✕ NEGATIVE

✕✕ STRONG NEGATIVE

Figure 9-10. Correlation matrix symbols.

MUCHs to a point where the objectives are achievable. However, before the tradeoff decision is made, the team should seek out alternatives to eliminate the trade-off altogether. This occurs through innovation or a research and development effort that may lead to a significant competitive advantage. The QFD effort is a valuable way to spin off long-term research and development projects in order to address key customer issues.

In the chocolate cake mix QFD, negative correlations indicate that "Moisture Content" and "Density of Cake" have a direct bearing on the "Taste Evaluation." Any changes in these requirements have a potential negative effect elsewhere. If the target values (HOW MUCHs) between moisture, density, and taste are mutually exclusive, we may have to adjust these values in order to optimize customer satisfaction. In contrast, a reduction in the "Number of Utensils Required" has a positive effect on "Time to Make."

Competitive Assessment

The COMPETITIVE ASSESSMENTS are a pair of graphs that depict item for item how competitive products compare with current company products. This is done for the WHATs as well as for the HOWs. The assessments are used to:

1. Establish the proper target values (HOW MUCHs).
2. Ensure good correlation between the WHATs and the HOWs. (Do we have good product requirements in place?)

The competitive assessment for the WHATs is called the customer competitive assessment, and should utilize customer-oriented information, gained through market surveys and other means. Engineers should avoid making this judgment because their technical knowledge is biasing. It is extremely important to understand the customer's *perception* of the various competitive products. Understanding customer perception is the key to product improvement. The information is plotted graphically on the right-hand side of the QFD chart in Figure 9-11. A company's product ratings may be "tied" together with a connecting line, which improves readability.

The competitive assessment of the HOWs is called the engineering competitive assessment, and should utilize the best engineering talent to analyze competitive products. It is strongly recommended that the product engineers be directly involved in this process in order to gain the most complete understanding of each competitive product. This information likewise is plotted graphically, in an area below the HOW MUCHs in Figure 9-11.

These two competitive assessments yield very powerful information. One would expect WHAT and HOW items that are strongly related also to exhibit a relationship in the competitive assessment. The assessments should be reasonably consistent with each other.

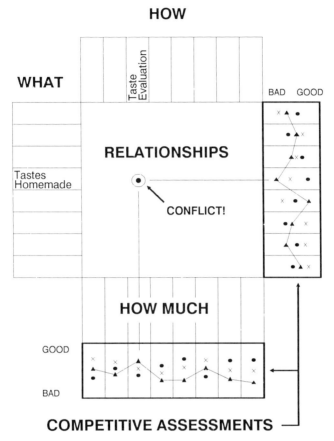

Figure 9-11. Competitive assessments (ASI 1987).

In the chocolate cake mix QFD example, the HOW of "Taste Evaluation," an internal taste-jury rating, is strongly related to the WHAT of "Tastes Home-made." The competitive assessments for these areas should be related. The "Taste Evaluation" technically rates the company's product a 4 (Good), with the competitors at 2 (Poor) and 1 (Bad). Meanwhile, the customer survey reports the exact opposite; the company's product is rated a 2 (Poor), with the competitors at 4 (Good) and 5 (Excellent). If the conflicts thus identified are not acted upon, the company may achieve superior performance to the in-house tests and product requirements, but fail to achieve expected results at the hands of the customer.

The competitive assessment also can be useful in determining the target values (HOW MUCHs) to be achieved. This is done by selecting values that not only are competitive, but reflect customer satisfaction.

Importance Ratings

Two types of importance ratings usually are brought into QFD charts, and they are effective in establishing priorities for the continuous improvement effort.

The first type of importance rating serves to establish the customer priorities for the wants (WHATs) and is referred to as the customer importance rating. It usually is derived from market research studies and can be obtained at the same time as the customer competitive assessment. This is an opportunity to understand how important the wants are to the customer—not to the engineer or the executive.

The second type of importance rating, referred to as the technical importance rating, usually is a computed value. The team establishes a weighting scheme for the various relationship symbols. A typical weighting scheme is:

9 = Strong relationship
3 = Medium relationship
1 = Weak relationship

The 9-3-1 weighting achieves a good variance between important and less important items although other weighting methods may be used. For each column (or HOW), the Customer Importance Rating is multiplied by the symbol weight, producing a value for each relationship. Summing these values vertically gives the technical importance rating.

The technical importance rating for the first column in Figure 9-12 is calculated as follows. The circle symbol weight (3) is multiplied by the customer importance rating (5), forming a relationship value of 15. The double circle symbol weight (9) is multiplied by the customer importance rating (2), forming a relationship value of 18. These two values (15 and 18) are added to form the technical importance rating, which is 33. The same process is repeated for each column.

The customer and technical importance ratings are not intended to be used literally, but rather to serve as a guide to establish product development priorities and to further cross-check the team's approach (i.e., do the numbers seem reasonable?).

Additional Rooms

QFD is a very creative process. Each team has the option of modifying the approach and placing additional information in the charts. Service complaints columns sometimes are added to help the team to judge where significant customer problems may exist. Organizational difficulty ratings may be used to measure the relative difficulty of accomplishing the HOWs. Some teams even place a correlation matrix (ROOF) on its side against the WHATs to establish con

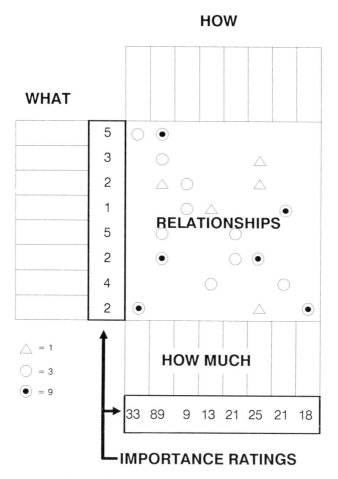

Figure 9-12. Importance ratings (ASI 1987).

flicts between the company and the customer. There is no ''right'' way to apply the technique, and the teams have creative license to apply it in a way that makes the most sense for their product.

Reviewing the Rooms

Creating a product planning matrix (''House of Quality'') is a rigorous endeavor. The chart certainly is difficult to understand at first glance, and it can be intimidating. As Figure 9-13 shows, however, QFD is made up of graphically depicted, common-sense elements that are crucial to effective product-planning

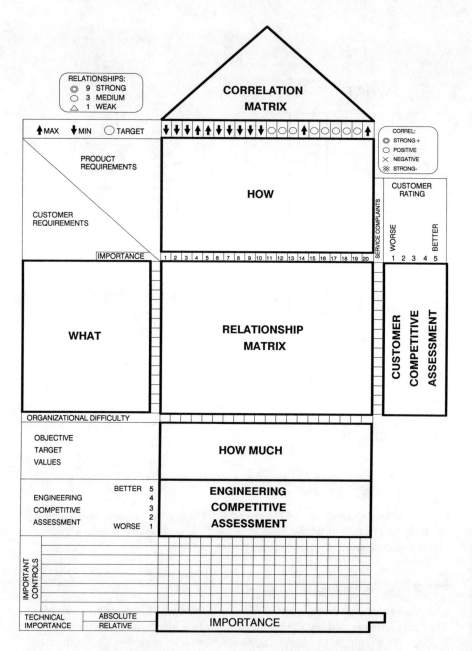

Figure 9-13. Summarized house of quality (ASI 1987).

decision making. In fact, much of the information discussed thus far already may be available in one's company; the key differences here are:

- Taking the time to pull the information together and *using* it.
- Working in cross-functional teams before there are problems (up-front planning).
- Using the "Voice of the Customer" systematically to drive the product development process.

A QFD product planning matrix is filled with valuable information. As discussed above, one can gain knowledge about:

1. Who the customers specifically are, and what they want (WHATs).
2. How government regulations and executive wants affect customer satisfaction (other wants).
3. How the company measures the achievement of the wants through product requirements (HOWs).
4. Key negative correlation decisions that must be addressed:
   - Trade-off decisions, by adjusting target values.
   - Research and development decisions to eliminate trade-offs.
   - Effective communications between affected departments.
5. Target values (HOW MUCHs) required to satisfy customers.
6. Competitive standing from a technical as well as a customer viewpoint, looking for consistency and product opportunities.
7. Establishment of long- and short-term product development strategies and priorities.
8. A retained knowledge base for new hires, transfers, and next generation product teams to build on.
9. Formalization of the communication (product development) process.

PHASES OF QFD

The product planning matrix ("House of Quality") contains the most critical information a company needs regarding its relationship to consumers and its competitive position in the marketplace; but in order to drive the voice of the customer throughout the company, a series of matrices, or phases, is utilized. The voice of the customer is systematically cascaded into the design, process (manufacturing), and production of the product and package.

Cascading from Chart to Chart

To translate the voice of the customer, a new chart is created in which the HOWs of the previous chart become the WHATs of the new chart. The HOW

MUCH values usually are carried along to the next chart to facilitate communication, ensuring that the objective values are not "lost" (see Figure 9-14).

QFD Roadmap of the Various Phases

The process of cascading from one chart to the next continues until each objective is refined to an actionable level. However, to keep the charts manageable in size, it is necessary to be selective about the items chosen for the next phase. The Pareto principle is utilized to determine the critical few items or HOWs. Only those HOWs that are *new* for the organization, *important* for customer satisfaction, or *difficult* to execute are taken to the next phase of QFD. It is not intended that every customer want be deployed into an infinite level of detail; the phases are to be utilized when appropriate. The cascading process *stops*

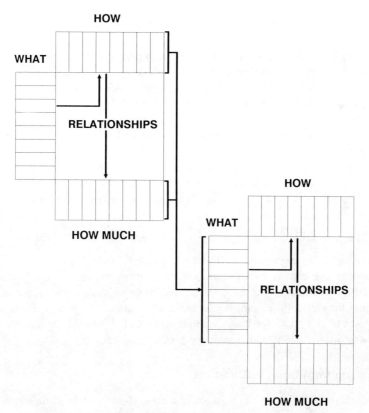

Figure 9-14. Cascading from one chart to another (ASI 1987).

when the team agrees that an item has been covered and the customer want achieved.

Figure 9-15 represents the QFD roadmap for deploying the voice of the customer. The figure shows that only critical items are "funneled" on to become the WHATs for the next phase. The roadmap defines two alternative roads that

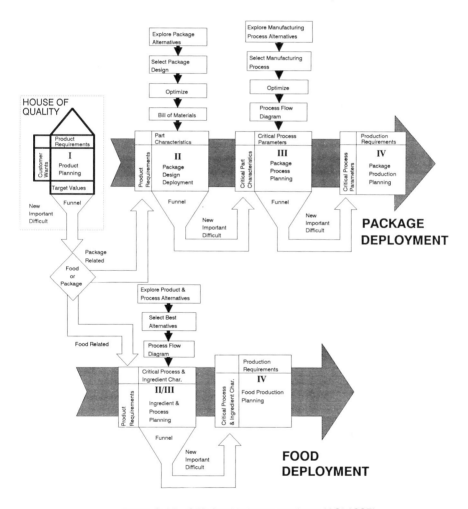

Quality Function Deployment in the Food Industry
(Roadmap for Deploying the Voice of the Customer)

Figure 9-15. QFD food industry roadmap (ASI 1987).

may be traversed. The "fork" in the road takes place at the exit from Product Planning (Phase I). The two roads are designated packaging deployment and food deployment.

Packaging Deployment

Packaging deployment refers to the activities involved in developing the wrapping, boxing, labeling, and delivery materials involved in food product development. The flow for the packaging deployment process is as follows:

- In Phase I, Product Planning, customer wants are evolved into Product Requirements. The critical *packaging-related* Product Requirements (HOWs) are carried on to the next chart (Phase II, Package Design).
- In Phase II, a package design is selected and optimized, and preliminary drawings are developed. From this information the team establishes critical part characteristics, which are now the HOWs. The critical part characteristics are carried on to the next chart (Phase III, Package Process Planning).
- In Phase III, the manufacturing process design is selected and optimized, and the process flow diagram is generated. From this information the team establishes critical process parameters. The process parameters in turn become the WHATs for Phase IV, Package Production Planning.
- Phase IV is the phase where day-to-day production controls are established, such as operator training, statistical process control requirements, preventive maintenance scheduling, mistake-proofing of equipment, and so on.

Food Deployment

Food deployment refers to the activities involved in developing the recipe, ingredients, and processing, as well as the production of foodstuffs in product development. The flow for the food deployment process is as follows:

- In Phase I, Product Planning, customer wants evolve into Product Requirements. The critical *food-related* Product Requirements (HOWs) are carried on to the next chart (Phase II/III, Ingredient and Process Planning).
- In Phase II/III, the food product and the method of processing are selected and optimized, and process flow diagrams are developed (formula card). From this information the team establishes critical process and ingredient characteristics, which are now the HOWs. The critical process and ingredient characteristics are carried on to the next chart (Phase IV, Food Production Planning).

- Phase IV is the phase where day-to-day food production controls are established, such as operator training, statistical process control requirements, preventive maintenance scheduling, mistake-proofing of the equipment, and so on.

Food Industry Examples of QFD

Figures 9-16 and 9-17 demonstrate package deployment and food deployment, respectively, using the chocolate cake mix QFD as an example.

Package Deployment Example

This example begins with the customer want of an "Easy to Open Box." The product requirement addressing that want is "Package Open Effort," which is targeted at 2.0 lbs. Package open effort becomes the WHAT for Phase II, where the package design is chosen and detailed. The team establishes that the "Glue Volume Dispensed" is a critical part characteristic, along with several other items. Glue volume dispensed and its target value are carried into Phase III, where the manufacturing process is selected and detailed. The critical process parameter of "Pump Pressure" and its target of X psi is selected to be carried into Phase IV. Pump pressure then is driven into the day-to-day production control requirements of the package manufacturing facility. Quality control (QC) checks are established, along with operator training and preventive maintenance on the pump.

Food Deployment Example

This example begins with the customer want of "Cake Not Heavy." The product requirement addressing that want is "Cake Density," which is targeted at 0.5 (g/cm^3). Cake density becomes the WHAT for Phase II/III, where the food design and the manufacturing process are chosen and detailed. The team establishes that the "Flour Amount Added" is a critical part characteristic, along with several other items. Flour amount added and its target value are carried into Phase IV, in order to specify day-to-day production control requirements of the food manufacturing facility. QC checks are established, along with preventive maintenance on the metering equipment.

The primary difference between package deployment and food deployment is that in food deployment Phases II and III are combined. This is done because, in the food industry, the end-product characteristics are defined by *both* the ingredient (design) and the manufacturing process. The two must be considered simultaneously.

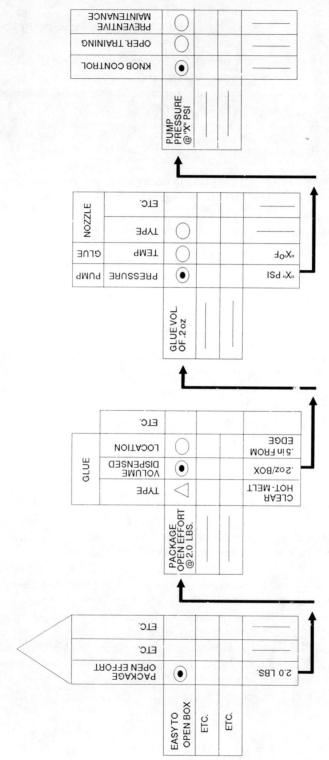

Figure 9-16. Package deployment example (ASI 1987).

Phase I
Product Planning

Phase II/III
Ingredient & Process
Planning

Phase IV
Food Production
Planning

Cake not heavy
Etc.
Etc.

Cake Density
.5g/cm 3

Cake Density of
.5g/cm3

Add Flour — Type — Enriched/bleached
Add Flour — Amount — 1 Cup
Add Baking Soda
Blend — Paddle Type — XXX
Blend — Speed — Medium
Oven — Temp — 350 Degrees F
Oven — Time — 35 Minutes

Metering Equip.
Add 1 cup flour/box

Knob Setting
Maintenance
Statistical Control

CONCLUSION

QFD, which has been utilized within the food industry since 1987, now is being viewed as an important element of a total quality management (TQM) system. Wider use of this technique and the sharing of innovations regarding the QFD process will benefit all food companies, thereby enhancing the competitiveness of U.S. food companies in the global market.

Companies that succeed in this undertaking never forget that the objective is to delight the customer, and not to make QFD charts. QFD is not the objective; rather it is the means to achieve the objective.

REFERENCES

Hauser, John R. and Clausing, Don. 1988. The House of Quality. *Harvard Business Review* 66(3): 63.

ASI. 1987. *Quality Function Deployment 3-Day Workshop Implementation Manual.* Dearborn, Mich.: American Supplier Institute (ASI).

Chapter 10

Product Excellence through Experimental Design

Anand M. Joglekar, Ph.D. and Alfred T. May

INTRODUCTION

Design of experiments is a body of knowledge, based upon statistical and other scientific disciplines, for efficient and effective planning of experiments and for making sound inferences from experimental data. In the 1920s, Sir R. A. Fisher (1925, 1935) developed the foundations for the design of experiments and successfully applied them in agricultural research. Since then, many researchers and practitioners have contributed to the growth of the subject and to its applications in industry. Particularly noteworthy are the contributions of Professor G. E. P. Box (Box, Hunter, and Hunter 1978; Box and Draper 1987) in developing optimization techniques and their applications in the chemical and allied industries, and the contributions of Dr. Genichi Taguchi (Taguchi and Wu 1980) in developing techniques for robust product design and their applications in the electronic and automotive industries.

Today, the design of experiments methodology is viewed as a quality technology for achieving product excellence at the lowest possible overall cost. It is a tool used to optimize product and process designs, to accelerate the development cycle, to reduce development costs, to improve the transition of products from research and development (R&D) to manufacturing, and to effectively troubleshoot manufacturing problems. It has been successfully but sporadically used in the United States in some chemical and food processing companies. More recently, it has been identified as a major technological reason for Japanese success in the automotive and electronic industries, in producing high-quality products at a low cost.

Over the years, inspection, statistical process control, and design of experiments have been used as three quality technologies to provide countermeasures against the causes of poor quality. The three fundamental causes of quality variation are: manufacturing variability, internal degradation of the product, and susceptibility of the product to external factors. The three principal stages of product development are: product design, process design, and manufacturing. Countermeasures against all three causes of quality variation can be

This chapter is based upon a paper published by the authors in *Cereal Foods World*, December 1987, Vol. 32, No. 12, © 1987 by the American Association of Cereal Chemists, Inc.

taken at the product design stage and, to a lesser extent, at the process design stage. During manufacturing, countermeasures can be taken only against manufacturing variability. Thus, quality becomes a primary concern of product and process designers. The role of design of experiments is to design quality into products and processes so that the need for expensive controls and inspection is reduced. For example, it is possible to design products to be robust against the effect of manufacturing variability, thereby preventing the production of poor-quality products.

In the United States, renewed emphasis on quality and increased competition are demanding the widespread use of the design of experiments methodology by engineers and scientists. In the past, such broad usage has been hampered by a lack of proper training of engineers and scientists and a lack of availability of tools to implement design of experiments. With the increased accessibility of microcomputers, this situation now can be dramatically changed.

This chapter has three major purposes: to identify the need to use design of experiments in product and process research and development (R&D) to achieve product excellence, to illustrate the design of experiments methodology, and to demonstrate how design of experiments can be made an integral part of product development by using microcomputer-based software.

DISADVANTAGES OF ONE-VARIABLE-AT-A-TIME APPROACH

The usual approach to product and process optimization is to conduct one-variable-at-a-time experiments. Although this approach is simple to plan and execute, it is not a good experimentation strategy in many situations. Its drawbacks include inability to determine the optimum, inability to determine interactions, and inefficiency of the experimentation.

Inability to Determine the Optimum

For example, consider a process where interest centers on determining the optimum time and temperature to maximize the process yield. On the basis of previous literature and experimentation, a temperature of 255°C is deemed reasonable. Following the one-variable-at-a-time approach, the temperature is held constant at 255°C, and the time is varied from 5 minutes to 25 minutes, with results that suggest that the best yield is obtained at 16.5 minutes (Figure 10-1).

To investigate the effect of temperature, the time is held constant at 16.5 minutes (because the best yield was obtained at that time), and the temperature is varied from 240°C to 280°C, with results suggesting that a temperature of 255°C gives the maximum yield (Figure 10-1). Thus the optimum time and temperature appear to be 16.5 minutes and 255°C, leading to a yield of 75 pounds per batch.

However, the above conclusion is incorrect. Figure 10-1 shows the actual

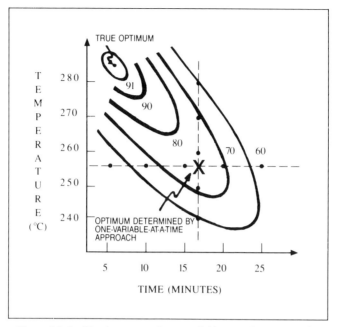

Figure 10-1. Disadvantage of one-variable-at-a-time approach.

contours of constant yield in the time–temperature domain. The optimum obtained by using the one-variable-at-a-time approach is considerably different from the real optimum. The penalty associated with not finding the true optimum is a loss of yield and a loss of productivity, as the true optimum requires only 30% of the time suggested by the one-variable-at-a-time approach.

Inability to Determine Interactions

In one-variable-at-a-time experimentation, only one variable is changed at a time, with all other variables kept constant; but the determination of interactions between two or more variables requires simultaneous changes in all variables. The inability to determine these interactions can cause very misleading conclusions.

Inefficiency

Relative efficiency is the ratio of the number of trials using the one-variable-at-a-time approach to the number of trials necessary to obtain the same amount of information using the design-of-experiments approach. The relative efficiency is known to increase with the number of variables being investigated. For two variables, the relative efficiency is 1.5; for five variables, the relative efficiency is 3.0; and efficiency continues to increase linearly with increasing numbers of variables. Because industrial experiments usually involve a large number of variables the use of designed experiments can substantially cut the costs of experimentation, by reducing the number of trials needed to achieve a given objective.

STRATEGY OF DESIGNED EXPERIMENTATION

The following is a brief review of some of the major principles of design of experiments. A detailed exposition of the subject is available (Box et al. 1978; Taguchi and Wu 1980; Joglekar 1988).

To ensure success, it is important to clearly identify the objectives to be achieved, to determine all the controllable product and process variables that could possibly help achieve those objectives, to identify noise variables against which stability may be desired, and to identify proper responses (dependent variables) to be measured. An effective experimentation strategy then can be developed.

The problem of product and process design optimization may be viewed as two-staged. In the first stage, screening, the objective is to efficiently determine the critical control variables from a collection of many potential variables. Two-level factorial and fractional factorial designs often are best suited for this purpose. In the second stage, optimization, the objective is to find the optimum settings of critical control factors so that the desired quality objectives are met. Multilevel response surface designs often are best suited for this purpose.

Factorial Designs

In two-level factorial designs, each variable is studied at only two levels, often called the (−) and (+) levels. The factorial experiment consists of conducting all possible combinations of variables and levels. For example, to study three variables (A, B, and C) at two levels each, eight combinations of variables and levels are necessary. Such an experiment is called a two-level factorial experiment. The eight combinations can be graphically represented by the corners of a cube.

From such a factorial experiment, the effects of each of the variables and all possible interactions can be determined. Thus, the effects of variables A, B, and C; the two-factor interactions AB, AC, and BC; and the three-factor interaction ABC all can be obtained. However, it is clear that as the number of variables increases, the number of trials for a factorial experiment increases geometrically, creating the need for fractional factorial designs.

Fractional Factorial Designs

Fractional factorial designs consist of appropriately chosen small fractions of the full factorial designs. They permit the study of a large number of variables in an economical number of trials (e.g., up to 7 variables in 8 trials or up to 15 variables in 16 trials). However, some of the effects then cannot be determined unambiguously.

For example, a fractional factorial design allows the study of three factors in only four trials. This constitutes a half fraction of the full factorial. From the four trials, the effects of variables A, B, and C can be estimated. However, the two-factor interactions cannot be independently estimated. For example, the BC interaction cannot be separately estimation from the effect of variable A ($A = BC$). Similarly, the effect of B is confused with the AC interaction, and the effect of C is confused with the AB interaction. The objective in designing fractional factorial experiments is to manage this confusion in such a way that effects expected to be important are not confused with each other.

Response Surface Designs

Once the critical variables are determined, response surface experiments are conducted to determine the optimum levels of variables. Near the optimum, the effect of each variable can be curvilinear (i.e., a peak in the response surface is expected). Hence, response surface designs have at least three levels of each variable. For more information, a full discussion of response surface designs should be consulted (Box and Draper 1987).

COMPUTER AIDED DESIGN OF EXPERIMENTS

Microcomputer-based software for the design of experiments is aimed at making the discipline of the design of experiments more readily available to scientists and engineers (Joglekar 1988). The authors have developed a software package called CADE (Joglekar and May 1987). The purpose of CADE is to provide a comprehensive design of experiments capability, in a user-friendly manner, to scientists and engineers to promote good experiment design and analysis practices. It allows scientists and engineers to concentrate on the technical aspects of the problem without being encumbered by the statistical details. The Discovery software is for the design and analysis of factorial and fractional factorial experiments; the Optimization software is for the design and analysis of response surface experiments. The Discovery and Optimization software packages were used in the cake formulation optimization study that follows.

SCREENING EXPERIMENTS TO IDENTIFY CRITICAL CAKE FORMULATION FACTORS

To illustrate the benefits of using the design of experiments methodology to achieve high quality in a food product and to demonstrate how it can be made an integral part of the product development process, an example is presented based on data obtained from a paper by Leo Kissell (1967). The sequential design of experiments approach consists of a fractional factorial design (16 trials) to identify the most important variables, followed by a response surface design (additional 9 trials) to optimize product quality. The design and analysis of the fractional factorial experiment are discussed in this section, with the design and analysis of the response surface experiment discussed in the next section on optimization of cake formulation.

Design of the Screening Experiment

Initially, CADE was used to design a fractional factorial experiment to evaluate six variables in 16 trials. The six variables were defined in terms of the following ratios:

Water ratio = A = weight of water/weight of remainder = $a/(b + c + d + e + f + g)$

Sugar ratio = B = weight of sugar/weight of remainder = $b/(c + d + e + f + g)$

Leavening ratio = C = weight of leavening/weight of remainder = $c/(d + e + f + g)$

Albumen ratio = D = weight of egg albumen/weight of remainder = $d/(e + f + g)$

Flour ratio = E = weight of flour/weight of remainder = $e/(f + g)$

Milk ratio = F = weight of nonfat dry milk (NFDM)/weight of remainder = f/g

where a, b, c, d, e, f, and g are the weights of water, sugar, leavening, egg albumen, flour, milk solids, and shortening, respectively. Ratios were chosen to ensure that the variables in the design would be independent of each other (Hackler, Kriegel and Hader 1956).

Two levels for each of the six ratios were used. These levels were: water ratio—0.386, 0.444; sugar ratio—0.709, 0.837; leavening ratio—0.032, 0.052; albumen ratio—0.03, 0.05; flour ratio—2.078, 2.538; and milk ratio—0.22, 0.38. Given the levels of the variables and the three responses to be measured, CADE automatically generates the log sheet shown in Figure 10-2, which identifies the 16 combinations of the six variables that constitute the designed fractional factorial experiment. Note also that none of the 16 trails is replicated. For 16 or more trials, replication may not be necessary, and a graphical method of determining significance can be used. The run order can be automatically randomized for executing the experiment. Randomization helps protect the experimenter against reaching erroneous conclusions due to extraneous sources of variability.

Data Collection

In the cake experiment, three responses were evaluated: cake volume, contour score, and internal score (Kissell 1967). The cake volume in cubic centimeters was measured by seed displacement. The contour score was evaluated on a 1–10 scale, with 1 being greatly sunken and 10 being highly peaked. The internal score was the sum of three properties: cell size, cell wall thickness, and uniformity of cell distribution, each of which was evaluated on a 0–4 scale. A summary of the data for the 16-run fractional factorial experiment also is shown in Figure 10-2.

Determination of Effects

The analysis begins with a summary of effects, which helps identify the critical variables and their effects on the response. The summary of effects for volume is given in Table 10-1. These effects are listed in rank order (largest to smallest), with the critical variables at the top. The variable effect is interpreted as the

		LOG SHEET				
Experiment Name: CAKE SCREENING EXPERIMENT		Int'l Qual-Tech, Ltd.				
Run Order	1	2	3	4	5	6
WATER	0.386	0.444	0.386	0.444	0.386	0.444
SUGAR	0.709	0.709	0.837	0.837	0.709	0.709
LEAVENING	0.032	0.032	0.032	0.032	0.052	0.052
ALBUMEN	0.030	0.030	0.030	0.030	0.030	0.030
FLOUR	2.078	2.538	2.538	2.078	2.538	2.078
DRY MILK	0.220	0.220	0.380	0.380	0.380	0.380
VOLUME	609	585	606	566	589	600
CONTOUR	7.3	7.8	6.8	8.5	3.0	4.5
INTERNAL	9.0	8.8	7.5	9.5	4.3	6.0
Run Order	7	8	9	10	11	12
WATER	0.386	0.444	0.386	0.444	0.386	0.444
SUGAR	0.837	0.837	0.709	0.709	0.837	0.837
LEAVENING	0.052	0.052	0.032	0.032	0.032	0.032
ALBUMEN	0.030	0.030	0.050	0.050	0.050	0.050
FLOUR	2.078	2.538	2.078	2.538	2.538	2.078
DRY MILK	0.220	0.220	0.380	0.380	0.220	0.220
VOLUME	526	567	609	584	585	554
CONTOUR	1.5	3.5	7.0	7.5	6.0	8.0
INTERNAL	3.0	5.5	9.0	8.3	8.8	9.0
Run Order	13	14	15	16		
WATER	0.386	0.444	0.386	0.444		
SUGAR	0.709	0.709	0.837	0.837		
LEAVENING	0.052	0.052	0.052	0.052		
ALBUMEN	0.050	0.050	0.050	0.050		
FLOUR	2.538	2.078	2.078	2.538		
DRY MILK	0.220	0.220	0.380	0.380		
VOLUME	578	586	505	548		
CONTOUR	3.0	4.5	1.5	3.0		
INTERNAL	5.0	6.8	3.0	5.3		

Figure 10-2. Designed screening experiment.

Table 10-1.   Summary of effects: screening experiment (volume).

Variables and interactions	Rank	Effect
B—Sugar	15	−35.3750
AC = BE	14	27.8750
C—Leavening	13	−24.8750
AE = BC = DF	12	−16.3750
D—Albumen	11	−12.3750
E—Flour	10	10.8750
BD = CF	9	−5.8750
AB = CE	8	5.3750
BF = CD	7	−3.8750
A—Water	6	−2.1250
F = NFDM	5	2.1250
ABD = CDE = ACF = BEF	4	1.8750
ACD = ABF = CEF = BDE	3	−1.1250
AD = EF	2	0.8750
AF = DE	1	−0.6250
Overall mean		574.8125

average change in the response as the variable is changed from its low level to its high level. For example, the largest effect (−35.375) on volume is due to sugar; this means that as sugar is increased from a low ratio of 0.709 to a high ratio of 0.837, the volume on the average decreases by 35.375 units. Similarly, leavening, albumen, and flour have relatively large effects.

In addition to the variable effects, there are some large interaction effects. Note that as a consequence of using a fractional factorial design to reduce the number of experimental trials, two-factor interactions are confounded with each other. For example, in Table 10-1, $AC = BE$ means that the observed effect can be attributed either to the interaction between water (A) and leavening (C) or to the interaction between sugar (B) and flour (E). This confusion between interactions can be resolved by methods discussed below under "Understanding Interactions."

Identification of Critical Factors

The second step in the analysis is the half-normal plot. This technique, which was described by Cuthbert Daniel (1959), is particularly effective in identifying statistically significant factors when there are at least 16 trials, and when there is no replication, as is the case in this experiment. If the observed effects and interactions are due solely to experimental error and are distributed normally they will fall along a straight line extending from the origin. Any effects appreciably to the right of this line can be considered to be statistically significant.

The half-normal plot for volume is shown in Figure 10-3. This plot shows that the variables sugar (B), leavening (C), albumen (D), and flour (E) have statistically significant effects. Furthermore, the confounded sets of interactions, $AC = BE$ and $AE = BC = DF$, also have statistically significant effects.

Understanding Interactions

The next step is to construct two-way tables to help demonstrate the nature of the significant interactions. For any designated two-factor interaction, a two-way table can be constructed to organize the observed results according to the levels of the two designated variables. Inspection of this table will help the user understand the nature of the interaction being evaluated. As an example, Table 10-2 shows the two-way table for the interaction between leavening and water. The table shows the four volumes obtained with each of the four combinations of leavening and water. At the 0.386 water ratio, increasing the leavening ratio decreased the volume by 52.75 cc, whereas at the 0.444 water ratio, increasing

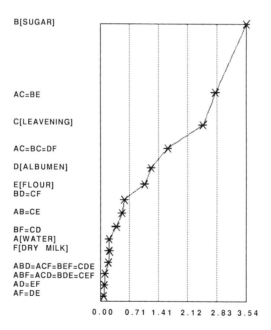

Magnitude of Effect (X 0.1)

Figure 10-3. Half-normal plot: screening experiment.

Table 10-2. Two-way table: leavening × water interaction.

.032(−)	LEAVENING	.052(+)	
			.386 (−)
609.00		589.00	
606.00		526.00	
609.00		578.00	
585.00		505.00	
602.25		549.50	
			WATER
585.00		600.00	
566.00		567.00	
584.00		586.00	
554.00		548.00	
572.25		575.25	
			.444 (+)

the leavening ratio increased volume by 3.0 cc. Thus, the effect of the leavening ratio depends on the water ratio, and the two variables are said to interact.

Owing to the fact that only a quarter fraction of the full factorial experiment was run, two-factor interactions were confounded (i.e., confused with each other). Three methods for identifying the active interaction among a set of confounded interactions are available (Joglekar 1988), and any one or a combination of them can be used. First, if the interaction in question involves one or two variables that are shown to be statistically significant, the interaction is likely to be significant. Second, if the results of the two-way table coincide with theoretical knowledge and prior experience, then a corresponding two-factor interaction is likely to exist. Third, additional trails can be planned that will help distinguish between two or more confounded interactions.

Two sets of confounded interactions were identified as being significant from the half-normal plot. One was $AC = BE$, and the other was $AE = BC = DF$. In the case of the confounded interaction $AE = BC = DF$, because variables B and C both were statistically significant, BC was selected as the most likely interaction. In the case of the confounded interaction $AC = BE$, an additional experimental trial was planned by CADE to help resolve the interaction. For this trial, water = 0.444, sugar = 0.837, leavening = 0.052, albumen = 0.050, flour = 2.078, and milk solids = 0.380. This trial corresponded to trial number 48 in Kissell's (1967) paper and had a volume of 535. The predicted values for this trial using first the AC interaction and then the BE interaction were 537.8

and 509.9, respectively. Because the prediction obtained using the AC interaction agrees very closely with the actual value of 535, the AC interaction was selected.

Model Building

After evaluation of the effects and the interactions, the model-building phase can begin. Statistically significant variables and interactions identified from the half-normal plot for volume were selected for the model. The variables of sugar, water, leavening, albumen, and flour, and the water $\times$ leavening and sugar $\times$ leavening interactions were selected for the model. Based on this selection, CADE then developed the following prediction equation (i.e., model):

$$V = 574.813 - 1.063(X1) - 17.688(X2) - 12.438(X3) - 8.188(X4)$$
$$+ 5.438(X5) + 13.98(X1X3) - 8.188(X2X3)$$

where:

V = Predicted value for volume
$X1$ = (Water ratio $-$ 0.415)/0.029
$X2$ = (Sugar ratio $-$ 0.773)/0.064
$X3$ = (Leavening ratio $-$ 0.042)/0.010
$X4$ = (Albumen ratio $-$ 0.040)/0.010
$X5$ = (Flour ratio $-$ 2.308)/0.23

Using this model, CADE then can predict the volume for any selected combination of variables. As an example for trial number 1 (i.e., run order 1 in Figure 10-2) the predicted value is 612.5 as compared to an observed value of 609.

Analysis of Variance

When a model has been selected, an analysis of variance is conducted to assess how well the model represents the data. Three key measures are used to evaluate the goodness of the model. One measure is % confidence, which measures the degree of confidence that the selected model cannot be attributed to experimental error. As a general rule, this value should be at least 95%; for the example, it is 99.98%. A second measure is % variation accounted for by the model, which is the percentage of the variation in the observed data that is explained by the model. As a general rule, this value should be at least 80%; for the example, it is 97.3%. A third measure is the coefficient of variation, which is the ratio of the standard error of the estimate to the mean value expressed as a percentage. This value should be small: for the example, it is 1.2%. The conclusion here is that the selected model adequately represents the data for volume.

Diagnostic Checking of Model

The model can be further checked by the analysis of residuals. For each trial, the residual (i.e., actual − predicted) and a standardized residual (i.e., residual/ standard error of estimate) are computed. If the value of the standardized residual exceeds 3, the data should be checked for errors. The residuals also can be plotted against run order, the predicted value, an experimental variable, or a user-defined variable. The purpose of these plots is to provide a diagnostic check of the assumptions underlying the analysis. As an example, a plot of the residuals versus predicted Y (volume) is given in Figure 10-4. The residuals appear to be randomly distributed about zero. If the plot showed a deterministic pattern or if the dispersion of the residuals changed with the predicted volume, then some of the assumptions underlying the analysis would be in question. For example, if the dispersion of the residuals increased as the volume increased, this would indicate that the assumption of uniform variance was not valid. Consequently, a log transformation of the data should be considered so that this assumption might be satisfied.

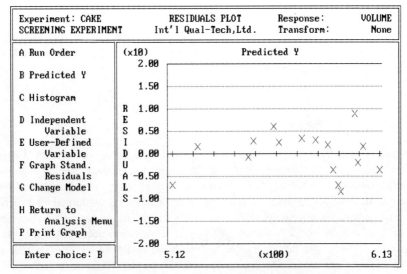

Figure 10-4. Residuals plot: screening experiment.

Identifying the Direction for Quality Improvement

The model thus developed can be displayed in graphical form by using cube plots. The cube plots for volume are given in Figure 10-5 and show that an increase in the sugar ratio decreases volume; however, the magnitude of the effect depends on the leavening ratio used. Furthermore, the effect of the water ratio also depends on the leavening ratio used; that is, increasing the water ratio decreases the volume at the low-leavening ratio but increases it at the high leavening ratio. Also, increasing the albumen ratio decreases volume, whereas from the effects table it is clear that increasing the flour ratio increases volume. Thus, the highest volumes are obtained with the low sugar, low water, low leavening, low albumen, and high flour ratios.

Summary of the Screening Experiment

The contour scores and internal scores were analyzed by using the same procedures as described for volume. The significant effects for volume, contour, and internal scores are summarized in Table 10-3, which shows that water had significant effects on volume (as a result of the water × leavening interaction), contour, and internal scores. Leavening also had significant effects on all three responses. Sugar had a significant effect on volume and was involved in an interaction with leavening. Albumen and flour also had significant effects on volume but not on the other two responses. From these results, the decision

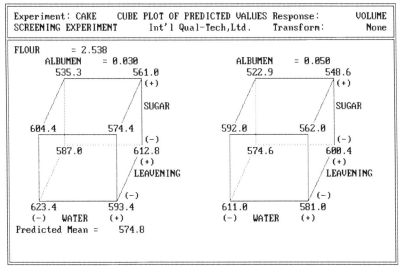

Figure 10-5. Cube plot: screening experiment.

Table 10-3. Summary of significant effects: screening experiment.

Variable	Low	High	Volume in cc	Contour 1–10 scale	Internal 0–12 scale
Water ratio	0.386	0.444		+1.4	+1.2
Sugar ratio	0.709	0.837	−35.4		
Leavening ratio	0.032	0.052	−24.9	−4.3	−3.9
Albumen ratio	0.030	0.050	−12.4		
Flour ratio	2.078	2.538	+10.9		
Dry milk ratio	0.220	0.380			
Water × leavening			+27.9		
Sugar × leavening			−16.4		

was made to optimize cake performance using water, sugar, leavening, and albumen as the variables for the response surface experiment.

OPTIMIZATION OF CAKE FORMULATION

Once the critical factors are identified, optimization experiments are conducted to determine the optimum levels of the critical factors (e.g., water, sugar, leavening, and albumen).

Design of Optimization Experiment

A central composite experiment was designed using CADE, and the designed experiment is shown in Table 10-4. The 25 trials for the central composite design involve five levels for each variable. Trials 1 through 16 are the factorial portion of the design, trials 17 through 24 are the star points, and trial 25 is the center point. The star and center points were added to the factorial design to provide an estimation of curvature. For an explanation of star and center points, see Box et al. (1987).

Model Building

The data for the response surface analysis also are given in Table 10-4. The first step is to fit a full response surface model, which includes all linear, interaction, and quadratic terms, to the data. For the cake optimization experiment, this full response surface model is the following:

$$V = b0 + b1(x1) + b2(x2) + b3(x3) + b4(x4) + b11(x1)^2$$
$$+ b22(x2)^2 + b33(x3)^2 + b44(x4)^2 + b12(x1x2) + b13(x1x3)$$
$$+ b14(x1x4) + b23(x2x3) + b24(x2x4) + b34(x3x4)$$

Table 10-4. Designed response surface experiment.

Trial Number	Run Order	Independent Variables				Responses		
		Water	Sugar	Leavening	Albumen	Volume	Contour	Internal
1	22	38.6000	70.900	3.200	3.000	609.0	7.3	9.0
2	14	44.4000	70.900	3.200	3.000	585.0	7.8	8.8
3	23	38.6000	83.700	3.200	3.000	606.0	6.8	7.5
4	10	44.4000	83.700	3.200	3.000	566.0	8.5	9.5
5	4	38.6000	70.900	5.200	3.000	589.0	3.0	4.3
6	7	44.4000	70.900	5.200	3.000	600.0	4.5	6.0
7	1	38.6000	83.700	5.200	3.000	526.0	1.5	3.0
8	5	44.4000	83.700	5.200	3.000	567.0	3.5	5.5
9	13	38.6000	70.900	3.200	5.000	609.0	7.0	9.0
10	16	44.4000	70.900	3.200	5.000	584.0	7.5	8.3
11	21	38.6000	83.700	3.200	5.000	585.0	6.0	8.8
12	2	44.4000	83.700	3.200	5.000	554.0	8.0	9.0
13	19	38.6000	70.900	5.200	5.000	578.0	3.0	5.0
14	3	44.4000	70.900	5.200	5.000	586.0	4.5	6.8
15	8	38.6000	83.700	5.200	5.000	505.0	1.5	3.0
16	11	44.4000	83.700	5.200	5.000	548.0	3.0	5.3
17	24	35.7000	77.300	4.200	4.000	557.0	2.0	5.3
18	9	47.3000	77.300	4.200	4.000	584.0	7.5	9.5
19	15	41.5000	64.500	4.200	4.000	634.0	7.3	8.8
20	12	41.5000	90.100	4.200	4.000	550.0	3.0	5.8
21	18	41.5000	77.300	2.200	4.000	534.0	7.5	9.8
22	6	41.5000	77.300	6.200	4.000	518.0	1.5	3.0
23	25	41.5000	77.300	4.200	2.000	622.0	6.0	7.3
24	20	41.5000	77.300	4.200	6.000	602.0	4.8	6.8
25	17	41.5000	77.300	4.200	4.000	605.0	6.0	7.8

where:

V = Estimated volume

$x_i = (X_i - \text{CP})/I$

X_i = The actual value of the variable

CP = The center point value of the variable

I = The high value for the factorial portion $-$ CP

bi = The coefficients estimated by least squares

$b0$ = The estimated value at the center point

The analysis of variance for volume, corresponding to this model, was computed, and the model was found to be adequate.

The estimates of the model coefficients for volume were computed, and the model was diagnostically checked by using the analysis of residuals. The contour scores and internal scores also were analyzed by using the same procedures as described for volume. The results for the analysis of variance and estimates

Table 10-5. Summary of results: response surface experiment.

	Volume in cc	Contour 1–10 scale	Internal 0–12 scale
Results of the Analysis of Variance:			
Model confidence %	99.96	99.93	99.98
Variation accounted for by the model%	95.13	93.76	96.4
Coefficient of variation %	1.9	15.2	8.2
Estimates of Model Coefficient:			
BO	605.0	6.0	7.8
A Water ratio	1.5	0.92	0.75
B Sugar ratio	−18.8	−0.60	−0.48
C Leavening ratio	−9.6	−1.93	−1.86
D Albumen ratio	−5.8	−0.20	0.02
A^2	−8.7	−.27	−0.14
B^2	−3.3	−0.17	−0.16
C^2	−19.8	−0.33	−0.39
D^2	1.7	−0.11	−0.22
AB	2.7	0.20	0.28
AC	13.9	0.11	0.44
AD	0.4	−0.01	−0.15
BC	−8.2	−0.32	−0.31
BD	−2.9	−0.08	−0.02
CD	−1.9	0.09	0.06

Underscore indicates that confidence level $\geq 95\%$.

of the model coefficients are given in Table 10-5. The results of the analysis of variance indicate that the response surface models for all three responses are statistically significant and account for most of the variation in the data. Table 10-5 also shows those model coefficients with confidence levels equal to or exceeding 95%.

Response Surface Plots

As the response surface models were statistically significant and accounted for most of the variability in the data, these models were used to generate response surface plots that show how key variables affect volume, contour, and internal score. Only two variables can be shown on any one response surface plot; therefore, it is essential to pick the variables so that the maximum amount of information is conveyed. Because water and leavening had strong interaction and quadratic effects, they were selected for the horizontal and vertical axes, respectively. Cross sections (i.e., slices through the multidimensional response surface) were taken at the low, mid, and high levels of albumen and sugar. For illustration, the response surface plot for volume at the midlevels of albumen (4.0) and sugar (77.3) is shown in Figure 10-6. A value of 0 means volume =

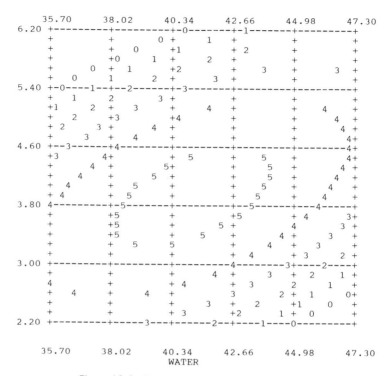

Figure 10-6. Response surface plot.

500; a value of 1 means volume = 520. An increment of 1 in value implies an increment of 20 in cake volume. The response surface plot for volume shows a hill-shaped surface with a clearly defined optimum.

Multi-response Optimization

The response surface plots having been completed for all three responses, overlay plots were generated to identify the regions in the experimental space where high-quality cake performance, as defined by Kissell, would be met. Kissell's criteria were: volume greater than 560, contour scores between 6 and 8, and internal score greater than 7.0. An X on an overlay plot indicates that all these acceptance criteria would be met. In addition to meeting these criteria, it would be ideal if the selected formulation also were tolerant to changes in ingredient levels, thereby reducing the need for extremely tight controls during manufacturing. Several overlay plots were generated by using different levels for sugar and albumen. The plot showing the greatest tolerance (i.e., having the largest region of X's) to variation in water and leavening is shown in Figure

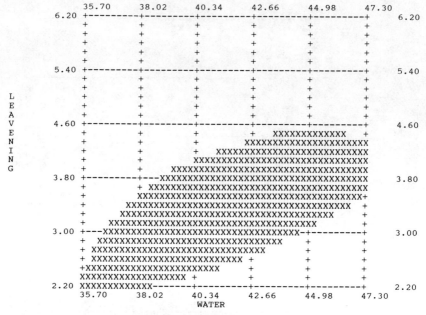

Figure 10-7. Overlay plot.

10-7. For this plot, sugar = 64.5 and albumen = 2.0. On the basis of this overlay plot, targets and tolerances were calculated as follows:

Water: target ratio 0.41 ± 0.025 (±6%) tolerance
Leavening: target ratio 0.034 ± 0.004 (±12%) tolerance

Because sugar and albumen are at their lowest levels, this is a relatively low-cost formulation as well.

A second overlay was obtained to evaluate tolerance to variation in albumen and sugar when water and leavening were at the target values. The selected formula was found to be tolerant to deviations in sugar and albumen.

Summary of Optimization Experiment

Thus, using the sequential approach and only 26 trials, a low-cost, tolerant, high-quality cake formulation was identified. For this formulation and the flour studied, the water ratio is 0.41, the leavening ratio is 0.034, the sugar ratio is 0.645, the albumen ratio is 0.02, the flour ratio is 2.538, and the dry milk ratio is 0.22. The predicted values for volume, contour, and internal scores are 624, 6.9, and 8.1, respectively.

CONCLUDING REMARKS

The example presented in this chapter deals with the application of the design of experiments methodology to the development of an optimum food product formulation. The design of experiments approach has broad applicability throughout the entire food industry, and some of these applications are briefly described below.

Other Applications

The design of experiments approach can be used by fundamental researchers to rapidly generate empirical knowledge to aid in the development of theoretical models. It can be used by market researchers to provide a clear direction for product development. In the hands of product developers, it is a major tool to develop robust products (e.g., products that meet the desired quality and cost objectives while simultaneously being tolerant to variations in raw materials, production processes, and consumer preparation factors). Process design engineers can apply these techniques to optimize production processes in order to reduce variability and enhance quality, reduce manufacturing costs, increase throughput, and reduce the need for extensive controls. It is a useful tool to reduce the cost of testing, such as sensory, analytical, and consumer tests, and to design improved measuring instruments. Production personnel can use this approach to troubleshoot manufacturing problems and to improve production plants in an evolutionary manner.

Economic Statistical Process Control

Once the product and process designs are completed, the goal during manufacturing is to monitor and control the manufacturing process and to continuously improve the process by reducing manufacturing variability. The principles of the design of experiments coupled with the economics and statistics of process control, form a methodology for achieving the above objectives. The authors (Joglekar and May 1989) have developed a software package, called ESPC (Economic Statistical Process Control), to easily implement the methodology in practice.

ESPC uses nested, crossed, and mixed designs to develop process capability studies. The advantage of these designs is that they allow total process variability to be decomposed into the different causes of variability, thereby identifying the key sources of variability. The concept of economic loss function (Taguchi and Wu 1980; Joglekar 1988; Joglekar and May 1989) then is used to quantify the economic loss due to process variability. Once the critical causes of variability and their economic impact are known, process improvement decisions (e.g., capital investment decisions) can be made on a sound economic basis. The notions of economic loss then are combined with the statistics of process control to design economically optimum process control charts aimed at monitoring and controlling the production process. ESPC thus constitutes a powerful methodology for achieving the most economic implementation of statistical process control in practice.

REFERENCES

Box, G. E. P. and Draper, N. R. 1987. *Empirical Model-Building and Response Surfaces*. New York: John Wiley & Sons, Inc.

Box, G. E. P., Hunter, W. G., and Hunter, J. S. 1978. *Statistics of Experimenters*. New York: John Wiley & Sons, Inc.

Daniel C. 1959. Use of half-normal plots in interpreting factorial two level experiments. *Technometrics* 1: 311–341.

Fisher, R. A. 1925. *Statistical Methods for Research Workers*, 1st edition. Oliver and Boyd.

Fisher, R. A. 1935. *The Design of Experiments*. Oliver and Boyd.

Hackler, W. C., Kriegel, W. W., and Hader, R. J. 1956. Effect of raw-material ratios on absorption of whiteware compositions. *Journal of the American Ceramic Society* 39: 20–25.

Joglekar, A. M. 1988. Computer-Aided Design of Experiments and Taguchi Techniques Course. 2820 Fountain Lane North, Minneapolis, Minn. 55447.

Joglekar, A. M. and May, A. T. 1987. CADE—Discovery and Optimization Software. Int'l Qual-Tech, Ltd., 2820 Fountain Lane North, Minneapolis, Minn. 55447.

Joglekar, A. M. and May, A. T. 1989. ESPC—Economic Statistical Process Control Software. Int'l Qual-Tech, Ltd., 2820 Fountain Lane North, Minneapolis, Minn. 55447.

Kissell L. T. 1967. Optimization of white layer formulation by a multiple-factor experimental design. *Cereal Chem.* 44: 253–268.

Taguchi, G. and Wu, Y. 1980. Introduction to off-line quality control. Central Japan Quality Control Association.

Chapter 11

Nutrition Promotion: The Role of Product Development and Marketing

Patricia D. Godfrey

The increasing emphasis on health and nutrition in the late twentieth century presents the food manufacturer with a tremendous opportunity to market healthy food products. The major purpose of this chapter is to increase the nutrition awareness of persons working in product development and marketing. An understanding of basic nutrition principles, dietary guidelines, and nutrition regulations will make the task of developing healthy foods easier.

NUTRITION SCIENCE

Nutrition is a young science, the majority of the nutrients recognized as essential to humans having been discovered during the last 70 years. It also is a complex science, whose issues have not all been resolved.

Nutrition History

The early nutrition science of the 1700s consisted of a quantitative approach, the measurement of energy. In the early 1800s, protein, fat, carbohydrate, and vitamins were defined. Minerals also were discovered, but only in the late nineteenth century were they found to be a dietary necessity. As the science developed, key discoveries were made: Chevreul found fat (triglycerides) to be composed of fatty acids and glycerol; protein was found to be essential; amino acids were identified, from the early 1800s until 1938, when the last essential amino acid was discovered. A new concept in the early 1900s was that of protein quality. In the early 1950s the relationship between fat and heart disease was proposed, and extensive fat research was begun. Years ago fats were regarded just as a source of energy; but then in the early 1900s fat-soluble vitamins were discovered, and linoleic acid was determined to be essential.

The acquisition of nutrition knowledge thus has been a slow and gradual process. Table 11-1 briefly summarizes the history of important nutrition discoveries.

The first stage in nutrition science was the identification of the 40 dietary essentials. This research led to the elimination of the diseases of undernutrition

Table 11-1.   Nutrition history.

Nutrient Discovery	Date
Energy (calories)—quantitative approach	Lavoisier 1783
Calorimetry—to determine calories	Liebig 1824
Classification of proximate nutrients as albuminous, olea-ginous, and saccharine (later called protein, fat, and carbohydrate)	Prout 1824
Protein foods (nitrogen-containing foods are essential to life)	Magendie 1816
Metabolic conversion of carbohydrate to fat	Boussingault 1845
Different proteins are not of equal value	1850s
Protein quality concept—BV (biological value)	Thomas 1909
Identification of eight essential amino acids	1810–1935
Chemical composition of triglycerides	1828
Fat-soluble vitamins	1913–1915
Linoleic is essential fatty acid	Burr and Burr 1929
Identification of glucose in the blood	1844
Identification of liver glycogen	1856
Definition of vitamins (it took two decades for people to understand that a lack of a food substance causes disease)	Funk 1912
Scurvy cured by lemon juice	Lind 1753
Beriberi associated with brown rice	Eijkmann 1896
Pellagra disease seen in maize diet	Hopkins 1906–1912
Vitamin C discovered	1917
Vitamins D and E discovered	1922
Vitamin B discovered	1926
Vitamin B_{12} discovered	1947

Source: *Nutrition Reviews Present Knowledge in Nutrition*, 5th edition (Olson et al. 1984).

(pellagra, scurvy, and rickets). Then the research emphasis shifted to diseases of overnutrition (such as obesity, cardiovascular disease, diabetes, etc.). These diseases are related to the overconsumption of foods high in fat, cholesterol, and calories. Current nutrition research is especially concerned with the diet and disease relationship.

Not everyone has believed in the diet–disease concept. As recently as 1979 there were differences of opinion on this issue. Congress and the United States Department of Agriculture (USDA) supported the idea that diet may prevent disease, but the National Institute of Health (NIH) did not consider the research to be strong enough to warrant any major conclusions. By 1979 there was a general consensus that diet was linked with certain diseases: salt with hypertension, sugar with dental caries, alcohol with liver disease. Obesity generally was regarded as bad for one's health, but there was no general agreement on the role of fat and cholesterol. In fact, scientists were questioning whether dietary modification would prevent heart disease. As George Mann commented:

"Since 1950 nutrition organizations and scientists have promoted low fat, low cholesterol, polyunsaturated diets, yet the cholesterolemia is unchanged. A generation of research on the diet–heart question has ended in disarray" (Olson 1980). In the 1970s the diet generally recommended was a low fat, low cholesterol diet with a polyunsaturated : saturated ratio of 1. Then, in the mid-1980s, the National Cholesterol Education Program was instrumental in changing the thinking about diet and health. It was decided at that time that diet was implicated as a risk factor for developing cardiovascular disease; and the dietary recommendation was a low fat, low cholesterol diet to decrease the blood cholesterol levels. It is now believed that there is a relationship between diet and disease, and that high blood cholesterol levels do increase the risk of developing heart disease.

Nutrition Requirements

First, researchers identified the necessary nutrients and their physiological effects; then the nutrient requirements were determined. [For further information, the reader may consult the excellent general nutrition reference book *Nutrition Reviews' Present Knowledge in Nutrition* (Olson et al. 1984).] This work led to the establishment of the Recommended Dietary Allowances (RDAs) in 1943 by the Food and Nutrition Board of the National Academy of Science.

The RDAs, which meet the needs of the majority of healthy persons in the United States, are reevaluated about every five years. The most recent release of the RDAs is the 10th edition, September 1989 (see Table 11-2). Because of a relative paucity of information on biotin, pantothenic acid, and trace minerals, these nutrients are not listed in the main RDA table but are provided in Table 11-3, which presents safe and adequate daily dietary intakes of selected vitamins and minerals.

RDAs are used for planning diets, to compare individual dietary intakes, and to estimate the nutrient adequacy of a diet. Another use of the RDAs was to establish the U.S. Recommended Daily Allowances (U.S. RDAs), which are guidelines for nutrition labeling.

The U.S. RDAs is the term that appears on food labels. These recommendations were developed in 1973 when nutrition labeling was initiated. The U.S. RDAs were based on the seventh (1968) edition of the RDAs and the 1968–1970 FDA Special Dietary Hearings. Usually the U.S. RDAs represent the highest RDA for the different population groups. The U.S. RDAs have not been changed since their origination in 1973. However, the entire label currently is being reevaluated by Congress and FDA, and the U.S. RDAs will be changed in the future. The percentages of U.S. RDAs for protein, vitamins, and minerals are listed on the lower portion of the nutrition panel on food packages.

The U.S. RDAs have four groupings, as shown in Table 11-4: adults and

Table 11-2. Food and Nutrition Board, National Academy of Sciences — National Research Council recommended dietary allowances,[a] revised 1989.

Designed for the maintenance of good nutrition of practically all healthy people in the United States

Category	Age (years) or Condition	Weight[b] (kg)	Weight[b] (lb)	Height[b] (cm)	Height[b] (in)	Protein (g)	Fat-Soluble Vitamins Vitamin A (µg RE)[c]	Vitamin D (µg)[d]	Vitamin E (mg α-TE)[e]	Vitamin K (µg)
Infants	0.0–0.5	6	13	60	24	13	375	7.5	3	5
	0.5–1.0	9	20	71	28	14	375	10	4	10
Children	1–3	13	29	90	35	16	400	10	6	15
	4–6	20	44	112	44	24	500	10	7	20
	7–10	28	62	132	52	28	700	10	7	30
Males	11–14	45	99	157	62	45	1,000	10	10	45
	15–18	66	145	176	69	59	1,000	10	10	65
	19–24	72	160	177	70	58	1,000	10	10	70
	25–50	79	174	176	70	63	1,000	5	10	80
	51+	77	170	173	68	63	1,000	5	10	80
Females	11–14	46	101	157	62	46	800	10	8	45
	15–18	55	120	163	64	44	800	10	8	55
	19–24	58	128	164	65	46	800	10	8	60
	25–50	63	138	163	64	50	800	5	8	65
	51+	65	143	160	63	50	800	5	8	65
Pregnant						60	800	10	10	65
Lactating	1st 6 months					65	1,300	10	12	65
	2nd 6 months					62	1,200	10	11	65

Category	Age (years) or Condition	Water-Soluble Vitamins							Minerals						
		Vitamin C (mg)	Thiamin (mg)	Riboflavin (mg)	Niacin (mg NE)[f]	Vitamin B$_6$ (mg)	Folate (μg)	Vitamin B$_{12}$ (μg)	Calcium (mg)	Phosphorus (mg)	Magnesium (mg)	Iron (mg)	Zinc (mg)	Iodine (μg)	Selenium (μg)
Infants	0.0–0.5	30	0.3	0.4	5	0.3	25	0.3	400	300	40	6	5	40	10
	0.5–1.0	35	0.4	0.5	6	0.6	35	0.5	600	500	60	10	5	50	15
Children	1–3	40	0.7	0.8	9	1.0	50	0.7	800	800	80	10	10	70	20
	4–6	45	0.9	1.1	12	1.1	75	1.0	800	800	120	10	10	90	20
	7–10	45	1.0	1.2	13	1.4	100	1.4	800	800	170	10	10	120	30
Males	11–14	50	1.3	1.5	17	1.7	150	2.0	1,200	1,200	270	12	15	150	40
	15–18	60	1.5	1.8	20	2.0	200	2.0	1,200	1,200	400	12	15	150	50
	19–24	60	1.5	1.7	19	2.0	200	2.0	1,200	1,200	350	10	15	150	70
	25–50	60	1.5	1.7	19	2.0	200	2.0	800	800	350	10	15	150	70
	51+	60	1.2	1.4	15	2.0	200	2.0	800	800	350	10	15	150	70
Females	11–14	50	1.1	1.3	15	1.4	150	2.0	1,200	1,200	280	15	12	150	45
	15–18	60	1.1	1.3	15	1.5	180	2.0	1,200	1,200	300	15	12	150	50
	19–24	60	1.1	1.3	15	1.6	180	2.0	1,200	1,200	280	15	12	150	55
	25–50	60	1.1	1.3	15	1.6	180	2.0	800	800	280	15	12	150	55
	51+	60	1.0	1.2	13	1.6	180	2.0	800	800	280	10	12	150	55
Pregnant		70	1.5	1.6	17	2.2	400	2.2	1,200	1,200	320	30	15	175	65
Lactating	1st 6 months	95	1.6	1.8	20	2.1	280	2.6	1,200	1,200	355	15	19	200	75
	2nd 6 months	90	1.6	1.7	20	2.1	260	2.6	1,200	1,200	340	15	16	200	75

[a]The allowances, expressed as average daily intakes over time, are intended to provide for individual variations among most normal persons as they live in the United States under usual environmental stresses. Diets should be based on a variety of common foods in order to provide other nutrients for which human requirements have been less well documented.

[b]Weights and heights of Reference Adults are actual medians for the U.S. population of the designated age, as reported by NHANES II. The median weights and heights of those under 19 years of age were taken from Hamill et al. (1979). The use of these figures does not imply that the height-to-weight ratios are ideal.

[c]Retinol equivalents. 1 retinol equivalent = 1 μg retinol or 6 μg β-carotene.

[d]As cholecalciferol. 10 μg cholecalciferol = 400 IU of vitamin D.

[e]α-Tocopherol equivalents. 1 mg d-α tocopherol = 1 α-TE.

[f]1 NE (niacin equivalent) is equal to 1 mg of niacin or 60 mg of dietary tryptophan.

Source: (National Research Council, 1989) Reprinted with permission.

235

Table 11-3. Estimated safe and adequate daily dietary intakes of selected vitamins and minerals.[a]

Category	Age (years)	Vitamins	
		Biotin (μg)	Pantothenic Acid (mg)
Infants	0–0.5	10	2
	0.5–1	15	3
Children and	1–3	20	3
adolescents	4–6	25	3–4
	7–10	30	4–5
	11+	30–100	4–7
Adults		30–100	4–7

Category	Age (years)	Trace Elements[b]				
		Copper (mg)	Manganese (mg)	Fluoride (mg)	Chromium (μg)	Molybdenum (μg)
Infants	0–0.5	0.4–0.6	0.3–0.6	0.1–0.5	10–40	15–30
	0.5–1	0.6–0.7	0.6–1.0	0.2–1.0	20–60	20–40
Children and	1–3	0.7–1.0	1.0–1.5	0.5–1.5	20–80	23–50
adolescents	4–6	1.0–1.5	1.5–2.0	1.0–2.5	30–120	30–75
	7–10	1.0–2.0	2.0–3.0	1.5–2.5	50–200	50–150
	11+	1.5–2.5	2.0–5.0	1.5–2.5	50–200	75–250
Adults		1.5–3.0	2.0–5.0	1.5–4.0	50–200	75–250

[a]Because there is less information on which to base allowances, these figures are not given in the main table of RDA and are provided here in the form of ranges of recommended intakes.
[b]Since the toxic levels for many trace elements may be only several times usual intakes, the upper levels for the trace elements given in this table should not be habitually exceeded.
Source: (National Research Council, 1989) Reprinted with permission.

children over 4 years; infants; children under 4 years; and lactating or pregnant women. Most product labels are based on the adult U.S. RDAs. Infant formulas and baby food use the infant and children U.S. RDAs. These U.S. RDAs and RDAs are useful guidelines for product development.

NUTRITION LEGISLATION

Food Fortification

History

The fortification of foods began in the early 1900s as a result of the discovery of the vitamin deficiency diseases pellagra, scurvy, rickets, goiter, and beriberi. Nutrition scientists discovered that an inadequate intake of vitamins and minerals contributed to these diseases. Food fortification was a public health measure to prevent nutritional deficiencies.

Table 11-4.   U.S. recommended daily allowances (U.S. RDAs).

	Adults and children over 4 years	Infants birth to 1 year	Children under 4 years	Lactating or pregnant women
Protein (low quality) g	65	28	65	65
(high quality) g	45	20	45	45
Vitamin A, IU	5,000	1,500	2,500	8,000
Vitamin C, mg	60	35	40	60
Thiamine, mg	1.5	0.5	0.7	1.7
Riboflavin, mg	1.7	0.6	0.8	2.0
Niacin, mg	20	8	9	20
Calcium, mg	1,000	600	800	1,300
Iron, mg	18	15	10	18
Vitamin D, IU	400	400	400	400
Vitamin E, IU	30	5	10	30
Vitamin B_6, mg	2.0	0.4	0.7	2.5
Folic acid, mg	0.4	0.1	0.2	0.8
Vitamin B_{12}, mcg	6	2	3	8
Phosphorus, mg	1,000	600	800	1,300
Iodine, mcg	150	45	70	150
Magnesium, mg	400	70	200	450
Zinc, mg	15	5	8	15
Copper, mg	2	0.6	1	2
Biotin, mg	0.3	0.05	0.15	0.3
Pantothenic acid, mcg	10	3	5	10

g = grams
mg = milligrams
IU = International Units
mcg = micrograms
Source: Code of Federal Regulations, Title 21 (Sections 101.9 and 105.3).

Table salt and milk were the first foods fortified; prior to 1936 only milk and salt were approved for fortification. Iodine was added to salt to prevent goiter, milk was fortified with vitamin D, which prevents rickets in infants.

A 1930s food consumption study found that U.S. diets were deficient in thiamine, riboflavin, niacin, and iron. In 1938 the American Medical Association (AMA) favored adding vitamins to staple foods but opposed indiscriminate food fortification.

Two milestones in food fortification were the development of food standards and the RDAs. The Federal Food, Drug and Cosmetic Act in 1938 established food standards, which ensured the nutrient integrity of foods and served as the basis for the fortification of foods. The standards allow or require nutrient addition. The FDA has enrichment standards for thiamine, riboflavin, niacin, vitamin A, vitamin D, iodine, and calcium in some foods (Table 11-5). A man-

Table 11-5. Food enrichment standards.

Food	Thiamine (B₁) mg/lb	Riboflavin (B₂) mg/lb	Niacin mg/lb	Iron mg/lb	Calcium mg/lb	Vitamin A IU	Vitamin D USP/lb	Iodine Part in 10,000
Flour	2.9	1.8	24	20	960*			
Bread, rolls, and buns	1.8	1.1	15	12.5	600*			
Farina	2–2.5	1.2–1.5	16–20	13 (not less than)	500* (not less than)		250* (not less than)	
Macaroni, noodles	4–5	1.7–2.2	27–34	13–16.5	500–625*		250–1,000*	
Rice	2–4	1.2–2.4	16–32	13–26	500–1,000*		250–1,000*	
Cornmeal, corn grits	2–3	1.2–1.8	16–24	13–26	500–750*		250–1,000*	
Cornmeal, self-rising	2–3	1.2–1.8	16–24	13–26	Not more than 1,750		250–1,000	
Milk						2,000 IU/quart	400 IU/quart	
Margarine						15,000 IU per lb		
Salt								0.5–1.0 part in 10,000

*That ingredient is optional.
Source: Code of Federal Regulations 21 Parts 100 to 169.

ufacturer is required to follow these enrichment standards when enriching a *standardized* food.

In 1943 the National Academy of Sciences Committee on Food and Nutrition developed the first table of Recommended Dietary Allowances (RDAs). This committee established minimum and maximum levels of thiamine, riboflavin, niacin, and iron enrichment for bread and flour. In 1942, FDA established a standard of identity for enriched flour. See Table 11-6 for additional historic information on food fortification.

Food fortification policies were developed early on. The Food and Nutrition Board of the National Research Council and AMA's Council on Food and Nutrition in 1961, 1968, and 1973 issued statements for food fortification criteria. The criteria are as follows:

1. The intake of the nutrient has to be below the desirable level in the diets of a significant number of people.
2. The food the nutrient is added to must be likely to be consumed by the needed population and must make a significant contribution to that population's diet.
3. An imbalance will not be created by the nutrient addition.
4. The nutrient addition is stable under normal storage and use.
5. The nutrient is physiologically available.
6. There has to be reasonable assurance that excessive intake will not occur and cause toxicity (Shank and Wilkening 1986).

Table 11-6.   History of food fortification.

Year	Historical Event
1930	AMA (American Medical Association) endorses addition of Vitamin D to milk, iodine to table salt.
1940	FNB (Food Nutrition Board) endorses addition of nutrients to flour.
1942	FDA (Food and Drug Association) issues enriched flour standard.
1943	War Food Administration requires enrichment of all bread and rolls. FNB recommends enrichment of cornmeal and grits. FDA issues statement of policy governing addition of nutrients to food.
1944	FDA expands enrichment program to include cornmeal, grits.
1946	FDA issues standards of enrichment for pasta products.
1952	FDA establishes enriched bread standard.
1962	FDA proposes regulations to permit only 12 nutrients to be added to food.
1966	FDA publishes final version of 1962 proposed regulations, limiting legal fortification to eight classes of food.
1969	White House Conference on Food, Nutrition, and Health recommends fortification of foods to meet nutritional needs.
1974	FDA proposes less restrictive rules for nutrient additions to foods.
1980	FDA promulgates 1974 proposals as a set of guidelines for food fortification.

Source: Development of Food Fortification (Watson 1981).

Regulations

FDA proposed nutrient fortification regulations in 1974, which were finalized in 1980. Foods that are fortified must follow these guidelines, which will prevent over- and underfortification:

1. A *nutritional deficiency* in a specific population group has been recognized by the scientific community. The enriched food has to be a suitable vehicle for the nutrient.
2. *Nutrients are lost* in processing, storage, or handling by at least 2% of the U.S. RDAs. All nutrients including protein, iodine, and vitamin D must be considered.
3. Nutrients are added to *fabricated food* in proportion to the total caloric content to balance vitamin, mineral, and protein content.
4. *Substitute* foods that replace traditional foods cannot be nutritionally inferior.
5. *Nutrient standards* of enrichment require added nutrients.

Meat, poultry, fish products, fresh produce, sugars, and snack foods are inappropriate for fortification.

Enrichment of foods is nutritionally significant and provides the U.S. diet with 40% of its thiamine, 15% of its riboflavin, 20% of its niacin, and 25% of its iron.

In the 1980s there was an increased interest in food fortification because of the health and fitness movement. Food manufacturers became zealous in marketing healthy nutritious products. Nutrition fortification is more difficult today than in the past when there were overt deficiency diseases. Now, it is difficult to decide what products to fortify with which nutrients.

Fortification Considerations

How does a manufacturer decide if a food should be fortified? It is necessary to decide what the purpose of the food product is and how it will be promoted (Borenstein 1984). Is the product a meal replacer, or a standardized food? Are there any negative aspects of fortification of this food? What are the nutrient interactions? Is there potential for safety and toxicity problems? Is the food a good vehicle for the nutrient? Is the source of the added nutrient physiologically available? Is it legal?

Sound decisions concerning food fortification require epidemiological nutritional research on the effects of individual nutrients. However, results from different studies may be inconclusive and conflicting. An example is the relationship between calcium intake and osteoporosis. It was suggested at the 1984

NIH Consensus Conference on Osteoporosis that increased calcium intake may prevent bone loss. This prompted a wave of calcium-fortified foods, such as orange juice and flour. The issue is whether these food products are a good vehicle for calcium fortification. Will adding calcium to the foods prevent bone loss? Further research needs to be done to address the role of calcium in bone loss.

The problem with fortifying foods is that the nutrients added may not be needed by everyone. Also, if too many foods are fortified with the same nutrient, overfortification and toxicity may be a problem. An example is the iron enrichment debate. The American Bakers Association had petitioned FDA in April 1970 to triple the standard of iron enrichment in food staples. This started the great iron enrichment debate, which lasted almost a decade. It was one of the hottest nutrition controversies ever argued. Nutritionists wanted iron super enrichment, but a group of physicians headed by Dr. Margaret Krikker protested because members of a subgroup of the population have hemochromatosis and absorb too much iron. Super enrichment would be dangerous to these people. FDA did not approve super enrichment of iron because it was not safe for all segments of the population (Anonymous 1978).

The food industry has to consider how fortifying its products will affect consumers. Is there a real need? According to Sandy Miller, formerly of the FDA: "The increased emphasis on health has increased the attention to nutrition and diet as a means of improving health. Fortifying foods may improve health. Food manufacturers have to be careful not to 'market nutrition' and exploit the consumer. For the first time, there is the beginning of widespread, indiscriminate fortification and enrichment. To keep nutritional order in the marketplace the food industry must shoulder the responsibility for policing its own action" (Miller 1987).

Another concern is the question of whether food is being fortified because of sales appeal or for the health benefit of the consumer. Food manufacturers must be careful not to engage in a nutrition horsepower race. Manufacturers have to be ethical when deciding to enrich foods. Enrichment can take the form of *fortification* to add nutrients that originally were not present in a food, or *restoration* to replace the nutrients lost during storage, processing, or handling. Fortification corrects a nutrient deficiency, whereas restoration assures that the nutrients in the processed food are equal to the original nutrients before processing (Anonymous 1982).

The level of fortification depends on its purpose. For example, if the food is a meal replacer, then 25 to 33% of the U.S. RDA of all known nutrients must be provided. The U.S. RDA is used as a basis for nutrient fortification levels.

Food manufacturers have flexibility in food fortification but must exercise responsibility in their decisions to market fortified foods.

A History of Nutrition Labeling

The 1969 White House Conference on Food, Nutrition, and Health was a landmark for nutrition awareness and nutrition policy. The conference addressed the country's nutrition problems of hunger, malnutrition, and nutrient deficiencies. The FDA labeling initiatives were an outcome of the recommendations from the White House conference. The FDA food labeling concerns were nutrition, ingredients, food fortification, and common or usual name issues. Nutrition labeling was introduced to help educate the consumer.

1973 Nutrition Labeling Regulations

In 1973 FDA finalized the nutrition labeling regulations for food products. The complete regulations were published in the *Federal Register* on January 19, 1973 (*Federal Register* 1973). A brief summary of these regulations is as follows:

- Nutrition labeling is voluntary. Exceptions occur if a nutrition claim is made on the product label or in advertising, or if the product is fortified. A nutrition claim includes any mention of calories, protein, carbohydrates, fat, vitamins, or minerals.
- When a product is nutrition-labeled, it follows the Code of Federal Regulations in title 21 parts 101.2 and 101.9.
- Nutrition information must appear on the principal display panel or nutrition panel, which is to the right of the principal display panel.
- A specific format and heading must be followed, and in a particular order.
- These items must be included in this order: nutrition information per serving, serving size, servings per container, calories, protein, carbohydrate, fat, and percentage of U.S. Recommended Daily Allowances of protein and seven vitamins and minerals, in this order: protein, vitamin A, vitamin C, thiamine, riboflavin, niacin, calcium, and iron. Originally the labeling of sodium was optional. Sodium labeling could be declared without triggering full nutrition labeling. When products were labeled with full nutrition, sodium could be included. In 1986 a new sodium regulation made sodium labeling mandatory, the order following fat. Other voluntary items which may be included are cholesterol, saturated and polyunsaturated fatty acids, vitamins D, E, B_6, B_{12}, folic acid, biotin, pantothenic acid, phosphorus, iodine, magnesium, zinc, potassium, and copper. However, if a label claim is made for one of these voluntary nutrients, then the food must be labeled.
- Serving size has to be listed according to a unit that the consumer can easily identify, such as a household measure (1 cookie, 1 tablespoon, or fluid ounces).
- FDA also established rounding rules. The U.S. RDA percentages are

labeled as follows: 2% increments up to and including 10%; 5% increments for 10 to 50%; 10% increments for over 50% of the U.S. RDA. Nutrients less than 2% of the U.S. RDA are declared as zero or as an asterisk. Special labeling rounding rules apply to sodium and potassium: use 0 when < 5 mg; round to the nearest 5 mg when 5 to 140 mg; round to the nearest 10 mg when > 140 mg (CFR Title 21; Moore and Wendt 1973).

The 1973 labeling regulations also established special dietary standards. When nutrients are added to food, then the following guidelines are used: If the food has less than 50% of the U.S. RDA, then food nutrition labeling rules are followed. If the food has 50 to 150% of the U.S. RDA for one or more nutrients, then it must follow special dietary supplement standards. A food that contains greater than 150% of the U.S. RDA is considered a drug (a medical food) and cannot be sold as a food or supplement.

The purpose of the food nutrition label was to provide the consumer with information on the nutrient content of food. The nutrition label was voluntary because FDA's role was to keep the food supply safe and to regulate, not to inform.

Government Enforcement of Labeling Regulations

The Food and Drug Association via the Federal Food, Drug and Cosmetic Act regulates most of the food labels. Advertising is regulated by the Federal Trade Commission. The USDA (United States Department of Agriculture) regulates meat, poultry, and egg products. Alcoholic beverages are governed by the Bureau of Alcohol, Tobacco and Firearms.

The major difference between FDA and USDA labeling is that the USDA allows for a shortened macronutrient format. The micronutrients (vitamins and minerals) are not required. The USDA also does not allow "and/or" labeling.

Nutrient Descriptors and Definitions Used in Food Labeling

The FDA has definitions for nutrient descriptors. These descriptors should help the consumer to better understand the nutrition label information. The majority of the food labeling descriptors and definitions that the FDA endorses are from 21 CFR 101. F. Edward Scarbrough, deputy director of the Food and Drug Administration summarized the FDA-allowed definitions. The *FDA labeling descriptors* are based on the following criteria:

- *Calories* (21 CFR 105.66): low calorie = <40 per serving and <0.4 per gram; reduced calorie = 33% less calories.
- *Sodium* (21 CFR 101.13): sodium-free = <5 mg per serving; very low

sodium = <35 mg; low sodium = <140 mg; reduced sodium = 75% less.

- *Cholesterol* (21 CFR 101.25): cholesterol-free = <2 mg per serving; low cholesterol = <20 mg; cholesterol reduced = 75% less.
- *Fat* (1988 letter): low fat = <2 g per serving and <10% fat on dry basis. FDA is working on a proposed fat labeling rule. *No fat* probably will be less than 0.5 gram per serving. *Low in saturated* fat will probably be less than 1 gram per serving.
- *Nutrients with a U.S. RDA* (based on FDA 1986 letter): (fair) source = 10% U.S. RDA; good source = 25% U.S. RDA; excellent source = 40% U.S. RDA.
- *Fiber* (based on 1986 letter): (fair) source = 2 g per serving; good source = 5 g; excellent source = 8 g.
- *Potassium* (based on 1988 opinion) (fair) source = 180 to 200 mg per serving (Scarbrough 1988).
- *Lite:* Representative Cooper proposed a bill (Lite Food Labeling Act) that defines lite as at least one-third reduction in calories, fat, or sodium. This and other lite/light bills, definitions, and regulatory proposals are being debated.

The USDA follows the above FDA regulations with the exception of the differences shown in the following *USDA labeling definitions*:

- A *lite/light* claim is a 25% reduction of fat or sodium.
- A *lean/lowfat* claim is for products that have no more than 10% fat.
- An *extra lean/low fat* claim is allowed for products with no more than 5% fat.
- *Low or reduced calorie* means at least a 25% reduction in calories; and if a comparative claim is being made, it has to be evaluated against a market basket survey or USDA Handbook 8 information.

These definitions are very helpful to the product development team in establishing criteria for healthy food products and for making nutritional claims. Such nutrition claims usually are "quantifiable claims."

Labeling Revisions in the 1990s

General Labeling Issues

The 1973 label was based on nutrient deficiencies and focused on micronutrients. The food label was reevaluated in 1978 by FDA, FTC (the Federal Trade Commission), and USDA. Five public hearings were held to get public input on nutrition, ingredients, and open dating. Also a nationwide food consumption survey was done. In 1981 FDA decided not to do a major label revision but rather to make changes on a regulation-by-regulation basis. Today, the label is 17 years old and is being reevaluated for current health concerns. Research now is concerned with macronutrients based on food overconsumption and chronic disease. Some of the current label's nutrients are not very significant to consumer health concerns.

Today's labeling issues are: Should the label be mandatory? Should some of the items (vitamins, minerals) be voluntary? Should some (cholesterol, fatty acids, fiber) be mandatory? Is the label too confusing because of numerics? Are graphics better? Will a new format be more understandable?

Do food standards need to be reevaluated? The purpose of food standards was to protect the quality of the food supply. They also may be anticompetitive and a hindrance to developing new foods. An example is the development of low-fat sour cream. The standard for sour cream specifies a minimum fat level. If a low-fat sour cream is developed with a lower fat content than the minimum, then it does not meet the standard and is misbranded if it is called sour cream. Standards limit researchers' flexibility in developing new products.

New labeling needs to be addressed because of the scientific diet reports (the Surgeon General's Report and the National Academy of Sciences Report) and the major nutrition legislation introduced by Congress in 1989. Representative Henry Waxman introduced the Nutrition Labeling and Education Act of 1989 in the House of Representatives. Senator Howard Metzenbaum introduced a similar bill in the Senate. The major point of Waxman's bill was mandatory nutrition labeling, to include calories, total fat, saturated fat, cholesterol, sodium, total carbohydrates, complex carbohydrates, sugar, protein, and dietary fiber. Senator Orrin Hatch went one step further when he introduced the Food and Nutrition Labeling Act of 1989, which included national uniformity. The major emphasis of national uniformity is that federal food labeling authority would preempt state food labeling authority.

On August 8, 1989, the FDA issued its "Food Labeling Advance Notice of Proposed Rulemaking." FDA asked for comments on this proposal, and to get additional feedback on labeling issues FDA held four hearings in the fall of 1989: on October 16 in Chicago to address the content of nutrition labeling; on November 1 in San Antonio to address ingredient labeling, food names, and nutrient descriptors; on December 7 in Seattle on health messages; and on December 13 in Atlanta on nutrition label format. The questions FDA is addressing in the proposed regulations are: (1) Do nutrition labeling requirements need to be revised? (2) Does the nutrition format need to change? (3) Should ingredient labeling change? (4) Do standards of identity need to change, and should common food descriptors such as "low fat" be defined? (5) How should health messages be labeled? (6) Is harmonization of USDA and FDA labeling requirements needed? In addition, FDA is trying to harmonize the U.S./ Canadian/international labeling rules (*Federal Register* 1989).

Cholesterol Labeling

A major consumer interest has been in cholesterol labeling. In the late 1980s, numerous manufacturers got on the cholesterol bandwagon, frequently labeling products in a misleading manner. Often only cholesterol would be labeled, and no information on saturated fat was provided. Some of the products did not contain cholesterol but were high in saturated fat.

A 1989 draft of a final cholesterol regulation by FDA addresses some of the current cholesterol labeling controversies. The labeling of food products that are high in total fat or high in saturated fat with a "no cholesterol statement" is misleading. The final draft would require a declaratory statement to be added to the label if a no cholesterol or low cholesterol claim were made. The statement would help to educate consumers and alert them to the fat content information. A product that is labeled "100% vegetable oil" also would require a declaratory statement of "see nutrition information on back for fat content." FDA is encouraging the voluntary declaration of cholesterol and fatty acids on food labels. However voluntary cholesterol labeling triggers mandatory nutrition labeling (calories, fat, etc.) (Department of Health and Human Services 1989).

Health Claims

Traditionally, health claims on labels have not been permitted by FDA. In 1938 Congress passed the Food, Drug and Cosmetic Act, which forbids false and misleading label statements. Health claims on foods also were prohibited via the nutrition labeling regulations in 1973. Prior to 1984 no explicit health claims were allowed.

In 1984, a major refocusing on health claims occurred due to the Kellogg All-Bran advertising campaign. The National Cancer Institute (NCI) reported that there was a relationship between dietary fiber intake and cancer. In 1984, NCI allowed Kellogg to use its name on food labels and in advertisements to back a high-fiber claim. The claim was that high-fiber foods (i.e., Kellogg All-Bran) are related to cancer prevention. Numerous companies followed Kellogg's example, and a proliferation of health claims on food products started. The problem with unauthorized health claims lay in enforcement. FDA did not take action on any health claims on food products, even on some claims that were questionable, and the result was advertising chaos, which intensified the need for FDA to finalize a health claim policy. Both consumer and industry pressure caused FDA to reevaluate its position. On August 4, 1987, FDA initiated a health claims proposal that was to allow manufacturers to provide "truthful" health messages on food labels. The proposal was very controversial and raised many questions: Is the label the appropriate place to provide health information? Will providing this information on the label create horsepower races and overfortification? This proposal was not approved by the Office of Management and Budget—the draft was thought to be too restrictive. (Department of Health and Human Services 1990).

Ethics

Health claims present an ethical dilemma. Where is the line drawn between freedom of speech and government control of misleading, fraudulent claims? The claims cannot be deceptive and must be supported by scientific investigation. It also is important to emphasize the total diet rather than single foods.

An example is the oat bran craze. Oat bran was implicated in reducing blood cholesterol. A study by the Northwestern University Medical School showed that there was a drop in blood cholesterol with a combined oat bran and low fat, low cholesterol diet (Van Horn et al. 1988). This finding was hyped by the news media, and a proliferation of food products were introduced containing oat bran, there being no health claims regulations to control the situation. Industry had not done a good job of self-regulation; a single food item had become a panacea for health. Soon afterward, rice bran and psyllium followed as "wonder foods" that would control cholesterol.

It is an interesting phenomenon that one food ingredient can drive product development and new product introductions. By June 1989 there were about 314 oat bran–containing products on the grocery shelves. The oat bran craze did demonstrate that consumers will change their eating habits if there is a perceived health benefit. In 1988 oat bran cereal sales were $124.4 million compared to $35.7 million in 1987 (Anonymous 1989). Will the oat bran popularity continue? Probably not. A recent study reported in the *New England Journal of Medicine* concluded that "oat bran has little cholesterol-lowering effect, that high fiber and lower-fiber grain supplements reduce serum cholesterol levels about equally, probably because they replace dietary fat" (Swain et al. 1990). A problem with this study, however, was that the cholesterol levels of the population group studied were normal to begin with, 176 mg%; the effect may be different on the hypercholesterolemic individual.

Are health claims for individual food ingredients warranted? Colin Campbell and Thomas O'Connor believe that "the unjustifiable specificity of information originated by the scientific community has been misleading in the marketplace" (Campbell and O'Connor 1988). The scientific reports often have qualifying information that is not included in labeling and advertising; so the question is whether a single food can really be linked with preventing disease.

FDA did respond to the health claims problem. On February 13, 1990, FDA published in the *Federal Register* a new health claims proposal entitled "Food Labeling; Health Messages and Label Statements; Reproposed Rule." This reproposed rule withdrew the 1987 proposal on health messages. FDA considered the 1987 proposal to be too "permissive," allowing unjustified label claims.

Six topic areas are suggested in the 1990 health message reproposal, which may be appropriate for health messages on food labels:

Fiber and cancer
Fiber and heart disease
Lipids and cancer
Lipids and heart disease
Sodium and hypertension
Calcium and osteoporosis

The FDA will develop scientific summaries, consumer health message summaries, model label statements, and a consumer guide to food labeling to support the health message policy.

The underlying tone of the health message policy is that the FDA will more closely monitor health messages on labels. Evaluation will be based on these considerations: (1) Is there enough scientific evidence to support the health message? (2) Do the beneficial attributes outweigh the negative effects? (3) Is the claim truthful, or is it exaggerated? And (4) Is the component enough to produce the claimed effect? However, this is a proposal and not yet a final rule.

In the future, we can expect to see health messages on labels, but they will be closely monitored and more useful to the consumer.

Dietary Recommendations

From 1977 to 1989, thirteen major dietary guideline reports were published by health, government, and professional organizations. The reports issued dietary recommendations for reducing the risk of chronic disease (Cronin and Shaw 1988).

The following list includes the name of each report, the date, and the organization that issued it:

1. Dietary Goals for the United States, 2nd edition, 1977, U.S. Senate Select Committee on Nutrition and Needs.
2. Healthy People: Surgeon General's Report on Health Promotion and Disease Prevention, 1979, U.S. Department of Health, Education, and Welfare.
3. Concepts of Nutrition and Health, 1979, AMA (American Medical Association).
4. Toward Healthful Diets, 1980, National Academy of Sciences.
5. Recommended Dietary Allowances, 9th edition, 1980, National Academy of Sciences, National Research Council.

6. Diet, Nutrition and Cancer, 1982, National Academy of Sciences.
7. Nutrition and Cancer, 1984, American Cancer Society.
8. Nutrition and Your Health: Dietary Guidelines for Americans, 2nd edition, 1985, USDA and Department of Health and Human Services.
9. Dietary Guidelines for Healthy American Adults, 1988, American Heart Association.
10. National Cancer Institute Dietary Guidelines, 1988, National Cancer Institute.
11. The Surgeon General's Report on Nutrition and Health, 1988, United States Department of Health and Human Services.
12. Diet and Health Implications for Reducing Chronic Disease Risk, 1989, National Research Council.
13. Recommended Dietary Allowances, 10th edition, 1989, National Academy of Sciences, National Research Council.

Summary of the Guidelines

Some of the reports give general dietary advice, whereas others emphasize ways to reduce the risk of heart disease and cancer. Generally, they all provide dietary recommendations on how to eat in a healthy manner. Many of the chronic degenerative diseases are covered, such as heart disease and cancer. The reports stress the importance of maintaining the ideal body weight and eating a variety of foods, which should provide all the essential nutrients. Most of the reports recommend reducing dietary cholesterol and fat, particularly saturated fat. Most recommend increasing the consumption of complex carbohydrates, such as starch and fiber. The American Cancer Society and the National Cancer Institute discuss the importance of β-carotene and vitamins A and C.

The USDA Dietary Guidelines recommend seven steps to improve one's general well-being:

- Eat a variety of food.
- Maintain a desirable body weight.
- Avoid too much fat, saturated fat, and cholesterol.
- Eat foods with adequate starch and fiber.
- Avoid too much sugar.
- Avoid too much sodium.
- If you drink alcoholic beverages, do so in moderation.

The two most useful reports to product development are "The Surgeon General's Report on Nutrition and Health" and the "Diet and Health Implications for Reducing Chronic Disease Risk." These reports not only are the most recent; they also provide developers with specific numbers and recommendations.

The Surgeon General's Report on Nutrition and Health

This report stated: "The main conclusion is that overconsumption of certain dietary components is a major concern for Americans. Many food factors are involved, chief among them is the disproportionate consumption of foods high in fats, often at the expense of foods high in complex carbohydrates and fiber—such as vegetables, fruits and whole grain products—that may be more conductive to health" (Surgeon General 1988). The five major recommendations the Surgeon General's nutrition and health report issued are: reduce consumption of fat, especially saturated fat and cholesterol; achieve and maintain an ideal body weight; increase complex carbohydrates and fiber in the diet with whole grains, cereals, vegetables, legumes and fruits; reduce sodium intake; and consume alcohol only in moderation.

Also, calcium should be increased in adolescent girls and adult women. Adequate iron consumption is especially important in children, adolescents, and women in childbearing years. And there is a practical admonition to "emphasize consumption of vegetables, fruits, and whole grain products—foods that are rich in complex carbohydrates and fiber and relatively low in calories—and of fish, skinless poultry and lean meats, and lowfat dairy products."

The following scientific evidence, which served as a basis for these guidelines, demonstrates that diet is associated with chronic disease:

- Dietary cholesterol and especially saturated fat raise blood cholesterol. Mono- and polyunsaturated fatty acids decrease blood cholesterol levels.
- Overweight increases the risk of developing diabetes, coronary heart disease, stroke, some cancer, and high blood pressure.
- Diverticulosis and some cancer rates are lower with a high-fiber, high-complex-carbohydrate diet. Water-soluble fiber may help to lower blood lipid and blood glucose levels. Vegetables and fruits, especially dark green, yellow, and cruciferous vegetables, may be protective against cancer (decrease the risk).
- A high-sodium diet is implicated in the incidence of stroke and high blood pressure.
- Increased alcohol consumption is associated with an increased incidence of liver disease, cancer, stroke, high blood pressure, and heart muscle problems.
- Decreased calcium intake early in life may increase the risk of osteoporosis earlier in life.
- Inadequate iron intake in children and women causes anemia.

Diet and Health Report

The most recent and the preeminent report is "Diet and Health Implications for Reducing Chronic Disease Risk," released in March 1989. This report is particularly valuable because of its quantitative recommendations.

The National Research Council decided to do a comprehensive review of the literature because of all the reports that had been released. A major goal was to reach a consensus on all the information. Also it was very important to consider competing risks arising from dietary recommendations (e.g., if meat and egg yolk were reduced to control fat and cholesterol, would a deficiency of iron result?).

The scientific results and conclusions of this report are too lengthy to discuss in this chapter. Instead, a simple summary of the report's eight dietary recommendations is included here:

1. *Fat:* Reduce total fat and saturated fat. Reduce fat to 30% or less of calories. Reduce saturated fatty acids to less than 10% of calories (7 to 8% is best). Reduce cholesterol to less than 300 mg/day. Substitute monounsaturated fatty acids for saturated. Polyunsaturated fatty acids should be 10% or less of calories (7% is the current U.S. amount, and this should be maintained).

2. *Carbohydrate:* Consumption of carbohydrates should be increased to 55% or more of total calories. This is accomplished by increasing complex carbohydrates. Eat five or more servings of vegetables and fruits (green and yellow vegetables and citrus fruits are especially important). Eat six or more servings of bread, cereals, and legumes.

3. *Protein:* The amount of protein intake should be moderate.

4. *Body weight:* Maintain your ideal body weight by a balance of food intake and exercise.

5. *Alcohol:* Consume less than 1 ounce of "pure" alcohol per day. In general alcohol should not be consumed; its intake definitely needs to be limited.

6. *Salt:* Salt intake should be 6 g or less per day (<2,400 mg of sodium).

7. *Calcium:* Consume adequate calcium at about the RDA amounts.

8. *Supplements:* Vitamin and mineral supplements generally are not needed.

The food industry needs to develop products that adhere to these guidelines. The major focus should be on fat, saturated fat, calories, sodium, cholesterol, and carbohydrates (fiber and complex). The major conclusions from these reports can be used as criteria in developing healthy food products and product literature.

INDUSTRY'S CHALLENGE

What role, if any, does industry have in changing the dietary habits of Americans? Do food manufacturers have a responsibility to change the food supply?

According to the Public Health Service, industry should be a key player. The Public Health Service report "Promoting Health/Preventing Disease: Year 2000 Objectives for the Nation," released in September 1989, includes industry in its objectives. In the "Summary of Objectives to Improve Nutrition," four of the objectives pertain to industry:

- Increase to at least 95% the proportion of school lunch and breakfast services with menus that are consistent with the Dietary Guidelines for Americans.
- Increase to at least 75% the proportion of institutional food service operations with menus that are consistent with the Dietary Guidelines for Americans.
- Increase to at least 5,000 brand items the availability of processed food products that are reduced in fat, saturated fat, and cholesterol (baseline was 2,500 in 1986).
- Increase to at least 5,000 brand items the availability of processed foods with lowered sodium (baseline was 2,150 in 1986).

The public health objectives indicate that "in order for food consumers to meet the objectives for reduction of dietary fat, saturated fat, cholesterol and sodium in their diets by the year 2000 it will be necessary to give them sufficient food choices" (Public Health Service 1989, p. 22).

A decade ago, nutrition did not play a significant role in product development. Today, the marketplace has evolved. Consumers are demanding taste, convenience, and nutrition in food products. Nutrition needs to be an added dimension of product development.

The food industry has slowly been making changes and cutting back on sodium and fat content. This is just the beginning. There needs to be more nutritious, palatable options available to consumers. Industry needs to move ahead quickly if the year 2000 objectives are to be met. Promotion and advertising materials must be truthful and carefully designed, reflecting the dietary guidelines and labeling regulations.

The traditional diet is changing, and industry needs to offer appropriate products to meet the new "American diet." Food manufacturers can accomplish this by following the nutrition principles, dietary guidelines, and labeling information suggestions outlined in this chapter. A constant awareness of new research and new ingredients is necessary if planners are to be successful and innovative.

The challenge to industry is to make the 1990s the decade of tasty, convenient, nutritious new products that successfully implement the dietary guidelines.

REFERENCES

Anonymous. 1978. Anatomy of a decision. *Nutrition Today* 29: 6–10.

Anonymous. 1982. The nutritive quality of processed foods: General policies for nutrient additions. *Nutrition Reviews* 40(3): 93–96.

Anonymous. 1989. Marketplace: Oat bran mania continues in new product introduction. Breads and cereals: Industry trends: Oat bran. *Food Engineering*, June, 29.

Borenstein, B. 1984. Rationale of fortification. Presentation at the AACC Short Course on Food Fortification, Oct. 1984, Minneapolis.

Campbell, C. and O'Connor, T. P. 1988. Health claims in food advertisements. *Journal of Nutrition Education* 20(2): 87–92.

Code of Federal Regulations 21 Parts 100 to 169.

Code of Federal Regulations, Title 21 (Sections 101.9 and 105.3).

Cronin, F. and Shaw, A. 1988. Summary of dietary recommendations for healthy Americans. *Nutrition Today*, Nov./Dec., 23(6): 26–34.

Department of Health and Human Services. 1989. Food labeling: Definitions of cholesterol free, low cholesterol and reduced cholesterol. Docket No. 84N-01531 21 CFR Part 101, FDA Jan. 1989.

Federal Register. Jan. 19, 1973. Regulations for the enforcement of the Federal Food, Drug and Cosmetic Act and the Fair Packaging and Labeling Act—food information panel. 21 CFR 38(13): 2124–2137.

Federal Register. Aug. 8, 1989. Food labeling; advance notice of proposed rulemaking. 21 CFR 54(151): 32610–32615.

Federal Register. Feb. 13, 1990. Food labeling; health messages and label statements; reproposed rule. 21 CFR 101 55(30): 5176–5192.

FAO/WHO (Food and Agriculture Organization/World Health Organization). 1973. Energy and protein requirements. Report of a Joint FAO/WHO Ad Hoc Expert Committee. Technical Report Services No. 552; FAO Nutrition Meetings Report Series 52. Rome: World Health Organization, 118 pp.

Hamill, P. V. V. et al. 1979. Physical growth. National Center for Health Statistics percentiles. *American Journal of Clinical Nutrition* 32: 607–629.

Miller, S. 1987. You said what? Paper presented at the annual meeting of the International Life Sciences Institute—Nutrition Foundation, Jan. 28, 1987, Naples, Fla.

Moore, J. L. and Wendt, P. F. 1973. Nutrition labeling—a summary and evaluation. *Journal of Nutrition Education* 5(2): 123–124.

National Research Council. 1989. *Diet and Health Implications for Reducing Chronic Disease Risk.* Washington, D.C.: National Academy Press.

Olson, R. E. 1980. Statement to the House Agriculture Subcommittee on Domestic Marketing, Consumer Relations and Nutrition. *Nutrition Today* 15(3): 12–18.

Olson, R. E. et al. 1984. *Nutrition Reviews Present Knowledge in Nutrition*, 5th edition. Washington D.C.: The Nutrition Foundation, Inc.

Public Health Service. 1989. Promoting health/preventing disease: Year 2000 objectives for the nation. Public Health Service, U.S. Department of Health and Human Services, Sept. 1989.

Scarbrough, E. F. 1988. An update on nutrition issues at FDA. Paper read at Journalist Conference, Dec. 1988, Washington, D.C.

Shank, F. and Wilkening, V. L. 1986. Considerations for food fortification policy. *Cereal Foods World* 31(10): 728–740.

Swain, J. F., Rouse, F., Curley, C., and Sacks, F. 1990. Comparison of effects of oat bran and low-fiber wheat. *New England Journal of Medicine* 322(3): 147–152.

Van Horn, L., Emidy, L., Liao, Y., Ballew, C., King, J., and Stamler, T. 1988. Serum lipid response to a fat-modified, oatmeal-enhanced diet. *Preventive Medicine* 17: 377–386.

RECOMMENDED READING

Department of Health and Human Services. 1989. Reproposal on health messages on food labels—proposed regulations, Nov. 29, 1989.

Ensminger, A. and M. E. 1983. *Food and Nutrition Encyclopedia*. Calif.: Pegus Press.

LaChance, P. 1973. A commentary on the new FDA nutrition labeling. *Nutrition Today* 8(1): 14–23.

National Research Council. 1989. *Recommended Dietary Allowances*, 10th edition. Washington, D.C.: National Academy Press.

Chapter 12

The History, Current Status, and Future of Nutritional Food Product Development

Mary K. Schmidl and Theodore P. Labuza

THE HISTORY OF NUTRIFICATION

Most physicians now have never seen human nutritional deficiency diseases such as pellagra, goiter, rickets, or scurvy. The dramatic reduction of these nutritional-related diseases in the twentieth century can be directly related to an active nutrition research program and government intervention, which stimulated the food industry to create nutritionally designed food products to supply the missing nutrients. With these problems solved, the current efforts of nutrition research and product development continue at an even greater pace, focusing on products that will help to reduce or control diet-related chronic diseases such as atherosclerosis or cancer, as well as the creation of specialty products for weight control and the hospitalized patient. Today a central issue is the controversy created by government limitations on health claims in the advertising and labeling of foods that were designed by industry because of current research findings on nutritional-related chronic disease (Labuza 1987). The early history of product development shows how the combined efforts of scientists, government officials, and the food industry led to the current activity in product development, and why the regulation of these products is difficult.

The restoration, enrichment, and fortification of foods with key nutrients have prevented untold cases of deficiency disease and death. Surveys of nutritional status such as those done in 1936 showed the U.S. population to be experiencing significantly low intakes of four nutrients: thiamine, riboflavin, niacin, and iron (Briggs and Calloway 1979). The decision was made to take governmental action to improve the nation's nutrition. Nutrition authorities faced with this problem decided to select foods to which these nutrients would be added. They decided on three criteria in choosing a food, namely: (1) it had to be consumed by nearly every American of any racial or cultural background; (2) it had to be inexpensive; (3) and the amounts consumed were not likely to be excessive. The food group they chose was the bread and cereals group, which includes pasta products such as macaroni, spaghetti, and noodles and grains such as wheat, corn, and rice (Austin 1978).

Paper #17,948 of the University of Minnesota Experiment Station. This work was supported in part by a grant from the Nutrasweet Co.

For years prior to this decision, nutritionists had been advocating the use of whole grain products, which contain significant amounts of the B vitamins and iron. A 1939 survey revealed that people truly preferred the refined breads and cereals, from which many of these nutrients were lost during processing. Therefore, enrichment standards were set in such a way that the amount of these nutrients added back to the refined products would make them approximately equivalent to the original whole grain products. The enrichment program, developed during the 1940s, called for the addition of these four nutrients to foods made from refined grains. As a consequence, the amount of thiamine contributed by these foods to the American diet increased from about 19% of the RDA in the 1930s to over 30% in the 1940s. There is no national law that requires enrichment; there are only standards of identity for enriched products specifying the amounts of required nutrients that can be added, such as those added when a cereal or bread product is to be identified as an enriched product. Twenty-seven states and Puerto Rico require enrichment with thiamine, riboflavin, niacin, and iron for all cereal grain products sold in their states. These laws are known as ''enrichment legislation'' (AMA 1951).

Today, the use of iodized table salt is recognized as an effective public health measure. Food grown in iodine-poor soil contains little or none of the element. In the United States, these areas generally are inland, such as the areas covering Michigan, Utah, and Idaho. In areas of endemic goiter, the beneficial effect of a small iodine supplement was demonstrated by Marine and Kimbell in 1918. With no need for laws or regulations, iodine was added to salt in Michigan in 1924; and by 1930, goiter was reduced from 38.2% to 9% in that population. Today, the use of iodized salt is recommended in all noncoastal regions where environmental and dietary levels are low. It is interesting to note that several other sources of iodine find their way into the U.S. diet. Iodates still are used as dough oxidizers in the continuous bread-making process, adding about 500 micrograms per 100 grams of bread. Dairy products accumulate iodine because of the use of iodine-containing disinfectants on cows, milking machines, and storage tanks and in cleaning-in-place techniques and because of iodine-containing additives in animal feeds (Food and Nutrition Board 1989). With the increased concern today over sodium intake and hypertension, these latter accidental sources and possibly some newly created food vehicle may become the major route for iodine ingestion.

Other examples of nutritional additions were the addition of vitamin D to milk to eliminate rickets in 1929 and the fortification of margarine with fish oil in 1939 to increase vitamin A to its level in butter (Briggs and Calloway 1979). Following World War II, FDA continued to promulgate standards, setting appropriate enrichment levels for such staple foods as dairy products and margarine. Food standards were written to specify, by chemical name, every ingredient that could lawfully be used in the standardized product. These ''recipe'' food standards were continued until the 1960s when, after enactment of the

Food Additives Amendment of 1958, FDA concluded that it had adequate control over the safety of food ingredients and thus could allow any "safe or suitable" functional ingredient to be used in standardized foods (Hutt and Hutt 1986). As a public health measure, in many states, milk is required to be fortified with 400 International Units of vitamin D per quart; the fortified product is known as vitamin D–enriched milk. Margarine, which has become a popular substitute for butter, often is fortified with vitamins A and D for the same reason.

By the 1970s, regulation of the fluoride content of water was part of the nutritional fortification program. By addition of fluorides in localities where there was a deficiency, prevention of tooth decay became a fully scientifically accepted, safe, economical, and efficient public health measure. By 1970, artificially fluoridated water was available to over 40% of the United States population and to millions in other parts of the world (McClure 1962 and 1970).

In the 1980s, two new developments occurred in the fortification of foods. As data became available showing the high incidence of osteoporosis in elderly women, technologists looked for a way to add calcium to the diet (Garn 1990). The elderly tend not to drink milk and may shun other dairy products such as cheese because of fat/calories. Thus it was decided to fortify orange juice with calcium, an onerous step because various calcium sources are insoluble in solution. At this point, not enough data are available to assess whether this fortification step will reduce the incidence of osteoporosis at rates equivalent to those of other measures.

The second development was the introduction of fiber, especially oat bran, into many different kinds of foods. The driving force was the relationship between fiber intake and reduced cholesterol and colon cancer (Klurfeld 1987; Anderson 1989). Most of the products being fortified are cereal baked goods although oat bran is being added to other products, such as liquid drink mixes and salad dressings. Because fiber is not considered an essential nutrient, there is much less support for this from some of the nutrition community compared to earlier fortification efforts, and as with the calcium in orange juice, fiber's long-term benefits are not yet known.

After the decisions have been made regarding the kind and amount of nutrients desired in the final product, the food technologist is faced with the challenge of adding them so that: (1) the product is not negatively affected in odor, flavor, or color; (2) the added nutrients are acceptably stable, with sufficient overages to compensate for losses in processing and storage; and (3) the process remains practical and economically viable. The more complex and abusive the processing conditions are, the more difficult it is to achieve these ends. The development of complete homogeneous mixtures is not always an easy task. In the case of vitamin or mineral fortification, the uniform mixing of a small amount of the nutrient into a large quantity of a food ingredient must be performed in an efficient and effective manner. For dry products, this usually is achieved through mixing verification over time. Samples of the product are analyzed at various time intervals to check for the amount added. Once this amount is consistent over a given time period, one can assume that the mix is homogeneous. This is easy to do with batch operations, but continuous systems may present more difficulty in obtaining the same degree of accuracy. During mixing, in storage, or during other processing techniques such as homogenization, heating, or extrusion, vitamins may be lost or become unavailable physiologically. Table 12-1 lists the vitamins and their relative sensitivities to environmental and/or processing conditions. These conditions should be considered during the developmental stage of the product.

LABEL REGULATIONS RELATED TO NUTRITIONAL PRODUCTS

RDAs

Recommended Dietary Allowances (RDA's) are the levels of intake of essential nutrients considered, in the judgement of the Committee on Dietary

Table 12-1. Relative sensitivities of vitamins to environmental conditions.

Vitamins	Sensitivity to Specific Stresses[a]				Optimal pH for greatest stability
	Heat	Light	Oxygen	Metals	
Oil-soluble:					
Vitamin A	+ + +	+ + +	+ + + +	+ + + +	
Vitamin D	+ + +	+ + +	+ + + +	+ + + +	
Vitamin E	+ +	+ +	+ + +	+ + +	
Vitamin K	+	+ + + +	+ + +		
Water-soluble:					
Ascorbic acid (Vitamin C)	+ + +	+ +	+ + + +[b]	+ + +	2–5
Thiamine (Vitamin B₁)	+ + + +	+ + +	+	+ + +	2
Riboflavin (Vitamin B₂)	+	+ + + +	+	+ + +	5
Niacin (Vitamin B₃)	+	+	+	+	3–7
Pyridoxine (Vitamin B₆)	+	+ + +	+	+	2
Cyanocobalamin (Vitamin B₁₂)	+	+ + +	+	+ +	4–5
Pantothenic acid	+ + +	+	+	+	4–5
Biotin	+	+	+	+	6–7
Folic acid	+	+ + +	+ + +	+ + +	7

[a] + = stable; + + + + = very unstable.
[b] Unstable in solution, stable in dry form.
(Adapted from Johnson, Gordon, and Borensten 1988)

Allowances of the Food and Nutrition Board (National Academy of Sciences) on the basis of available scientific knowledge, to be adequate to meet the known nutritional needs of practically all healthy persons. (Food and Nutrition Board 1980)

RDAs are recommendations for the average daily amounts of nutrients that population groups should consume over a period of time; they should not be confused with requirements for a specific individual. Differences in the specific nutrient requirements of individuals generally are not known; so RDAs (except for energy) are set to exceed the requirements of most healthy individuals and thereby ensure that the needs of nearly all in the population are met. Intakes below the recommended allowance for a nutrient are not necessarily inadequate, but the risk of having an inadequate intake increases to the extent that the intake is less than the level recommended as safe (Food and Nutrition Board 1989).

The United States Recommended Daily Allowances (U.S. RDAs) were designed to be used for food labeling (Code of Federal Regulations Title 21 CFR 101.9(a)) and became effective in 1975. According to this regulation, if a nutrient is added to a food and/or a nutritional claim is made either in advertising or on the package, nutrition labeling is mandatory. The specific nutrition information and its format on the label are specified in the regulation. The government is considering alternative formats for nutrition labeling to make the information more easily understood and utilized by consumers, and an official proposal to revise the present cholesterol and nutrition labeling format has been made (55 FR 29456, July 19, 1990). The U.S. RDAs (Table 12-2) are based on the NRC (National Research Council) RDAs that were promulgated in 1968. Since 1968, the RDAs have been updated three times, with the latest addition being published in 1989. Although the FDA-required nutritional labels are based on the 1968 RDAs the new proposal uses new reference values (RDI's). Changing the basis, as is being proposed, could require a long regulatory procedure and might increase the cost of foods because of label copy costs.

Medical Foods Labeling

Our knowledge base in the area of nutrition and health-related diseases has grown much larger over the past 50 years. As noted earlier, we no longer have to be concerned with nutritional deficiency diseases or the establishment of basic requirements such as the RDAs, although the requirements remain the foundation of our know-how and are continuously updated (approximately every five years). Therefore, in recent years the focus of nutrition has become more medically oriented, not only in the area of chronic disease states as related to dietary intake (cardiovascular disease, cancer, obesity), but also with respect to special niche populations such as infants, the critically ill, and the elderly. A number of health problems can be improved upon or controlled by nutritional support or food modification. Specialty medical food products are brought to market

Table 12-2. Comparison of NRC-RDAs and U.S. RDAs

	NRC RDA[a]	U.S. RDA[b]
Protein, g	63	65[c]
Vitamin A, IU	5,000	5,000
Vitamin C, mg	45	60
Thiamine, mg	1.4	1.5
Riboflavin, mg	1.6	1.7
Niacin, mg	19	20
Calcium, mg	800	1,000
Iron, mg	10	18
Vitamin D, IU	400	400
Vitamin E, IU	15	30
Vitamin B_6, mg	2.0	2.0
Folacin, mg	0.2	0.4
Vitamin B_{12}, mcg	2	6
Phosphorous, mg	800	1,000
Iodine, mcg	130	150
Magnesium, mg	350	400
Zinc, mg	15	15
Copper, mg	[d]	2
Biotin, mg	[d]	0.3
Pantothenic acid, mg	[d]	10

[a]Based on male 25–50 years, 1989.
[b]Adults and children over 4 years.
[c]Based on protein efficiency ratio less than that of casein.
[d]No NRC-RDA established, but there are recommended safe and adequate levels.

through the cooperative product development efforts of the medical community, nutritionists, dietitians, and food technologists. Some products are available to the average consumer and found on the grocery shelf, whereas others can be obtained only through closely monitored medically controlled programs. The regulation of these foods is complex. The September 1989 issue of the *Food Drug Cosmetic Law Journal* was devoted solely to medical foods (*FDC Law J.*, Vol. 44).

Prior to 1972, many of the dietary items to be used under a physician's care were classified as drugs. This meant that under the existing law these items had to undergo the same extensive documentation related to the chemistry, biological effects, apparent efficacy, and lack of toxicity that was required for all other new drugs, before obtaining FDA approval for manufacture and sale. In 1972, many of these drug items were reclassified as foods for special dietary uses and placed under the jurisdiction of FDA's Bureau of Foods (now known as the Center for Food Safety and Applied Nutrition). These regulations are administered under Section 105 of Title 21 of the Code of Federal Regulations. Categories include hypoallergenic foods (21 CFR 105.62), infant foods (21 CFR 105.65), foods relating to caloric reduction for weight control (21 CFR 105.66), foods for diabetics (21 CFR 105.67), and foods for regulation of sodium intake (21 CFR 105.69). These categories really do not cover the broad category of enteral products (which will be discussed below), so the latter area is legally quite gray. This omission was intended to foster product development and to extend the availability of medical foods by relaxing the need for New Drug Approvals (Chopra 1977).

Since 1972, the regulatory status of medical food products has been clouded, especially in light of the re-proposed health claims labeling regulations prepared by the FDA in 1989. At this point, it is not known with certainty how FDA intends to categorize guidelines governing the definition, manufacture, distribution, and use of "medical foods." To revert to drug standards for special dietary foods would be regressive and counterproductive. Although in the past there was growing evidence that FDA was in the process of writing a new regulation, more recently FDA has made it clear that it would not regulate this area but would more stringently regulate the manufacture of products under Good Manufacturing Practices (21 CFR 110). FDA also suggested that manufacturers should do shelf-life testing to ensure that products meet the labeled nutrient values (Anonymous 1988a).

Calorie-Controlled Food Label Claims

Under 21 CFR 105.66(a)(1), a food may be labeled "low calorie" only if a single serving contains 40 or fewer calories and contains no more than 0.4 calorie per gram. If a food is labeled "reduced calorie," according to 21 CFR 105.66(d)(1), it must be at least one-third lower in calories than a similar food in which the calories are not reduced, and it must not be nutritionally inferior to the original food. "Nutritional inferiority" is defined in 21 CFR 101.3 as any reduction in an amount equal to 2% or more of the U.S. RDA (per average serving) of the required labeled nutrients present in the food. The required essential nutrients for nutritional labeling include protein, vitamins A, C, B_1, and B_2, niacin, calcium, and iron. A reduction in the calories or fat content of a food does not result in its being nutritionally inferior from a legal standpoint. If the food label suggests that calories have been reduced, it must show the number of calories the product contains versus the number of calories in an unmodified version of the product, and it must meet either the low or the reduced calorie standard. If the food is naturally low in calories, such as carrots, it cannot be labeled "low calorie carrots" because that would mean that these carrots are lower in calories than any other carrots (21 CFR 105.66(a)(1)).

The USDA, which regulates meat, poultry, and egg products, has stricter labeling requirements than FDA's, (Brewington 1989), which became effective in April 1987 to more accurately reveal the fat content of foods containing meat. Under USDA Policy Memo 70B, the following claims are specified: "extra lean" (less than 5% fat by weight); "lean" and "low fat" (less than 10% fat by weight); and "light," "lite," "leaner," and "lower fat" (at least 25% less fat than similar products). However, ground hamburger can be lean if it has less than 22.5% fat. Whenever any of these terms is used on the product label, the amount of fat in the product must be declared. Also if a comparison is made (i.e., "lower fat"), a statement explaining this comparison must be included on the label. With respect to "light" reduced or low calorie meat products, USDA requires a 25% reduction (Policy Memo 71A). The guidelines for nutritional labeling are the same as for FDA, but, if relevant, USDA requires that the stated values shown on the label be given for "as cooked" as well as uncooked. The USDA also has modified its stance on standards of identity for processed meats. Prior to 1987, sausages could contain no more than 30% fat by weight, and the amount of added water was limited to prevent processors from selling water as meat. Under new guidelines, the total fat plus added water cannot exceed 40% with the fat still at a maximum of 30%; thus lower-fat sausages now can be legally produced.

Specific Health Claims on Labels

The basic regulations related to health claims made for foods other than the medical foods noted above are very complex, as noted by Labuza (1987) and Hutt and Hutt (1986). The basic tenet of the Food and Drug Administration has been that any disease-related claim—other than those allowed and claims related to those areas such as calorie claims, nutritional labeling including cholesterol and fatty acid values, and so on—makes the food a drug and therefore illegal unless a new drug application is made. Over the past 40 years the FDA has aggressively exercised its authority in this area, especially against products made by the so-called health food industry. In some cases the government has lost, as in the case the FDA took against a sugar producer who fortified sucrose with 19 vitamins and minerals and sold it as "non-empty-calorie" table sugar. The courts ruled that this product was legal since there was nothing in the law that prevented such combinations or claims.

For the most part, the food industry as a whole had not pursued a health claims approach on food labels and was content not to make any health claims other than those allowed. They did, however, begin to make claims in the electronic and print media where the FTC has authority and had allowed health claims to be made based on certain substantiation guidelines. Other factors also worked for change: the increased awareness of consumers of the relationship between diet and chronic disease because of instant mass communication, efforts on the part of consumer groups to get the food industry to tell more about the healthfulness of products on the package label, and the efforts of some federal agencies to promote public health in the news media. Then, in 1986, one major food company, with the blessings of the Federal Trade Commission and the National Cancer Institute, challenged the FDA by putting a cancer-prevention-related claim on the package label of a cereal fortified with dietary fiber. That action led to a series of other food companies selling foods with similar chronic-disease-related health claims on their package labels. In addition, several private health organizations set up a process by which they would give a seal of approval that could be put on the package label for foods meeting their specific dietary guidelines (e.g., if the product had less than 30% of its calories from fat, it would be approved as a food healthy for the heart). Both FDA and USDA oppose this seal-of-approval approach. One result is a major controversy within the government between FDA and other agencies as well as a conflict between FDA, the food industry, and the private health-related organizations that has not been resolved.

In February of 1990 the FDA published proposed guidelines for the health claims they will allow on food package labels (Feb. 13, *Federal Register*). The outcome of these label claim proposals is in doubt, and whatever happens may have a major impact on the types of foods that the food industry will be willing to create to meet consumer health needs.

RESTRICTED-CALORIE WEIGHT CONTROL TOTAL DIET PRODUCTS

Introduction

It is clear that obesity is a significant problem in American society; excess body fat is associated with many chronic diseases including hypertension, hyperlipidemia, cardiovascular disease, gout, diabetes, gallstones, and cancer. (American Heart Association 1986, JAMA, 1988). Approaches to weight control vary considerably in their effectiveness in decreasing body fat as well as in their associated health risks which can range from the mild to severe (sudden death). This is due to the fact that weight loss is still a subjective science. Weight-reducing diets published in the scientific literature and a myriad of diets published in the popular press are available to help individuals achieve weight loss as well as for subsequent weight maintenance (Wadden, Van Itallie, and Blackburn 1990). In some diets, energy intake is severely restricted, the most extreme case being fasting; whereas, in others, energy intake is not specified, but dietary components are manipulated, ranging from nutritionally balanced to unbalanced energy-restricted diets in addition to an emphasis on specific foods (e.g., the grapefruit diet) that may or may not have any effect at all except a psychological one (Mirkin and Shore 1981).

Any diet that reduces energy intake below energy expenditure should produce a weight loss if it is maintained for a long enough (but safe) time period. Therefore, most diets, if followed, are effective—at least in the short-term. They differ, however, in their risks. Few Americans diet under close supervision of their physicians; people are more likely to adopt popular weight-reducing diets promoted in books or magazines.

Liquid Protein Diets

In the mid 1970s extremely low-energy, predigested liquid protein preparations, consisting of protein (collagen) of low biological value, were developed for over-the-counter sales. Despite the promotional claims for these products, muscle mass was not preserved, and extreme side effects occurred, including 58 deaths among women who had been on the diet for two to three months. The mechanism by which the liquid protein and fasting caused the deaths has been the subject of much speculation and investigation. Deficiencies of potassium, magnesium, sulfur-containing amino acids, copper, and selenium, resulting in possible heart muscle abnormalities, have all been suggested (Lintigua et al. 1980; Klevay 1979, Blackburn, 1978).

In an attempt to develop a regulatory solution to the problem, FDA in August 1984 published new regulations, 21 CFR 101.17(d), requiring warning labels on protein weight reduction products that provide 400 calories or less per day and derive 50% of their calories from protein. The required statement reads: "Warning. Very low calorie protein diets (below 400 calories per day) may cause serious illness or death. Do not use for weight reduction without medical supervision. Use with particular care if you are taking medication. Not for use by infants, children, or pregnant women." Depending on the diet product, other statements also may be required to warn consumers that the products are not designed for use in weight reduction unless taken under medical supervision (Frattali 1984, Broomfield, 1988.) Wadden et al. (1983) reviewed conditions that the physician should be aware of in using these diets.

Improved Low-Energy Diet Products

Several improved forms of low-energy diets providing 300 to 600 kcal have been developed since the 1970s. They contain protein with added vitamins, minerals, and, in some cases, a small amount of carbohydrate. Many physicians consider very low-energy diets to be potentially dangerous and recommend their use only for select patients under close medical supervision. Examples of programs and products in this area would be the Optifast® powder manufactured by Sandoz Nutrition Corporation, Minneapolis, Minnesota, and HMR-500® manufactured by Health Management Resources, Boston, Massachusetts. These products can be obtained only through medically supervised physician-monitored programs. The FDA, American Dietetic Association, American Institute of Nutrition, and pharmaceutical companies are concerned about the unsupervised use of these diets by the general public. A balanced diet that provides a daily energy deficit of 500 to 1,000 kcal/day will allow a recommended weight loss of about 1 to 2 pounds of fat per week. Between 80 and 120% of the Recommended Dietary Allowances (RDAs) for most nutrients can be met by consuming a properly selected diet of 1,200 kcal daily. When the energy intake falls below 1,200 kcal/day, a multiple vitamin and mineral supplement is necessary. An ideal low-energy balanced diet (between 1,000 and 1,200 kcal) should provide 100% of the RDA for vitamins and minerals, at least 100 grams carbohydrates (preferably complex carbohydrate), at least 15 to 25 grams of essential fatty acids, and 0.8 to 1.0 gram of high-quality protein per kilogram of ideal body weight per day. Furthermore, the diet should be economical, convenient to prepare, and compatible with the individual's lifestyle.

LOW-CALORIE/REDUCED-CALORIE FOOD PRODUCTS

Introduction

Every year hundreds of products are developed in the United States that are reduced in fat or calories compared to their standard counterparts. A product can be ''sugar-free'' and not be reduced in calories, as long as the package makes it clear that the item is not intended for weight control. Some products are labeled ''light,'' which may only mean that they have a certain amount of sodium removed or are of a certain color (beer) or density (chips). Despite the existence of some low fat dairy products (skim milk), and the proliferation of a variety of low-fat snacks and low-calorie beverages, researchers continue to be interested in finding ways to substitute for or reduce the caloric value of foods. The reduction of carbohydrates or fat can be accomplished by (1) the addition of water and other ingredients such as gums or thickeners to maintain functional properties and supply the equivalent mouthfeel and taste; or (2) the addition of noncaloric or low-caloric fat or sugar substitutes, such as aspartame (Nutrasweet®), Olestra®, Simplesse®, or other new fat substitutes; (3) the removal of sugars and fat; and (4) a combination of the above methods.

Reduced-Calorie Sweeteners

Fructose and high fructose corn syrup (HFCS) are being used to replace sucrose in many food items because of their higher sweetness per equivalent weight. The amount required for replacement depends on the product and serving temperature. A product with 90% HFCS replacing an equivalent weight of sucrose can be 20% to 60% sweeter than sucrose; so less HFCS can be used. However, fructose is a reducing sugar, whereas sucrose is not. If nonenzymatic browning is not desirable in a product that contains protein, fructose should be limited or avoided.

Aspartame, commercially known as Nutrasweet® (Nutrasweet Co., Chicago), a nutritive sweetener (4 calories/gram) comprised of the methyl ester of aspartic acid and phenylalanine, is approximately 200 times sweeter than sucrose (Dziezak 1986). Its sweetness varies, depending on the food product it is used in; and because of its sweetness intensity, the amount used contributes few to no calories. Unfortunately, a number of technological factors preclude the extremely broad usage of aspartame. Temperature, pH, and moisture conditions are critical to the stability of aspartame, which self-degrades very rapidly. For example, products containing aspartame generally will lose all sweetness when baked or thermally processed. Its stability is best within a pH range of 3 to 5, with optimum stability at pH 5.2. At pH 3.4 and lower, hydrolysis of the dipeptide is observed, and above pH 5.0, cyclization to diketopiperazine (DKP) occurs (Vetsch 1985; Stamp and Labuza 1989). Aspartame also reacts with reducing sugars (as do other proteins) in the presence of heat and moisture. Further, aspartame will not contribute bulk or mouthfeel or lower water activity (inhibit microbiological growth) as sugar would in many solid foods; so it is necessary to use other technologies with aspartame to ensure stability.

Saccharin has 300 to 400 times the sweetness of sucrose, and has been used as a commercial nonnutritive sweetener since 1900 (Dziezak 1986). It has bitter, metallic, and astringent aftertastes and is better accepted in a mixture with aspartame rather than alone (Beck 1980). It is a weak carcinogen, but it has been exempted from being banned in the United States by the Food and Drug Administration by a moratorium passed and extended by Congress (21 CFR 105.66(b)(1)). Aside from its use in conjunction with aspartame in soft drinks, it may be used in tabletop sweeteners, dry beverage blends, canned fruits, gelatin desserts, cooked and instant puddings, salad dressings, jams, jellies, preserves, and baked goods (Dziezak 1986).

Acesulfame-K® (potassium salt of acesulfame) is a noncaloric sweetener with 200 times the sweetening power of sucrose, marketed by Hoechst Celanese Corporation, Somerville, New Jersey, under the Sunette® brand name. In July 1988, FDA approved acesulfame for use in dry foods including chewing gum. FDA approval is pending for use of the sweetener in confections. Hoechst will seek additional FDA approvals for use of the sweetener in liquid products and baked goods (Anonymous 1988b).

Use of the three above-mentioned high-intensity sweeteners is permitted in foods in the United States. Cyclamate, discovered in 1937, has 30 to 60 times the sweetness of sucrose (Dziezak 1986). It is not useful by itself because of an unpleasant aftertaste, whereas a blend with saccharin (10 parts cyclamate to 1 of saccharin) has been very successful. Its use has been prohibited in the United States since September 1970, because of its having been suspected of carcinogenicity and taken off the GRAS list. In 1985 the National Academy of Science/National Research Council concluded that cyclamate was not a carcinogen but may serve as a promoter or co-carcinogen. Testing continues in an effort to define conditions whereby it may be approved in the United States (Lecos 1985), but other countries such as Canada have not banned its use.

Bulking Agents and Fibers

Bulking agents and fibers are ingredients that can be used to lower the caloric content of a food. The concept of providing an ingredient that contains no or low amounts of calories to produce products low in calories is not a new one. In many respects, air and water can be considered bulking agents. During the process of extrusion, air often is used to expand or bulk a product, and water is used as the major ingredient in many products jointly with high-intensity sweeteners to keep the calorie content low.

Polydextrose is classified as a bulking agent with a calorie level of 1 kcal/g. Cooley and Livesey (1987) suggest that its caloric value may be higher than this because of microbiological digestion in the gastrointestinal tract. It can be combined with noncaloric or low-caloric sweeteners to reduce the calorie content by 50% or more, but not to the level of 0.4 kcal/g required to qualify a product as a low-calorie food. It is approved as a multipurpose food additive, whose applications include use in frozen desserts, puddings, baked goods, frostings, hard candies, and soft, chewy candies (Dziezak 1986). Other ingredients that combine sweetness with bulking properties and new bulking agents have been synthesized and are being proposed for approval by the FDA (Anonymous 1988b).

Dietary fiber is a term used to describe the complex carbohydrates and lignin that make up the structure of plant cells. These carbohydrates have diverse properties, but by definition they cannot be digested by human gastrointestinal enzymes. They contribute few or no calories unless acted upon by bacterial action to produce volatile fatty acids, as occurs with pectin (Slavin 1987). In addition to reducing or replacing calories and acting as a bulking agent, different sources of dietary fiber may offer the human body protection from many diet-related diseases, such as coronary heart disease, diabetes, diverticulosis, and cancer (Klurfeld 1987; Anderson 1989).

The technological challenge of adding fiber to a food is complex. Many or most food fiber ingredients have the ability to bind or hold water; therefore, when added to a liquid food system, they increase its viscosity. A fiber with a low water holding capacity (WHC), when added to a beverage system, may result in a gritty texture. Ideally, many fibers could be incorporated into cookies, crackers, granola bars, cereals, or wafers, where their functionality is best utilized, to give "crispness" or additional texture to the food. Examples include most cereal brans and cellulose derivatives. To alleviate the flavor problems with added fiber, aspartame can be utilized, which also replaces carbohydrates or fat to decrease the caloric content so that a double effect occurs. This type of replacement currently is being done by General Mills (Minneapolis) in its high-fiber cereal, Fiber One®, which has only 60 calories per ounce.

Synthetic Fat Replacers

LaBarge (1988) and Gillis (1988) reviewed the major industrial efforts now under way to find appropriate low-calorie or noncaloric substitutes for fats and oils in food products. The two approaches currently receiving the most attention are (1) replacing fat with a combination of water with surface-active lipids or nonlipids (such as modified carbohydrates or proteins), the latter having emulsifying or high-swell gel properties and a lower food energy value; and (2) replacement of fat with noncaloric compounds that have fatlike properties similar to those of ordinary lipids, but whose ester bonds are modified (e.g., glycerol ethers, pseudofats, and carbohydrate fatty acid esters) so as to reduce their biological availability (at least to human gut enzymes).

Efforts focused on potential fat replacements are concentrated on triglyceride analogs, esterified polycarboxylic acids, and polyether analogs that cannot by hydrolyzed by the intestinal lipases. Because of their inability to be digested, they cannot be utilized for calories. One such compound currently under intensive investigation is sucrose polyester, also known as Olestra® (Procter & Gamble, Cincinnati, Ohio). Olestra is a mixture of octa-, hepta-, and hexa-esters of sucrose formed by the reaction of sucrose with long-chain fatty acids. The substance is not metabolized by the body and thus is noncaloric. The company has several use patents, including shortening and oils, margarines, beverages, salted snacks, and low-calorie baked goods (Toma, Curtis, and Sobotor 1988), but has not received FDA approval for the compound.

Another possible fat substitute, Simplesse® recently was developed by the NutraSweet Co. It is produced by microparticulation (reshaping into round particles) of milk and egg proteins. The process produces protein particles that are so small (0.1–2.0 microns) that they are perceived as a fluid with the mouthfeel of fat. Simplesse® contributes 1.3 kcal/g in its equal-weight replacement of fat, thus resulting in a significant calorie reduction. The company petitioned FDA for use of the substitute in salad dressing, mayonnaise, ice cream, yogurt, sour cream dips, and cheese spreads (Best 1988). Like other proteins, this protein is denatured by heat; so it is not currently recommended for use in products that must undergo heat treatment (Altschul 1989). In February 1990, FDA gave approval for its use in frozen dairy-type desserts. Kraft General Foods has announced that it has a similar protein product available for use.

Separation Technology

The separation of fat from foods is probably one of the oldest processing techniques available to reduce the calorie content of a food. Fats contain nine calories per gram, whereas protein and carbohydrates provide four calories per gram. The trimming of fat from the outer portion of a steak is the simplest example of a separation process. Another common separation technique is the centrifugation of milk to produce 2%, 1%, and nonfat milk. Skim milk has a caloric density that is 57% that of whole milk, but the percentage of calories from fat for skim milk is only one-tenth that of whole milk.

The mechanical separation of fat to produce skim milk, which then is introduced into other dairy products to reduce their fat content and caloric density, may have reached a practical limit of application. Further progress in enhancing the acceptance of existing low-fat products and in reducing their fat content even further may depend on the use of mechanical separation in conjunction with another technology such as flavor enhancement, the use of extraction technology (supercritical CO_2) or the addition of nonfat substitutes.

The use of separation technology can be very complex, especially in combination with reformation processing. Surimi (imitation seafood products) processing utilizes these technologies to develop a unique food system especially low in fat (less than 0.1 g/100 g of product). White fish (generally pollack) are skinned, deboned, washed, and rinsed to eliminate fat, blood, and water-soluble proteins, leaving only the muscular protein, which is then cooked to form a gel (called ''kamaboko'' by the Japanese who originally developed the process). In one such imitation food, a small amount of crab meat is mixed with the white fish paste and cryo-protective agents such as sugars. It is then spread into a wide, flat shape, and heated to allow the proteins to interact to form a shellfish-like texture. After it has cooled, the material is cut into thin strips, which then are wrapped in an edible cellulosic film containing a reddish coloring to simulate crab pigment. The product is vacuum-packed and then flash-frozen (Lee 1986). It should be noted that surimi is labeled ''imitation'' because it contains lower amounts of protein (by more than 2%) compared to its counterpart; adding non-fish protein would remove this pejorative label, but would interfere with the proper setting of the texture. More research is needed in this area.

The concept of simply not adding oil or a carbohydrate to lower calories sounds easy but often is not. Canned tuna, salmon, and sardines packed in water are examples of not adding oil. The replacement of oil with water changes the heat penetration rate during the sterilization process (Ababouch and Busta 1987). Oil decreases the conductivity and increases the resistance to heat. Therefore, a new process must be developed and optimized for such products for maximum quality and flavor. The same would apply to canned fruits packed in water or their own juice versus heavy syrup.

Portion Control

Sales of gourmet of ''good-tasting'' calorie-controlled entrees in the frozen market have increased in recent years (Schmidl 1985). Basically, the serving size is decreased, and spices are added to enhance appearance, mouthfeel, and flavor. Frozen or shelf-stable complete meals contribute to dieting in two ways:

they provide portion control—the amount available to be eaten is controlled by the size of the package—and they can have a lower fat content than that normally achieved by cooking at home (Altschul 1989). For persons trying to control their intake, these meals appear to be useful tools (Berkowitz, Agras, and Arnow 1989). For purposes of reducing fat intake, a complete meal should have as low a fat content as is consistent with its being palatable.

Emulsion Technology

Development of reduced-calorie mayonnaise, margarines, salad dressings, mousses, and whipped toppings is based on emulsion technology and the addition of unique functional ingredients. For low-calorie salad dressings, modified food starches and gums, such as xanthan and carrageenan, are used to impart a fatlike mouthfeel and viscosity, to suspend spices and flavor, and to replace the calories normally contributed by the oil. More recently, very low dextrose equivalent maltodextrins have been suggested as replacements for the oils in margarines and salad dressings. As noted earlier, micro-particulated protein also is being evaluated for this function.

In recent years, reduced-calorie margarine has become more popular. The fat content has been decreased, in some cases, from 80% (minimum amount of fat permitted in margarine) to 40% fat and 60% water. Usually these margarines do not contain milk or the proteins that would enhance microbial spoilage due to increased water activity. Most have added sorbates and benzoates to prevent spoilage from some organisms, especially molds, which can grow on fatty emulsions. Some products also contain hydrocolloids as stabilizers, as well as BHA and BHT as antioxidants. Reduced-calorie margarines are not as good as other margarines for frying, as they contain too much water, which causes spattering (Schmidl and Labuza 1985).

Lower-calorie whipped toppings and "lite mousses" obtain their structure and smooth texture by the use of unique functional proteins such as whey, sodium caseinate, modified soy proteins, and vegetable gums. Monoglycerides, acetylated or lactylated monoglycerides, hydroxylated lecithin, and polysorbate esters are the most common emulsifiers used to achieve the desired texture. Aspartame and artificial flavors also can be added to improve palatability. Citrates and phosphates may be used to aid in protein stabilization.

Future Needs

To continue to meet the needs of the consumer for lite, reduced-, or low-calorie foods, much research still is needed. Examples of these needs are: (1) fibers that contribute positive health benefits, but no negative physiological, textural, or flavor characteristics; (2) advanced technologies to remove fats and cholesterol from animal and vegetable foods (such as supercritical CO_2 extraction); (3) new or improved safe sweeteners that are economical, are not carcinogenic, impart sweetness in all food systems, and are stable throughout processing and storage; and (4) edible oils and fats that are functional in food systems, contain few (or no) calories, and do not interfere with absorption of other dietary nutrients.

CLINICAL NUTRITION PRODUCTS

Introduction

Nutritional products used in hospital and nursing-home settings have become an important aid to the medical profession. Because a wide variety of products could be made, some standards have been created. For example, the American Society for Parenteral and Enteral Nutrition (ASPEN) has published standards for the food systems used for hospitalized pediatric patients (Anonymous 1989). Developments in the field are due to advances that have occurred in three areas (Bistrian and Jaksic 1989). First, a growing knowledge of human physiology and biochemistry has resulted in a fairly comprehensive understanding of the nutritional requirements of health versus those of the disease state, as well as of certain in-born errors of metabolism (Levy 1989). Second, new food technologies and an understanding of physical chemical principles such as emulsion and surface chemistry have been applied to the development of specialized infusion solutions and specialized food products containing various nutrients. Third, there has been considerable improvement in surgical techniques and medical devices for the intravenous administration and tube feeding of parenteral and enteral products (Shenkin and Wretlind 1978; Bistrian and Jaksic 1989, Dudrick, 1972).

A key to understanding the development of nutritional products for clinical use is to recognize that the nutritional and physiological requirements of a hospitalized patient generally are fairly different from those of the average, healthy individual. For example, (1) patients usually have an increased need for calories (Kinney 1976); (2) patients usually have an increased need for protein as a result of trauma or sepsis (Bistrian et al. 1974); (3) patients with a disease of, resections of, or obstructions of the gastrointestinal tract will have a decreased ability to absorb nutrients; (4) hospitalized patients lack mobility, which can affect the biochemical requirements for specific nutrients such as calcium; and (5) patients may have a disease or malfunction of the food/nutrient processing organs (e.g., stomach, intestine, liver, pancreas, or kidney), which can greatly alter nutritional requirements. Even though the basic principles of supplying nutrients to the hospitalized patient now are firmly established, there still are many problem areas that await solution through future research.

Oral Feeding Products

Historical Development

The recent evolution of enteral (oral) feedings—either by normal mouth feeding or by nasal/oral tube feeding (gavage)—as a nutritional intervention tool has been dramatic. Liquid systems that are available for these oral diets allow the physician to support nearly every patient need. They range from palatable supplements to special formulations designed to manipulate metabolism at a biochemical level.

To some physicians, the products utilized in enteral feeding represent a blending of common foodstuffs that must have evolved from the work of hospital dietitians; but such an assumption is far from reality. In fact, perhaps the most useful formulas, those of an "elemental" nature, are spinoffs of the NASA program (Winitz et al. 1965).

Of particular importance to those involved with the medical and nutritional concerns of the first U.S. astronauts were considerations related to elimination of the human waste products of astronauts confined to the small capsule. Urine, unlike fecal material, presents few problems. A potential solution to the fecal waste problem arose from two sources: emerging studies demonstrating nearly complete absorption of nutrients from the first portion of the jejunum, and ongoing investigations conducted by the National Cancer Institute (NCI) relative to the effect of crystalline amino acid diets on cell growth (Borgstrom et al. 1957; Greenstein et al. 1957). For researchers involved with solving the astronauts' problems, an obvious way to deal with bowel movements was to remove the need for them. The goal was to deliver a nutrient solution to the jejunum that would not require digestion and would be completely absorbed in the upper gastrointestinal tract. If nothing ever reached the colon, there would be no need for bowel movements. The formulation would be "elemental," e.g., simple amino acids and sugars and essential micronutrients, with absolutely no residue.

One of the most difficult problems was that amino acids were not readily available in crystalline form at that time. However, J. P. Greenstein from NCI had considerable experience and interest in this area and agreed to work with the NASA contractors to help get amino acids prepared (Greenstein et al. 1957). The final result was a concentrated solution (2,200 mOsm/L) a liter of which could supply all the protein nitrogen needs for an astronaut for nearly a month (Winitz et al. 1965). Unfortunately, the ability of the gut to handle hyperosmolar loads was not well understood at that time. Initial administration of the solution to volunteers resulted in explosive diarrhea and vomiting, symptoms also experienced by the astronauts. These effects eliminated the use of elemental diets in space travel; however, the clinical applications of a nutrient solution that required absolutely no digestion and only a few inches of jejunum for absorption were recognized. A hospitalized patient who did not have a pancreatic exocrine function, bile acids, ileum, colon, and so on, still could absorb nutrients if they were in the simplest form. The doctor could feed above or below a fistula, inflamed bowel, obstructed pancreatic and bile ducts, and other pathologic states. One major application could use with the short bowel syndrome. In fact, one of the early studies was entitled "Use of the 'Space Diet' in the Management of a Patient with Extreme Short Bowel Syndrome" (Thompson et al. 1969). Diets currently available include not only this first effort (Vivonex®, Norwich-Eaton, Norwich, New York), but also a multitude of other products that provide the physician with the tools required to treat nearly all patients (Table 12-3) in need of calories, proteins, carbohydrates, fats, vitamins, and minerals.

Types of Enteral Products

There are many types of processed enteral food products (Schmidl, Massaro, and Labuza 1988). Classifications vary, but on the basis of composition, they include elemental, blenderized, milk-based, lactose-free, chemically defined, special-formulation, supplemental, and modular products (Mountford and Cristol 1989). Dorf (1989) recently reviewed those products available for tube-feeding the young child. To develop these products properly, one needs to have not only knowledge of nutritional requirements and clinical nutrition, but also a great depth of knowledge in the areas of thermal processing, emulsion technology, spray drying, and agglomeration (instantizing technology). Table 12-4 compares some complete nutritional products on the basis of calories.

Table 12-3. Clinical problems for which defined-formula diets may be appropriate.

Inborn errors of metabolism	Hypermetabolic states
Phenylketonurics	Severe trauma
Maple syrup urine disease	Major burns
Gastrointestinal disease	Incidental uses
Ulcerative colitis	Preoperative bowel preparation
Granulomatous bowel disease	Nonallergenic food source
Chronic partial obstruction	Food supplement
Malabsorption syndromes	Toilet management problems
Short bowel syndrome	Protection of bowel mucosa against
Infantile diarrhea	damaging agents
Fistulas	Feeding of premature infants
Pancreatitis	Feeding of anorexic patients
Renal failure	

Adapted from Shils, Bloch, and Chernoff (1976).

Table 12-4.   Clinical nutritional products comparison per 1,000 kilocalories.

	Compleat B® (Sandoz)	Sustacal + Milk® (Mead Johnson)	Ensure® (Ross)	Precision® Isotonic Powder (Sandoz)
Protein				
g	40.0	60.3	35.0	30.0
source	Beef	Nonfat milk	Na and Ca caseinate 30.6 g Soy protein 38.4 g	Egg white solids
Fat				
g	40.0	24.4	35.0	31.3 Vegetable oil
source	Corn oil	Milk fat	Corn oil	Mono–di-glycerides
Carbohydrate				
total g.	120.0	134.4	136.7	150.0
source	Sucrose 23 g Maltodextrin 73.4 g Vegetables Fruits Orange juice Lactose 24.4 g	Sucrose 36.2 g Corn syrup solids 11.8 g Lactose 85.8 g	Corn syrup solids 98.3 g Sucrose 38.4 g	Maltodextrin sugars
Minerals				
Calcium, mg	625.0	1,611.2	500	667
Phosphorus, mg	1,687.5	1,333.4	500	667
Magnesium, mg	250.0	375.0	200	266
Iron, mg	11.3	16.7	9	12
Iodine, mcg	93.8	138.9	75	100
Copper, mg	1.3	1.9	1	1.3
Manganese, mg	2.5	2.8	2	2.7
Zinc, mg	9.4	13.9	15	10
Sodium, mEq	67.9	40.2	30.4	34.8
Potassium, mEq	33.7	64.8	30.8	25.6
Chloride, mEq	22.9	37.6	28.2	30.1
Volume for 100% RDAs	1,600 ml	NA	1920 ml	1,560 ml
Volume to give 1,000 cal	1,000 ml	NA	1960 ml	1,042 ml
mOsm/kg	490	756	450	300

Adapted from Shils et al., 1976.

Elemental Diets.   An elemental diet can be defined as a formula that delivers to the intestinal absorptive surface a complete mix of nutrients that can be absorbed with little or no additional activity required of the gut and appended organs. To date, only a few products meet these criteria. They are primarily composed of simple sugars and crystalline L-amino acids (e.g., Vivonex®, Norwich-Eaton, Norwich, New York, and Stresstein®, Sandoz Nutrition). One product (Vital®, Ross Laboratories, Columbus, Ohio) contains crystalline amino acids as well as di- and tripeptides. There is some evidence in the literature that these short peptides are absorbed by transport mechanisms different from those for single amino acids (Mathews and Adibi 1976). The advantage is that the increased rate of absorption of peptides can lead to an improved nitrogen balance. The optimal amino acid compositions in these formulas have yet to be thoroughly confirmed.

The main advantage of elemental diets is that virtually no digestion is necessary. It is most likely that these diets result in minimal stimulation of the pancreatic, biliary, and small intestinal secretions. This allows the diet to be used in conditions such as pancreatitis and gastrointestinal fistulas, and where bowel rest is desired. In addition, these diets are nonallergenic and thus are potentially useful in cases of food allergies. The disadvantages of these formulas are similar to those of chemically defined formulas, which also are expensive. Some elemental diets may cost ten times as much as intact protein diets. These formulas also can create osmolar complications that, along with generally poor taste, result in poor oral acceptance by patients.

Blenderized diets.   Blenderized formulas are created by mixing various foods together and blending them at high shear rates to form a liquid slurry. The commercial formulas are nutritionally complete, contain proteins (usually meat or milk proteins), have moderate to high residue levels (contain natural fiber sources), and are thermally processed for stability. A blenderized diet is appropriate for the patient who has an anatomically intact and functionally sound intestinal tract but who also finds it difficult to swallow food. Examples of these products are Compleat® and Compleat Modified® produced by Sandoz Nutrition (Table 12-4) and Vitaneed®, produced by Sherwood Medical (Buena Park, California).

The advantages of these products are that they generally contain all known essential vitamins and minerals, trace elements, and micronutrients, and they should usually restore or maintain normal bowel movements. Disadvantages include: (1) the requirement for bowel movements; (2) the high viscosity, which makes passage through small feeding tubes difficult when gravity feed is used; (3) a need for complete digestive capabilities; (4) potential thermally induced reactions between the components during processing; (5) loss of some nutrients during storage because of chemical reactions such as NEB and ascorbic acid–induced reactions; and, in some cases, (6) the high lactose content if milk is used. As noted, the thermal processing of the blend to produce a shelf-stable sterile product can result in significant chemical reactions and off-flavor development. Research using high-temperature/short-time (HTST) or ultra-high-temperature (UHT) methods would be recommended and should improve overall quality. Research also is needed on the stability of the nutrients during distribution. The availability of natural ingredients has improved over the years, but seasonal variation in the composition of the ingredients must be closely monitored by the process manufacturer to ensure control over the nutrient content.

Milk-based enteral products. There are a wide variety of milk-based products (which contain lactose because of their milk base). Most are nutritionally complete products with a generous amount of protein, and they are most useful as an oral nutritional supplement for patients who for many reasons have difficulty in meeting their full nutritional requirements through normal oral intake. Meritene® (Sandoz Nutrition) and Sustacal® (Mead-Johnson, Evansville, Indiana (Table 12-4)) are products of this nature that have been on the market for more than 50 years. They come in powder form or as a liquid that is retorted to create a shelf-stable sterile product. The liquid Meritene® product is provided as a liquid in an aseptic flexible package. Hydrogen peroxide is used to sterilize the packaging material (Tetra-Pak, Lund, Sweden) prior to filling of the sterile liquid. This product is being made for use in Canada (Schmidl et al. 1988). This type of packaging system makes for a less expensive, lighter-weight container than the common can, and it also occupies less space on the hospital storage shelf when compared to a liquid canned product. In addition, the low-viscosity milk base lends itself to HTST processing, whereas there is more concern for the sterilization of viscous slurries in blenderized food products because they require more thermal processing, which can degrade the flavor and the nutritional components.

There are many advantages to using these products, including excellent taste as compared to the blenderized food products. They are well accepted by patients for oral supplemental use and also are relatively inexpensive. The chief disadvantage is that they contain lactose. Frequently, the critically ill patient begins to develop dysfunction due to lactase deficiency secondary to brush border atrophy and/or damage. In many cases, the classic symptoms of lactose intolerance, including diarrhea, abdominal bloating, and cramping, often are confused with more serious or unresolved pathologic states. Failure to recognize the true nature of the complaints will result in an unnecessary delay in implementation of the metabolic support process by changing the formula.

Lactose-free. Lactose-free formulas are most often the "ideal" tube-feeding formulas, as they are nutritionally complete products, are low in cost, create few osmolality problems, contain no lactose, and offer a broad range of choices relative to protein source, fat, and carbohydrate content. Most of these products, such as Liquid Ensure® (Ross Laboratories (Table 12-4)) or Liquid Resource® (Sandoz Nutrition), have been designed specifically for tube feeding and have added flavors. The major protein source includes sodium and calcium caseinate and soy protein isolate. Some products also are designed to be isotonic (300–330 mOsm/kg) and thus may be more easily tolerated by certain patient populations. Products such as Ensure Plus® (Ross Laboratories), Resource Plus® (Sandoz Nutrition), and Magnacal® (Sherwood Medical), which are higher in osmolality than other formulas in this group, are more calorically dense, with 1.5 and 2.0 kcal/mL, respectively; hence, more nutrition can be provided in less fluid volume. This is accomplished through the addition of more fat and less water to these formulas. All of these products come in retorted containers. The containers may be steel cans, Tetra-Pak (aseptic boxes), or, more recently, polypropylene multilaminate spikeable (they can receive spike administration sets) containers (known as Closed System Containers). The Closed System Container (spike and hang bottle) usually comes in a 1,000-mL size and can be used for tube feeding simply by using a piercing spike connected to the proper tubing to feed the patient.

There are very few specific disadvantages of these products; however, caution must be maintained in using the more calorically dense formulas because their high osmolarity without additional free water may lead to the development of the hyperosmolar syndrome, a precursor of the dumping syndrome that can lead to an electrolyte imbalance.

Chemically defined formulas. Chemically defined products are formulations that use purified ingredients but are not totally elemental. They require a minimum amount of digestion. For example, the powdered protein products usually contain egg albumin and require pancreatic enzyme activity prior to absorption to digest the protein into the absorbable amino acids. Generally, these products are high in carbohydrates but vary in protein content, and many are low in fat content. Most, if not all, are virtually fiber-free. The low fat content makes them suitable for conditions associated with fat malabsorption. The advantages of these products are that they can be used under conditions in which only minimal digestion is possible, and, because of their low fat content, due to lack of lipase for digestion by the patient, they can be used as a supplement when the patient is on a clear liquid diet. The disadvantages are that they are more expensive than previously mentioned diets; they can create osmolar complications, as they are relatively high in osmolarity (600 mOsm/kg), and they generally have poor taste, resulting in poor acceptance by patients if they are administered by mouth. These products generally are produced as a blended dry powder that requires reconstitution in cold water prior to use. Generally they have a caloric density of 1 cal/mL (Schmidl et al. 1988).

Specialized diets—disease-specific. This category includes products designed for specific organ failure such as kidney or liver failure, hereditary disease, or other disease-specific disorders. Renal-failure products usually contain only essential amino acids, thus limiting the delivery of nonessential nitrogen while supporting anabolism and limiting catabolism. They must contain histidine, which is essential in treating renal failure because of the body's inability to synthesize this amino acid. They are calorically dense (2 cal/mL) and are essentially free of sodium and potassium because these electrolytes depend on the kidney for their removal from the body.

Stress formulas (e.g., Stresstein BCAA®, Sandoz Nutrition) used for mul-

Stress formulas (e.g., Stresstein BCAA®, Sandoz Nutrition) used for multiple-trauma and burn patients contain high levels of branched-chain amino acids (BCAAs) such as leucine, isoleucine, and valine as their nitrogen source. The mechanism by which these amino acids function physiologically is not known. One general explanation is that, under normal nutritional and physiological conditions, fuel requirements of the peripheral tissues largely are met by glucose and fatty acids. Amino acids generally contribute little toward overall fuel economy at these times. However, during those abnormal metabolic states induced by trauma or sepsis, fat mobilization and utilization and glucose utilization are decreased as a result of hormonal changes precipitated by the disease. Under these conditions, BCAAs derived from muscle protein catabolism become an important and significant potential source of fuel. When the BCAA undergoes deamination, the free amino group is transaminated into other organic precursors, yielding alanine and glutamine (Cerra et al. 1983). The alanine is released from the muscle and is transported to the liver, where it is taken up and rapidly converted to glucose by the associated gluconeogenic metabolic pathways. Additionally, the oxidative decarboxylation of the ketoacids to form thioesters of coenzyme A allows this organic moiety to be readily utilized by the tricarboxylic acid cycle for energy in the muscle cells (Freund et al. 1979; Echenique et al. 1984; Blackburn et al. 1979).

Additionally, there are formulations for specific disease states caused by genetic defects, such as phenylketonuria (PKU) and maple syrup urine disease (MSUD) (Levy 1989; Dorf 1989). There also are formulas that increase the calories from fat to reduce the respiratory quotient (RQ), important for those with respiratory distress. Impact® (Sandoz Nutrition) is a unique ready-to-use enteral formula enriched with arginine, ribonucleic acid, and fish oils. It has been shown that supplemental dietary arginine strongly stimulates lymphocyte reactivity in healthy humans and in surgical patients. More recently, supplemental arginine has been shown to increase the T-lymphocyte response to mitogens in cancer patients (Daly et al. 1988).

Of additional interest is recent work showing that when ribonucleic acids (RNA) are added to the diet, they appear to be vital to the maintenance of normal cellular immunity and act to increase host resistance. Additionally, nucleotide-supplemented diets fed to mice have demonstrated an improved ability of macrophages to fight bacterial infection compared with mice fed a nucleotide-free diet (Carver, Cox, and Barness 1990). Finally, fish oil high in eicosapentaenoic acid (EPA) and docosahexanenoic acid (DHA) along with a decrease of linoleic acid may be beneficial due to lack of suppression of the immune system (Alexander et al. 1986).

High-Calorie Fat Emulsion Products

Many patients have an increased caloric requirement because of their condition (e.g., burn, sepsis), so that there is a need for high-energy liquid enteral and parenteral products. Because of the osmotic limitation of sugars, either in the gut or when supplied directly into the bloodstream, it becomes necessary for the energy source to be comprised of fat. In some cases, up to 50% of the calories may come from fat (e.g., respiratory stress patients). Therefore, many products require emulsion technology for their development.

It should be noted that it is easy to form an emulsion in a commercial homogenizer, given the proper ingredients, but that during storage, physical changes in the dispersed fat or oil droplets can take place, with subsequent disruption of the emulsion through creaming, flocculation, and coalescence. The creaming phenomenon involves the flotation or sedimentation of dispersed emulsified droplets, eventually changing the system into two emulsion layers, one richer in fat (top layer) and the other poorer (lower phase). Creaming is dependent on: the density difference between the continuous and dispersed phases; the viscosity of the continuous phase, which unfortunately cannot be very high if the product is to be gravity-fed; and the droplet size, which in the case of an intravenous product must be one micron or less in diameter, the same size as chylomicrons, so that the fat particle will be recognized by lipoprotein lipase in the bloodstream and metabolized by the body (Hallberg 1965). For direct feeding, especially for patients with pulmonary problems, the stabilization of the fat emulsion also is critical, as stress can occur if the fat is not delivered to the gut in the proper proportion.

The velocity, V, of creaming (separating out of the droplets) can be expressed by Stokes' law (Sherman 1968):

$$V = \frac{2 g_c r^2}{9\eta} \left[\rho_{con} - \rho_{dis} \right]$$

where:

V = velocity of separation
g_c = gravitational constant
r = radius of droplet
η = viscosity of continuous phase
ρ_{con} = density of continuous phase
ρ_{dis} = density of dispersed phase (oil)

Flocculation is the agglomeration of droplets to form loose and irregular clusters. Because flocculation increases the effective droplet size (i.e., radius), the rate of creaming also increases in proportion to the square of the droplet size. Generally, agglomerated droplets can be redispersed by mixing or shaking (adding energy), as weak interdroplet (van der Waals) forces are responsible for flocculation.

Coalescence, the irreversible union of small droplets to yield larger ones, can occur after flocculation if the stabilizing interfacial film of emulsifying agent(s) is ruptured. Coalescence is a kinetically spontaneous process because of a lower total surface free energy when two particles combine into one. This ultimately leads to separation of the two phases into two distinct layers because as the radius (r) increases, the creaming rate increases. The rate of coalescence is governed by the resistance of the emulsifier interfacial layer to shear and distortion, which may arise during agitation or freezing of the emulsion. Hence, fat emulsions are sterilized by using slow agitation, and the product label copy usually states "Do Not Freeze." Emulsions can be stabilized against creaming, flocculation, and coalescence by introducing a strong interfacial film around each droplet, adding electric charges to the droplet surfaces, and increasing the viscosity of the continuous phase. Examples of emulsifiers used include unhydroxylated and hydroxylated lecithins, polyglycerol esters, polysorbates, and mono- and diglycerides, some of which cannot be used for intravenous feeding. It should be noted that sterile liquid formulas that supply total nutritional needs (TPN or Total Parenteral Nutrition products) and contain fat are now available, and they have kept people alive for over three years when used as the sole nutrient source.

Nonenzymatic Browning

Another technological hurdle to consider with these as well as some of the previously mentioned products is the Maillard browning reaction (Labuza and Schmidl 1986). The Maillard reaction, or nonenzymatic browning (NEB), an irreversible reaction between reducing sugars and proteins or amino acids, is difficult to control in many liquid food systems because of the high concentrations of reactive compounds present (i.e., free amino acids and reducing sugars). The concentrations of amino acids and glucose cannot be diluted to prevent or slow browning because of nutritional and caloric requirements. It is of great importance that from 20 to 40% of the essential amino acids can be lost in storage because of the browning reaction, thus increasing the need for extra fortification (Kaanane and Labuza 1989). Methods to control browning are still under major investigation, including the use of sulfites and cysteine (Labuza and Massaro 1990). The presence of Maillard reaction products in solutions also leads to questions about the ultimate fate of these compounds in the body after oral or intravenous administration. Little is known about the potential toxicity of Maillard compounds although there is evidence for carcinogenicity and their role in atherosclerosis (Baynes 1989), as well as the problem of increased zinc excretion if fed intravenously (Stegink et al. 1981).

INFANT FORMULA DIETARY FOODS

Introduction

The key textbook covering general aspects and problems of infant nutrition has recently been revised (Ledenthal 1989). The ideal food for infants is human milk, and until the twentieth century, there was virtually no safe and reliable alternative to breast feeding. In the late 1800s, survival rates for hospitalized infants who did not have access to human milk were lower than 20% (Anderson, Chernin, and Fisher 1982). As the understanding of the nutritional requirements of infants increased, various infant feeding preparations were formulated. The need to modify the composition and to heat-treat cow's milk plus the appearance of sanitary standards for milk handling were key aspects of the development of alternate feeding methods in the late nineteenth century (Sarrett 1981).

Human milk is the ideal model for infant formulas. To evaluate the performance of infant formulas against human milk, one must understand how the evaluation is made. The following criteria have been used to evaluate the suitability of nutritional products for infants: (1) infant growth rate as evidenced by weight, length, and head circumference; (2) composition of formula (comparison of nutrient levels); and (3) performance of the formula during feeding (evaluation of bioavailability). The use of modern infant formulas can result in infant growth rates similar to those achieved with human milk. Because of recent nutritional guidelines and regulatory requirements (AAP 1976; FDA 1982, 21 CFR Part 106) all such formulas must meet certain minimum compositional standards. As advances are made in knowledge of the effects of product formulation and processing on the bioavailability of nutrients, the development scientist can work more closely with the nutritionist and clinician to design infant products with even greater improvements.

Regulations

Infant formulas are designed to meet specific nutritional needs; however, all infant formulas must meet certain nutritional minimums unless specifically exempted from coverage under the Infant Formula Act (U.S. Congress 1980). The Food and Drug Administration also is responsible for administration of the infant formula regulations (FDA 1982). These regulations specify certain minimum testing requirements and good manufacturing practices that must be met prior to product distribution (21 CFR Part 106) along with the nutritional requirements based on the infant U.S. RDAs. Generally, after a new infant formula has been clinically tested and the complete composition confirmed during the start-up of manufacturing, the manufacturer must continue to ensure that each subsequent batch of product meets compositional specifications, by (1) testing each batch for the full label claim and/or (2) verifying the addition of certain vitamins and minerals via validated premix systems. It is safe to say that the industrial, government, and academic involvement in the nutritional analysis of infant formulas cannot be matched by the effort put into any other food product (AOAC 1985).

Infant Formulas—Current Practices

Introduction

Current infant formulas, which are available as either dry powders, sterile liquids, or sterile concentrates, are significantly different in composition from cow's milk, which, by itself, may be inappropriate for feeding infants. Modern formulas have been modified to provide all of the nutrients known to be required by the infant, at levels that support growth and development similar to that shown by infants fed human milk. They provide well-absorbable protein and fat ingredients plus adequate vitamins and minerals, and they simulate the low-protein, low-electrolyte, low-solute content of breast milk (Sarrett 1981). Early infant formulas used skim milk, which was diluted with water to achieve the proper protein and electrolyte concentrations, and carbohydrate and fat, which were added back to maintain adequate caloric levels (typically, 0.67 kcal/mL).

Manufacturing Process

The preparation of a sterilized concentrated infant formula and other nutritional liquid diets may be achieved in the following manner: (a) The following ingredients are blended into water at 60°C: lactose, nonfat dry milk, lipids (usually a blend of soybean and coconut oils), carrageenan, trace minerals, and vitamins to yield a final composition in 72 g/L of fat, 145 g/L of carbohydrate, and 31 g/L of protein. (b) The mix is homogenized at 70°C, first at 70 kg/cm^2 and then at 280 kg/cm^2. (c) The mix is cooled to 5°C. (d) The product is placed into containers and hermetically sealed, and then is thermally processed for 12.1 minutes at 121°C or the equivalent. Instead of thermal processing, the mix can be pasteurized and then spray-dried and agglomerated into a readily water-soluble powder. The liquid product is mixed with an equal volume of water for infant feeding (Rowley and Richardson 1985). Today, depending upon the special requirements of the growing infant, specialized protein, fat, and carbohydrate systems may be employed. Additionally, vitamin and mineral fortifications will depend upon the specific nutritional needs of the infant and the need to maintain minimum levels throughout product shelf life.

An infant formula designed for infants can use many ingredients, examples of which are listed in Table 12-5. In the United States, liquid infant formulas (ready to feed and concentrates) are much more popular than are the powdered products, primarily because of their convenience. Conversely, in the world market, the powdered products predominate because of the extra shipping costs involved with the liquid products. Many of the same formulation and processing considerations affecting the physical characteristics of the liquids also affect the powdered product characteristics, as do the final spray-drying conditions.

Table 12-5. Specific ingredients used in infant formulas.

Sources	Ingredient
Nitrogen	Milk protein, sodium caseinate, calcium caseinate, protein hydrolyzates from whey or caseinates, crystalline amino acids, whey proteins.
Carbohydrates	Lactose, sucrose, maltodextrins, carrageenan.
Fat	Coconut oil, soybean oils, medium chain triglycerides, soy lecithin, mono- and diglycerides.
Minerals	Calcium phosphate tribasic, potassium citrate, sodium citrate, magnesium chloride, calcium carbonate, potassium chloride, zinc sulfate, ferrous sulfate, cupric sulfate, manganese sulfate.
Vitamins	Ascorbic acid, niacinamide, choline chloride, m-inositol, alpha-tocopheryl acetate, calcium pantothenate, riboflavin, vitamin A palmitate, thiamine chloride hydrochloride, pyridoxine hydrochloride, biotin, folic acid, phylloquionone, vitamin D_3, cyanocobalamin.
Others	Ribonucleic acids, flavors.

Developments in Infant Formulas

In the past five years many novel (but possibly essential) nutrients have been used to fortify infant formula products. These compounds include carnitine, taurine, and ribonucleic acids. Carnitine's daily requirement is unknown for all mammalian species including humans; it is synthesized in the liver from the essential amino acids lysine and methionine. Although it had always been assumed that individuals eating a diet containing sufficient levels of the essential amino acids would synthesize adequate amounts of carnitine, it has recently become apparent that there are individuals with a systemic carnitine deficiency. It has been found that during the normal development of the newborn rat, there is an increase in the carnitine concentration of plasma, cardiac muscle, and skeletal muscle. It also has been shown that at least a portion of the carnitine in the newborn rat comes from the mother's milk. It is not known if the newborn infant liver is capable of synthesizing carnitine from lysine and methionine if dietary carnitine is not provided. Because all the long-chain fatty acids supplied in the diet must be transported into the mitochondria via the carnitine system before they can be oxidized to produce energy, adequate tissue carnitine levels are essential for these individuals. Even if the diet contains adequate levels of lysine and methionine, the liver of an infant may have experienced impairment of the carnitine biosynthetic machinery, and thus the patient may suffer from carnitine deficiency. Therefore, in recent years infant formulas have been fortified with this nutrient (FASEB 1983 and Fritz 1959).

The precise biological role of taurine is unknown apart from its conjugation with bile acids and xenobiotics. Evidence is accumulating, however, that taurine may have a more general biological role in development and membrane stability. Furthermore, there is a dietary requirement for taurine in the human infant, which is suggested because of the low plasma taurine concentration levels found in infants fed formulas (non-taurine-fortified) versus those infants fed human milk (Gaull 1982). Hayes, Stephan, and Sturman (1980) suggest that taurine is difficult for infants to synthesize because their enzymatic pathways are not yet completed. It also has been shown that carnitine has a favorable effect on carbohydrate metabolism.

Infants fed nucleotide-fortified formulas demonstrated increased bifidobacteria levels and decreased levels of enterobacteria (Gil et al. 1986). Exogenous nucleotides have been reported to help produce long-chain polyunsaturated fatty acids to be integrated into the nervous system development and help maintain high levels of high density lipoproteins. The development of immunoglobulins to be added to infant formulas is the next step for this dynamic field (Fomon and Ziegler 1989).

FOODS FOR THE ELDERLY

Introduction

In the past, the elderly received little attention as a target population for specialized food products, but the situation has changed in the past few decades with the increased numbers in the elderly population. Effective medical care and the prevention of childhood and other infectious diseases have extended life expectancy and left the chronic diseases usually associated with old age (cancer, cardiovascular diseases, and cerebrovascular diseases) as the major cause of death.

As a matter of convenience, the elderly may be defined as persons 65 years old and over, which is the period in life when most are "retired," and major alterations in lifestyle occur. In addition, many physiological functions slow down at this time. For example, basal metabolic rate, heart output, lung capacity, nerve conduction, and many other functions drop noticeably over the later decades in life (Shock 1962). In spite of these changes, eating habits and often the amount of food eaten do not change significantly, contributing to obesity.

Social and phychological factors can alter lifestyles and, ultimately, dietary habits. For example, economic pressures often increase as a result of lower income during retirement. Living alone often changes eating habits, and lack of motivation in preparing regular meals is common. Living arrangements are critical for the elderly. Many live independent lives without assistance from others; some are healthy; some are bedridden or institutionalized. Other considerations are anxiety and depression that may result from pressures of everyday living that are unique to the elderly. All these factors can seriously influence the elderly person's dietary intake, wants, and needs (Roe 1983).

Like most of the U.S. population, the elderly are becoming better motivated to maintain good health. They are especially conscious of health because of the debilitating aspects of aging and the associated medical costs. Today close to 19% of the U.S. population is "retired," and this percentage is increasing as a result of improved medical care, a better food supply, and a better understanding of diet over the past decades (IFT, 1986). Thus, consideration of the relationship of diet to disease is essential (e.g., saturated fats and atherosclerosis, sodium and hypertension, low fiber and cancer, dairy products and lactose intolerance). Recent work on the consequences of the consumption of Maillard reaction products as well as oxidized lipids on aging suggests that significant work on controlling these reactions in any food is critical (Baynes 1989).

Anticipating an ever increasing elderly population and increasing societal awareness of the needs of the maturing American, the food industry has a role in meeting the nutritional needs and wants of this population group. A particular concern is that the increased taste and odor threshold of the elderly must be taken into account in producing appealing and tasteful foods for this group (Schiffman 1984). This must be done without increasing the sodium burden or adding excess sweeteners, which would only increase unwanted calories. To maintain laxation, a higher fiber content also is desirable in foods for the elderly (Shock 1962).

Special Products

Product opportunities abound in several categories. Examples of products for older people with heart disease include low-salt bread and crackers; low-fat, low-salt cheeses; low-fat meats; and low-salt soups. Products directed toward the problem of obesity include reduced-calorie desserts and nutrient-dense foods. On the other hand, because loss of body mass occurs in many elderly people, high-caloric supplements also are needed. High-fiber foods can help control constipation. Osteoporosis can be addressed through calcium in orange juice and vitamin D–fortified foods, and lactose-free dairy products can address the problem of lactose intolerance. Dwyer (1989) has recently reviewed the nutritional approaches to cancer treatment of the elderly. The product ideas suggested here are certainly not a complete list, and many new products will appear in the future.

FRONTIERS

A broad range of food products have been produced by various food technologies for use in the nutrition/health care arena. By understanding the basic principles of formulation, food processing, and clinical nutrition, researchers can utilize these modalities to prevent the wastage of body mass, to help to prevent, control, and/or alleviate acute and chronic disease conditions, and to provide proper nutrition to most population groups. Food technologists should be aware of the challenging frontiers in this area, knowing that someday they may help to create better-quality and more stable products that will maintain health and/ or be used to help in disease conditions. Of critical significance are issues raised by the National Academy of Science report "Designing Foods," which discusses future trends and developments in the creation of nutritionally based products (NAS 1989). Specific items of interest are the breeding of animals that have less fat and more unsaturated fats, as well as transgenic animals with specific nutrient changes (e.g., increase of calcium in the muscle mass), and the development of genetically engineered dairy starter cultures that will digest the cholesterol from butter fat during the fermentation of cheese to make a no-cholesterol product. Genetic engineering of the ingredients available to the food technologist in the future certainly will contribute to significant modifications, making it possible to engineer food products consistent with optimal consumer health and well-being. The major concerns—which certainly will have an impact on what products will be needed and what the industry will be able to market— are the need for better evidence relating specific dietary components to health and the need for a regulatory climate that will allow proper and valid claims to be made about the healthfulness of specific foods.

REFERENCES

AAP, 1976. Commentary on breast feeding and infant formulas, including proposal of standards for formulas. American Academy of Pediatrics, Committee on Nutrition. *Pediatrics* 57: 278.

Ababouch, L. and Busta, F. F. 1987. The effect of thermal treatment in oils on bacterial spore survival in oil. *J. Appl. Bacteriol.* 62: 491.

Alexander, J. W., Saito, H., Ogle, C. K., and Trock, O. 1986. The importance of lipid type in the diet after burn injury. *Ann. Surg.* 204: 1–8.

Altschul, A. 1989. Low calorie foods. *Food Technology* 43(4): 113.

AMA. 1951. *Handbook of Nutrition: A Symposium*, 2nd edition, p. 679. New York: The Blakiston Company.

AMA. 1988. Council report: Treatment of obesity in adults. *JAMA* 260: 2547.

Anderson, J. 1989. Recent advances in carbohydrate nutrition and metabolism in diabetes mellitus. *J. Am. College Nutri.* 8(5): 615–675.

Anderson, S. A., Chernin, H. I., and Fisher, K. D. 1982. History and current status of infant formulas. *Am. J. Clin. Nutri.* 35: 381.

Anonymous. 1989. Standards for nutrition support. *Nutri. in Clinical Practice* 4: 33–37.

Anonymous. 1988a. FDA 1988/89 compliance policy program. *Food Chem. News* 18(Apr.): 45.

Anonymous. 1988b. FDA clears Hoechst's non-caloric sweetener for use in dry foods. *Food Technology* 42(10): 108.

AOAC. 1985. Production, regulation and analysis of infant formulas. *Proceedings* of the Topical Conference, Assn. of Official Analytical Chemists, Arlington, Va.

Austin, J. E. 1978. Cereal fortification reconsidered. *Cereal Foods World* 23(5): 229.

Baynes, J. 1989. *The Maillard Reaction in Aging, Diabetes and Nutrition.* New York: A. R. Liss Press Inc.

Beck, K. M. 1980. Nonnutritive sweeteners: saccharin and cyclamate. In *CRC Handbook of Food Additions*, 2nd edition, ed. T. E. Furia, p. 125. Roca Raton, Fla.: CRC Press.

Berkowitz, R., Agras, W. S., and Arnow, B. 1989. The use of prepackaged food during realimentation following a very low calorie diet. Presented at the Optifast postgraduate course, San Antonio, Tex.

Best, D. 1988. Fats and oil crystallize formulation opportunities. *Prepared Foods* 157(5): 168.

Bistrian, B. R., Blackburn, G. L., Hallowell, E., and Heddle, R. 1974. Protein status of general surgical patients. *JAMA* 230: 858.

Bistrian, B. R. and Jaksic, T. 1989. Advances in hospital nutrition. *J. Am. College Nutri.* 8(5): 35-125.

Blackburn, G. L. 1978. The liquid protein controversy—a closer look at the facts. *Obesity and Bariatric Med.* 7: 25.

Blackburn, G. L., Moldawer, L. L., Usui, S., Bothe, A., O'Keefe, S. J. D., and Bistrian, B. R. 1979. Branched chain amino acid administration and metabolism during starvation, injury, and infection. *Surgery* 86: 307.

Borgstrom, B., Dahlquist, A., Lundh, G. and Sjoval, J. 1957. Studies of intestinal digestion and absorption in humans. *J. Clin. Invest.* 36: 1521.

Brewington, C. R. 1989. Labeling claims for meat and poultry products. *Food Drug Cosmetic Law J.* 44: 325.

Briggs, G. and Calloway, D. 1979. *Bogert's Nutrition and Physical Fitness*, 10th edition. Philadelphia: W. B. Saunders Publishing Company.

Broomfield, I., Chopra, R., Sheinbaum, R. C., Borrovis, G. G., Silverman, A., Schoenfield, L. J., and Marks, J. W. 1988. Effects of ursodeoxycholic acid and aspirin on the formulation of lithogenic bile and gallstones during loss of weight. *New Eng. J. Med.* 319: 1567.

Carver, J., Cox, W., and Barness, L. 1990. Dietary nucleotide effects upon murine natural killers cell activity and macrophage activation. *J. Parenteral and Enteral Nutri.* 14: 18-22.

Cerra, F. B., Mazuski, J., Teasley, K., Nuwer, N., Lysne, J., Shronts, E., and Konstantinides, F. 1983. Nitrogen retention in critically ill patients is proportional to the branched chain amino acid load. *Crit. Care Med.* 11: 775.

Chopra, J. G., 1977. Regulatory status of medical foods. In *Defined Medical Diets*, ed. M. Shils, p. 149. Chicago, IL: American Medical Association.

Committee on Nutrition, AAP. 1980. On the feeding of supplementary foods to infants. *Pediatrics* 65: 1178-1181.

Cooley, S. and Livesey, F. 1987. The metabolizable energy value of polydextrose in a mixed diet fed to rats. *Brit. J. Nutri.* 57: 235.

Daly, J. M., Reynolds, J., Thom, A., et al. 1988. Immune and metabolic effects of arginine in the surgical patient. *Ann. Surg.* 208: 512-522.

Dorf, A. 1989. Tube feeding the young child: Current practices and concerns of pediatric nutritionists. *J. Am. Dietetic Assn.* 89(11): 1658.

Dudrick, S. J., Steiger, E., Long, J. M., Ruberg, R. L., Allen, T. R., Vars, H. M., and Rhoads, J. E. 1972. General principles and techniques of administration in complete parenteral nutrition. In *Parenteral Nutrition*, ed. A. W. Wilkinson, p. 222. Baltimore: Williams and Wilkin Co.

Dwyer, J. 1989. The spectrum of dietary and nutritional approaches to cancer. *Nutrition* 5:197.

Dziezak, J. 1986. Sweeteners and product development. *Food Technology* 40(1): 112-130.

Echenique, M. M., Bistrian, B. R., Moldower, L. L., Palombo, J. D., Miller, M. M., and Blackburn, G. L. 1984. Improvement in amino acid use in critically ill patients with parenteral formulas enriched with branched chain amino acids. *Surg. Gynec. Obst.* 159: 233.

FDA. 1982. Infant formula: quality control procedures. Food and Drug Administration. *Federal Register* 47, 17016.

Federation of American Societies for Experimental Biology (FASEB). 1983. Health effects of dietary carnitine. Life Science Research Office Contract #FDA 223-79-2275.

Fomon, S. and Ziegler, E. E. 1989. Upper limits of nutrients in infant formulas. *J. Nutri.* 119: 125.

Food and Nutrition Board. 1989. *Recommended Dietary Allowances*, 10th edition. Washington, D.C.: National Research Council, National Academy of Science.

Food and Nutrition Board. 1980. *Recommended Dietary Allowances*, 9th edition. Washington, D.C.: National Research Council, National Academy of Science.

Frattali, V. P. 1984. Weight reduction products and practice—a nutrition review. *Assn. Food and Drug Officials* 48: 12–20.

Freund, H., Atamian, S., Holroyde, J., and Fischer, J. E. 1979. Plasma amino acids as predictors of severity and outcome of sepsis. *Ann. Surg.* 190: 571.

Fritz, I. B. 1959. Action of carnitine on long chain fatty acid oxidation by the liver. *Am. J. Physiol.* 197: 297.

Garn, S. 1990. Will calcium supplementation preserve bone integrity? *Nutrition Reviews* 48(1): 26.

Gaull, G. E. 1982. Taurine in the nutrition of the human infant. *Acta Paediatr. Scand. Suppl.* 269 38: 38–40.

Gil, A., Corral, E., Martinez, A., and Molina, J. A. 1986. Effects of dietary nucleotides on the microbial pattern of faeces in a term newborn infant. *J. Clin. Nutri. Gastroenterol.* 1: 3–8.

Gillis, A. 1988. Fat substitutes create new issues. *JOACS* 65: 1708.

Greenstein, J. P., Birnbaum, S. M., Winitz, M., and Otey, M. C. 1957. Quantitative nutritional studies with water-soluble, chemically defined diets. I. Growth, reproduction and lactation in rats. *Arch. Biophys.* 72: 396.

Hallberg, D. 1965. Elimination of exogenous lipids from the bloodstream. An experimental methodological and clinical study in dog and man. *Acta Physiol. Scand. Suppl.* 254 65: 1.

Hayes, K. G., Stephan, Z. F., and Sturman, J. A. 1980. Growth depression in taurine-depleted infant monkeys. *J. Nutri.* 110: 2058–2064.

IFT. 1986. Nutrition and the elderly. A scientific status summary by the Institute of Food Technologists Expert Panel on Food Safety and Nutrition. *Food Technology* 40(9): 81.

Johnson, L., Gordon, H., and Borensten, B. 1988. Vitamin and mineral fortification of breakfast cereal. *Cereal Foods World* 33(3): 278.

Kaanane, A. and Labuza, T. P. 1989. *The Maillard Reaction in Foods in Aging, Diabetes and Nutrition.* New York: J. R. Liss Press, J. Baynes Edition.

Kinney, J. M. 1976. Energy requirements for parenteral nutrition. In *Total Parenteral Nutrition.* ed. J. E. Fischer, p. 1335. Boston: Little, Brown.

Klevay, L. M. 1979. Copper deficiency with a liquid protein diet? *New Engl. J. Med.* 300: 241.

Klurfeld, D. 1987. The role of dietary fiber in gastrointestinal disease. *J. Am. Dietetic Assn.* 87(9): 1173.

LaBarge, R. G. 1988. The search for a low-calorie oil. *Food Technology* 42(1): 84.

Labuza, T. P. 1987. A perspective on health claims in food labeling. *Cereal Foods World* 32: 276.

Labuza, T. P. and Massaro, S. 1990. Browning and amino acid losses in total parenteral nutrition systems with specific reference to cysteine. *J. Food Science* 55: 821.

Labuza, T. P. and Schmidl, M. K. 1986. Advances in the control of the browning in foods. In *Role of Chemistry on the Quality of Processed Foods.* ed. O. Fennema, W. Chang, and C. Liu. Westport, Conn.: Food and Nutrition Press.

Lecos, C. W. 1985. Sweeteners minus calories—controversy. *FDA Consumer* 19(2): 18.

Ledenthal, E. ed. 1989. Nutrition in infancy. In *Textbook of Gastroenterology*, 2nd edition. New York: Raven Press.

Lee, C. 1986. Surimi manufacturing and fabrication of surimi-based products. *Food Technology* 41(3): 115.

Levy, H. 1989. Nutrition therapy for selected inborn errors of metabolism. *J. Am. College Nutri.* 8(3): 545–605.

Lintigua, R. A., Amatruda, J. M., Biddle, T. L., Forbes, G. B., and Lockwood, D. H. 1980. Cardiac arrhythmias associated with a liquiprotein diet for the treatment of obesity. *N. Engl. J. Med.* 303: 735.

Marine, D. and Kimbell, O. P. 1912. The prevention of simple goiter in man. *J. Lab. Clin. Med.* 3: 40. (reprinted in Nutrition Reviews 33: 272, 1975).

Mathews, D. M. and Adibi, S. A. 1976. Progress in gastroenterology—peptide absorption. *Gastroenterol.* 71: 151.

McClure, F. J. 1970. *Water Fluoridation*. Washington, D.C.: Superintendent of Documents.

McClure, F. J. 1962. *Fluoride Drinking Waters*. Public Health Service Publication 825. Washington, D.C.: Superintendent of Documents.

Mirkin, G. B. and Shore, R. N. 1981. The Beverly Hills diet: danger of the newest weight loss fad. *JAMA* 242(2): 235.

Mountford, M. and Cristol, C. 1989. The enteral formula market in the United States. *Food Drug Cosmetic Law J.* 44: 503–515.

NAS Board on Agriculture. 1989. *Designing Foods*. Washington, D.C.: National Academy of Science Press.

Roe, D. A. 1983. *Geriatric Nutrition*. Englewood Cliffs, N.J.: Prentice-Hall.

Rowley, B. O. and Richardson, T. 1985. Protein lipid interaction in concentrated infant formula. *J. Dairy Sci.* 68(12): 3180–3188.

Sarrett, H. P. 1981. The modern infant formula. In *Infant and Child Feeding*, ed. J. T. Bond, L. J. Filer, Jr., G. A. Leveille, A. M. Thomson, and W. B. Weil, Jr., p. 99. New York: Academic Press.

Schiffman, S. S. and Coney, E. 1984. Changes in taste and smell with age. Nutritional aspects. In *Nutrition in Gerontology* ed. J. M. Ordy, D. Hann, and R. Alfred Slater, p. 43. New York: Raner Press.

Schmidl, M. 1985. Weight control—an American pastime. *Cereal Foods World* 30(3): 212.

Schmidl, M. K. and Labuza, T. P. 1985. Low calorie formulations: cutting calories keeping quality. *Prepared Foods* Oct.: 118–120.

Schmidl, M. K., Massaro, S., and Labuza, T. P. 1988. Parenteral and enteral food systems. *Food Technology* 42(7): 77.

Shenkin, A. and Wretlind, A. 1978. Parenteral nutrition. *World Rev. Nutri. Diet.* 28: 1.

Sherman, P. 1968. *Emulsion Science*. New York: Academic Press.

Shils, M. E., Bloch, A. S., and Chernoff, R. 1976. Liquid and formulas for oral and tube feeding. *Clin. Bull.* 6(4): 151–158.

Shock, N. W. 1962. The physiology of aging. *Sci. Am.* 206(10): 100.

Slavin, J. L. 1987. Dietary fiber, classification, chemical analyses and food sources. *J. Am. Dietetic Assn.* 87(9): 1165.

Stamp, J. A. and Labuza, T. P. 1989. Mass spectrometric determination of aspartame decomposition products. *Food Additives and Contaminants* 6: 397.

Stegink, L. D., Freeman, J. B., DenBesten, L., and Filer, L. 1981. Maillard reaction products in parenteral nutrition. In *Maillard Reactions in Food*, ed. C. Eriksson. New York: Pergamon Press.

Thompson, W. R., Stephens, R. V., Randall, H. T., and Bowen, J. R. 1969. Use of the "space diet'' in the management of a patient with extreme short bowel syndrome. *Am. J. Surg.* 117: 449.

Toma, R. B., Curtis, D. J., and Sobotor, C. 1988. Sucrose polyester: its metabolic role and possible future applications. *Food Technology* 42(1): 93.

Vetsch, W. 1985. Aspartame: technical considerations and predicted use. *Food Chem.* 16(3, 4): 245.

Wadden, T. A., Stunkard, A. J., Brownell, K. D., and Van Itallie, T. B. 1983. Very-low-calorie diets: their efficacy, safety and future. *JAMA* 250(2): 833.

Wadden, T., Van Itallie, T., and Blackburn, G. 1990. Responsible and irresponsible use of very-low-calorie diets in the treatment of obesity. *JAMA* 263(1): 83.

Winitz, M., Graff, J., Gallagher, N., Narken, A., and Seedman, D. A. 1965. Evaluation of chemical diets as nutrition for man-in-space. *Nature* 205: 741.

Chapter 13

Foodservice New Products: "I don't think we're in commodities anymore, Toto"

Kristin S. Ferguson

THE FOODSERVICE ENVIRONMENT

Foodservice manufacturers generally have viewed any meal prepared anyplace and served anywhere other than the home as falling within the foodservice market. Now, even the home, the last bastion of the retail food manufacturer, is being invaded by innovative foodservice operations intent on capitalizing on ever more blurred market segments—invaded in ways that demonstrate the changing nature of the food industry.

Nearly two decades ago, in 1974, the foodservice functions of most food manufacturers were referred to in ways that were less than endearing to food-service professionals: "institutional sales," "commodity sales," bulk sales." Some large food companies even abandoned most of their value-added food-service efforts, considering them low-growth areas not worthy of capital investment. At that time, about 59% of the U.S. food dollar was spent in retail: items and ingredients purchased for preparation and consumption at home. By 1989, that share had dropped to an estimated 53% (Technomic 1989).

From a food manufacturing perspective, and depending on how one categorizes certain segments, that percentage may have become even lower. For example, look at the "in-store deli" segment. A consumer stops by the deli counter at the supermarket to pick up two orders of lasagna for dinner. The counter attendant puts the orders in a microwavable container, the consumer pays at the checkout counter, and the supermarket rings up a sale, a retail sale. Or is it retail? The lasagna is served from a half-size steam table tray, the same tray of lasagna the manufacturer's foodservice division sells to hospitals, colleges, and other "traditional" foodservice outlets. So maybe it is a foodservice sale—or maybe it is both. It is a matter of perspective. In-store delis are a rapidly growing market segment (or subsegment) in the food industry. If that lasagna sale is a "retail" sale, then maybe 53% is still a good figure. But if it is a foodservice sale, then perhaps 53% is too high; perhaps 52% or even 51% would be more accurate.

The point of this illustration is not to debate who gets to tally up the food sales dollar. That may be relevant to a fast-food/quick-service operation or a retail-oriented manufacturer who has "lost" a sale to the in-store deli, but it does not matter here. Rather this discussion seeks to illustrate something of the complexity of the food industry, the increasingly blurred nature of market segments, the growing reach of foodservice manufacturers, and, perhaps, the occasional mutability of certain statistics in the food industry.

To go further, look at Table 13-1 as one way to sector, or segment, the food industry. In this scenario, a typical large foodservice manufacturer might well address product development efforts toward *all* the sectors, though not as discrete segments because a product that is successful in one sector is likely to have market and sales potential in another. Such multiple-sector use is uppermost in the mind in most foodservice product development efforts, but adaptability of product is the key. Take, for example, a chicken nugget. In the quickservice or midscale restaurant segments, it is developed for preparation with a deep-fryer. Speed of reconstitution is a key factor for these segments. But frying is anathema to most healthcare operations such as hospitals and nursing homes, and is impractical if not impossible for an in-flight feeding operation. The product, then, must be adapted so that it can be reconstituted either through baking or microwaving without loss of quality.

These discrete segments also are unlikely to reflect how a foodservice manufacturer is structured to deal with the marketplace. A sales force is likely to be organized with one or more of the following divisions:

1. *Zone manager/regional manager system,* to manage sales efforts with, and through, the broker/distributor network (the Food Sales Wests, the Syscos, the S. E. Rykoffs), which deals with the majority of foodservice operations—restaurants, healthcare institutions, drinking establishments— at the regional and local level.

Table 13-1. Food industry market segments.

Commercial Sector	Noncommercial Sector
Convenience stores	Business/industry (cafeterias)
Drinking establishments	Colleges/universities
Industrial (basic ingredients:	Correctional facilities
flour, chicken parts, etc.)	Hospitals/healthcare
Lodging/hotel/motel	In-flight feeding
Recreation/theme parks	Military/government
Restaurants	Nursing homes
• Upscale	Schools (primary/secondary)
• Midscale	
• Quick service	
Supermarkets/groceries	
Wholesale clubs/warehouses	

2. *National accounts* (and/or chain accounts and/or key accounts), to work with the large multi-unit, multistate operations—corporate operations that have manufacturer relationship requirements that cannot be handled adequately or efficiently by the zone/regional system; for example, such organizations as Marriott Corporation (resorts, hotels, motels, restaurants), Grand Metropolitan (Burger King), and General Mills (Red Lobster, Olive Garden).

3. *Wholesale clubs/warehouse clubs,* to work with a rapidly growing, but still evolving segment where special characteristics and developing demographics bases require specialized attention.

4. *"Deli" sales,* to deal with the special requirements of convenience stores (often franchisees) and in-store (in-supermarket) delis.

5. *Military/government sales,* which requires special familiarity with convoluted government and military procurement systems and their often complicated bidding systems.

6. *Primary and secondary schools,* which must deal with government-mandated nutrition requirements utilization of government surplus products, special bidding requirements, and a chronic shortage of funds.

Obviously, the size of the manufacturer will determine whether all of these divisions exist, or some of them, or whether one super salesperson wears all the hats (and lives out of a suitcase and travels 99% of the time).

However the sales force might be organized, the marketing efforts and marketing communications and advertising in foodservice reflect both the multiplicity of segments and the *businesses* that constitute the customers in those segments. If there is a single, essential difference between a retail manufacturer's and a foodservice manufacturer's marketing and product communications efforts, it is the latter's business-to-business focus and almost complete absence of communications with the ultimate consumer. This is not to suggest that the consumer is an afterthought; but here the focus of effort is on the user, not the consumer, of the product. It is the users (cooks, chefs, banquet managers, hospital foodservice directors, and so on) and the people who deal directly with the users (distributors, franchisors, chain owners) who determine if the sale is made.

In foodservice, product quality generally is of the highest importance just as it is in retail, and the product must meet any trends and fashions of taste that reflect the dynamics of the consuming public. But the form the product takes, what packaging it is in, how the product is reconstituted, what kind of equipment it requires are concerns of the user, not the consumer. Perhaps the most unusual aspect of foodservice manufacturing is that the customer is not the person who eats the product; and, though the product must be palatable, have good plate presentation, present good price/value perception, and so on, everything else about it is geared to the people who use it. Consequently, the marketing and selling effort is a business-to-business concern, and that makes for a product development chain altogether different from that of retail manufacturing.

FOODSERVICE PRODUCT DEVELOPMENT

The Development Process

Every foodservice company, every food company, collects and analyzes several categories of financial information to assess its progress toward corporate goals. Senior management usually establishes specific corporate growth targets to be met over the next year or three years or five years: "We're targeting compound growth of 20% year-over-year for the next X years." This target generally is passed down the hierarchy to those managers who actually have to execute the plans to achieve that growth. Those lower managers also are likely to be the first to ascertain when a discrepancy appears between their best-case forecasts and plans for sales growth of existing product lines and senior management's stated (often publicly) objectives. Therein lies the key role of the product development process: to ensure that a stream of new products is available as necessary so that the growth stream of corporate sales will match or exceed the stated growth stream of corporate objectives. Consistent failure to do so causes loss-of-face at the senior level and, often, loss-of-job at the lower level.

Such an ideal scenario is necessarily an oversimplification because the assessment of goal attainment is an ongoing process, as the new product/product development process would be. Moreover, most foodservice manufacturers are unlikely to have either a by-the-book or even a formalized new product development process.

In any case, there probably is a general consensus in the food industry on the general attributes of a new product. In the main, it is something that is not merely an extension of an existing product line, no matter how cleverly conceived; something that the company does not currently sell; something that is not wildly outside the manufacturer's existing line of business, such as a product line that would more rationally be dealt with as a new venture. Some might add that changes or improvements in the formulation of existing products, such as those that might be necessitated by a change in packaging technology, create new products.

The development of the retortable tray is an example of this. The retortable tray offers substantially improved product shelf life and reduced storage costs, making it attractive to operators and users in several market segments. The retort process, however, requires reformulation of existing products so they can be reconstituted properly in a new package. Using lasagna again to illustrate, a manufacturer of frozen foodservice lasagna would assemble cooked ingredients in a half-size steam table pan, freeze the product, and distribute it for reconstitution on site. To be retortable, this manufacturer's frozen lasagna product would require reformulation with starches, noodles, cheeses, and so on, that would tolerate being canned—the essence of the retort process—with little, if any, loss of product quality. The company would be selling essentially the same lasagna as its frozen product, albeit reformulated, but the market for this product likely would be altogether different from the market for the frozen product. Is this a new product then? Only the most intractable purist would say no.

Whatever the definition, there is little difference between retail and foodservice manufacturing in the way that new products are defined. Any difference between them lies in the *process* of development itself.

There is a "purist" or an ideal approach to the new product development process, and thousands of courses and seminars reflecting it have been taught or attended by various levels of corporate management. The approach is likely to begin with an explication of the product life cycle or some variant of it, and then outline traditional aspects of the development process, including idea generation, concept testing, prototype development and testing, and so on; and then the seminar leader explains why that approach is wrong and how it really should be done—the new paradigm. The variations among the process models (which the reader probably can find in any number of scholarly books and articles) usually are minor and probably are irrelevant to the practical course of events, but they help sell seminars and keep consultants in business. In any case, let us refer to this ideal approach as the traditionalist's model of the product development process. The most likely site of the pure traditionalist's approach in the food industry is in consumer-oriented retail-foods megacorporations, primarily because they have the asset base to support the necessary bureaucratic organizational elements. They provide models to which smaller but growing manufacturers often aspire.

For purposes of comparison, we can use a metaphor in which these large corporations are represented by a conventional warfare model, and the typical foodservice outfit, regardless of size, is a guerrilla warfare, seat-of-the-pants-flying, do-what-works practitioner. Take it for granted that the conventional retail model has greater research sophistication in practice; that is has more, and more specialized, research personnel; that it has research practices and methodologies that sometimes are not practical, and often are not possible in the foodservice environment; that it has a different essential focus for its research and development efforts—the consumer—given the main objective of ensuring product success. Take it for granted also that the typical guerrilla foodservice operation, whether by choice or more likely by necessity, redefines the terms "lean," "mean," and "opportunistic."

This process model is what we might call "formally informal." It is *formal* in the sense that the elements are, in part or as a whole, critical to ensuring product development success. Just as they are in a highly sophisticated retail megacorporation, experience shows across the industry that certain procedures are critical; that if a foodservice manufacturer fails to do certain things, ignores certain data, fails to understand the nature of the industry and of its own busi- -ness, then the probability of success is diminished, and risk is increased. This is so notwithstanding the fact that many foodservice new products, because of the nature of the industry, are virtually guaranteed some level of success. It is *informal* in the sense that it is most often an ongoing, free-flowing process in foodservice, neither enhanced nor constrained by the presence of a formal organizational structure, whether bureaucratic or not. In essence, the guerrilla foodservice model of product development is a *process*, not a *structure*.

The point of this analysis is that the emphasis in foodservice is on a more or less formal process with certain informal features. There is no large product development department; development teams are organized on an ad hoc, this-is-the-project, this-is-what-we-need, this-is-who-can-do-it basis. Ultimately, the goal is to achieve and enjoy the successful results of the process.

The Three Phases of New Product Development

The process in general consists of three phases. Phase I, *sourcing* or *intelligence gathering*, is an ongoing practice conducted, first, for its own sake, to keep abreast of any kind of relevant change in end-user behavior as that affects eating habits; and, second, as it specifically relates to elements and projects of the other phases. Intelligence gathering of necessity must deal with sources both internal to and external to the manufacturer—with areas where the impetus for collecting information, regardless of the object source, is generated internally by the manufacturer's own personnel, and with areas where the impetus for a new product is external, from a customer or a potential customer, for example, to which the manufacturer's personnel must respond. Phase II, *refining, developing, and planning*, makes concrete the new products ideas generated from intelligence collection. (This is the "go with it" or "you must be kidding" phase.) Phase III, *implementation*, is producing, marketing, and selling those viable, defensible survivors of Phase II.

Sourcing and Intelligence Gathering

The internally driven aspect of new product sourcing is more unstructured than its external counterpart, its informality due in part to the absence of externally imposed organizational constraints, the development practices of others, and, as we shall see, certain customers in particular. Marketing and research and development (R & D) play the key roles at this stage. Marketing has particular responsibility for keeping tabs on the changing foodservice environment, and the trade press plays a vital role in providing this information.

Over the years as the complexity of foodservice has increased, publications have appeared that address their editorial focus respectively to all segments of the foodservice industry, and to key related areas such as distributor operations, convenience store operations, school foodservice, and so on. In turn, the editors, publishers, and reporters pride themselves, justifiably, on keeping track of even the slightest nuance of change in technology, demographics, eating habits, and lifestyles, and keeping an editorial eye on trends and fads, tastes, and styles as they might affect the industry. Certain publications, such as *Restaurants and Institutions*, also conduct periodic detailed research studies on issues of concern to the industry or to particular segments.

Trade associations, foremost among them the International Food Manufacturers Association (IFMA) and the National Restaurant Association (NRA), also serve as sources of general information and occasionally of hard data on specific issues. IFMA, as its name implies, is the predominant manufacturers' association. As such, its meetings and gatherings provide a major venue for gossip (a valuable source of information, properly evaluated) and competitor checks. IFMA also sponsors substantial research efforts. Its major ongoing effort is the annual *Industry Forecast and Outlook*, and special studies and reports are prepared by staff and committees composed of IFMA's industry members. IFMA issues *Forecast and Outlook* in conjunction with Technomic, Inc., the preeminent industry consulting group. Technomic also conducts a wide range of valuable industry studies and research projects for its member companies.

NRA is an operator-oriented trade association, but manufacturers compose a significant element of its membership. In fact, membership is a prerequisite for participating in NRA shows. The association's annual show in Chicago provides the nation's largest showcase for foodservice manufacturers to present their products directly to a wide audience of chefs, cooks, school foodservice directors, hotel/motel managers, and other operators. As such, not only is it a ready source of information and gossip on what competitors are doing, but it also provides an ongoing perspective and a source of valuable feedback on what operators are doing, the key to a major segment of the industry.

These association shows and meetings and the many others sponsored by other industry trade groups and publications—the Chain Operators Exchange (COEX), sponsored by IFMA, the Multi-Unit Food Service Operators (MUFSO) show, sponsored by *Nation's Restaurant News*, the ASFSA annual convention and show, sponsored by the American School Food Service Association, and so on—also provide venues for other major elements of the information-gathering process: eating out at various finer restaurants (never an onerous task); talking with cooks, chefs, owners, and others about their plans and their needs; and seeing first hand how a trend-on-paper translates into a trendy (sometimes) establishment. Not insignificantly, the meetings also allow manufacturers to experience regional differences in taste and the impact such differences have on idea generation and product development. Any manufacturer intent on developing a barbeque (or BBQ) anything, for example, had best be aware of North Carolina barbeque and Texas barbeque—a twain that surely will never meet.

It is precisely this kind of "market research" information that proves invaluable in the new products idea-generation process. And contrary to the results achieved by a consumer/retail manufacturer, this approach is likely to be far more productive than either a formal internally generated evaluation or consultant-conducted market research study. It gives the alert marketer key insights into what really is happening in the marketplace. Besides, the lack of homogeneity in the marketplace, the presence of multiple market segments in at least two discrete sectors, renders many of the market research methodologies that are utilized by consumer-oriented manufacturers impractical for the foodservice manufacturer, from the standpoint of both cost and utility of results.

For the typical foodservice manufacturer, this informal process is augmented by more formal research efforts. R&D departments, as the "research" part of their program, conduct taste and sensory studies. And occasionally, new product consultants will be engaged to assist in translating this market research, as it is, into specific product prototypes.

Whatever the source, these market data provides most of the seed stock from which marketers and research technologists and scientists generate their contributions to the new product process. In foodservice, basic food research is not a likely source of new products because most foodservice manufacturers have neither the time, the available staff, the resources, nor often the inclination to engage in it, regardless of their corporate size. That may be fortunate or unfortunate, depending on one's perspective on the issue. To the extent that basic research exists in foodservice, it exists in those large corporations with both retail and foodservice manufacturing where foodservice "borrows" basic research capability from the retail side as necessary, as available, and if desired. R&D's larger task at this stage is to keep informed of new technologies, new processes, new ingredients, new user equipment, and so on, which might turn otherwise good but unusable ideas into new products winners.

Production generally plays no significant role in the idea sourcing phase. It is important, though, that production personnel continually make known the production constraints that would torpedo an idea, before any significant investment is made of time or other resources.

Sales personnel play a supplemental but significant role in the sourcing phase. They are the regular interface between the company and its customers, and thus are a ready conduit for information and ideas. Likewise, they also serve as informal testers and feedback generators with the brokers, distributors, and operators with whom they regularly deal: product ideas and concepts can be easily discussed on a "what if" basis without suggestion of commitment on either side. "What if we had a product like this? Would you use it? Could you sell it? What kind of demand do you think there might be? Would it need to be changed?"

Sales also functions as a channel for specific product requests or demands, as the case may be, from customers, the most common external source of ideas. Distributors may need something specific to fill a gap in their product line. Operators may need a special product that can fill a menu need and yet be utilized within their particular operational and equipment constraints. This, as noted earlier, is the more structured part of Phase I because the manufacturer must be responsive in all cases to the constraints imposed by the customer's circumstances. Sales, in fact, through its relationship with national accounts, or key accounts or chain accounts (those multiunit/multistate chains, large quick-service operations such as McDonalds or Burger King, or very specialized large customers such as Disney), is the major coordinating point for external sourcing of ideas and requests.

National accounts are different in almost all ways from other regular food-service customers, such as distributors, and not just in their size alone. Manufacturers generally will segregate their national account business—according to the size of the customer, its maturity in its segment of the industry, the importance of its business, and the special attention it needs (or demands)—into more than one level, say Tier I and Tier II national accounts. The larger, Tier I, players such as McDonalds pride themselves, justifiably, on the sophistication of their own operations. They have their own research and development staffs and their own marketing staffs. Consequently, the "ideas" that they present to a manufacturer most often are in the form of an already existing prototype. At this stage, what the manufacturer gives them in return is market intelligence: regional taste preferences, information on consumer trends and tastes.

Tier II national accounts invariably are smaller, often growing, promising chains that have yet to develop their own sophisticated research and development capabilities. That lack, properly exploited, can work to the advantage of both the chain and the manufacturer. For example, development costs can be transferred to the manufacturer in exchange for the possibility of preferred-supplier status. The manufacturer in turn may offer deficit spending in the early stages if the account shows promising growth potential.

Regardless of the category—distributor, Tier I or Tier II national account—these accounts also come to the manufacturer for other reasons. First and most obvious, they are not themselves manufacturers, and it is not in their business interest to become so. Second, but particularly so for distributors and smaller, less developed national accounts, they consider the manufacturer to be the product development innovator, the idea generator in the area of concern. This is to the manufacturer's advantage as long as it continues to be the innovator; but, all other things being equal, as soon as the manufacturer ceases to be innovative, the account will move to another manufacturer who is.

With these accounts, sales serves readily as nurturer and hand-holder, and as the conduit for ideas between the account and the manufacturer's marketing and R&D functions. Marketing, in its turn, serves as the manufacturer's internal coordinator of the external idea, leading it through the relevant parts of Phase II—refining, developing, and planning for the product. Even in those circumstances where the manufacturer–account relationship does not develop further, these externally generated ideas may yet develop into products for the manufacturer that are applicable to other segments of the industry.

Refining, Developing, Planning

Once an idea reaches that point where it is deemed to represent a potentially viable new product, a number of Phase II activities kick in more or less simultaneously: refining the idea into a workable concept, developing the necessary prototype and production model, planning the various aspects of marketing and selling it. The following is one scenario of how this might proceed.

Marketing coordinates the concept development process working closely with R&D. More "what ifs" are conducted with sales, brokers, and distributors, while R&D develops the hand-made "gold standard" prototype. In part, this entails conducting taste and reconstitution tests internally and, if deemed necessary (perhaps with a higher-risk product), externally with focus groups. At this stage R&D also conducts initial production feasibility and production cost studies, establishing the ingredient base and availability, and, with marketing, the reconstitution status. Will the product be fully cooked, partially cooked, raw? Frozen or fresh? Marketing, meanwhile, conducts the initial volume, price, and sales estimates with input from sales, and a preliminary pro forma budget statement may be developed.

Marketing also commences segment studies and risk studies if necessary. Segment studies determine what market segment is the most probable for initial product focus, but quite often the appropriate segment is obvious as a product of the idea generation and concept development efforts. If the segment is not obvious, it may be determined, for example, that introduction into a noncommercial segment is the low-risk way to go, with later rollover into commercial segments. The results of this determination, in any case, are useful later in determining the initial product advertising strategy.

Risk studies determine probable additional capital investment, existing production capability versus projected production needs, and so on, as they relate to estimated probable product acceptance and profitability. As a general rule, the higher the investment is, the higher the risk, all other things being equal. As with segment studies, there are occasional products for which risk studies are moot: additional capital investment is so low, and probability of acceptance is so high, as to put the product into an enviable "no-brainer" category.

Once the gold standard is made, the development team, with R&D in the lead, immediately focuses on developing the production model and running pilot plant tests. The object here is to make a production model as close as possible, given production exigencies, to the gold standard. In any case, numerous attempts and additional focus group studies and product refining may be required to develop an acceptable production model. It is at this point that marketing most often initiates serious development work with its advertising agency.

The advertising agency's primary function here is to assist in developing the initial advertising concepts, a preliminary plan for introducing the product that covers probable magazine placement (which ones, when, how often), other promotional materials and programs (use of free-standing inserts, user response cards, or direct mail pieces), and initial estimates of program cost. This latter, given marketing's input of its probable budget, usually equals the proposed budget plus 10 to 15 percent—just to make sure the job is done right. Whatever the case, once this planning has been completed and the necessary compromises have been worked out, the agency at marketing's direction proceeds with testing ad concepts, developing the promotional materials, and finalizing the overall plan.

If all has gone well and the product has not been shelved for any of myriad reasons, then the manufacturer should have three things at this point: an acceptable production model, an understanding of the product's risks and prospects, and a developed program for initial introduction. The next step is the test market. However, this was essentially a scenario for a middle-of-the-road, midlevel risk product. With a low-risk product, the steps might be fewer; and with a high-risk product, they might be repeated and fed back many times for further refinement.

Test marketing, in particular determining the number of markets in which the product is to be tested before full rollout, is a direct function of the risk assessment. As with the "no-brainers" mentioned above, a low-risk product often generates its own special test market program: "Slap it on the price list and see if it sticks." (It usually does.) But with higher-risk products, a more detailed strategy is necessary. Quite often the use of multiple test markets is called for, which entails testing the advertising in the markets, producing and distributing the product to the markets, and closely monitoring distributor sales and repeat sales—the keys to end-user response.

In the worst case, the product is a complete and unmitigated dud, and the manufacturer tries to extricate itself as quietly as possible. That is an *extremely* unlikely prospect, though not unheard of in the foodservice industry. A more likely case if problems develop in test market is that marketing will rush in to conduct detailed focus groups to define the problem, and the product will be pulled back for refinement and reintroduction. The best case, and the most common, is that everything goes as hoped, and the product is ready for Phase III—rolling it out to waiting customers, implementing the master plan so well developed by marketing and sales to achieve complete domination of the market segment.

The products that are generated from external sourcing, from customer requests, and from national or chain accounts follow a different, more limited path through Phase II. Larger national accounts, for example, present the manufacturer with their own gold standard, and they are generally not interested in having the manufacturer tinker with it. Instead, the manufacturer's responsibility is to develop a production model for it. Even with customer requests where there is no offered prototype, the customer generally has specific product qualities in mind, which determine the constitution of the gold standard and in turn the production model. These customers also are not likely to be interested in the manufacturer's marketing support (though they may want marketing funds), and they almost certainly are not interested in the advertising agency's input. What remains is developing the product, determining the product's costs in light of the customer's desired selling price, producing it, getting it to the customer, and assuring the customer that the manufacturer has the capacity and the intent to be a supplier over the life of the product. The risk for the manufacturer in this relationship is that it is entered most often with *no* guarantee that the manufacturer will be the prime supplier, and the development costs must be borne with this prospect in mind. In some instances, the manufacturer has not been the supplier; but fortunately, from the manufacturer's perspective, this situation rarely occurs.

Yet even with winning—and landing a large national account certainly is winning—there may also be losing in a certain sense. Most products developed specifically for a customer are proprietary. Most customers use such a product only in the market segment in which they operate. The proprietary nature of the product and the usual manufacturer–customer relationship constrain the manufacturer from using that product in other appropriate market segments— and there might be many. The relationship does not constrain the manufacturer's competition from developing a knock-off and quickly moving to those segments, however. (For example, how many chicken nuggets are now in the market?) The manufacturer's recourse, to the extent that it exists, is to reformulate—*very carefully* and over time—in the hope of capitalizing on those markets. Most manufacturers would likely concur that, all things considered, these special accounts are worth the effort.

Another product outcome of these Phase II efforts should be mentioned here— the special case of what are called niche products. Occasionally it is determined that after all the effort, the research, the refinement, and the determination of excellent profit prospects, the actual market for the product is going to be smaller than was hoped. Two possible reasons for this, both pertaining to the nature of the product itself, are (1) the regionality of the product and (2) that its place within a segment and across segments, once it is fully introduced, has "natural" growth constraints on it. Regionality refers to matters of taste, particularly regional differences in taste; and taste often is a significant barrier to the transportability of a product. As mentioned earlier, barbeque is an excellent example of this. An example of the latter phenomenon is the product (e.g., an appetizer-type product) whose place or niche is a small part of a larger trend or pattern. Suppose that a product is a good product, will have repeat sales, and will guarantee good profit and return on investment; whether it is a niche product often is a function of the size of the manufacturer and of economies, or rather diseconomies, of scale. A niche product to a large national manufacturer may be the product-line mainstay to a smaller regional manufacturer. To a large manufacturer, a market may be too small to be practical; but to the niche manufacturer, it may be *the* market. A case may be made for the time when such niche products, developed by a large manufacturer, may be sold to a regional manufacturer or a manufacturer who specializes in those products.

Implementation: Marketing and Selling

Foodservice marketers have three main tasks: they must identify the targets toward which their marketing efforts will be most effective in getting products to market; they must identify and define the problems they will encounter in cost-effectively reaching those targets; they must develop and execute the programs that will most efficiently solve the problems.

The ultimate target (as discussed in the first section of the chapter) of foodservice marketing and selling efforts is the user of the product—the restaurant operator, the hospital or school foodservice director. Consumers influence that user to the extent that the user's buying patterns are derivative of consumer behavior; and that behavior has been, and apparently in the future will be, favorable to the foodservice industry. However, identifying the target in foodservice is one thing; selling that target is something else. By the very nature and structure of the industry, the user, with very few exceptions, buys only what is available through the distributor. If the distributor does not offer it, the user does not buy it.

The users do have some leverage. They can encourage, insist, even demand that their distributor carry a product. Sometimes that works, but the decision ultimately is the distributor's. The task of Phase III, of implementing the marketing and selling programs, is to influence that buying decision in the manufacturer's favor. Therein lies the problem: reaching the distributor and influencing the buying decision.

Television is an extraordinary medium for influencing consumer behavior; but it is considered extraordinarily ineffective, if not irrelevant, in influencing foodservice buying decisions. On a cost-to-results basis, it would be prohibitively expensive. Instead, a manufacturer reaches the distributor and influences the buying decision by the old-fashioned, pretelevision way: through printed words and pictures and through face-to-face, one-on-one contact.

Getting the distributor to buy is just the first step; helping the distributor to sell effectively also is necessary. With the ever-growing complexity of today's value-added foodservice products, the effective marketing program must address both in the most cost-effective manner possible.

Marketing has three main approaches to influencing the distributor's buying decisions and three useful weapons: hit them from above, hit them from below, and hit them directly, using as weapons the trade press and direct mail—good old words and pictures—and a good sales force as partners in the effort.

Influencing the distributor from above entails getting the most out of the manufacturer's sales force and the brokers with whom they work. Brokers function as the manufacturer's agents in representing products to distributors. Their major utility is that they are on the scene, available on a regular basis to work with the distributors, assist them in understanding the products, and encourage them to carry products. The sales force works both through and alongside the broker.

The essence of effective selling for both sales force and broker is product knowledge: where it fits on the manu, how it is used, what advantages the product has over the competition and to the user. Is it labor-saving? Does it give good price/value, and good price markup? The higher the level of product knowledge with the sales force and the broker, the easier their selling job is, and the easier it is for them to demonstrate to the distributors how they will benefit the distributors' sales efforts. Marketing's job is to ensure that product knowledge is there, with regular training programs, brochures and specification sheets, incentive and promotional programs aimed at the broker, programs that the broker can use with the distributor.

The operator provides excellent leverage to the manufacturer in getting at the distributor from below. If the operator is "sold" on trying a product, that desire is directed to the distributor, and that makes the distributor's selling job easier. The operator, though, is not always easy to reach. Sales can do this, but that almost involves the old-fashioned door-to-door cold-call approach, which is not an effective use of their time or of the manufacturer's resources. The sheer number of operators would require an enormous sales force. The distributor *does* make these calls, but the distributor also represents a large number of manufacturers with an even larger list of products. It is better for the manufacturer to ensure directly that the operator knows of the product rather than to rely solely on the distributor. And the best way to do this is to provide direct advertising and information to the operator through the trade press and direct mail.

The advertising agency is critical in this effort. The object is to provide as much appealing information as possible in the most cost-effective way. Advertising in the industry magazines most often read by operators—*Restaurant Business, Nation's Restaurant News, Restaurant Hospitality, Restaurants and Institutions* in the commercial sector; *School Food Service Journal, Food-*

Service Director, and *Food Management* for the noncommercial sector—is the best means of visually presenting the product and essential basic information about it to the operator. However, that is not a tightly focused approach, whereas direct mail is very specific. With direct mail, the manufacturer can ensure that the right person in the right operation gets the information—although this approach is only as good as the mailing list. Fortunately for marketers, agencies have media buyers and direct mail specialists whose job it is to advise on the best mix of the two.

The third assault on the distributor is direct. Advertising in those magazines, such as *Institutional Distribution* and *The Foodservice Distributor*, that are directed to distributors supplements the face-to-face contact efforts of the broker and the manufacturer's sales force. However, an effective marketing program also provides the distributor with materials and promotions that make the distributor's job easier and keep the manufacturer's products in the distributor's mind. These materials cover everything from product specification sheets to point-of-sale materials, table tents, and menu clips that the distributor sales representative (DSR) can show to the operator. The promotions provide pecuniary incentives to the distributor to carry the product.

Helping the distributor to sell effectively is a productive supplement to encouraging the buying decision and to reinforcing the long-term relationship. This assistance comes in two forms. The first is designed into the product itself and its packaging. The greatest detriment to a repeat sale—aside from a poor product—is a product that is difficult for the operator to use. With the increasing complexity of value-added products, it is imperative that a degree of fault tolerance be built into the product. First, it must be there so that if the product is not reconstituted exactly according to package directions, which, for example, must now cover microwaves, conventional ovens, convection ovens, and deep fryers, it will not turn to unusable garbage in front of the operator's eyes. Second, it must be there so that if something goes wrong—mishandling or whatever—during the distribution process and the operator's storage, the product will not upset the customer even if it is reconstituted wrong. Likewise, the packaging needs to be protective against most natural kinds of abuse, and the instructions must be readable by native speakers of several different languages and understandable by anyone.

The second form of assistance is in training for the DSRs and promotional assistance, as noted, to the distributor. Adequate product knowledge is as important at the DSR level as anywhere in the sales chain, for the DSR is the person who has most frequent contact with the operator. To ensure this, marketing and its agency design DSR training programs that cover all aspects of the product from packaging and instructions on reconstitution methods to how to sell. The program utilizes videos, hands-on training sessions with the DSRs, samplings of the product, and materials that the DSR can use to demonstrate the product to the operator, such as suggested plate presentations and recipe cards.

There is an intentional circularity to these efforts, which is intended to help these people—the broker, the distributor, the operator—help themselves and help each other. There also is an obvious benefit to the manufacturer. If marketing's programs can help the sales force and the broker, then they can help the distributor, who can help *and* sell the operator; and it helps the distributor, and the broker, and the manufacturer for the operator to be sold. This kind of assistance is the ultimate goal of these efforts.

Marketing and selling to national accounts, like product development, differs from routine practice. Although it is to the manufacturer's advantage to be proactive in maintaining the relationship, its nature is such that the manufacturer's activities are most often reactive to the customer's needs and wants.

Marketing's involvement with national accounts, regardless of their size, is always on an ad hoc basis: at the customer's request and to assist with a special problem. Marketing is almost never involved with quick-service national accounts; rather it is involved with those customers who might be in hotel/motel/lodging operations or who perhaps operate a national chain of midscale family restaurants. In these instances, marketing services are likely to entail, as examples, developing specific programs of point-of-sale materials, brochures, and posters; or developing training manuals and how-to-handle-the-product programs. Whatever the case, the involvement will be at the specific customer's request, channeled through sales.

Sales is the dominant point of interaction between the manufacturer and the customer; the main tasks of the people in this function are to keep information flowing between the two and to maintain the relationship. They do this by keeping the customer up-to-date on the manufacturer's activities and capabilities, and by getting the customer's people into the manufacturer's operations and plants for familiarization tours. The other side of this coin is that sales is in the perfect position to gather intelligence, legitimately acquired, about the customer's activities and future plans. This can help the manufacturer open the door to future product opportunities.

TRENDS AND DIRECTIONS, PROBLEMS AND OPPORTUNITIES

Product development is by definition a future-oriented practice. In an ideal food industry world, products would be developed in response to specific, clearly identified market opportunities, discovered through perfect knowledge of the market and customer behavior. In the practical world, manufacturers can at best attempt to approximate this ideal. That is what they—the marketers, the R&D scientist, the sales people—try to do every day. The object of research, whether market or product research, is to try to realize as fully as possible what future developments, in one month or five years, will affect the manufacturer's opportunities and consequently the products, and to translate that information into state-of-the-art products.

No one needs to be reminded, though everyone constantly is, of products that were market-researched and concept-tested to a fare-thee-well; ''new'' Coke and the Edsel come easily to mind. These products serve a useful, practical purpose in reminding manufacturers of the need to remain constantly grounded in reality. They also serve as reminders that there are three specific facts about the future and future efforts that everyone should constantly keep in mind when engaging in any kind of research and product development, or marketing and selling effort.

First, very little of the future will be like the past, no matter how much one might wish it otherwise. The products that got a manufacturer where it is today are not the products that will carry it into the future. And as both product and market segments change, there will be an increasing blurring of market segments. Old segments, old reliables, will dissolve; new ones with new labels and fuzzier boundaries will replace them. Complexity will increase. And as those segments blur, as the distinction fades between what is a foodservice ''market'' and what is a retail ''market,'' so will the competition between retail manufacturers and foodservice manufacturers increase. That may be competition, well-funded competition, much more intense than foodservice manufacturers have ever faced from intra-industry competitors. It will likely be both a problem and an opportunity for foodservice manufacturers.

Just as the segments and their nature will change, so are the labor economics of the industry changing. As noted early in the chapter, the ultimate foodservice customer has been the person who eats away from home for whatever reason, by choice or of necessity. That, by definition, entails someone serving that customer whether in a quick-service or an upscale restaurant or a hospital or a college cafeteria: laborers and employees, servers and preparers. If current directions are clues, that scenario means labor problems, particularly in the areas of cost and availability. To the operator, it is beneficial to transfer these costs and problems wherever and whenever possible to the manufacturer. To the manufacturer, there are and will continue to be opportunities in producing value-added, labor-saving products.

Second, nothing is likely to be what manufacturers, marketers, and R&D scientists think it is going to be, in spite of their best efforts to divine it. Every marketing department and R&D department should keep a can of the new Coke and a photograph of an Edsel on permanent display.

Finally, the speed with which things change and the dimensions of those changes will be faster and greater than ever before. We should fasten our seat belts and enjoy the ride.

REFERENCE

Technomic, Inc. 1989. Positioning for Market Success, Official Conference *Proceedings*, IFMA Eighteenth Annual Foodservice Forecast and Outlook Seminars, Sept. 15, 19, 22 1989, San Francisco, Calif., Rosemont, Ill., East Elmhurst, N.Y.

RECOMMENDED READING

The overwhelming majority of writings on the food industry are devoted to consumer products general manufacturing. That body of literature dedicated to foodservice is operator-oriented, and it is not recommended unless the reader desires to run a restaurant or a related food enterprise.

Some titles of general interest on the food industry and elements of it are:

Connor, John M. 1988. *Food Processing: An Industrial Powerhouse in Transition.* Lexington, Mass.: Lexington Book.
Earle, Mary D., ed. 1985. *Product and Process Development in the Food Industry.* New York: Harwood Academic Publishers. Division of Grune & Stratton.
Mallowe, Charles A., Jr. and McLaughlin, Daniel J. eds. 1971. *Food Marketing and Distribution.* New York: Lebhar-Friedman Books.

All of the literature of specific interest to members of the foodservice manufacturing industry currently comes from either the trade press or from trade associations. Publications of the latter generally are restricted to association members. The reader familiar with these publications will have a far greater grasp of the breadth and complexity of the industry than one whose reading excludes them.

For general reading, see:

Advertising Age. Chicago: Crain Communications, Inc.
Adweek's Marketing Week. New York: A/S/M Communications, Inc.

For the operator-oriented, commercial sector, see:

Nation's Restaurant News. New York: Lebhar-Friedman, Inc.
Restaurant Business. New York: Bill Communications, Inc.
Restaurant Hospitality. Cleveland, Ohio: Penton Publishing.
Restaurants & Institutions. Denver, Colo.: Cahners Publishing Co.

For the operator-oriented, noncommercial sector, see:

Food Management. Cleveland, Ohio: Edgell Communications, Inc.
FoodService Director. New York: Bill Communications, Inc.
School Food Service Journal. Englewood, Colo.: American School Food Service Association.

For distributor-oriented reading, see:

Foodservice Distributor. Cleveland, Ohio: Penton Publishing.
Institutional Distribution. New York: Bill Communications, Inc.

For other, more specialized publications of interest, see:

Convenience Store News. New York: BMT Publications, Inc.
Food Engineering. Radnor, Pa.: Chilton Company.
Food-Processing. Chicago: Putman Publishing Co.
Foodservice Product News. New York: Young-Conway Publications.
Prepared Foods. Chicago: Gorman Publishing Co.

Chapter 14

The Role of the Flavor Supplier

Robert C. Pellegrino

INTRODUCTION

The taste of foods and beverages has been a cultural rallying point for people throughout the ages. Recipes are passed down from one generation to the next so that critical mixtures of spices and other cooking ingredients are not lost. We begin being exposed to flavors early in our lives and quickly develop tastes that we like and those that we dislike. In later years, we often taste something that rekindles a memory from some other time in our lives. Regional differences in tastes develop as people in a particular area are exposed to the same combinations of ingredients and cooking techniques over and over again. All people have strong opinions about the taste or flavor of the foods and beverages they consume. In a new food product being developed, the flavor is of critical importance to its successful acceptance by the consumer. The flavor industry exists to assist product developers at food and beverage companies to develop customized flavors for the new products they intend to market.

The flavor industry has always been somewhat mysterious; most consumers do not understand that specialized companies create and manufacture the flavors in the food products they purchase. However, the historical roots of the industry can be easily discerned by looking at the spice traders of the Orient or the botanical extract manufacturers of Europe. As time progressed and these materials were analyzed, an understanding of the active ingredients, or key chemical components, of these spices and herbs developed. The active ingredients are those compounds that give a plant, spice, or herb its characteristic taste. Some examples are: menthol, the active ingredient of peppermint; eugenol, the active aromatic chemical of clove; and methyl salicylate, the active component of wintergreen. These and other aromatic chemicals eventually were commercially synthesized from petroleum sources, and the synthetic ingredients were combined to develop particular mixtures that impart flavor character to foods and beverages. The flavor industry developed as the demand for flavoring mixtures increased.

The individuals within the flavor industry who create taste profiles by combining aromatic ingredients are called flavorists or flavor chemists. The flavorist's challenge to put together unique combinations of flavoring materials will always be one of the creative frontiers of the food industry. The individual who can excel in the development of flavors must have a strong knowledge of the aromatic materials that can be utilized and their individual and combined organoleptic qualities. As important as the ability to recall taste characteristics is the artistic flair required to create new combinations of materials to produce a desired flavor effect. In many ways, the flavorist's work with aromatic chemicals is similar to an artist's use of paints. Flavor chemists truly are the food industry's creative artists. They blend artistic and scientific skills to achieve one of the most significant attributes a food product must possess, its flavor.

The formative training of flavorists takes years. In their training they learn the taste and smell characteristics of more than 4,000 synthetic ingredients and 2,000 natural materials approved for use in food products. The education of a flavorist never ends, as he or she continues to learn to utilize new combinations to produce unique flavors for food bases. The learning process involves the characterization of taste by a terminology that consists of descriptors (or notes) such as green, seedy, fatty, and nutty. As they taste individual aromatic chemicals, flavorists discover what is known as the threshold level—the minimum level of the aromatic material at which the character or notes it possesses are recognized.

As the product developer and the flavorist work to achieve a particular flavor for a development project, an understanding of this flavor language becomes a critical factor in their communication. By speaking in flavor nomenclature, a product developer can guide the flavorist to achieve specific desired characteristics. To be successful in custom designing a flavor for a new product, the flavorist must completely understand the challenge of the project. The communication of this information to the flavor company is critical; it is provided by the food product developer to the sales person who represents the flavor company.

THE ROLE OF THE SALES PERSON

Most flavor companies are represented directly by sales personnel at food and beverage manufacturers. These sales people or account managers must understand the product development process. In order to be effective, they need to be personable and trustworthy, and they must have excellent communication skills. These qualities are all important because the product developer will give the sales person a very detailed description of the project on which the manufacturer is working. The product developer would be reluctant to share this information with someone who was not likable or trustworthy. By sharing such information with a sales person, the product developer is providing confidential information on the food company's new product plans. Ethical treatment of the information provided to the sales person is essential to the flavor supplier's long-term success. A product developer who has worked with a sales person on a successful project will be confident that the sales person will help to secure the proper flavor on future occasions.

The sales person's primary mission is to maintain contact with all product developers at their accounts. The sales person will initiate sample requests and work closely with the product developer to advise flavorists of flavor requirements. The most advantageous situation for the flavorist occurs when the product developer provides the base of a food product that has been developed. It gives the flavorist the ability to clearly see the flavor challenge and evaluate creations. Whether the base is provided or not, it is very important that the product developer provide the sales person with the following information:

- A description of the flavor character desired:
  - The target audience for the product.
  - The target or gold standard.
- The form of the flavor required:
  - Liquid.
  - Powder.
  - Paste.
- Processing conditions for the product.
- The manner in which the product will be reconstituted.
- Whether natural, natural WONF (With Other Natural Flavors), or artificial flavor is desired.
- Flavor cost/use guidelines.
- Critical dates of the project:
  - Marketing showing.
  - Consumer tests.
  - Launch date.
  - When the submission is needed.
- Stability tests to be done.
- The quantity of flavor required.
- Other considerations:
  - Kosher considerations.
  - Ingredients that must be avoided.

This information is highly confidential and must be treated as such by the sales person as well as by the organization that receives these project details.

The type of project information needed and normally provided to the sales person can be more clearly seen by using some examples. The descriptions of the flavor desired for a project might be "concord" grape, "fuzzy" peach, or "milk" chocolate. The target audience might be children as opposed to the entire family. If a powder is required, the flavor normally will be spray-dried on a carrier system containing maltodextrins, modified food starch, or vegetable gum. The processing conditions should describe the temperatures at which the flavor will need to survive. If a natural flavor is required, the product developer should specify whether a WONF is acceptable. A WONF flavor normally is what a flavor company will supply if a natural is requested. A WONF flavor will contain not only ingredients derived from the name source but other natural ingredients as well. An orange WONF would contain naturally produced aromatic chemicals such as ethyl butyrate or acetaldehyde. A natural non-WONF orange flavor would be composed of fractions of orange oil. Cost/use guidelines should be specified in terms of price per unit for the flavor.

In a later section, we present a detailed example of what happens today when a flavor supplier receives a flavor request for a project outlined as above. In general, the project would be assigned to a flavor chemist who would discuss it with the sales person. The flavorist develops one or two flavors and sends them to the product developer for evaluation.

The product developer evaluates the flavor, and then is contacted by the sales person for feedback. It is important that the product developer communicate to the sales person in "flavor language" as much as possible. An initial submission of a strawberry flavor might be "too green," a cherry flavor "too medicinal," or a chocolate flavor "too dirty." These descriptors all have meaning to the flavorist. The sales person will communicate this feedback to the flavorist, who can modify the flavor by manipulating the materials in the formula or adding new components. If the wrong words are used in the feedback, a product developer might get a second submission that is still further from the target. This is why the ability of the sales person to communicate effectively is essential to success.

The flavor sales person is the food company's representative to the flavor organization, and manages the resources of the flavor company on behalf of the food company to ensure that the product developer's objectives are met. Once the flavorist is successful in developing a flavor for the new product, the sales person will be contacted to provide pricing, product specifications, and labeling information. At this point, the project picks up momentum, and the sales person is busily involved in ensuring that the product developer has all the information and product needed. Pilot plant runs usually are scheduled, in which larger quantities (5–50 pounds) of flavor are required. It will be provided by a "sample or small order department" within the flavor company.

After the research part of the project is done, the sales person will meet with the purchasing group to coordinate the plant needs for the flavor. She or he will communicate the amount of lead time the flavor company needs in providing a first order. Beyond that, the sales person will work with purchasing to determine annual requirements for the flavor, to ensure that the food company's production schedule will be met. The complexity of the flavor and of food product development demands that the flavor sales person be technically capable of discussing the project. This need has led the flavor companies to recruit product developers and appoint some of their own technical personnel as sales people. The most successful flavor sales people are those who "stay on top" of all the needs of the product developer, as well as those of the food companies' purchasing and manufacturing locations.

HOW FLAVOR COMPANIES HAVE CHANGED

There was a time when grocery stores had just three or four aisles, and the number of products they offered was very limited. Beginning in the 1960s and continuing through the 1980s, a great expansion occurred in the size of grocery stores and the shelf space available for food products. In the food industry, this was an era of product proliferation, with one product after another finding its way onto the shelves. Much of the development activity merely involved adding a new flavor to an existing line. There was tremendous demand on the flavor companies to respond quickly by creating and submitting new flavors for these products and modifying them to fit a certain taste profile.

During this time, food technology was dominated by the development of dry mix products that the consumer prepared at home, and the challenge for the flavor companies was primarily "creative." The flavorists used their creative skills to design a flavor for incorporation into the dry mix to achieve particular organoleptic characteristics described by the food product developer. Sales persons routinely called on product developers to determine the nature of the flavors needed for their projects. Most product developers fail to recognize that flavors behave entirely differently according to the bases into which they are incorporated. The flavor components must be adjusted to accommodate the individual base. The numbers of product development projects that the food companies had in progress were plentiful, and the technical demands on the flavor were fairly simple. The sales person communicated this request to a flavor chemist, who either selected a flavor or two he or she deemed appropriate as a starting point or created new ones. After the submission was made in such a case, the sales person would contact the product developer for feedback or a description of the product developer's evaluation. The feedback discussion revolved around whether the character of the flavor was the desirable one or not. The product developer would suggest modifications of the flavor by describing flavor notes that should be increased or decreased. Revisions were made until the correct taste profile was delivered by the flavorist. Most of the flavors thus developed were artificial—artificial flavors being those composed of synthetic aromatic chemicals (those not derived from natural sources) approved for use in food products. The aromatic chemicals approved for use in flavors are found on GRAS (Generally Recognized As Safe) lists. These lists have been issued by FEMA (Flavor Extract Manufacturers Association) and are recognized by the FDA as safe for use in food and beverages.

In many ways, the 1960s and 1970s were the golden era of the food and flavor industry because the technology involved was relatively simple, and there were a large number of product proliferations. Food products survived longer because computer scanning at the checkout counter did not exist. The cost of launching new products was far less than it is today. Many opportunities existed, and the competition among flavor companies was based on service and creativity.

In the 1980s, there was significant change. A rise in the number of dual-income families led to a demand for "ready to consume" products. New food technologies such as aseptic or extrusion processing were being utilized to develop these food products. A dramatic expansion of frozen, shelf-stable, and refrigerated products with new packaging took place. More and more American households had microwave ovens to prepare food products. Consumers' demand for "natural," "reduced-calorie," and "low-fat" products became very significant.

The demands for these new food products caught both food and flavor companies somewhat by surprise. The product development and flavor challenges could not be solved in the short times that had been typical for project assignments. The evolution of new technologies utilized in the food industry is still having a tremendous impact on the flavor industry. The challenge for flavor development was no longer just "creative." The flavor needed to have stability through the extreme heat experienced in UHT (ultra-high-temperature) and extrusion processing, in high moisture or low acid environments, and through microwave preparation. Much of today's demand for flavors is for "naturals." Many of the ingredients required to produce a "high-quality" natural flavor were not available to meet this demand, which created a need within flavor organizations that they become basic sources of natural raw materials. More and more flavors were being requested that would develop through a cooking process, such as the flavor of roast beef or baked bread. These flavors cannot be created merely by combining aromatic materials. A thorough knowledge of the chemistry behind these processes is required in order to simulate reactions among flavor materials that will "form" these flavor profiles.

The change in the food technology being employed in the development of new products has altered the way that flavor suppliers operate. Most noticeable has been the requirement for dramatic expansion of the technical capabilities of the flavor companies. The flavor chemists are still the central figures of these organizations, but today's leading flavor companies' research staffs contain food scientists, analytical chemists, and natural products chemists to support their efforts. The time needed to solve problems related to the microwave, the extruder, and UHT processing, along with reduced-calorie (low-fat, non-sugar-sweetened) foods and natural flavors is quite extensive. Applied research programs in which development personnel in flavor companies are finding solutions to such problems have become commonplace. Flavor suppliers are continually working on natural materials development, flavor protection systems, and the development of analytical data to enhance their ability to create higher-quality flavors. Food and beverage companies have become "lean and mean" and they are depending on the technical personnel of the flavor suppliers to collaborate more closely than ever in their product development effort. Development teams and time lines are being established today between the flavor suppliers and food companies so that they can face the technical challenges of a new food product program together. Thus it is important to understand the functions within the technical groups at flavor companies, a subject we address in the following section.

THE ROLE OF THE TECHNICAL GROUP

Leading flavor companies' research staffs contain a diverse group of technical personnel to solve flavor challenges related to the new product development efforts of food and beverage companies. The flavor chemist is still the key individual within these organizations, who puts ingredients together to customize a flavor profile for a particular application. The flavorist's effort today is complemented by technical personnel who can assist in providing data and materials that can be used in the new creations. Flavor chemists being trained today must have a very extensive knowledge of chemistry; they need to understand and predict the interactions of all the flavor ingredients they employ with food products.

A strong analytical effort with increasingly sophisticated instrumentation provides input about what the components are that produce a certain aroma or taste. A flavorist will indicate a specific area in a gas chromatographic (GC) analysis, based upon his or her interest in the aroma of a particular peak, and the analytical chemist will attempt to identify that component for the flavorist. There are basically two different types of detectors used in GC analysis: flame ionization and thermal conductivity detectors. The flame ionization detection technique is the more precise one, and it interfaces with a mass spectrometer that can identify individual aromatic chemicals by comparison against standards. Thermal conductivity detection allows the flavorist to "smell through" a GC run and odor-assess the components. The analytical group also evaluates the stability of a flavor by "looking" at how it changes with time in a food or beverage. This approach allows researchers to identify and remove ingredients that are not stable, or to develop an understanding of off notes being formed.

Food scientists work closely with flavor chemists to evaluate newly developed flavor creations to ensure that the flavors survive the food processing or are compatible with a particular base. Variations in sweetening systems, starches, gums, salt, fats, and oils in the base have a significant impact on the flavor's perception and its performance. By supplying the base, the product developer increases the ability of the flavorist to customize a flavor for that particular application. Most flavor companies have added pilot food processing equipment to enhance their ability to design flavors that withstand these processes. The food scientists within flavor companies have become an important link for the product developer. Normally these food scientists have come out of the food industry into the flavor industry. They have been added to provide a specialized expertise, to facilitate flavor development by understanding the application. A flavor company's food scientists speak a common language regarding the processing conditions and ingredients utilized in the food product. They are a key resource for the flavorists in their pursuit of understanding the interaction and the compatibility of the flavor with the base. Rigorous screening of flavors by the food scientist in these technically complex bases and processing conditions becomes a critical factor for success. In cases where a base is not provided, the food scientist may design a base in which the flavor can be screened. Food scientists in the flavor company may put together product demonstrations for food or beverage companies, showing new flavors or concepts that have been developed.

Natural products chemistry is a discipline that came to the flavor industry in the early 1980s. The demand for natural flavors triggered a need to develop new approaches to produce natural materials for the flavorists to utilize. Natural products personnel normally have advanced degrees in enzymology, microbiology, or biochemistry. They utilize fermentation, enzyme modification, or Maillard reaction techniques to develop natural flavor bases to which flavorists can add aromatic components to create the finished flavor. The flavor base develops through the interaction of ingredients over time with temperature, or flavors are produced by microorganisms. Common starting ingredients utilized are amino acids, autolyzed yeasts, sugars, fats, or enzymes. Examples of flavors that would be developed by utilizing such approaches are roast coffee, fried chicken, or caramel. Increasingly, the creation of flavors of the future will involve a collaboration between a natural product chemist who develops a base and a flavorist who creatively formulates a topnote that complements it.

These are the skills that large flavor companies have added to their technical staffs. The changing food technology has made the challenge of most flavor projects more complex than ever before. The artistic aspect of the flavorists remains, but their efforts must be supported by these other disciplines. Today, the research personnel within flavor companies are working to accomplish two missions: to satisfy a flavor need for a specific customer project and to develop technical approaches to longer-term flavor-related problems. In order to understand how these skills are utilized, we shall examine how a complex flavor project might be handled by a flavor company today.

AN EXAMPLE OF A FLAVOR DEVELOPMENT PROJECT

A flavor account manager visits a food product developer to discuss an important new major project. The product developer provides information relating to the objectives of the project, the base, and when initial submissions are needed. Unflavored base is provided, and a "gold standard" target product is discussed and evaluated. The initial submission is needed in two weeks, as the first marketing showing of the new product prototype is scheduled in five or six weeks. The sales person returns to his or her office, writes up a call report on the details of the project, and ships the base to the lab. What happens next is a bit different from one flavor company to the next, but generally major new development projects are handled in the following manner.

The sales report will be electronically transmitted to the flavor company's research administrator by computer. This will allow the project information to be permanently captured and quickly referenced as the project continues. This information provides a basis for research, pricing, regulatory, and manufacturing considerations related to the flavors developed for the project. The quality and comprehensiveness of the report are important to the project's successful execution. At times, product developers will present their own write-ups specifying the objectives of the food company's project and the pertinent technical issues that must be considered.

The sales person's report will be reviewed by a technical group to judge whether an ''off the shelf'' library sample may satisfy the project requirements. Library samples have been tested in various application media, and paneling work has been done to establish the flavors with the highest taste preferences. Descriptors such as ripe, jammy, candylike, roasted, and so on, are indicated for these samples to help one select a flavor for submission. Over time, flavor companies develop thousands of flavor formulations. The flavor library will contain 10 to 20 variations of major flavor types (e.g., strawberry, chocolate). This number is needed because flavors perform differently, depending on the base and the application. The sample library information exists in a computerized database in such a manner that the technical requirements are input, and possible flavor selections are indicated. If a base has been provided or the characteristics of the base have been disclosed (and a base can be modeled), several library flavors that appear to be possibilities will be applied to the base so that those most suitable for the project can be selected. An advantage of sending samples ''off the shelf'' is that this provides flavors to the product developer quickly. It is a way of ''getting on the map'' and providing the basis for a feedback dialogue between the sales person and the product developer vis-à-vis the evaluation of the samples submitted.

If the project is very technically complex in nature, or if the research staff is not satisfied with library flavors evaluated in the base, a development project will be initiated and assigned to a flavorist. In a situation where a gold-standard flavor target has been provided (and time permits), the flavor chemist will request the analytical department to conduct a GC–mass spectrometer analysis to indicate the approximate chemical composition of the flavor of the target. Flavor analytical groups have established mass spectrometer databases that allow them to compare aromatic chemical spectra standards with the profile of components that exist in the target flavor system. If the gold standard is a finished product, an extraction and concentration of the flavor from the product will be made with an organic solvent to prepare the sample for the GC analysis. The analysis will indicate the peak number, the retention time, the identity of the peak, and the approximate concentration. If the flavor has been extracted from the product, the analytical results will indicate the flavor that remains in the finished product. The flavor incorporated into the product might be different from the target flavor, as it may have changed in the food processing or during the shelf life. Sometimes the flavorist will "smell through the peaks" of a GC run, using thermal conductivity detection to determine critical aromas of the flavor profile. Sometimes the flavorist can identify a component by its aroma when the instruments cannot detect it because of the low concentration of the material. GC analytical techniques normally allow a flavorist to get about 80% of the way to the formulation of the flavor of the gold standard. They must develop the unknown part by using their organoleptic experience and creativity.

The flavorist may review the analytical results with a natural products chemist to determine if the components in the gold standard flavor were the result of a reaction or processing of the ingredients. If this is the case, the natural products chemist will develop a base for the flavorist by processing, reacting, or extracting materials. The flavorist will begin to create a flavor by formulating materials that she or he knows are in the product from the analysis, or that she or he organoleptically senses must be added to produce a particular taste or aroma effect. Once initial flavor prototypes have been developed, the flavorist will work with a food scientist to apply the flavor creation to the base and subject it to any processing conditions required to transform it into a finished product. Sometimes the food scientist or the flavorist will suggest base modifications to the product developer so that the base is more compatible with the flavor and the overall project objective. Accelerated stability testing may be done if it is a critical factor. Normally stability testing is a responsibility shouldered by the food company. The flavorist will use ingredients in the formulation that experience indicates will likely be stable in the particular base.

Many times flavorists will formulate a flavor into parts, as they are better able to manipulate those parts to achieve the particular effect they seek. An example of this might be a strawberry flavor that has been formulated into green, fruity, sweet, and sour parts, each of which will be composed of many aromatic chemicals or natural isolates. Once the particular characteristic or note is achieved in each part, the parts are combined to create the total flavor. By adjusting the relationship of the parts, the flavor character can be altered. Fine adjustments can be made once the parts are in balance with each other, by adding aromatic chemicals or natural isolates one at a time to produce a desired effect. Revisions are made based on the organoleptic evaluation of the flavor in the base relative to the gold standard.

An efficient way to achieve rapid flavor development involves visits to a flavor company by product developers. The sales person normally will accompany the product developer on such a visit to facilitate discussions concerning the project. The project will have been worked on by a flavorist in advance of the visit. The flavorist and the product developer will taste the unflavored base and the target to describe the desired flavor attributes of the target. The product developer then will taste the parts of the flavor that the flavorist has created. They will establish a common nomenclature on the notes the components possess and their relationship to the gold-standard flavor profile. They will taste the finished flavor, which is the combination of the parts, and will discuss modifications needed. This discussion revolves around which components need to be increased or decreased, as well as any flavor character that needs to be added or eliminated. Usually these modifications can be done quickly if there is an up-front understanding of the project objective, and if the purpose of the visit is clearly defined. Many variations can be made with the product developer's guidance while he or she is in the flavorist's laboratory. Modifications are made throughout the work session, and the product developer will leave the flavor company with flavor samples to try after returning home.

When processing of a food product is necessary to evaluate its flavor and the flavor company does not have the necessary equipment, a flavorist may visit the food company with a "flavor kit" containing components thought to be workable. The flavorist will "run" the flavor in the product with the developer at the food company's pilot lab or manufacturing facility. The flavorist will manipulate the parts of the flavor brought to the facility to understand those elements being lost or accentuated as a result of the processing, but it will not be possible to develop the final flavor at the food company. The flavorist will return home with a clear picture of the formula design required to accomplish the flavor objective, and will put together one or two formulations for the product developer to try. The product developer then will "run" the flavors and the unflavored control, and will send samples of the products of these runs (including the unflavored control) to the flavorist for evaluation. This will enable the flavorist to understand how the flavor survived the processing, and the flavorist will make adjustments based on an organoleptic and/or analytical evaluation of key flavor components that have been lost or are too strong.

Some product development projects do not identify a gold standard but rather indicate a flavor profile type and a target audience (e.g., tropical punch flavor for a child's beverage). Here the creativity and experience of the flavorist and the food scientist become extremely important to successful development of the flavor. From projects they have worked on previously, they will have developed an understanding of the types of flavors that work in particular applications, as well as attributes of the flavor that the target audience prefers. In this example, children prefer a high impact, and the flavorist will build aromatics into the flavor to provide such a profile. It would be typical in these types of projects to conduct panel sensory studies to determine how the target audience perceives (or scores) the flavor that has been developed. This job is made easier if the food product developer shares with the flavorist the type of questions that might be asked of the sensory test panel.

Once the flavor (or two or three variations) has been developed and screened to the satisfaction of the flavorist and the food scientist, samples will be submitted. The feedback process will begin among the developer, the sales person, and the flavorist. Modifications will be made until the developer selects a flavor or flavor variations to show to marketing personnel associated with the new product. The marketing group will decide whether the new product prototype is ready for testing with consumers. Normally a range of products with different flavor variations is shown by the product developer, and two or three are selected for further testing. If prototypes are not judged to be acceptable by marketing, revision work will be required in either the base, the flavor, or both. Once the consumer testing is conducted, further flavor revisions may be required if the sensory scores do not achieve a targeted level.

During the period of product testing, the issues of pricing, ingredient labeling, product certification, specification development, and manufacturing lead times will be worked out between the food company and the flavor supplier through the sales person. Today formulas are computerized at most flavor companies. Once the product developer has selected a flavor, the flavorist will input into the computer the formula that has been created. If new ingredients are used, they must be coded. Costing systems have been designed to develop a product cost based on the ingredients used, the product yield, and the anticipated manufacturing costs. For a completely new flavor, it might take a day or so to get a price, but prices for library flavors can be provided immediately.

It is extremely important that the flavor supplier understand the manner in which the food company's quality assurance personnel will test the flavor to ensure its conformance to product specifications. If particular analytical tests are to be conducted, the product developer or Q.A. personnel should so advise the flavor supplier. By understanding the product specifications and any testing that will be conducted, can avoid future problems or product rejections.

FLAVOR PURCHASE AND BEYOND

Once the food or beverage company has decided to market the new product, the product developer and any purchasing and manufacturing personnel to be involved in the product launch should provide input to the sales person in terms of the flavor requirements. Both the estimated volume of flavor needed initially and the annual volume projected are very important. The flavor company will utilize this information to ensure that it can secure the raw materials needed to produce the flavor. If the food company issues a contract to purchase a specified amount of the flavor, the flavor company will contract for a sufficient quantity of materials to produce the volume of flavor specified in the contract. This will lock in the cost and availability of materials, which in the case of natural flavors is a particularly important consideration. If production of the flavor does not require specially processed ingredients, and it is made by "compounding" (weighing and mixing) aromatic materials, the demand on the operations group of the flavor company is fairly routine. However, if the flavor contains natural ingredients that must be prepared or specially processed to develop a flavor base, the challenge to produce the flavor in a short lead time becomes more difficult. It is becoming increasingly important for the product developer and purchasing to work in close partnership with the flavor company through the sales person on the supply needs for the flavor. They must have a dialogue on the lead time required by the flavor supplier to manufacture the flavor.

With the consolidation that is occurring among companies within the food industry, there is increased discussion about limiting the number of suppliers with whom food and beverage companies will do business. The impetus for this is coming primarily from the purchasing and manufacturing areas because it will allow them to capture the cost savings of increased flavor volumes from a smaller group of suppliers. This appears to be a trend that is becoming important in the product development community as well. Within the research groups of food companies there exists less staff to develop new food products that involve complex technical issues. From the point of view of product development personnel, there is an increasing need to work more closely than ever with suppliers to resolve flavor designs for new products. The flavor companies continue to add food scientists to their own staff, as it has become important to demonstrate the flavor to the product developer in a finished product. This approach allows instant feedback and shortens the product development process.

Another recent development is an increase in the number of exclusive collaborations established between flavor and food companies. If projects are longer-term and extremely complex, food companies are choosing to work in close partnership with two and sometimes only one flavor supplier to develop an exclusive flavor for new products. If the flavor company succeeds in the development and a product goes to market, the food company normally will guarantee that the flavor company will "enjoy" its business for two years. At that point, some food companies might utilize alternate supplier programs to leverage the price they pay for the flavor. However, it is wise for the food company first to ask the flavor company to submit a cost-reduced version of the product, as this sets up a potential win–win situation for the food company and the flavor supplier. The flavor company will reduce the cost of the flavor, and it also will retain the business.

In the future, a closer working relationship will be necessary between flavor suppliers and food companies. The trust and confidence they place in each other will always be vital to successful new product development. The food companies can help secure the relationship between the two by letting the flavor companies understand their product directions. This will allow the flavor companies to understand the resources they need to add, as well as the basic technologies they need to develop. One thing is clear: the flavor development related to a new food product will always involve creativity, scientific knowledge, and a quick response. The role of the flavor supplier is essential to the successful execution of a food company's mission to develop new products.

RECOMMENDED READING

Furia, Thomas and Bellanca, Nicolo. 1975. *Fenaroli's Handbook of Flavor Ingredients*, Vols. I and II. Cleveland, Ohio: CRC Press Inc.

Heath, Henry. 1981. *Source Book of Flavors*. Westport, Conn.: Avi Publishing Co., Inc.

Heath, Henry and Reineccius, Gary. 1986. *Flavor Chemistry and Technology*. Westport, Conn: Avi Publishing Co., Inc.

Chapter 15

Industry–University Synergy: A Multifaceted Opportunity for the Industrial Product Developer

Myron Solberg, Jack L. Rossen, and Robert B. Leslie

IDENTIFYING THE RESOURCE

The products of universities are new knowledge and educated people, both of which are critical to food product development. New knowledge is the underpinning of future commercial products; and for the food industries, it comes from basic and applied science disciplines. Educated people are able to transform new knowledge into useful end products that fill consumer needs, whether they be related to convenience, safety, aesthetics, or healthfulness.

There is a long tradition of industry–university interaction in food process and product development. An early example in the United States was the cooperation between William Lyman Underwood of the Underwood Company, a manufacturer of tinned foods, and Samuel Cate Prescott of the Massachusetts Institute of Technology. Their cooperation led to a scientific understanding of canned food spoilage and process requirements, which resulted in safe and wholesome canned vegetables, available throughout the year and able to fill the nutritional requirements of urban populations. The ultimate accomplishment was the development of a well-industrialized nation in the period just before and during the early part of the twentieth century.

The university, then, is a real resource. To understand its potential, one must be familiar with the roles universities play in society, as discussed in the following paragraphs.

Function of the University

Teaching

The agricultural strength of the United States is supported by the land-grant university system. The three-component mission of the land-grant universities incorporates teaching, research, and extension.

This is publication No. C10535-1-90 of the New Jersey Agricultural Experiment Station supported by state funds and the Center for Advanced Food Technology (CAFT). The Center for Advanced Food Technology is a New Jersey Commission on Science and Technology Center.

Traditional teaching of food science is accomplished in more than 50 U.S. universities. The Institute of Food Technologists (IFT) developed guidelines for acceptable undergraduate programs leading to the bachelor of science degree, and it evaluates applications from university departments whose programs are thought to meet the criteria. Box 15-1 outlines the existing criteria, which periodically are reviewed and revised by the IFT Education Committee. At the graduate level, approximately 50 schools offer the master of science, the doctor of science, and/or the doctor of philosophy degree with a variety of food science and related programs.

The common educational path is that of the full-time student attending classes and/or carrying on research during the normal workday hours. This system exists in nearly all institutions of higher learning and is the source of degreed persons entering the work force.

Nontraditional university education is the area where industrially employed food product developers are given the opportunity to sharpen their skills. One route is to take an intensive short course designed to update the student's knowledge base or to introduce new knowledge. This serves the dual purpose of providing knowledge to the attendees and giving them the opportunity to get to know some experts, thus establishing a potential source of knowledge for the future.

Another route is the entry of the fully employed-in-industry person into a formal evening program leading to food science degrees at the master's or the doctor's level. A few U.S. universities, located near large concentrations of food industry facilities, have provided this opportunity for growth and development to industrial scientists and technologists. For example, a program of this type has existed at Rutgers University in New Brunswick, New Jersey, since the early 1970s when the faculty of the graduate program recognized the need for it. They accepted the obligation to maintain a competitive food industry in New Jersey by agreeing to teach all graduate courses after 4:30 P.M. and to eliminate residency requirements for graduate degrees. Additionally, the faculty agreed that a student could carry out degree-qualifying research in a company laboratory, provided that the results would be publishable, and that the faculty advisor would have prescheduled free access to the work area.

This radical departure from the norm evolved one further step in the early 1980s. One company in the area requested that a series of graduate-level courses be taught at the company site for its employees. Students paid regular university tuition, the company paid the university for faculty members' time, and an extra amount was provided for expenses and departmental discretionary use. In the early 1990s, this program is evolving into a Video Cassette Recorder (VCR) program that will be provided to multiple company locations with in-person interaction sessions at central off-campus sites.

The impact of the total program has been extraordinary. The traditional grad-

Box 15-1.   IFT undergraduate curriculum minimum standards, 1977 revision.

Organization and Budget: administered by an independent administrative unit with an adequate budget.

Faculty: minimum of four with earned doctoral degrees or extensive professional experience.

Facilities: up-to-date laboratories to conduct chemical, engineering, and microbiological exercises required. Pilot plant to teach unit operations and unit processes. Adequate library facilities and holdings.

Required Courses in Food Science and Technology:

Food Chemistry—lecture and laboratory (prerequisites: four chemistry courses including organic and biochemistry).

Food Analysis—lecture and laboratory (prerequisites: four chemistry courses and one food chemistry course).

Food Microbiology—lecture and laboratory (prerequisite: one general microbiology course).

Food Engineering—lecture and laboratory (prerequisites: one physics and two mathematics courses).

Food Processing—two courses with lecture and laboratory.

Other Required Courses:

Chemistry—two courses in general chemistry, one course in organic chemistry, one course in biochemistry.

Biological Sciences—one course in general biology, one course in general microbiology.

Nutrition—one course.

Mathematics—two courses including concepts of calculus.

Statistics—one course.

Physics—one course.

Communications—two courses.

Humanities and Social Sciences—four courses.

uate-student group is large and strong. The nontraditional component of the program has conferred many master of science degrees and a few doctor of philosophy degrees, whereas the traditional program has conferred the vast majority of the doctoral degrees during the two decades. The state of New Jersey has maintained a strong food processing presence with a concentration of research and development activities. The food science program at Rutgers has become one of the largest, strongest, and most highly respected in the world.

Research

Research activity and productivity are the keys to graduate education in the universities, which are the traditional source of the knowledge base needed for food process and product development. Traditional balanced programs in food chemistry, food biology, and food engineering underlie the success of the exemplary food science programs in universities. Discipline-oriented research, using foods as models and generating mechanistic and molecular understanding, has strengthened these programs. The people who gain this knowledge then play a leading role in turning the industrial applications into both improved and new products.

University research is led by faculty members utilizing the creativity, skills, and enthusiasm of graduate students, postdoctoral researchers, and technicians. One faculty member may be the designated principal investigator for several research projects. The faculty may adopt different philosophical approaches to research: Some may choose to develop research of extraordinary depth in an attempt to elucidate molecular-level phenomena involved in the development of cell structure, such as cell membrane or cell wall synthesis, mechanisms of nutrient transport into cells, inhibition of cellular respiration, or maintenance of cellular concentration gradients. Others may choose to conduct phenomenological research based upon the measurement of observed results without an in-depth understanding of processes. Some may develop empirically based mathematical models, while others develop molecular-interaction-based mathematical models of food systems during processing.

The university system is designed to foster individualism in the belief that it assures creativity and originality. The end product of this activity is defined as scholarly work, which may be quantitated by numbers of publications and the quality of the reported discoveries—measured by numbers of citations by other authors, invitations to speak at national and international meetings, and job offers from other universities.

Historically, food scientists chose to specialize in commodities or processes. This resulted in dairy, meat, bakery, fish, and fruit and vegetable experts, as well as canning, freezing, dehydration, curing, and other experts. However, the commodity approach, though still alive in some universities, has given way to the discipline approach; expertise now is identified in proteins, lipids, carbohydrates, nutrition, microbiology, flavors, colors, rheology, psychophysics, material properties, material and energy transport, and more.

The modern approach allows one to solve problems and create products through understanding rather than from experience alone. Knowledge is transferred across all commodities. For example, researchers now recognize that the principles of a molecular structure's relationship to the functional quality of moistness are similar whether the product is bread dough, meat batter, surimi, been curd, or cheese.

The university with a wide coverage of discipline areas within the food science program obviously is a potential source of the knowledge required by product developers. The availability of broad discipline coverage across an entire university also offers other opportunities. Utilizing the knowledge provided by food scientists simplifies matters to some extent for product developers, as their language of communication resembles the language of the industrial user. Obtaining the same knowledge from nonfood scientists may require the assistance of a sophisticated translator from the potential user company.

The bottom line is that research capability exists within the universities—the ability to generate knowledge leading to more complete understanding of the chemical and physical phenomena that are critical to food process and food product development.

It is necessary for universities to continue the generation of such understanding, and adequate funding of the research needed to provide this knowledge is essential. Funds must be derived from potential users who are benefiting from existing knowledge. This includes state and federal governments representing the indirect beneficiaries, the consumers, and industry representing the direct beneficiaries.

Extension

The extension component of the U.S. land-grant universities was the unique aspect differentiating the land-grant universities from all other universities worldwide. The traditional role of extension is to translate the relatively esoteric knowledge generated in the university and encourage its application to field problems. The system was created and exploited in production agriculture. It provided the know-how for effective fertilization, irrigation, pesticide application, seed development, artificial insemination, sanitary milk handling, and much more.

The extension function generally is implemented through an organization of agents in the field who are supported by specialists residing in the university. The specialists are responsible for transferring information to the agents in response to problems, to implement improvements in present practices. The system was well established in the agricultural community long before there was an identifiable "food science." Thus the food industry developed largely without agricultural extension support.

When food science extension became a reality, its role was technology transfer, and its implementation was principally the task of the extension specialists working directly between the university and the processor. The large national or multinational food processor does not need the extension specialist, as it employs people with equivalent expertise. The extension specialist thus interacts primarily with small companies, home food preservers, supermarkets, and restaurants. Every state in the nation has its own "cooperative extension program." Each program is targeted toward fulfilling the needs of its state.

Food science extension specialists often provide a valuable service to food companies of all sizes in continuing education. Extension programs develop workshops, training programs, symposia, and seminars.

Technology and information transfer is the extension specialist's function. The resource is available to all persons and companies within the state and is supported jointly by the federal and state governments.

Industry–University Interface

Benefits for Industry

The university is a source of people, facilities, and knowledge. The people tend to be creative, industrious, and entrepreneurial as successful university faculty. They tend to be willing to share their knowledge and their time in the often naive belief that this will lead to research support. When it does lead to research funding, they provide an opportunity for a company to gain information without major capital investment and without having to commit its personnel to potential short-term residency. Industrial support of research gives a company the opportunity to become familiar with students working in areas of interest to it and lets it have the first chance to make employment offers to them.

Facilities can be made available to the company at the university, in the pilot plant or in the laboratory. Often there are unique opportunities in both places. Pilot plant equipment may be instrumented for research and thus may provide information not attainable from a standard rental or even from equipment within one's own facility. Instrumentation and the expertise to operate it and interpret the results often exist at the university, but may not be available within the company. This instrumentation may be more advanced than similar instruments in company laboratories, or it may include instruments that are truly niche-research-oriented and thus do not exist in corporate laboratories, including consulting companies.

Companies can arrange to use pilot plant equipment, to have samples analyzed on various instruments, and to obtain an interpretation of the results without significant capital investment and without employing highly specialized personnel. This arrangement also allows company personnel to meet graduate and undergraduate students and to develop a relationship that permits the evaluation of capabilities and could influence a student's employment decision in favor of the company.

At one time, many universities had little to offer in state-of-the-art equipment and instrumentation. This situation has changed considerably in recent years and continues to improve.

Knowledge residing in the university needs to be extracted so that it can be applied industrially. An occasional visit may whet the appetite, but serious knowledge acquisition is the result of significant interaction. The support of a research effort provides legitimate opportunity for far-ranging discussions. When a university faculty member considers a problem, the answer or discussion it engenders is an integration of knowledge derived from research supported by a variety of sources. This same kind of know-how is applied to any project being supported by a company. Direct support of research offers the supporter access to the information generated with a significant lead time relative to those who will get it from its formal presentation or publication. The information may have been generated by using a model of much greater significance to the sponsor than to other interested companies; and the sponsor has the opportunity to negotiate certain patent benefits, going all the way to exclusivity. These benefits may be based upon certain up-front fees or on other terms. Such arrangements will vary from one university to another.

Benefits for Academe

The industry–university interface provides the academician with a source of funds for carrying out research and for the resultant education of graduate students. The industrial component provides enlightenment about the kinds of problems existing in the product development arena and thus an opportunity for the academician to identify missing fundamental knowledge. This, in turn, provides an opportunity for a research focus on areas that will attract industrial attention and generate investment.

The academician becomes familiar with the industrial scientists, technologists, and engineers and thus is better able to assist students in finding industrial employment. The expertise of the academician is recognized by persons in industry, and the opportunity develops for a consulting arrangement. Such an activity provides the faculty member with income as well as knowledge about industrial practice. This industrial knowledge can become an important part of the faculty member's teaching by allowing the use of real examples in support of concepts. The academician can become a better teacher by learning to explain concepts in easily understandable terms.

The university scientist also gains an increased understanding of the functions of the industrial scientist and can better prepare students for the transition they will make when they move from academe to industry. This will prevent the disappointments that are possible for both the new Ph.D. and the company when unreal expectations exist.

TAPPING THE RESOURCE

Knowing the components and philosophies of a resource is the key to tapping it. The university usually consists of teaching, research, and extension components; and identifying those people, facilities, and programs will allow use of its potential. No regular updating of such information is published. The IFT maintains a list of universities and colleges with approved undergraduate programs, published annually as a part of a booklet entitled *IFT Administered Fellowship/Scholarship Program: Program Description and Application Instructions*, available from the Scholarships Department of the Institute of Food Technologists, 221 North LaSalle Street, Chicago, Illinois 60601. Listings of universities and colleges with designations of expertise areas, commodity specialties, and mechanisms for industrial interaction appear from time to time in industry trade magazines. *Prepared Foods* magazine, in April 1987, presented such information in an article prepared by Daniel Best and Nancy McCue of the magazine staff, entitled "Industry and Academia: Forging a New Relationship." A table in the article incorporates information about 22 universities, describing such topics as confidentiality, expertise, and food categories. Also, more detailed descriptions are provided for four other universities.

A need exists for the development of an academic source book for food science and technology. The industrial benefit of such a publication could be significant.

Based on a knowledge of what is generally available and some idea of what may be specifically available, this section considers mechanisms for utilizing the resource.

Traditional Routes

Consultants

The university scientist may serve as a consultant to a company, and as a consultant could be expected to charge from $500 to $1,500 per day plus expenses, depending upon the level of expertise possessed. The benefits of hiring a consultant include a rapid rate of information transfer, a minimal risk of proprietary information leakage, and a potential for the development and monitoring of an in-company effort. The negatives include the singularity of the individual human's knowledge, and the availability of just the existing knowledge with no opportunity to generate new knowledge.

Cooperative Extension Specialists

The extension specialist is available to act in a manner similar to that of a consultant, with his or her activities generally restricted to use by in-state residents or companies. Often the extension specialist will request that the help seeker come to the university, thus increasing the specialist's productivity. The transfer of information offered by the extension specialist involves no fees; but should there be a need to carry out analyses or small research investigations, fees may be charged to cover supplies and technician time. After being presented with the industrial need, the extension specialist may recommend a consultant or the development of a cooperative project with one or more faculty members, or some other approach that would result in costs.

The advantages of working with an extension specialist are greatest when the problem being considered is one that can be solved through the use of existing technology. In such a case, answers are obtained quickly and without charge. The extension specialist also will analyze the more complex problems and recommend routes to solutions, thus providing the equivalent of a free problem evaluation session.

Agricultural Experiment Stations (AESs)

The AES is the research arm that traditionally provided information to the extension specialist, who would then carry it to the user. AESs are components of land-grant universities. In some states they are separated from the teaching departments, whereas in others they are fully integrated with the departments, with faculty partially included in the teaching budget and partially in the AES research budget.

The AES activity is directed toward state problems and often is supported by funds specifically designated by legislatures for the development of individual crops or individual industrial sectors. Many state problems are national and global problems as well.

An industry within a state may apply pressure to the legislature to encourage the support of research in areas of its specific interest.

Every AES project, nationwide, is reported upon annually. The brief reports are entered into a national computerized database known as the CRIS system. Key-word searches of the CRIS database are possible mechanisms for identifying where, who, and what as related to a wide variety of research topics of interest to food scientists in both academic and industrial environments.

One-on-One Projects

A company may establish a funded research project with a university scientist within a university. The university scientist who has special expertise or unique instrumentation may undertake the project through any of several routes. If the project requires unique analytical skills and instrumentation, the results may be provided on a fee-for-service basis.

Fee-for-service charges will be based upon costs for labor, materials, instrument depreciation, indirect costs or overhead, and some price assigned to "expertise." Research universities are required to operate under the rules of sound fiscal management. The use of a university fee for service capability is justifiable for a company that has not invested capital for instruments and facilities and has not employed the necessary expertise. The university provides an opportunity for evaluating the efficacy of concepts or hypotheses without major investments.

Similar motivation may result in a company's funding a full-fledged research project. Again the absence of both capital investment and the need to employ expertise makes the prospects interesting to the company. The university's interest is twofold: first, to provide educational opportunity to students and, second, to provide new knowledge for incorporation into the discipline. Supporting a graduate student and providing that student with a thesis or dissertation opportunity is a university goal. This reflects itself in the need for a project to be no less than one year in duration and preferably two or three years. To be suitable for the support of a graduate student, the research must be publishable. For the research to be highly useful to the company, there may be a need for the use of proprietary formulations in the studies. This dilemma is resolvable; a frequently utilized solution is to conduct the work with the proprietary formulation and with a model formulation simultaneously, with reporting in the scientific literature of the model results.

The funding of a research project within a university may take a variety of formats. Of greatest benefit to both the sponsor and the university is the research contract. In this format, the expectations of both parties are clearly spelled out and agreed upon before the work is begun. The costs for a one-graduate-student project research contract may vary greatly from one university to another and within a university, based upon the sponsor's requirements for the handling of resulting intellectual property. Typical cost ranges are presented in Table 15-1. The faculty salary cost will vary from some universities that consider it matching funds to others that charge it fully, including fringe benefits and indirect (overhead) charges. The salary cost, when charged, will vary with the level of expertise of the individual. Graduate students' salaries vary from one university to another, as does the cost of fringe benefits charged to salaries. Some universities waive tuition fees, whereas others charge tuition fully to a project. Indirect costs vary greatly from one university to another. Most universities have their base indirect costs assigned by federal government auditors. The federal indirect cost

Table 15-1. Typical range of costs for a one-graduate-student research project in a university.

	Low	Average	High
Salaries:			
Faculty member (10%)	0	4,000	8,000
Graduate student (50%)	8,000	12,000	15,000
Fringe Benefits (20–27%)	1,600	3,000	5,670
Other Costs:			
Tuition	0	6,000	10,000
Supplies & operating	3,000	7,500	10,000
Travel	500	1,000	1,500
Indirect Costs:			
40–140%	5,240	16,750	67,430
TOTAL	18,340	50,250	117,600

level is based upon the university's physical plant and research facilities value, and the university uses this established rate as its base for all negotiations with industrial sponsors. The rate may decrease as the sponsor moves toward more desirable generic and basic research, and it will increase as proprietary rights are sought. All patents usually are assigned to the university. Sponsor exclusivity of any sort will affect the indirect cost rate, with the highest rate being for exclusive license without fee. Negotiating points for indirect cost reductions include prior agreement to pay all patenting costs, first right of refusal rather than exclusive use, nonexclusive license, license fees to be negotiated after invention occurs, and other similar items.

The opposite extreme to the research contract is the specified gift or grant-in-aide. This mechanism is one in which a sum of money is provided with no legal expectations in support of the research efforts of a particular university faculty researcher. Such a grant usually will bear no indirect costs. The benefits derived by the grantor include a legitimatized opportunity to engage the researcher in discussions and an opportunity to suggest areas of potentially mutual interest. The many possible arrangements between the two extremes described offer numerous opportunities for negotiation between companies and universities in the search for mutually beneficial relationships.

Departmental Interaction Projects

The interdisciplinary nature of food science provides an opportunity for inter-departmental cooperation on research projects, and a sponsoring company can stimulate such interaction. The researchers benefit from a reduction of university procedural requirements, and the company may benefit by funding a shared technician who will assist several faculty researchers. However, departmental interaction projects generally will involve a greater investment of funds than projects not involving such interaction because each faculty researcher will expect a graduate student to be supported in order to accomplish his or her part of the cooperation. Thus, although such an opportunity exists within the university environment, its utilization may be limited.

The need for such interdisciplinary research activities has not gone unnoticed. The search for economically feasible means to achieve such objectives has spawned a variety of new approaches. These have taken on the identification of centers or institutes, which we discuss next.

Alternate Approaches

Overview — Centers and Institutes

The successful university center or institute is one that complements the traditional department structure within the university and/or the research and development function of industry. A primary principle must be that the center or institute carries out activities that a department or company could not accomplish on its own. These activities should provide increased opportunities for the benefit of both university departments and their faculty members and for corporate R&D units and industrial scientists, technologists, and engineers.

Centers and institutes often are established across departmental lines and even university lines. They sometimes are designed to bridge between industry and the university. They may be organized to carry out unique cross-disciplinary research or to provide a regionalized source of expensive expertise, equipment, or instrumentation. Sometimes they may make available unique opportunities for entrepreneurs or small businesses to obtain product or process development assistance along with marketing sales, accounting, government relations, and other required support leading to business development. There are numerous paths that may be or have been taken by developing or developed centers and institutes.

Classical Institutes

The classical university or government institute has tended to focus upon an area of expertise where narrowness, rather than breadth, is its strength. A critical mass of researchers are housed together to provide a stimulating and competitive environment so that scientific or technological frontiers are advanced. The mission is to gain new knowledge. Funding is, in part or totally, the traditional one-on-one type, which may be provided by industry, government, foundations, or endowments. Scientists or faculty members function as research leaders or principal investigators. They develop teams of technicians and postdoctoral associates. Often there are opportunities to have predoctoral graduate research students in the group through affiliation with university graduate programs or departments. The facilities and equipment usually are not connected with a university department, however. The faculty will have a university department affiliation, but their participation in teaching will be decided by their own preferences with little or no stimulation from the institute director.

The classical institute provided the foundation for many new approaches, which tend to be called centers although some have retained the institute designation.

The long-established institutes or centers have many operational formats and must continue to evolve as they maintain viability in a continually changing environment. Several of those institutions were selected for description here to illustrate the many permutations that are possible and the adaptability of the various systems.

Established Centers and Institutes Evolving

USDA's Agricultural Research.   The food science discipline had within its traditional structure some of the earliest forerunners of the new approaches. The first of these were government-sponsored and -operated laboratories such as the U.S. Department of Agriculture's Regional Utilization Laboratories. Founded in 1940, these laboratories of the Agricultural Research Service (ARS) were dedicated to developing ways to increase the utilization of various crops that were yielding harvests above the consumers' level of demand. Organized and funded by the government and staffed with civil service scientists, these laboratories were independent of universities and attempted to interest industry in their discoveries and developments. The four USDA Regional Laboratories now are called Regional Research Centers (RRC) and have maintained their mission of commodity-oriented utilization directed toward the region in which they are located. The Northern RRC concentrates on grains and fermentations. Fruits and vegetables are the focus of the Western RRC. The Southern RRC works on cotton, cottonseed, fibers, and soybeans. The widest range of subjects is addressed by the Eastern RRC, which directs attention to hides and leather, wool, dairy products, meats, vegetables, and the all-encompassing area of food safety. In addition to the four Regional Research Centers, ARS has research activities at nearly 130 locations throughout the United States, employing nearly 8,000 people. The general research aim continues to be one of direct assistance to the consumer, the university, and the industry. These research centers now compete for funding from government agencies. The Regional Research Centers recently have been directed to increase their interaction with industry and to direct effort toward both the food and the nonfood use of agricultural commodities. They are initiating cooperative and sponsored research arrangements with industrial firms in which there is a cost-sharing scheme. Exclusivity of patent rights and limited-time confidentiality arrangements are being negotiated with corporations. They are a resource for industry that awaits exploitation. At the same time, they sponsor research at universities under contracts when such a transfer of funds is appropriate.

UK's Institute for Food Research.   The Institute for Food Research (IFR) in Great Britain is comparable to the USDA ARS, but it demonstrates some significant differences. The IFR is one of eight institutes that constitute the laboratory facilities of the Agricultural and Food Research Council (AFRC). The AFRC is an independent body established by Royal Charter, which is funded principally from the "Science Budget" of the U.K. Department of Education and Science (DES). In addition to its DES funding, AFRC receives "commissions" and the associated funding from the Ministry of Agriculture,

Fisheries and Food (MAFF). AFRC also undertakes research for industry and other bodies. Its research program is carried out by using the scientists and facilities in its own institutes or in U.K. university departments via research grants.

At the time of writing, the IFR is going through a period of consolidation restructuring and retargeting. Its intrinsic scientific potential, in terms of people skills and facilities, is being updated to the highest international standards. The focus of the work is being directed toward developing the generic science base with less emphasis on specific commodity-oriented work. Within the changed focus of the IFR, greater emphasis will be given to providing high-quality, impartial scientific input to issues that impinge more directly upon the food consumer rather than the food manufacturer.

The IFR now is moving toward a position of independence, aiming for "arms-length" relationships with industry, consumer bodies, and government in order to maintain impartiality in its research and advisory roles. The technical program of the institute includes food structure : functionality : processing relationships, with increasing emphasis being given to food safety, nutrition, and food quality and with new initiatives in biotechnology.

The emerging relationships between diet and health require food products with scientifically endorsed nutritional claims. IFR will serve these needs for the consumer, the manufacturer, and the regulatory authorities. IFR has established clinical links with many of the preeminent medical research schools, and has established strong collaborative programs in dietary and physiological factors affecting iron and zinc absorption in infants and adults, effects of dietary fiber on human gastrointestinal function, and carbohydrate and lipid metabolism of fiber-enriched foods. It is conceivable that the research now considered strategic by the government funding agencies will give rise to the precompetitive programs of the food industry of the twenty-first century.

UK's Research Associations.   Another approach, also originating in the United Kingdom, was that of the Research Association. The Research Association (RA) focused on helping an industry in short-term problem solving, with the generation of new knowledge as an objective but one of considerably less priority than problem resolution. Three Research Associations are described here: the Leatherhead Food Research Association, the Campden Food and Drink Research Association, and the Flour Milling and Baking Research Association.

The Leatherhead Food RA was founded in 1919 to improve food production through research. The majority of the work carried out in the early days was government-funded, but the proportion has decreased over the years, with a shift in emphasis toward industry-funded contract work. In effect, Leatherhead Food RA and the other food RAs now are owned by their members in the food industry. The Leatherhead technical program consists of work of a confidential nature done with, or for, a single member or small groups of member companies; technical programs selected, guided, and monitored by its R&D panels, on which expert technical representatives of the member companies are well represented; and strategic work, funded by membership contributions and government.

Membership has grown from the original U.K. base to about 750 members in about 40 countries worldwide. The Leatherhead Food RA has earned a national and international reputation, as well as substantial revenues, by developing the capability to provide a wealth of legislative, scientific, technical, and market information, on an international basis. The Leatherhead RA is best known for its information service. In the area of new product development, the Leatherhead Food RA provides a complete package from original concept, through development and pilot production, to sensory analysis and consumer acceptance studies. Extensive analytical resources provide essential support services, ranging from nutritional labeling to problem solving, such as the identification of spoilage and foreign bodies.

Leatherhead's experienced staff operate in strict confidence in high-quality laboratories and processing facilities. These facilities are of significant value to small to medium-sized companies, which see them as cost-effective alternatives to establishing their own in-house capabilities.

The Campden Food and Drink RA was established in 1919 as the Campden Experimental Factory. Within a few years its mission gained focus, and it was renamed as a Fruit and Vegetable Preservation unit. Fruit and Vegetable Preservation remained in its name until 1972 when it became the Campden Food Preservation RA; then, in 1988, it became the Campden Food and Drink RA.

Campden, as do the other RAs, derives its income from membership subscriptions, government contracted (or commissioned) work, and confidential work done on behalf of individual members, or groups of members. It has approximately 500 members, who contribute 20% of its annual funding. The government provides 30% of its funds, with 50% derived from confidential contracts. The 200 staff members are organized into scientific divisions covering Agriculture and Sensory Quality, Microbiology and Food Hygiene, Food Technology, and Food Science.

Research funded by members is controlled through membership panels to meet their long- and short-term needs, with additional benefits of cost sharing. Results of government-sponsored research are available to members. Group-sponsored project results are confidential to those participants directly involved.

Campden offers a special "Acorn" membership designed to give companies access to technical advisory services without incurring the cost of employing specialist staff. This introduction to Campden's services is available for a two-year period to help small businesses become established in the food and catering industries.

Because of the strong membership base and its long-established commitment to food preservation, this RA has been able to develop an effective accommodation between providing shorter-term direct support to the membership and establishing some longer-term commitment to acquiring in-depth scientific knowledge in certain key areas related to the preservation of food quality and safety.

The Flour Milling and Baking Research Association (FMBRA) was formed in Chorleywood in 1967. This RA carries out scientific research and provides technical support to over 500 member companies both in the United Kingdom and overseas.

Members' subscriptions and contract work carried out for MAFF have formed the two main sources of finance. In response to the government's revised approach to the funding of public sector research and development, FMBRA has broadened its financial base and now attracts grants from the Homegrown Cereals Authority, the Department of Trade and Industry (DTI), and European Economic Community (EEC) R&D programs.

FMBRA has built up a range of specialist equipment to serve the needs of the cereal processing sector of the food industry, and it also has maintained a commitment to basic research to underpin its applied work in milling and baking.

With over 600 journal titles and 7,000 books, the FMBRA library is probably the foremost collection of flour milling and baking publications in Europe. FMBRA also maintains a unique computer-held database, now comprising over 38,000 items of industrial relevance and available both on and off line. The current literature is scanned, and abstracts of relevant material are prepared and published in hard-copy format every two months. This RA provides members with full information on legislation and with help in interpreting its implications. It also plays an important role in providing information to the government when existing legislation is under review or new legislation is proposed, and it helps trade associations formulate their views on proposed legislation.

Japan's National Food Research Institute. The National Food Research Institute (NFRI), in Tsukuba Science City, Japan, is today's form of what started in 1934 as the Rice Utilization Research Laboratory. Funded completely by the government, Ministry of Agriculture, Forestry and Fisheries, this institute has eight research divisions. The mission is to provide the base of knowledge needed to establish sophisticated processing techniques and more convenient and effective supply systems for food. The research efforts of approximately 110 researchers currently are concentrated in biotechnology and microbiology, engineering, quality evaluation and preservation, and foods and their components.

The basic and applied research conducted within the NFRI is published in the scientific literature. The institute has no financial involvement with industry. The expertise within the institute and the research results often are transferred to industry through the unique system of Japanese Research and Development Associations, wherein university experts serve as members of an advisory group or planning committee. Four of these associations are described in Table 15-2. The Ministry of Agriculture, Forestry and Fisheries matches the industrial investment, which must be a cooperative effort of at least two companies. One of the companies would be the ultimate user of the technology and the other the manufacturer of the technological innovation.

Sweden's SIK—the Swedish Food Institute. The Swedish Food Institute, SIK, located in Goteborg, Sweden, was established in 1947. SIK has approximately 90 member companies, which comprise the food industry trade association. The majority are from the Scandinavian countries, but there is meaningful international representation. The activities of SIK are financed by the member companies and the Swedish Government through the National Board for Technical Development. The objectives of SIK clearly recognize the commercial needs of the member companies, contributing to them through research which enables the food industry in general to produce foods that are in line with the evolving needs of consumers. SIK anticipated a growing demand for contract and consultancy work and recognized that a strengthening of its resources was required to meet this need so that its commitment to "continuous long-term research" was not diluted.

In early 1990, the research level of effort, going from basic to applied, consisted of 12% in competitive grants obtained by SIK researchers, primarily from the Forestry and Agricultural Research Council (SJFR); 50% in joint government–industry research and development, with the National Board for Technical Development (STU) providing the government input; 20% in industrial multi-sponsor projects, which are fully paid for with industrial funds; and 13% in proprietary industrial contracts. The remaining 5% of activity was in education through the housing of the Chalmers University of Technology Department of Food Sciences in SIK.

The SIK program is developed triennially and involves close cooperation of the institute with the industrial committee of the trade association. The industrial committee is responsible for conducting a comprehensive survey of member company needs, which then are reflected in a draft drawn up by a SIK management committee. The resulting program outline is discussed in a planning group representing the trade association, SIK, and STU. Implementation of the agreed-upon program is the responsibility of the SIK management research committee, which exercises administrative control over SIK's heads of research.

SIK has a good record of identifying important generic areas and maintaining continuous involvement in them over a sustained period, leading to genuine in-depth understanding. Two examples would be microwave heating, where a collaborative project on packaging for microwave ovens attracted 20 companies to

Table 15-2. Listing of projects undertaken within the Japanese Research and Development Association format in which at least two industry partners cooperate on each project and the Ministry of Agriculture, Forestry and Fisheries subsidizes approximately 50% of the annual cost.

The Japanese Research and Development Association for:	Initiation date	Annual investment (yen)	Number of companies	Number of projects	Number of academic experts	Partnership functions
Improvement of enzymes in food industry	November 1988	200 million	12	6	9	1) Food/enzyme function manufacturer 2) Computer manufacturer
Bioreactor system	March 1984	not available	54	20	15	1) Food manufacturer 2) Enzyme manufacturer 3) Plant engineering company 4) Biosensor manufacturer
High separation system in food industry	October 1989	300 million	44	22	not available	1) Food manufacturer 2) Separator and refiner manufacturer
Sensing system in food industry	October 1989	500 million	36	18	not available	1) Food manufacturer 2) Sensor manufacturer

participate, and aseptic processing, where SIK was given the responsibility for coordinating a large, joint Nordic project.

The 1989–92 three-year program is directed toward enabling greater industrial use of natural ingredients and mild process conditions without sacrificing nutritional value, sensory quality, and safety. Toward this end, SIK has consolidated its research program from 28 projects to 7 comprehensive projects, in the areas of food macromolecule structure and function, quality changes, process and storage effects on flavor and aroma, sensory measurement and significance, microbiological safety, heat transfer, and nutrient bioavailability.

Wisconsin's Food Research Institute.   The Food Research Institute (FRI), located in Madison, Wisconsin (USA), was founded in 1946 at the University of Chicago and moved to the University of Wisconsin in 1966. The FRI mission always has been to conduct research on food safety. Its $3.0 million annual budget is derived from the State of Wisconsin, the food industry, and the federal government. The state funds salaries, facilities, and facility operation and maintenance to the extent of nearly $1.0 million annually. Federal government grants and contracts are competitively acquired, usually by individual researchers or small groups of researchers, and amount to approximately $1.0 million each year. The major portion of the industrial funding is generated in the form of unrestricted gifts in support of FRI research, with the size of the gifts based upon annual sales figures of the companies. In response to these gifts, the contributing companies receive newsletters and other direct communications, are invited to periodic on-campus meetings, and are invited to the annual meeting of the institute, where there are technical presentations designed to show attendees the leading edge of food safety research and concerns. This effort is accomplished with the help of internal and external speakers. Another portion of industrial support comes from company-sponsored projects.

The FRI is fully integrated with the University of Wisconsin's Department of Food Microbiology and Toxicology. The eight faculty members of the department are the eight full-time members of the institute. Located in a land-grant university, the faculty have responsibilities in research, teaching, and public service. The food safety emphasis is generally reflective of concerns within the United States. At present four of the faculty are engaged in research on bacterial pathogens, with the other four working individually in each of the other areas of interest, including toxic fungi, viruses, toxicology, and nutritional food safety. Thus, 75% of the effort is in microbiology, and 25% is in toxicology and nutrition.

The FRI is dedicated to the accomplishment of research that is basic in nature and leads to increasing knowledge in the discipline base. The faculty members operate in a traditional mode, with each one responsible for his or her own research program. The acute sense of the FRI faculty to recognize and even anticipate the food safety concerns of the public, the regulatory agencies, and corporations has been demonstrated for many years and contributes to its recognized role as an unbiased source of food safety information.

The New Centers

The new centers are a phenomenon of the United States and its goals in international competitiveness. Within the food field, all of the centers are integral parts of universities. Many of the centers have translated the national goal to more provincial goals related to state competitiveness. This focus is expressed as new jobs that result from industrial development and spill over into improved quality of life. The centers are all products of the 1980s, and thus, in most cases, are far from mature; so the mechanisms whereby industry may extract its maximum benefit from them still are not fully developed.

The centers must not assume any role that is competitive with industry. They must complement industry and stimulate industrial research and development. As integral components of a university, they must promote university objectives in terms of education, adding to the knowledge base, and of public service, transferring new knowledge and technology to the industrial user.

The centers must not impinge upon the traditional functions of departments. Therefore, centers need to be established with goals and missions that are beyond the reach of university departments. One such theme, around which many centers are built, is the cross- or multi-disciplinary research program. This may take the form of many disciplines using an expensive instrument and its associated expertise or several disciplines contributing from their base knowledge to solve problems of such complexity that no one discipline could handle them. When a center seeks industrial or governmental financial support, it should not be at the expense of departmental research, but rather should contribute to and expand departments. The center should catalyze departmental growth and development in research capability, research quality, student quality, and departmental reputation.

Some centers were established within states as technology transfer or technology extension centers, with their success dependent upon entrepreneurial business start-ups and the growth of existing small businesses. Such centers border on the gray area separating industry and university functions. The primary benefits of such centers to universities are the availability of facilities for research in process design and development, and the hands-on educational experiences they offer students at various levels within the educational system. The key benefit for entrepreneurs and small business is the availability of a site where partially subsidized product development can be carried out in the presence of experts, so that some potential pitfalls can be avoided. The entrepreneur and the small business generally are undercapitalized and cannot afford a full-service food product development consulting organization. When a finished product has a professionally prepared appearance, a business's potential for generating capital improves dramatically. The potential for developing a company with a cash flow that then can be invested in new product development on a sound industrial basis is justification for the concept of these centers from an industry viewpoint. Without university involvement, such future industrial development would not be possible.

Several examples of the new centers have been selected for inclusion in this section.

Rutgers University's Center for Advanced Food Technology (CAFT).   CAFT is an initiative of the New Jersey Commission on Science and Technology, a state body within the Department of Commerce, Energy and Economic Development. Founded in 1984 and located on the New Brunswick campus of Rutgers University, CAFT is an industry–university–government research cooperative supported by the State of New Jersey, the university, food-related industries, and the federal government. CAFT's basic research and engineering program is interdisciplinary and precompetitive. It has 19 member companies, each of which provides one representative to an industrial advisory board that assists in policy matters and the identification of research directions. Project proposals in identified researchable areas are developed cooperatively each year by industrial and academic scientists and engineers. Research is conducted in the university by faculty research leaders with a project manager who serves as coordinator for the interdisciplinary team, which represents as many as eight departments in a single project. Monthly coordination meetings and quarterly accomplishments review meetings encourage interdisciplinary and industry–university interaction. The annual basic research budget is over $2.5 million, with $1.5 million derived from the state, $650,000 from industrial members, and $400,000 from the university. Three research projects are supported with these funds. They are concentrated on water relations in food systems, centered around water mobility and chemical reaction in restricted water environments; physical forces in food systems, focused on extrusion cooking and new concepts for in-line sensing of moisture; and rheological properties in food processes. More than 100 people are directly involved in the basic research effort.

CAFT's advanced technology development, demonstration, and transfer program consists of a state-supported component oriented toward increasing the competitiveness of small and medium-sized companies within the state through advanced process technology. There is also a federal government–supported component dedicated to the development and demonstration of highly automated and flexible thermostabilization processes to manufacture high-quality shelf-stable foods. This component is assisted by an industrial coalition of 16 companies, who provide guidance and know-how relative to the industrial state-of-the art. This minimizes the probability of doing research in areas where technology is already available and implemented. The annual budget for the full program is approximately $2.5 million, of which $2.3 million is provided by the federal government, $50,000 by industry, and $150,000 by the state government. Approximately 30 people are involved in this multidisciplinary program, which is still in its evolving stage.

A third program under the CAFT umbrella is the instrument support facilities program. There are three facilities in the program, with each managed by a CAFT staff member and all three administered by a CAFT senior scientific staff member. The mission of the facilities is to provide instrumentation support to CAFT funded projects, to other university projects, to affiliated company projects, and to nonaffiliated company projects. All work is done on a fee-for-service basis. Incoming work from non-university projects is screened for suitability, and routine problems that can be handled by area consulting laboratories are directed to those facilities.

The facilities are dedicated to mass spectrometry, rheology, and spectroscopy and calorimetry. Each facility is equipped with approximately $1.0 million worth of instrumentation provided by the state government and gifts from instrument manufacturers. The annual operating budget of the facilities, exclusive of depreciation, is approximately $350,000. The facilities serve as a resource that benefits many researchers from the university, industry, and both state and federal government laboratories. The complete CAFT organization interacts on various levels with more than 100 industrial firms from all over the world. It supports approximately 50 graduate students working toward advanced degrees as well as many postdoctoral fellows, thus preparing a variety of people in various disciplines for entry into the food industry professional labor force. The center has no faculty. All faculty are assigned to discipline departments and have an affiliation with the center. CAFT has a new 32,000-square-foot research and pilot plant facility that houses administrative offices and some CAFT affiliated faculty. The vast majority of CAFT research is carried out in the discipline departments, where researchers are in the midst of a critical mass of their own kind and interact across disciplines through research and coordination meetings. A regular industrial presence at coordination meetings increases the rate of information transfer and shortens the time from discovery to implementation.

CAFT communicates with its affiliated companies through newsletters, semiannual research accomplishments reports, annual project proposals, preprints of manuscripts prepared for submission to journals, regular scheduled meetings, unscheduled visits, and a videotape review of one project every six months.

CAFT offers numerous routes for members of industry to interact and gain information that could improve the industrial product developer's progress. There is a need for the industrial representative to recognize new knowledge and translate it into industrial application. The ability to take information developed for one purpose and use it in a totally unrelated area is a creative skill that separates the great users of knowledge from the good ones. Knowledgeable and visionary individuals must invest their time to get the most out of precompetitive university programs. CAFT's $6 million program provides an excellent opportunity for industrial product developers.

North Carolina State University's Center for Aseptic Processing and Packaging Studies (CAPPS). CAPPS is the only National Science Foundation Industry–University Cooperative Research Center directed toward food research. Founded in 1987 on NCSU's Raleigh campus, CAPPS is a component of the Food Science Department and shares the department's 40,000 square feet of pilot plant and $2 million in aseptic processing and packaging equipment. Its cooperation with Michigan State University, Ohio State University, and Virginia Polytechnic Institute and State University makes CAPPS a cross-university center. With nine member companies, including both the Food and Drug Administration and the USDA Agricultural Research Service, CAPPS sponsors 14 projects involving 40 people, among them six graduate and two undergraduate students. A total budget slightly greater than $800,000 is derived from the four cooperating universities (25%), NSF (25%), member companies (37%), industrial sponsor-shared projects (10%), and matching funds from the Virginia Center for Innovative Technology (3%). Industrial member commitments are for a minimum of two years, and research projects are established with minimum life expectancies of two years. Two projects have been completed. Research projects are ongoing on meat flavor and texture, new package sterilization systems, determining thermal properties, time–temperature profile measurement, flavor migration, seal integrity testing, and chlorophyll stability. Formal industry interaction takes place during the semiannual industrial advisory board meetings, where research progress is reported orally, and through written bimonthly project reports and semiannual comprehensive accomplishments reports.

CAPPS has a strong industrial advisory board that votes on project proposal suitability. Recommendations for project funding are for a one-year period; renewal requires a new proposal and a new vote by the board. The results of all research carried out under the center's auspices are shared among all of the members, whether the research is supported by pooled funds or by a single industrial sponsor.

The research activities are all interrelated with their focus upon aseptic processing and packaging, but no attempt is made to integrate researchers. Thus the program is the traditional one of university departmental research but differs from that model in having a common-subject-matter orientation. It further differs through its seeking out appropriate talent at any university, so that it brings a wide variety of expertise together at its formal meetings, where interaction is encouraged.

CAPPS participates in presenting the Better Process Control School in Aseptic

Processing and Packaging, which provides certification to operators of aseptic processing plants.

This young center offers much opportunity to product developers seeking the advantages of aseptic processing and packaging. The potential for breakthroughs in this exciting field is great, and those companies that obtain cutting-edge knowledge first can gain immeasurably over their competition.

Purdue University's Whistler Center for Carbohydrate Research (WCCR). Since 1986, the WCCR, in West Lafayette, Indiana, has been dedicated to furthering the utilization of carbohydrates through an increased understanding of their chemical, physical, and biological properties and through the training of young scientists to work with carbohydrates. Sharing facilities in the Food Science Department, the four permanent faculty members with an academic assignment in Food Science direct the activities of 13 postdoctoral and 10 pre-doctoral researchers. An additional 20 faculty from various university departments are associated with the center. They participate in seminars and provide assistance and guidance but are not supported by center funds.

An industrial consortium currently consisting of seven companies provides a minimum entry fee of $125,000 each, which is placed into a permanent fund if the company agrees to that. This fund is designed to insure the permanence of the center, as the primary goal of the permanent fund is to support a professional chair. Consortium fees that cannot enter the permanent fund and current interest from the permanent fund are used at the discretion of the director to support postdoctoral researchers while other project funds are being sought, thus assuring the availability of quality researchers for rapid start-up of short-term or long-term projects.

The current annual budget of WCCR is approximately $1.25 million. Faculty salaries are provided by the university, with all other support derived from industry or government funding agencies.

The expertise of the faculty is in structure–function relationships in polysaccharides and gums with almost complete emphasis on the molecular and three-dimensional structure aspect. Research support is exclusively of the traditional one supporter: one principal investigator type, with ideas for research originated in-house by the researcher. The center has one National Institutes of Health, one National Science Foundation, and two State of Indiana supported projects. There are also competitive grants in the center from the National Dairy Promotion Board, the Sugar Association, and the Corn Syrup Refiners Association. A few short-term industrial single-sponsor projects round out the program. Center researchers cannot agree to give up the right to publish results but can agree to publication delays.

Members companies are given special treatment by center staff, but a company does not need to be a member in order to sponsor research. Companies have realized major benefits by establishing relationships with potential employees and with faculty. Member companies are provided with knowledge of research results at appropriate times, which approximate quarterly reports.

This young center is still growing and intends to add expertise in the functional property, enzyme, and biochemical modification and organic chemistry areas.

Massachusetts Institute of Technology's (MIT) Industrial Liaison Program (ILP)   Although the ILP is neither a center nor an institute, its existence since 1948 and its mission to encourage long-term mutually beneficial relationships between academics and the industrial community make it an essential component of any attempt to identify sources of industrial opportunity in a university setting. ILP covers the full scope of corporation interests as it represents the totality of MIT programs. Approximately 270 member companies contribute varying amounts based upon revenues. The fees total approximately $8 million annually.

Management of the industry–academe interaction is in the hands of Industrial Liaison Officers (ILOs), who are assigned a portfolio of companies. The officer's job is to get to know the research, technical, and strategic interests of member companies, to acquire a broad knowledge of MIT programs, and to match up companies with programs that will be of interest to them. The ILO will help a member company to meet faculty involved in areas of interest by arranging one-on-one meetings for visiting industrial member-company representatives. The ILO will make arrangements for and sponsor the travel of faculty to a member company to present a seminar. The ILO will select appropriate publications or preprints of publications to forward to carefully targeted individuals in member companies.

The ILP organizes three symposia each year on topics of emerging interest, to which member companies are invited without charge. A comprehensive directory of research at MIT, a newsletter that attempts to cover all that is new at MIT, and a list of publications are disseminated to all member companies.

A major objective of the ILP activity is to encourage companies to invest in research at MIT. This is accomplished by exposing its programs and faculty to a wide range of corporate representatives. In addition to providing the faculty with an opportunity for industrial research support, the ILP divides up approximately 10% of its revenues among those faculty who provide support to the ILP. Credits for such support are given for submitting a preprint or a publication, meeting with a visiting member, speaking at a symposium, or traveling to a member company. The funds given to faculty may be used for professional development. Approximately 50% of the revenues supports the ILP operations, and the remaining 40% is placed in the president's unrestricted funds pool for use throughout MIT.

The dissolution of the Food Science program and its successor Department of Applied Biological Sciences in 1988 has dispersed food-related programs into a variety of departments and has diminished them considerably. However, the diversity of the MIT faculty and their quality continues to provide an opportunity for the food product developer to seek out new concepts which could be translated into food related uses.

University of Nebraska's Food Processing Center (FPC). Established in 1983, the Food Processing Center on the Lincoln campus of the University of Nebraska is directed toward assisting food entrepreneurs and companies. Although Nebraska entrepreneurs and small companies are entitled to assistance without charge, any company—irrespective of its geographic location—can arrange for contract support and assistance.

The range of assistance extends from product development and processing through marketing and business development. The center activities incorporate research, service, and education. FPC has 8 technical staff people and 20 collaborating professionals. Center activities have resulted in the development of new food processing facilities, new retail food businesses, improved quality standards, and increased energy efficiency in processing. Entrepreneurs have been helped with feasibility studies, sensory evaluation, prototype development, packaging, and marketing. The educational objective is carried out through a variety of workshops, conferences, and short courses covering sanitation, marketing, energy conservation, and better process control. Companies are charged fees for participation in these educational activities.

The center has an advisory council with representatives from industry, state government, center staff, and collaborating departments. The advisory council provides guidance relative to industrial interests and needs. Representatives volunteer for participation on the council.

FPC's budget includes $220,000 per year from the state, of which 90% is used for technical and marketing staff salaries and the remainder for operations. The center also had $300,000 in industrial and federal government grants and contracts. The federal funds are USDA-derived to assist start-up activities for businesses. The industrial contracts are principally from large companies and are directed toward technical research and product development. The center operates almost exclusively with staff personnel and is permitted to carry out proprietary work with full confidentiality. To round out the activities of the technical staff, the center will carry out limited amounts of custom processing and preparation of test packs for market studies.

The FPC shares newly built facilities with various departments and has available pilot plants for meat and poultry, fruits and vegetables, cereals and oil seeds, dairy and fermentation. There is also a packaging room, and both chemical and microbiological analytical services are available. The analytical services offered for general use are only those that are highly specialized and unique to the university environment. Routine analytical support is provided when required as part of a larger in-house project.

Faculty involvement is minimal and is fully voluntary. Faculty are credited with an hourly rate for their volunteered time, and the funds are transferred into discretionary accounts to be used for program development.

FPC provides the industrial food product developer with opportunities that are different from those offered by any of the previously described centers. Technical research, analytical services, product development assistance, marketing, and business development are available from FPC.

University of Minnesota's and South Dakota State University's Dairy Foods Research Center (DFRC).   In existence since 1988, this Minnesota and South Dakota Dairy Foods Research Center is one of six similar centers established throughout the United States. (Others may be found in the listing of U.S. centers in the appendix to this chapter.) It was created as an initiative of the National Dairy Promotion and Research Board, with base funding derived from a 1984 congressional act that requires that 15 cents be contributed by milk producers for each 100 pounds of milk produced. Oversight responsibility for the research utilization of the funds resides in the USDA. Of each 15 cents contributed, 10 cents stay within the state generating the funds and is used by the State Dairy Promotion Board, while the remaining 5 cents is transferred to the National Board.

The university center is required to secure funds, matching those given by the national board, from both the university and the state board and industry sources. The division of funds in the center is 75% for the University of Minnesota and 25% for South Dakota State University. All funding commitments are for five years. The National Dairy Promotion and Research Board provides the center with $400,000 annually. The state boards allocate $267,000, and company members (numbering 15) pay $5,000 each for a total of $70,000. There is an additional $63,000 in single-industrial-sponsor-funded research. The university's contribution of $400,000 is from experiment station research funds, which become committed to the program for five years. These were principally funds that were supporting appropriate research and did not represent new funds in a strict sense.

The $1.2 million budget supports 26 projects. At the University of Minnesota there are 15 faculty, 25 graduate students, two postdoctoral researchers, and one technician involved in center research. The program at South Dakota State University involves five faculty, three graduate students, and one postdoctoral researcher.

The research thrusts are in four areas: genetics of dairy culture microorganisms, dairy food safety, dairy product processing and shelf life, and chemical and sensory analysis of dairy products. The research is carried out in facilities that the center shares with the appropriate food science departments at the universities.

The industrial members are represented on an advisory committee, and a subgroup of the advisory committee serves as a technical advisory committee (TAC). Research proposals generated by faculty are reviewed by the TAC, which recommends whether or not to fund the research. The TAC recommendations are provided to the full advisory committee at the annual meeting for input and approval. Researchers prepare an annual summary report that is published as part of the center's annual report. Distribution of the annual report, which contains "unfinished" research results, is limited to member companies. Member companies attend an annual meeting where each project's accomplishments are presented.

All of the faculty involved in the center are from the two university food science departments. The research is carried out in the general format of one faculty researcher–one project although there are a few multifaculty projects.

The center provides an opportunity for the generation of new knowledge related to dairy products. Improved mechanisms are being sought for determining the kind of new knowledge industry needs for its future well-being. There is good potential for dairy-oriented product developers to gain knowledge from interaction with this center or any of the other dairy and dairy foods research centers of the type described.

Illinois Institute of Technology's (IIT) National Center for Food Safety and Technology (NCFST). The National Center for Food Safety and Technology was established in 1989 by a cooperative agreement between the U.S. Food and Drug Administration (FDA) and IIT. Located in the Argo, Illinois, facilities of CPC International's Moffett Technical Center, which was given to IIT, the center has more than 100,000 square feet, including 56,000 square feet of pilot plant facilities. Staffed with 14 FDA and two IIT professionals, the center is divided into four research units: food process engineering, packaging, biotechnology, and quality assurance.

Support for the center is derived from FDA for staff salaries and in the form of research contracts, from IIT in facilities, and from the food-related industries in the form of contributions and contracts. The center is too new to be accurately described in monetary terms; it is still in the policy development stage. It has a technical advisory committee and a policy committee containing industrial representation from companies that have participated in the center's development.

The NCFST is tending toward a significant dependence upon industrial research contracts. It has established policy that permits proprietary and confidential research to be carried out with no obligation to publish the results.

The center offers opportunities that are quite different from those at publicly funded universities, which were described previously.

New Approaches in Europe

The UK's LINK Scheme.   The LINK initiative represents a major new approach by the U.K. Government to the funding of research in support of the nation's science base and industrial competitiveness. Through LINK, various U.K. government departments provide up to half the cost of collaborative research programs between industry and the science base in research institutes and universities.

The overall aim of LINK is to accelerate the commercial exploitation of government-funded research. The LINK initiative focuses on advances in science and engineering with particular commercial promise. It is designed to stimulate collaboration between industrial and science-base partners on projects in key areas of science and technology.

The Food Processing Sciences Program, a LINK initiative program, was announced in September 1988 and is jointly sponsored by two government departments (DTI, MAFF) with funding of up to £7 million over five years for collaborative research projects. A requirement for support is that DTI and MAFF contributions be matched by an equivalent contribution from the industrial partners in the joint academic : industry consortia.

The program is managed by a committee of academics and industrialists, together with DTI and MAFF officials. A particular responsibility of the committee is to decide which projects and consortia are worthy of LINK support. A program manager with food industry experience is assisting the committee in the day-to-day management of the program.

The broad technical aims of the LINK Food Processing Program are to encourage collaborative R&D in relevant bioscience, process development, process modeling, and control. Four priority areas were identified: structure/ function relationships in foods, predictive modeling of food material behavior during processing, approaches for on-line sensor development (moisture, foreign bodies, microorganisms, appearance), and food biotechnology.

A variation of the LINK program developed in 1988 with the formation of the Amorphous-Crystalline Transitions in Foods (ACTIF) club, which is an ongoing scientific program at the Department of Applied Biochemistry and Food Science, Sutton Bonnington (Faculty of Agriculture of the University of Nottingham). The ACTIF club represents a significant U.K. development in building university–industry–government linkages relevant to the food industry. The research program is generated via discussion among the club members (currently ten food companies) with input from the academic partner. It is funded, on an equal basis, by membership contributions and MAFF. The ACTIF concept calls for a core program of research into the glassy state behavior of food polymers, together with confidential satellite projects between individual companies or groups of companies and members. In terms of demonstrating the feasibility and benefit of shared precompetitive research and establishing precedents for the treatment of intellectual property rights, ACTIF is forging new routes.

European Economic Community's FLAIR Program. Precompetitive research programs have a prominent role as the year 1992 and the Single European Market approach. The concept of engaging in meaningful collaborative research is consistent with both national and community-wide desires to increase industrial efficiency and competitiveness and to ensure food safety and quality for the consumer.

Within the overall framework program for community activities in research the development is the FLAIR (Food Linked Agro-Industrial Research) Program. There are two modes of collaboration in the FLAIR program, shared cost and concerted actions.

In the shared-cost mode, the consortium, containing both academic and industrial partners, may claim up to 50% of the total cost of a research project. Research institutes or associations that are funded principally or exclusively by industrial organizations are considered as industrial participants. All projects must include participants from more than one EC member state.

For concerted-action proposals the objective is to coordinate research that is already taking place in the different countries through the organization of meetings, consultation with national experts, and diffusion of information on the progress and results of the projects. Normally, for such actions, the appropriate European Economic Community Commission will pay 100% of the coordination costs for participants from member states, but it will not contribute toward research expenses. Participants in concerted actions can be industrial firms, cooperative groupings of such firms, and research institutions and universities that are established in the Community or in certain nonmember European countries. Industrial participation is not obligatory, but priority would be given to projects with an industrial partner, or research establishments principally funded by industrial organizations. Concerted actions normally would involve groups from a significant number of countries.

The technical areas in which the research programs (whether shared-cost or concerted-action) are envisaged include the assessment and enhancement of food quality, food hygiene, safety and toxicological aspects, and nutrition and wholesomeness aspects.

In-Depth Evaluation of New Approaches

The development of the modern centers and institutes was a natural event spawned by the economics and the politics of the moment. Stimulated by the diminishing traditional federal government base for research, a professed government desire for increased competitiveness, a period of state government well-being, and a food industry in turmoil from mergers and limited buy-outs and thus withdrawing from in-house research, both universities and governments recognized the opportunity to try new approaches. Government investment could be leveraged by industrial funds to provide universities with increased sources of revenue to conduct research and strengthen the educational infrastructure. The interaction resulting from the industry–university partnerships would assure rapid knowledge and technology transfer and minimize the time from discovery to utilization for profit. The result would be increased industrial competitiveness and profit, increased employment of the population, increased tax revenues for governments, increased funds for university development, and an elevated quality of life for the general population.

The universities would be doing what they do best, obtaining new discipline-oriented knowledge. Industrial involvement would assure that the new knowledge was in areas where needs were evident and critical. Industry would do what it does best, convert the new knowledge into proprietary applications leading to profit. Government would catalyze the optimization of the activities of the two components, resulting in new heights of food quality, safety, and health.

With few exceptions, the resulting organizations have been modeled upon traditional lines. The major new approaches have been in the establishment of multi-participant partnerships and a subsequent leveraging of each partner's monetary investment. Another widespread development has been the welcoming of industrial involvement in university research activity or planning and a diminishing of academic fears of industrial ''contamination'' of the search for knowledge. The research, in most cases, continues to be one faculty member:one project, which is the traditional academic mode. The research results generally remain publishable, as publication is the major route through which researcher recognition is achieved. The academics generally have made concessions, permitting publication delays of up to one year for their research results. Most center models have grouped projects into thrust areas in an attempt to demonstrate team approaches. All of the new centers have established industrial advisory units. These units vary in their ability to influence center activity, from being purely advisory to evaluating proposed research and voting on whether or not to recommend funding. The most surprising aspect to many academics has been the industrial interaction's focus on relatively long-term research and the search for new knowledge. This approach has been stimulated by the general policy of centers to pool funds and openly share research results among groups of industrial partners. The few centers that permit confidential and nonpublishable research to be conducted tend to be directed into short-range research and technical development under relatively tight control by the sponsoring company.

Nearly universal to the new centers is an increased level of communication, necessitated by the industrial involvement. To satisfy industry's short-term approaches to profit, the bits and pieces of long-range research need to be taken back to the company laboratories on a regular basis for incorporation into their developmental research. The skill of the industrial scientist in recognizing the potential benefit of bits and pieces of new knowledge determines the level of satisfaction that a company perceives from its participation in a center program. If research results are provided frequently, the probability of a useful information transfer action is increased. The frequency range of scheduled industry–university interaction meetings is from monthly in CAFT to annually in the DFRCs, with the majority of centers scheduling semiannual or quarterly exchanges.

The Rutgers University CAFT model has produced a number of innovations that do not appear in any other centers, among them perhaps the most innovative development within a university setting, the integrated project team (IPT) approach and the ensuing monthly study group meetings. The primary doctrines of the IPT system include industry–academe interaction in the development of an integrated project, with a university project manager coordinating the efforts of many faculty research leaders and the inputs from many industrial scientists and engineers. This activity leads to a comprehensive project proposal and monthly study group meetings, with attendance of all faculty research leaders and some industry professionals, thus assuring at least minimal interaction between faculty researchers and input from industry. The IPTs consist of faculty from a variety of disciplines located on several of the five New Brunswick campuses of Rutgers University. Neighboring university faculty have been incorporated into the IPT if specific expertise was required and was not available at the Rutgers campuses. One of the CAFT projects has members of eight different departments from two universities interacting. No project has fewer than four interacting departments. The involvement of industry researchers and developers in proposal development ensures that the basic research is focused toward new knowledge that, when available, will be put to use in the industrial environment. The multidisciplinary interactions ensure that difficult problems are viewed from a wide variety of perspectives at the monthly study group meetings, as ways to overcome the problems are generated.

Each faculty research leader is encouraged to publish independently as well as in subgroups within the open scientific literature. The semiannual written reports of the IPT are integrated by the project manager and appear as a single project accomplishments report.

The system works. The program is successful in the eyes of the industrial members, the university, the state government, and the faculty participants.

The industrial product developer can tap the resource of this system most effectively by investing time in it. Specific researcher identification can be made by observing presentations at quarterly accomplishment meetings or discussions at monthly study groups or from reading semiannual project reports. The time spent with researchers who are generating pieces of the whole that may be of special and immediate industrial interest can clarify and verify a potential application. Because non-food-science-discipline researchers, such as chemists, biochemists, mechanical engineers, and others, have been interacting with food scientists and engineers, and because they have been working on food-related problems and discussing their work in terms of food, communication between the food product developer and the nonfood academic is simplified. There now exists a much more common language and a mutual understanding of needs. The efficiency of such information transfer from non-food-science researchers to food product developers is unique to the CAFT model.

There are, of course, negative aspects of the new approaches, which have been analyzed. These are regarded as obstacles to be overcome. Among them are such issues as intellectual property ownership, research direction, management, rate of progress, and others. The next section addresses these obstacles. The benefit of making a low investment for large quantities of research effort is a strong weighting factor, as is the breadth of talent available without a need for capital investment.

SURMOUNTING THE OBSTACLES

Throughout this chapter, obstacles to industry–university interactions have been pointed out. Here some of the potential roadblocks are brought together and analyzed. Some of the problems are industry-identified, whereas others are of the academic variety. Both types of concerns need to be satisfied if successful interactions are to be achieved.

Intellectual Property

Every industrial firm considering participation in a center program raises the question of intellectual property ownership. The general guidelines within which almost all centers function are similar. The ownership of patents and copyrights resides in the university or the center. In membership-type centers where pooled funds are supporting research, full-paying-member companies often will be eligible for a free but nonexclusive license, or some portion of their membership fee will be used to offset licensing fees. In some centers, the member companies will vote, after reading a disclosure, on whether to divert research funds to the cost of patenting and patent maintenance. A negative vote will allow a group of members to undertake patenting costs, and only they would be entitled to the benefits previously described. When no group of members is willing to bear the patenting costs, the university could pay them, and all licensing would carry a fee. Should be university decide not to pay for patenting, the inventor would be given the rights to take any action desired. The license fees that are collected provide a percentage to the inventor, with the remainder often going to the center for further division and disbursement to departments, colleges, and the university. Such arrangements, as described, often are discussed at great length by corporate and university legal counsel before they are accepted. Experience has shown that, almost without exception, they are approved by the corporate counsel and made binding in the membership agreement. Some faculty researchers have questioned the arrangements, claiming that the free license of members denies them their share as inventors. This problem generally is satisfied by pointing out the industrial contribution that allowed the work to be done in the first place, and that the licenses to members are nonexclusive so that the opportunity for fee income exists.

When a company supports a single-sponsor project, negotiations will be carried out before the research agreement is established concerning the disposition of intellectual property. Many universities will accept multiples of normal indirect costs, which become up-front payments, in return for offering an exclusive license. Lesser multiples of indirect costs might be charged for a right of first refusal with a performance clause. In brief, there are many possible arrangements. Serious negotiations by reasonable people from industry and the university almost always result in an agreement.

Focusing of Research

Single-sponsor research projects permit industrial focusing to a greater extent than member-sponsored projects. A major fear faculty often express is that they will lose their freedom, whereas industrial sponsors fear loss of control. There are overriding factors that eliminate these fears, however. In single-sponsor projects, if either partner feels the perceived danger to be too great, that partner can choose not to enter into any agreement. In member-supported research, the fact that all information is being shared between competitive companies motivates the members to drive the research decidedly toward the basic side so that it remains precompetitive. Thus each company assumes the obligation of taking the new knowledge and making it proprietary on an in-house applications-oriented basis. In many member-sponsored centers, the involvement of the industrial members in project evaluation and the regular interaction that ensues provides the opportunity to keep research headed toward previously agreed-upon goals with the recognition that in research redirections usually are necessary. A research project that does not require changes and the development of new paths toward its goals is considered not to have incorporated a reasonable amount of risk into its planning.

The fears about control, whether it be too much or too little, may assume mythical proportions for both parties and should not be taken lightly.

Research Management

The industrial concern is often "lack of management," whereas the academic concern is "micro management." Neither concern represents reality. Research does not progress in the absence of management, but techniques differ greatly between industry and university environments because of dissimilar constraints. When these differences are understood, expectations are clarified, and compromises may be reached. The key factor is that the underlying academic goals are the education of students and the generation of new knowledge. When both parties to an industry–university research project keep the academic goals in constant view, a satisfactory management scheme can be developed and implemented. The academic route often provides much more information for the industrial sponsor than could have been envisioned when the project was proposed and formulated.

Membership-type centers impose management demands upon faculty researchers that usually are greater than would be experienced in single-sponsor departmental-type research. This is so because of the need for frequent communication and transfer of information to the industrial firms, who now are supporting longer-range, higher-risk, basic and precompetitive research. The justification for such research support within a company often depends upon the shorter-term benefits derived from the research effort. The need to ensure that such short-term benefits are realized is the driving force behind the increased level of effort demanded of faculty researchers in such programs.

Significantly more management is imposed upon interdisciplinary membership-type projects because of the need for the research parts to mesh to create the whole. This requires that faculty researchers interact and meet routinely to keep the research on track. Accomplishing this requires coordination, which in the CAFT model is effected by a project manager who conducts frequent meetings of research subgroups as well as the full researcher team. The quarterly and semiannual meetings of the membership centers demand more frequent formal reporting by researchers than traditionally is customary.

When the faculty researcher understands the industrial needs, and when the industrial scientist or engineer understands the magnitude of the new rules under which the faculty research is trying to operate, adequate cooperation can result.

Integrated interdisciplinary research is not for all faculty researchers. Those who do not see the benefits of cross-disciplinary interaction cannot be brought into such research projects. In some cases, the faculty fear that recognition of their work will be clouded by the multiplicity of faculty potentially involved in a single publication. Such a diminution of credit could impact one's promotion if an unenlightened performance evaluator were involved. Such fears are not ungrounded. The burden falls on center directors and deans to clear the smokescreen and obtain a firm commitment for faculty support by the university administration. This is happening on many campuses. A powerful force behind this is the National Science Foundation, as it continues to promote cross-disciplinary centers in a significant manner.

Rate of Progress

The industrial perception is that university research moves slowly, if at all, whereas the academics believe that industry expects significant progress on a daily basis. A factor underlying these perceptions is that industrial research moves steadily, whereas university research progresses in spurts. The integration of the area under industry's steady, day-in and day-out, research curve is often equaled and indeed even exceeded by the integration of the area under the intermittent but extremely high peaks of university research. There is a difference between the work of an eight-hour-per-day worker and that of a graduate student—who will take time off for courses, studying for examinations, and other professional and educational endeavors, but once in the laboratory will work day and night, motivated to complete the research, obtain a degree, and move to the next stage of professional development.

Two factors can be most disappointing to an industrial sponsor who does not have realistic expectations, and both are characteristic of the project initiation stage. It is here that the enthusiasm of the industrial partner is at a peak—the funds have been allocated, and the company is eager to get going; but universities just are not set up with a waiting pool of graduate students ready to jump into a research project. Graduate students often are available only at the beginning of the semester, and the best graduate students can be attracted only when funds are available—approximately ten months prior to the anticipated date of their arrival. A second difficulty is that the new graduate student does not become productive in the laboratory for at least four or five months, and often is only marginally productive during the entire first year of his or her graduate career. This problem often can be overcome by incorporating 50% of the time of a technician or a postdoctoral researcher into the first project year and scheduling that individual to work either full-time or part-time during start-up. Such personnel often are available in a researchers' laboratory and can be moved to a new project as an earlier project is moving toward maturity.

The industrial and the academic goals are likely to be reached in the same time-frame for projects of the same degree of complexity. A three-month-long industry project has no place in a university environment, however. The greatest potential for equivalency of effort comes in a two-year project. Projects that last longer than two years usually will yield more cost-effective results in a university environment than in an industrial laboratory.

EVALUATING COSTS, BENEFITS, AND RISKS

Industrial Viewpoint

An industrial firm contemplating the initiation of an industry–university cooperative program of any type must enter into the program with realistic expectations. Education is a primary university function, and any research project that is undertaken must have some educational value. Short-term projects cannot be handled effectively in a university environment; the motivation of university researchers is different from that of industrial researchers. Through a joint project, an industrial firm can gain access to faculty knowledge, and it can evaluate for potential employment those students who have acquired expertise closely related to the company interests. Research in a university is not cheap, but it can be very cost-effective; moreover, capital investment can be avoided in terms of space, instrumentation, and intellectual capacity.

Basic research of a precompetitive nature, carried out in a membership-type center using pooled industrial funds and subsidized by government funds, is the most cost-effective mechanism for the early acquisition of any new knowledge that might exist. The leveraging of the investment can be in the hundred-times category. Obtaining information in a timely and efficient manner will require an investment above and beyond the basic membership fee. To achieve the ultimate in-depth search for relevant new knowledge being generated in basic research projects, it may be necessary to assign a company scientist or engineer to participate in a hands-on way in the actual research project. Such a gift of manpower would speed up research progress and ensure the transfer of important new findings to the company on a real-time basis.

Academic Viewpoint

An academic contemplating entry into an industry–university cooperative venture must have realistic expectations. A plan must exist, at least in one's mind, for maintaining academic objectives. It is unrealistic to think that entry into a contract will permit a research effort to take any direction other than one that can be clearly shown to support the defined objective. The academic must be available to the sponsor for interaction and information transfer on a fairly frequent basis.

The industrial input into the effort, in terms of people and information, can be a distinct advantage. The individual faculty member can benefit from the opportunity to broaden his or her understanding of the problems and concerns of industry by learning the significance of the research activities and by obtaining a set of real examples to enhance his or her teaching presentations. The student working on a sponsored project also gains from an expanded view of the research application.

Industry cannot be overlooked as a source of research funds, whether for a single-sponsor project or a multidisciplinary membership-sponsored source. A combination of center-sponsored cross-disciplinary research, single-industrial-sponsor research, and single-sponsor government research is an ideal blend of support to carry a researcher through the ups and downs of the research funding process.

CONCLUDING REMARKS

Many routes exist whereby the industrial product developer can tap into the university and generate a true synergy. An understanding of the university and its motivating factors is essential so that realistic expectations can be established. Academe produces new knowledge in small pieces as a research project progresses; and it is these pieces that provide the product developer with concepts for applications, and that satisfy the industrial requirement for short-term justification. Obtaining these gems of knowledge requires work and the investment of time and money. Just sponsoring a project and then sitting back for a year until a report is provided often produces less than satisfying results. Visiting regularly, interacting with professors and students, and even participating in the actual research will ensure for the industrial sponsor the transfer of all that is learned, and will increase the level of mutual satisfaction.

The newer industry–university centers build upon the concept of the older institutes and centers, which have been a resource for food industry product developers for many years. The perceived obstacles for industry–university interaction and cooperation are more myth than reality. Much of the mystery is attributable to a communication gap, resulting in fear of the unknown.

The benefits to both the industrial product developer and the university researcher are numerous and recognizable. Industrial use of the academic resource continues to expand as barriers on both sides break down. Industrial competitiveness in global markets is a driving force, providing the stimulus for a highly cost-effective industry–university cooperative research effort.

APPENDIX

List of University Food-Related Centers and Institutes in the United States (compiled by Dr. Steve Taylor of the University of Nebraska).

Dr. D. M. Barbano
Northeast Dairy Foods Research Center
Department of Food Science
Cornell University   (joint with University
  of Vermont)
105 Stocking Hall
Ithaca, NY 14853-7201
607/255-2899

Dr. Winston Bash
Food Industry Center
Ohio State University
2121 Fyffe Road
Columbus, OH 43210
614/292-7004

Dr. James BeMiller
Whistler Center for Carbohydrate Research
Purdue University
Smith Hall
West Lafayette, IN 47907
317/494-5684

Dr. Reuben B. Beverly
Center for Urban Agricultural Research
Department of Horticulture
Georgia Experiment Station
Griffin, GA 30223
404/228-7243

Dr. Richard Brimhall
Ezra Taft Benson Agriculture and Food
   Institute
Brigham Young University
B-49
Provo, UT 84604
602/378-2607

Dr. Alfred A. Bushway
Food Science Cooperative Research Unit
Department of Food Science
208 Holmes Hall
University of Maine
Orono, ME 04469
207/581-1629

Dr. Dean O. Cliver
WHO Collaborating Centre on Food Virology
University of Wisconsin
1925 Willow Drive
Madison, WI 53706
608/263-6937

Dr. Brendan J. Donnelly
Northern Crops Institute
North Dakota State University
Box 5183 SU Station
Fargo, ND 58105
701/237-7736

Dr. Donald L. Downing
New York State Food Venture Center
Cornell University
Agricultural Experiment Station
Geneva, NY 14456
315/787-2273

Dr. Charles P. Gerba
Microbial Analytical Laboratory
Department of Nutrition and Food Science
University of Arizona
Tucson, AZ 85721
602/621-6906

Dr. Richard Hahn
Kansas Value Added Center
Kansas State University
Umberger Hall 307
Manhattan, KS 66506
913/532-7033

Dr. William C. Haines
Food Industry Institute
Michigan State University
201 Food Science
East Lansing, MI 48824
517/355-8295

Dr. Herbert O. Hultin
Office of Marine Resources
Marine Food Program
University of Massachusetts Marine Station
P.O. Box 7128, Lanesville
Gloucester, MA 01930
617/281-1930

Dr. Lawrence A. Johnson
Food Crops Processing Research Center
Iowa State University
Dairy Industry Building
Ames, IA 50011
515/294-4365

Dr. Gerald Kuhn
USDA Center of Excellence on Home Food
   Preservation
Pennsylvania State University
Department of Food Science
116 Borland Laboratory
University Park, PA 16602
814/863-2965

Dr. Richard Lechowich
National Center for Food Safety and
   Technology
Illinois Institute of Technology
Chicago, IL 60616-3793
312/567-3001

Dr. Jong S. Lee
University of Alaska
Fishery Industry Technical Center
202 Center Street, Ste. 201
Kodiak, AK 99615
907/486-6034

Dr. David R. Lineback
Southeast Dairy Foods Research Center
North Carolina State University   (joint with
  Mississippi State University)
Box 7624
Raleigh, NC 27695-7624
919/847-8165

Dr. Edmund W. Lusas
Food Protein Research and Development
  Center
Texas A&M University, FM-183
College Station, TX 77843-2476
409/845-2741

Dr. Joseph A. Maga
Food Research and Development Center
Department of Food Science and Human
  Nutrition
Colorado State University
Fort Collins, CO 80523
303/491-6705

Dr. Don Naumann
University of Missouri
Missouri Center for Agricultural Products
  Technology
122 Eckles Hall
Columbia, MO 65211
314/882-2639

Dr. Philip E. Nelson
Purdue University
Center for Value-Added Research
Department of Food Science
Smith Hall
West Lafayette, IN 47907
317/494-8257

Dr. O. Robert Noyes
California Polytechnic State University
  (joint with University of California–Davis)
Dairy Research Center
Food Science and Nutrition Department
San Luis Obispo, CA 93407
805/756-2997

Dr. Dennis G. Olson
Meat Irradiation Technology Center and
  Meat Export Research Center
Iowa State University
215 Meat Laboratory
Ames, IA 50011
515/294-1055

Dr. Norman Olson
Center for Dairy Research
University of Wisconsin
Babcock Hall
Madison, WI 53706
608/263-2001

Dr. Michael Pariza
University of Wisconsin
Food Research Institute
1925 Willow Drive
Madison, WI 53706
608/263-7777

Dr. Jeffrey K. Kondo·
Western Dairy Foods Research Center
Utah State University   (joint with
  Oregon State University and Brigham
  Young University)
Logan, UT 84321
801/750-2113

Dr. Louis B. Rockland
Food Science Research Center
Chapman College
333 No. Glassell Street
Orange, CA 92666
714/997-6649

Dr. Charles Shannon
Food and Fibre Center
Mississippi State University
P.O. Box 5446
Mississippi State, MS 39762
601/352-2160

Dr. Robert L. Shewfelt
Postharvest Systems Laboratory
University of Georgia
Griffin, GA 30223-1797
404/228-7284

Dr. Myron Solberg
Center for Advanced Food Technology
  (CAFT)
P.O. Box 231
Rutgers University
New Brunswick, NJ 08903
908/932-8306

Dr. Kenneth R. Swartzel
Center for Aseptic Processing and Packaging
  Studies
Department of Food Science
North Carolina State University
Box 7624
Raleigh, NC 27695-7624
919/737-7249

Dr. Steve L. Taylor
Food Processing Center
University of Nebraska
Lincoln, NE 68583-0919
402/472-2833

Dr. James E. Tillotson
Food Policy Institute
Tufts University
School of Nutrition
Medford, MA 02155
617/381-3222

Dr. Daniel Wang
Biotechnology Process Engineering Center
Room 20A-207
Massachusetts Institute of Technology
Cambridge, MA 02139
617/253-0805

Dr. Joseph Warthesen
Minnesota–South Dakota Dairy Foods
  Research Center
Department of Food Science and Nutrition
University of Minnesota   (joint with South
  Dakota State University)
St. Paul, MN 55108
612/624-3224

Chapter 16

Protection of Intellectual Property

Burton A. Amernick

INTRODUCTION

Over the years innovation in food technology has contributed greatly to changes in the way we live and has resulted in many of the innovators becoming household names. One of the more famous was Louis Pasteur, who is credited with being the founder of microbiological sciences. He introduced heat treatment to preserve various foods and drinks including milk and beer, a treatment still referred to as "pasteurization."

In 1873, Pasteur was granted U.S. patent 135245 entitled "Improvement in Brewing Beer and Ale" and U.S. patent 141072 entitled "Improvements in the Manufacture and Preservation of Beer and in the Treatment of Yeast and Wort, Together with Apparatus for the Same" for his inventions concerned with pasteurization.

Like Pasteur, many other inventors in food technology have relied upon the patent laws to protect their innovations. The existence of a patent system has enabled many inventors to obtain the necessary financing to refine their inventions into useful commercial products or processes, which, in turn, have benefited the public in general.

The case of Procter & Gamble Co. against Nabisco Brands Inc., Keebler, Co, and Frito-Lay Inc. is one example of the role of patents in food technology. Procter & Gamble sued Nabisco, Keebler, and Frito-Lay for infringement of U.S. Patent 4455333 and for unfair competition including alleged trade secret theft. The subject matter of the case was a dual-textured cookie that was crispy on the outside and chewy on the inside. The suit was settled, before trial, in September 1989, with the defendants agreeing to pay a total of 125 million dollars to Procter & Gamble—at that time the largest reported settlement in a patent case.

Some understanding of the patent system seems essential for persons involved with technology, especially in view of the relative expense associated with research and development and in view of the relatively rapid changes in technology that are occurring. It is hoped that the following discussion will provide the reader with some appreciation of factors that are considered in evaluating patentability, as well as the underlying reasons for a patent system.

BASIC DISTINCTIONS BETWEEN PATENTS, COPYRIGHTS, TRADEMARKS, AND TRADE SECRETS

Intellectual Property Rights

Property refers to the ownership of something whereby the owner has the right to exclude others from that property. One category of property is referred to as intellectual property. The legal protection for intellectual property for the most part falls into four general areas, depending upon the intellectual property involved. These areas are patents, trade secrets, copyrights, and trademarks. Patent and copyright protection is provided by specially enacted federal statutes. Trademark rights are acquired by use of the mark, without the need to depend upon specifically enacted laws. However, added advantages are acquired by registering a mark under the federal Trademark Law and/or individual state laws. Trade secret protection is not dependent upon statutory law, but upon tradition or case law. The patent laws and copyright laws enacted by Congress are based upon Article 1, Section 8, of the Constitution of the United States, which states:

> The Congress shall have the power to promote the progress of science and useful arts, by securing for limited times to authors and inventors the exclusive rights to their respective writings and discoveries.

The patent laws are intended to afford protection to inventors for innovation in technology. To be patentable, as will be discussed below, an innovation must satisfy the criteria established by the patent laws.

Copyrights

Copyright protection is granted for original works of authorship fixed in any tangible medium of expression from which the work is or can be communicated, either directly or with the aid of a machine.

Works of authorship include the following categories:

1. Literary works.
2. Musical works, including any accompanying words.
3. Dramatic works, including any accompanying music.
4. Pantomimes and choreographic works.
5. Pictorial, graphic, and sculptural works.
6. Motion pictures and other audiovisual works.
7. Sound recordings.

Copyright protection extends to the particular manner in which an idea is expressed, but it does not extend to the underlying ideas. For instance, a copyright in a written description of a process for producing a new food product can prevent someone from describing it in the same manner as covered by the copyright, but it does not prevent others from actually practicing the process. In fact, the copyright does not even preclude another from describing the process by using a different written expression. On the other hand, patent protection for a new process is intended to prevent others from practicing the process but not from making copies of the written description of the process that would appear in the patent.

Registration of copyrights is under the jurisdiction of the Copyright Office. In general, the duration of a copyright is the author's life plus 50 years. Prior to March 1, 1989, in order to secure copyright protection for published works, a copyright notice on the work was required. Such a notice consists of the following three elements:

1. Copyright symbol (the letter "C" in a circle), or the word "copyright," or the abbreviation "Copr."
2. The year of the first publication.
3. The name of the owner of copyright.

Works published on or after March 1, 1989, no longer require the copyright notice.

Certain enhanced legal rights are obtained by using the copyright notice and by registering the copyright with the Copyright Office.

Trademarks

A trademark is a word or symbol or a combination thereof used by a manufacturer or a vendor in connection with a product. A service mark is similar to a trademark except that it is used to identify the services performed by a particular entity and distinguish them from those of competitors.

The primary objective for affording trademark and service mark protection is to identify to the purchasing public that the goods or services are those of a single source and to distinguish them from similar goods or services of others. Through use, trademarks and service marks become a guarantee that goods or services marketed under the mark meet a particular standard of quality. Even though trademarks and service marks can be extremely valuable business assets, the primary reason for their protection is to prevent confusion in the minds of consumers.

Trademark and service mark rights are created by use of the mark. Moreover, the legal rights can be enhanced by obtaining a federal registration for the mark and, to a much lesser extent, obtaining state registrations. Once a trademark or service mark is federally registered, such fact can be indicated by placing the registration symbol ® or "Reg. U.S. Pat. and Trad. Off." or "Registered in

U.S. Patent and Trademark Office'' after the mark. The United States Patent and Trademark Office has jurisdiction over federal registration of trademarks and service marks. The constitutional basis for the federal trademark laws is the commerce clause of the Constitution, which gives Congress the right to regulate, inter alia, interstate commerce. The exclusive rights of trademarks and service marks can continue indefinitely if used properly.

A tradename is a name used to identify a business entity, as distinct from trademarks and service marks, which are used to identify products and services, respectively, of a business entity. Tradenames are not registerable under the federal trademark laws. When a name is used as both a tradename and a trademark or service mark, the name is capable of being registered as a trademark or service mark. If the name is used only as a tradename, protection usually is available under state laws protecting against unfair competition.

Trade Secrets

There are no federal trade secret laws. Accordingly, legal protection of trade secrets depends upon prior cases and upon specific state laws where available. A number of states have enacted laws concerning trade secret protection. A trade secret can be envisioned as any formula, pattern, device, or compilation of information that is used in one's business and which give him or her an opportunity to obtain an advantage over competitors who do not know or use it. The subject matter of a trade secret must be secret so that, except by the use of improper means, there would be difficulty in acquiring the information. Information susceptible to trade secret protection includes that associated with a technology as well as other types of information such as secret business and financial information. On the other hand, patents are concerned only with technology.

The subject matter of a trade secret must be new, but the difference between the prior knowledge and the trade secret need not be so great as the difference required to merit a patent. Manufacturing processes can best be protected by maintaining such a secret.

THE PATENT SYSTEM WAS CREATED TO PROMOTE THE PROGRESS OF TECHNOLOGY

The underlying philosophy for establishing a patent system is to speed up the progress of "useful arts" (i.e., technology). Article 1, Section 8, of the Constitution (see quotation, above) is the basis for the patent and copyright laws.

Pursuant to this authorization, Congress enacted the patent laws, which are intended to encourage people to use their efforts to solve technological problems for the benefit of the public in general, such as in the form of new and more effective products and new procedures. In food technology, the desire is for new food products that are more nutritious, less expensive, less susceptible to spoilage, better manufacturing methods, improved methods for testing such as quality control procedures, and improved and/or less expensive equipment for these purposes.

To promote the progress of technology, the patent laws require full disclosure of the invention, thereby adding to the sum of available useful knowledge. This disclosure is especially important because an invention in one area can help advance the technology in another area. Advances in biochemistry, for example, have made it possible to produce new materials that have shown promise in the food processing industry. For instance, it is now possible profitably to produce high-fructose corn sweeteners employing enzymes (glucose isomerase, invertase, or amylase) produced by biotechnology. The use of biotechnology makes available larger quantities of the enzymes. It has been suggested that researchers might produce flavor and aroma chemicals such as lactones and terpenoids by microorganisms. Hybrid yeast strains are used in brewing processes.

Furthermore, computers now are being used extensively in controlling and investigating food processes, and robots are being used to perform the more routine jobs. The advent of the microwave oven greatly expanded the prepared frozen meal market, a development that in turn has led to innumerable new food products.

In 1988, the United States Patent and Trademark Office (referred to as the Patent Office) granted the first patent (Leder and Stewart 1988) directed to new nonhuman mammals, one example being a mouse. The animals of this invention are intended to be used to test materials, including food additives, suspected of being carcinogens. Because the animals are supposed to possess a propensity to develop tumors, the test should be very sensitive.

A PATENT IS A CONTRACT

A patent is a contract between the inventor and the public. In the United States, the public is represented by the government, specifically the United States Patent and Trademark Office.

As with any contract, each party gives up something of value and in return receives something of value. With patents, the government gives to the inventor the right to exclude others from ''practicing'' the invention, that is, from making, using, or selling the invention as claimed for a limited period of time. This period of time in the United States is 17 years from the date of the patent grant. For food additives, color additives, drugs, and medical devices this period can be extended up to five years associated with delays at the U.S. Food and Drug Administration (FDA) or at the Animal and Plant Health Inspection Service in obtaining approval to market. In many other countries, patents expire 20 years from the filing data of the applications.

The patent right sometimes is thought of as a negative right because the inventor is not given the right to practice the invention, but instead receives the right to prevent others from doing so. In fact, even the inventor could be prevented from practicing the invention. For instance, a patented invention for a new food additive or color additive cannot necessarily be commercialized, as such substances are subject to regulation under the Federal Food, Drug and Cosmetic Act. Also, one's patented invention could be dominated by a more basic prior patent having broad coverage encompassing the later invention. By way of example, assume that Inventor A invents and patents a new compound X and describes X as being useful as a fabric dye. Inventor B later discovers that compound X is useful in a process to produce a powdered dried food product. Because the compound is patented by Inventor A, the process to produce the powdered food product using compound X cannot be practiced by Inventor B without permission from Inventor A to do so, such as by obtaining a license. Likewise, Inventor A cannot practice the process of preparing the powdered food using compound X without permission from Inventor B. Often in these situations, the parties cross-license each other.

This so-called negative right is not unique to patents. The use of any property that one owns is restrictive to some extent. For instance, buying a car gives a person the right to prevent others from using it, but not the right to drive it. For the car to be driven, it must be registered and the driver licensed. Even then there are restrictions on how and where it can be driven such as speed limits and one-way streets.

Likewise, it is not necessary to obtain a patent in order to practice an invention. As discussed above, the right to do something will be dictated by other factors such as government restrictions and rights of others.

In return for these rights, the inventor gives to the public a full written description of the invention.

WHAT CAN BE PATENTED

Because patents are created by specifically enacted laws (the U.S. patent laws are found in Title 35 of the United States Code, referred to as 35 U.S.C.), what can be patented and the requirements that must be satisfied are stated herein. With respect to subject matter capable of being patented, the law is written very broadly. In particular, whoever invents or discovers any new and useful process, machine, manufacture, or composition or matter, or any new and useful improvement thereof, may obtain a patent, provided that all of the other conditions and requirements of the patent laws are met (35 U.S.C. 101). In fact, it has been stated that the language used to define patentable subject matter is intended to "include anything under the sun that is made by man" (Diamond v. Chakrabarty 1980). Nevertheless there are limits. The laws of nature, methods of doing business, printed matter per se, materials found in nature, physical phenomena, and abstract ideas are not patentable.

Inventions falling within the above categories of patentable subject matter and applicable to food technology include:

- Compounds and compositions, including those that have been genetically engineered.
- Methods of manufacturing food products.
- Methods of treating food products to alter properties, such as decaffeinating coffee beans, producing reduced-calorie beer, or increasing the shelf life of a food product.

The Supreme Court in 1980 decided that living matter could be patented (Diamond v. Chakrabarty 1980). The invention in that case was a human-made, genetically engineered bacterium capable of breaking down multiple components of crude oil, and therefore potentially useful in treating oil spills. The court held that genetically engineered microorganisms are capable of being patented.

Subsequent to this, patents were granted for even higher forms of living matter, including seeds and plants (Ex parte Hibberd 1985). The Patent and Trademark Office Board of Patent Appeals and Interferences (The Board) decided in a case that a new polyploid (more than two sets of chromosomes) oyster was subject matter capable of being patented (Ex parte Allen 1987). However, the patent was not granted for other reasons. After that decision, the Commissioner of Patents and Trademarks issued a notice stating that "non-naturally occurring nonhuman multicellular living organisms, including animals, are patentable subject matter" (Quigg 1987). After this notice, there were complaints from animal rights groups along with hearings in Congress, during which time the Patent Office placed a moratorium on granting such patents. The Patent Office then granted its first animal patent (Leder and Stewart 1988). As noted above, this patent is concerned with certain strains of mammals that have a propensity to develop tumors, and they are intended to be used in tests of materials suspected of being carcinogenic. Accordingly, they could be of use in evaluating the potential safeness of a proposed food additive or coloring agent.

UTILITY

A requirement for patentability is that the invention must be useful (35 U.S. C. 101). The utility does not need to be refined to the extend that the invention is commercial, as long as the invention performs to some reasonable extent. To a large degree, the questions of utility arise in chemical cases, and especially with pharmaceutical inventions. However, the question of whether the invention satisfies the utility requirement sometimes arises for other inventions. This issue is raised when the nature of the invention is such that its asserted utility or operativeness appears to contravene established scientific principles or current knowledge of the available technology. If the invention is such that persons working in the involved technology area, once made aware of the invention, would be skeptical about its operativeness, then the invention is one in which utility is an issue.

A food example involved an invention concerned with a method for enhancing the flavor and increasing the specific gravity of a beverage such as a fruit juice, coffee, or tea, by passing the beverage through a magnetic field (Fregeau v. Mossinghoff 1985). The Patent Office took the position that the nature of the invention was such that utility was at issue, and thus shifted the burden to the patent applicant to establish operativeness.

In fact, in this case the applicant admitted that the invention was "one about which those of ordinary skill in the flavor chemistry art would be skeptical when first hearing of it." The applicant then submitted evidence in the form of declarations from a university professor in food science who had carried out taste tests and tests for detecting physical property changes of various beverages subjected to the magnetic field. However, the evidence was found to be insufficient to overcome the refusal and warrant the granting of a patent because the observed differences in physical properties were only minimal, and they did not establish change due to any magneto-chemical effect other than change due to extrinsic factors such as variations in the ambient conditions or experimental error. The taste tests were not deemed to be statistically significant.

In addition, in certain situations, mainly drug cases, the Patent Office under the utility requirement required the patent applicant to prove that the invention was safe for its intended purpose. This requirement to prove safety was challenged in court and was found, in the case of drugs, to be the responsibility of the Food and Drug Administration, not the Patent Office (In re Watson 1975). In that case, safety was deemed not to be a criterion for patentability. However, an invention unsafe for use by reason of toxicity or danger to the point of causing immediate death under all conditions of its sole contemplated use would be lacking in utility and therefore unpatentable.

TO BE PATENTABLE THE INVENTION MUST BE NEW

Another requirement that an invention must satisfy to be patentable is that it must be new or novel (35 U.S.C. 102). Because patents are creatures of statutes, those conditions, referred to as "prior art," that defeat the novelty of an invention are likewise defined in the patent laws. Only the more typically encountered ones are mentioned below. (A discussion of all such conditions can be found in Amernick *Patent Law for the Nonlawyer*, 1986).

Probably the two most common categories of prior art are printed publications and patents. The publications and patents can be from any country and in any language. A patent or publication that describes one's invention and is prior in time to it defeats the novelty of the invention. Upon the granting of a U.S. patent, the date that can be used for prior art purposes reverts back to its filing date.

In the event that a printed publication or patent describes an invention and is more than one year old when the patent application is filed in a patent office, such prior description will render the invention of that patent application unpatentable no matter when the invention was actually made. In fact, the patent or publication could even be by the inventor, but when such has appeared more than one year before the actual filing of the patent application, granting of a patent is precluded. This situation is referred to as a "statutory bar" because no matter whose patent or publication it is, and no matter when the invention was made, a patent is barred. In essence, then, the United States gives the inventor a one-year grace period after patenting or publication to file an application, provided that the invention was made prior to the patent or publication. However, most other countries do not give any grace period; so the patent application must already be on file before the invention is publicly disclosed in order to be patentable in most other countries. Often an inventor desires to present or publish a paper describing some discovery, but to preserve foreign rights, the paper should not be published until a patent application has been filed. After filing of the application, the paper can be published without affecting the rights.

Public use or public knowledge of an invention in the United States prior to one's invention renders it unpatentable. Moreover a patent is precluded if the invention was in public use or on sale in the United States more than one year prior to the filing of the patent application. The public use or on-sale activity could even by done by the inventor, but when it is more than one year before the filing of the patent application, such activity will prevent granting of a patent. This one-year period is an attempt to balance the desire for early disclosure of the invention to the public and the need to give the inventor some limited time to determine whether pursuing patent protection is justified.

Furthermore, the making of the invention in the United States before the patent applicant's invention by another who has not abandoned, suppressed, or concealed the invention precludes the applicant from getting a patent.

U.S. law further requires that the actual inventor(s) file the application and be named and sign an oath confirming inventorship. This is true even though the inventor(s) may be obligated to assign the patent to another, such as the inventor's employer.

INVENTIONS MUST BE NONOBVIOUS TO BE PATENTABLE

The above-discussed novelty-defeating prior art items presuppose that the exact subject matter for which a patent is being sought is described by a single prior art item. However, even if the invention is not fully described by a single prior art item, it still may not be patentable. In particular, the patent law also requires that the invention be nonobvious (35 U.S.C. 103). An invention is not patentable if the differences between the subject matter sought to be patented and the prior art are such that the subject matter as a whole would have been obvious at the time the invention was made to a person of ordinary skill in the technology or art that is the subject matter of the invention.

Obviousness is to be evaluated without the luxury of the hindsight gained from becoming aware of the invention after it has been made. Instead, it is determined only with information that existed as of that earlier point in time when the invention actually was made.

In evaluating whether an invention is obvious or nonobvious, factual inquiries are made for the following purposes:

1. To determine the scope and content of the prior art.
2. To determine the differences between the prior art and the subject matter (patent application claims) in question.
3. To determine the level of ordinary skill in the pertinent art.

The person of "ordinary skill" is a somewhat hypothetical person determined on a case-by-case basis, taking into account such factors as level of experience and educational background of persons working in that field of technology most closely related to that of the invention.

In addition, the following considerations should be taken into account, as they may be relevant with respect to the nonobviousness of the invention:

1. Commercial success of the invention.
2. Long-felt but unfulfilled need in the prior art.
3. Failures of others in the art.

Although the existence of any of these latter considerations can be used to bolster the arguments for the nonobviousness of an invention, the lack of such considerations does not indicate obviousness.

One example of a food technology invention demonstrating nonobviousness was concerned with the addition of substantially pure 2-methyl-2-pentenoic acid (referred to as 2M2PA) to foods to impart a strawberry flavor (In re Kratz 1979). Although 2M2PA is one of the many components of natural strawberries, there was no basis in the prior art for selecting it and using it in a composition to impart a strawberry flavor. Because the ability of 2M2PA to provide a strawberry flavor was not predictable from the prior art, the invention was nonobvious and patentable.

CONTENTS OF THE PATENT DOCUMENT

Basic Components

What must be included in the patent document itself is also specified by the statute. In particular, a specification containing a written description of the invention and at least one claim is required (35 U.S.C. 112). If the invention is of the type that needs a drawing to be understood, such as machines and electronic circuitry, drawings are required as well as a discussion thereof. In addition, an abstract is included as an aid to those searching the patent literature.

The written disclosure of the invention, in addition to needing a description of the invention, must satisfy an "enablement requirement" and a "best mode" requirement (35 U.S.C. 112).

Enablement

The enablement requirement provides that the specification must contain a written description of the manner and process of making and using the invention in such full, clear, concise, and exact terms as to enable any person skilled in the art to which the invention pertains to make and use the invention. This is part of the consideration given up by the inventor to the public in exchange for receiving the patent right. Although some experimentation might be required to make and use the invention from this written description, the enablement requirement still will be satisfied. However, such experimentation must not amount to what would be deemed undue experimentation. If so, the enablement requirement would not be met, thereby precluding the grant of a valid patent.

Many inventions in the biotechnology field such as newly synthesized microorganisms cannot be adequately disclosed in writing to enable those skilled in the art to make them without undue experimentation to satisfy the enablement requirement. In such an event, this requirement of the law can be complied with by depositing a sample of the invention (e.g., a microorganism) with a recognized depository such as the American Type Culture Collection or the National Research Culture Collection, along with a reference to the deposit in the patent application.

Best Mode

The specification also must set forth the best mode contemplated by the inventor for carrying out the invention. It does not actually have to be the best way but only that which the inventor believes to be the best. This requirement is to prevent concealment by an inventor of his or her preferred way of practicing the invention while still taking advantage of the rights afforded by the patent.

Claims

The claims of the patent represent what the inventor gets out of the patent. The claims define what the patent holder can prevent others from doing (making, using, or selling). The claims are to particularly point out and distinctly claim the subject matter that the inventor regards as the invention. The claims of a patent should not be confused with technical claims of performance. The claims of a patent set forth the limits or metes and bounds of the technical property being protected. The claims are compared to the prior art to evaluate patentability and compared to another's activity to determine whether infringement exists.

In order for infringement to exist, an accused activity must employ all of the features stated in a claim. However, infringement is not avoided if all of the claim features are practiced along with some additional feature not recited in the claim.

Each claim appears as a single sentence, but in actuality is the object of the sentence "What I claim is" or "What is claimed is."

Oath

Also required to complete a patent application is an oath or declaration signed by the inventor(s) stating that he/she or they made the invention claimed. The application must be completed and then reviewed and understood by the inventor(s) prior to the signing. Incorrect designation of inventorship can invalidate a patent. However, errors of inventorship that occurred without deceptive intention can be corrected and the patent rights saved.

The oath signed by the inventor also recognizes the inventor's duty of candor to the Patent and Trademark Office, which requires bringing to the attention of the Patent and Trademark Office information such as prior art that would be important for the patent examiner to be aware of when evaluating the patentability of the invention in question. The examination process at the Patent and Trademark Office is not intended to be an adversarial one, but one where both the applicant and the examiner have the same objective of having a valid patent granted.

PATENT EXAMINERS

At the present time, there are about 1,500 patent examiners with at least a bachelor's degree in engineering or science. The examining corp is separated into the three major engineering disciplines (chemical, electrical and mechanical), and each of the subdivisions is divided into a number of individual groups. Each group is responsible for a particular area of technology, which in turn is composed of a number of subgroups referred to as "Art Units." Each "Art Unit" is headed by a senior examiner, referred to as a "Supervisory Primary Examiner," The amount of authority and the freedom of action an examiner can have depend upon the particular examiner's experience.

Group 130 handles patent applications concerned with food technology, and Group 180 handles those concerned with biotechnology.

INTERNATIONAL PATENT TREATIES

Paris Convention

The United States is a member of both the Paris Convention of 1883 for the Protection of Industrial Property and the Patent Cooperation Treaty (PCT). With respect to the Paris Convention, a patent application has a convention year that begins upon the filing of the first application on the subject invention. By filing a corresponding patent application within the convention year in a Paris Convention country, a convention priority date (i.e., the same date it was originally filed in the United States) is given to the foreign application by the foreign country.

Another important provision of the Paris Convention is that a member country cannot give patent rights to its own citizens that differ from the rights it grants to citizens of another member country.

Currently, there are about 95 member countries of the Paris Convention, including most of the important industrial countries.

Patent Cooperation Treaty

The Patent Cooperation Treaty provides a procedure for filing patent applications in a number of countries (about 43 countries are members). It does not provide for substantive changes in the laws of the individual member countries. The treaty provides for the filing of one application in one patent office, referred to as the "receiving office," and designating those member countries of interest. The initial filing can be in any language. However, sometime after filing, depending upon the countries designated, translations will be required.

Accordingly, a U.S. citizen or resident can file such an application in English and in the United States Patent and Trademark Office. There is a standard format for the application, and it will be recognized as a regular national filing in as many member countries as are designated by the applicant. After certain requirements are met, such as the payment of national fees, the application will be examined according to the procedures of each of the named countries.

European Patent Convention

Since 1978, pursuant to the European Patent Convention, a European patent application naming one or more of the European member countries of the convention can be filed in the European Patent Office in Munich, Germany. The European Patent Convention provides for one examination and the grant of a single patent and certificate stating that such has been granted. A European patent has the effect of a national patent in each of the named countries. Enforcement of these patent rights then can be conducted in the individual courts of each country designated.

CONCLUSION

The patent system serves to promote the progress of technology by encouraging invention and by making available to the public information on new and more effective products and processes. Because products of research can result in patentable inventions, persons involved in research including researchers and managers should be familiar with the patent laws and procedures.

REFERENCES

Amernick, Burton A. 1986. *Patent Law for the Nonlawyer.* New York: Van Nostrand Reinhold.

Diamond v. Chakrabarty, 447, U.S. 303 1980.

Ex parte Allen, 2 U.S.P.Q. 2nd 1425 (United States Patent and Trademark Office Board of Patent Appeals and Interferences, 1987).

Ex parte Hibberd, 227 U.S.P.Q. 443 (United States Patent and Trademark Office Board of Patent Appeals and Interferences, 1985).

Fregeau v. Mossinghoff, 227 U.S.P.Q. 848 (Court of Appeals, Federal Circuit, 1985).

In re Kratz, 201 U.S.P.Q. 71 (Court of Customs and Patent Appeals, 1979).

In re Watson, 186 U.S.P.Q. 11 (Court of Customs and Patent Appeals, 1975).

Leder, Philip and Stewart, Timothy. 1988. U.S. Patent 4736866. Entitled "Transgenic non-human Mammals." Assigned to President and Fellows of Harvard College.

Quigg, Donald. Apr. 21, 1987. *Official Gazette of United States Patent and Trademark Office,* Vol. 1077, p. 24.

Chapter 17

Focal Issues in Food Science and Engineering

Marcus Karel

INTRODUCTION

Innovations in food product development depend heavily on consumer acceptance and other nontechnical factors. The key aspects of food technological innovations include:

1. The real and/or perceived needs and wants of the consumer.
2. Legal and other regulatory issues.
3. The availability of adequate consumer education through various channels, especially the news media.
4. Economic issues.
5. Scientific and engineering advances.

Before discussing science and technology, we propose to review some of the nontechnological factors.

Consumer

The attitudes of the consuming public are perhaps the most important factor in food product development. Consumer concerns involve primarily issues of health, safety, and convenience (Graham, Green and Roberts 1988). The role of dietary factors in maintaining good health and promoting longevity is being recognized as a key factor in public health, by the public as well as by medical experts. The complexity of diet–health interactions makes it difficult, however, to formulate a simple set of guidelines with respect to desirable diets. The field is wide open to promoters of specific dietary measures, some of which are meritorious, and some of which seem of little value. The consumer thus is extremely susceptible to diet fashions. The nutrients that consumers especially perceive to be related to good health include calcium, fiber (including oats and psyllium), and omega-3 fatty acids. Currently, diet-related health concerns focus particularly on pesticide residues, cholesterol, aluminum, tropical oils, and sulfites.

Another major consumer "need" is convenience. Changing life-styles have generated a demand for fast foods, snacks (including snacks with controlled nutrient content), microwavable foods, and prepackaged prepared portion-controlled foods. However, the desire for convenience is coupled with increased attention to perceived quality. The perception of quality is, of course, subjective; nevertheless, the appearance of "gourmet" prepared foods, and the widespread acceptance of previously "ethnic" foods has resulted in improving quality standards for convenience foods.

Finally the consumer is limited in his or her choice of foods by their cost.

Legal and Regulatory Issues

The marketing of food is regulated by a complex of laws and regulations that are administered by several agencies within several departments of the U.S. government (Hui 1979). As a result, the development of new food products and processes requires costly and often very lengthy regulatory reviews. It is not unusual to see lags of decades between the time when a process or ingredient is perfected and the granting of regulatory approval for its introduction to commercial practice.

Media and Consumer Education

The considerable attention paid by the consumer to the relations, whether real or alleged, between diet and health has resulted in some confusion. A desirable solution to the resultant misinformation and conflicts may be found in consumer education. Unfortunately, however, the inherent characteristics of the news media make such education difficult, as the emphasis often is on sensational, "newsworthy," or dramatic aspects of the issues that are presented (Seltzer 1989).

Advertising should be an equally effective medium for consumer education, but unfortunately it often produces miseducation. Both industry and consumer groups have often been irresponsible in oversimplifying, and on occasion misrepresenting, scientific evidence in presenting their points of view. Public disillusionment with "authoritative" pronouncements from established sources—whether from government, universities, churches, or professional societies—makes public education in the sciences a difficult and often thankless task.

The complexity of the issues involved, and the public airing of various conflicts within the scientific community, have conditioned the public to be skeptical about established views, in spite of a rather naive acceptance of heterodoxy.

It is the responsibility of the food scientist to continue to present facts as he or she sees them, without oversimplification and in spite of occasional distrust of the public. In the long run, truth tells.

Economic Issues

Industry's development of new food products and processes is driven by the profit motive. Therefore, it is not sufficient just to excel at convincing consumers to purchase one product in preference to others; it is equally important to reduce the cost of the product to the producer.

The most prominent feature of the present industrial economy is its global nature. Raw materials are available from every corner of the world, a situation that has led to a substantial lessening of the danger of catastrophic shortages of raw materials. As an example, the severe cold wave of December 1989 destroyed much of the Florida citrus crop, but the impact of that crop failure was mitigated by an abundance of Brazilian oranges. The food industry also has been able to overcome some labor cost increases by either importing labor for agricultural tasks (e.g., guest workers in California or in Europe) or importing staples from far-flung regions. This globality has greatly increased the requirements for quality control of imported staples, and also has resulted in occasional crises (e.g., Chilean grapes contaminated with cyanide) and some real dangers of transfer of microbial pathogens or of other contaminants. The global nature of the food supply requires the constant vigilance of industrial quality control systems and of government regulatory agencies.

Another characteristic of the industrial scene, in the food industry as well as in other industries, is an accelerating trend toward automation and computer control of production, storage, and distribution of foods.

Scientific and Engineering Advances

The needs, constraints, and incentives for innovation are in themselves inadequate to produce technical innovations. One also must have the requisite backing of scientific advances. In many cases, in fact, scientific advances generate the recognition or the development of needs and incentives.

Three scientific revolutions have occurred in recent decades that are likely to revolutionize the food industry: advances in computer science, in genetic engineering, and in material science.

The advances in the availability of computer hardware and software have had an enormous impact on the practices of the food industry and related industries. One of the greatest and most visible impacts has been in the area of analytical and industrial instrumentation. The capabilities of modern analytical methodologies, whether mass spectrometry, HPLC, gas chromatography, or the various spectroscopic techniques, depend on computers. Advances in instrumentation are dominated by software capable of performing a range of tasks from simulation of molecular motion through collection, calculation, and recording of various analytical data. Process control and automated manufacturing also depend on modern high-speed computers (Saguy et al., 1990).

Another area of computer influence is that of inventory and control in storage, distribution, and merchandising. We are all familiar with barcode systems, where scanners allow checkout counter personnel to display and record prices, batch numbers, and other pre-encoded characteristics of merchandise. First-in, first-out inventory management is becoming more feasible, and just on the horizon are systems that will integrate effects of time and temperature, thus allowing management of inventory on the basis of "most-aged," first-out systems (Wells and Singh 1989).

Computers have been extremely useful in automation and process control, as well as computer-assisted-design (CAD) and computer-assisted-manufacturing (CAM), in the chemical industry. The food industry has initiated such applications, but many of these applications are limited by lack of quantitative methodology for measurement, control, and optimization of food properties. The complexity of food properties requiring measurement and control demands new approaches; and one of these approaches to the adaptation of complex systems to computer-operated control is the use of "expert systems"—a branch of artificial intelligence. A recent symposium of the Institute of Food Technologists (IFT) was devoted entirely to this topic (Whitney 1989).

The second scientific revolution affecting the food industry is genetic engineering, which itself is part of biotechnology. The ability to shape life at will is still, fortunately perhaps, limited to lower organisms. However, it now is possible, for instance, to transfer the capability of producing a given enzyme from higher organisms to microorganisms. A key feature of this research is that it is possible to transfer the ability to produce specific enzymes from organisms that are inefficient in terms of this production (e.g., mammals) to more efficient producers (e.g., microorganisms). This ability to affect the genetics to produce specific compounds is of considerable importance in product development, as it generates a potential for new sources of food components (e.g., flavors).

Genetic engineering speeds up breeding. Much of the traditional genetics work cannot be modified to achieve aims in a much shorter time span, but traditional breeding is greatly facilitated by the fact that researchers know the function of individual genes and can clone them.

The third area in which there have been significant advances affecting food industry innovations is the material science of foods. This discipline provides a basis for understanding the relations between food structure and composition and the functional properties of food. It provides a foundation for the development of engineered foods. The importance of these advances need not be stressed in this age of "re-formed" meats, surimi, diet drinks containing artificial sweeteners, and fat substitutes. The underlying concept of engineered food is the delivery of desired functionality (e.g., sweetness, fatlike mouthfeel, texture, or a particular color and appearance) through an appropriate choice of ingredients selected on the basis of their chemical composition and/or physical structure, rather than solely through selection of preexisting plant or animal products that fortuitously have the needed properties.

The above scientific advances, however, do not automatically guarantee progress in the food industry. Bridges must be provided for the transfer of technologies and their adaptation to specific needs of the industry and of the consumer. List 17-1 summarizes some of the approaches urgently needing to be undertaken by the food industry. The current state of progress in the industry is not entirely satisfactory, as for a number of reasons many of the major U.S. industries have been forced to concentrate on relatively short-term financial goals. Consequently, basic research efforts in the material science of foods have been reduced or postponed. On the other hand, there has been significant investment in the development of technologies likely to improve efficiencies and to increase profits on a short-term basis.

Most of the research of the food industry has been oriented toward process improvement and is directed primarily to computer applications. However, this work also will require new developments in material science. One very important development—needed to tie computer technology and material science technology to the ability to produce foods in a reproducible, quality-conscious way—would be the ability to measure on-line whatever quality characteristic is desired. Key needs are appropriate sensors.

Basic research in biotechnology does continue in small U.S. venture-capital-funded companies, some of which also are making important advances in material science. The most concentrated efforts, however, are under way overseas. In Europe, multinational companies, in particular Nestlé and Unilever, are the leaders; and in Japan, Mitsubishi, Ajinomoto, Suntory, and several other companies seem to continue to strengthen their basic research.

SOME SPECIFIC TECHNOLOGICAL DEVELOPMENTS AND THEIR STATUS

Supercritical Fluid Extraction and Other Applications of Supercritical Fluids

Supercritical fluid applications have received considerable attention in recent years and are the subject of much intensive work (McHugh and Krukonis 1986).

List 17-1.   What food industry must do to utilize scientific advances.

1. Develop a major effort to relate the function of ingredients in food products to their physicochemical properties, molecular structure, and biological activity.
2. Specify its requirements for "engineered" ingredients in molecular terms.
3. Come to grips with the issue of natural vs. "nature-identical" sources.
4. Be willing to take a long-term view in research and development.
5. Develop sensors for properties that need to be controlled, and which can be used in a computer-assisted control and automation.
6. Develop an understanding of the processes (biosynthesis, biodegradation, chemical reactions) involved in generating key ingredients (e.g., flavors).

The principles of operation and key advantages of the process are shown in List 17-2. Recently, much attention has been devoted to the potential for cholesterol removal from butter and from eggs using relatively mild, nontoxic solvents. The market for cholesterol-free egg is expanding, with $100 million spent on egg-substitutes in 1989 (Sperber 1989). Cornell University is reported to have achieved 98% reduction of cholesterol in butter, and is working on "cholesterol-free" beef tallow. Michel Foods of Minneapolis has been collaborating with the University of Wisconsin and with Phasex Corporation in developing methodology and potential markets. According to Sperber (1989), one of the technology-generating companies (Supercritical Processing, Inc.) estimates operating costs of 0.2 to 0.4 dollar per pound for cholesterol removal from butterfat. The future of this particular application, however, seems very uncertain, and demonstrates the main disadvantage of the process, namely, its high cost. The reduction of the cholesterol content in butter by a factor of 10 may cost as much as two dollars per pound of butterfat—surely a prohibitive cost.

Other applications, however—in particular, the extraction of expensive volatile flavors and the removal of much more of the soluble compounds from expensive new materials (e.g., caffeine from coffee)—seem quite promising.

Food Irradiation

Ionizing radiation—in particular, gamma rays from radioactive isotopes such as cobalt 60, or electrons or X rays generated by accelerators—is effective in destroying or sterilizing insects, in preventing sprouting of tubers, in softening cellulose-containing plant materials, and especially in pasteurizing or sterilizing foods. In common with other sterilizing procedures, irradiation also can produce side effects, especially an off flavor in some food materials. The safety of application of irradiation and the methodology of processing with minimal side

List 17-2. Supercritical fluid extraction.

Principle:

- Gases at high pressure and temperature have potential as solvents for a number of extractive processes (separation, purification, detoxification) or as reaction media (oxidation of organic waste products in supercritical water).
- The process requires operation at high pressures and, in case of water, at high temperatures.

Major advantages:

- Ease of removal of solvent
- Solvent nontoxicity (CO_2, water)
- Unusual solubility properties

Major disadvantage:

- Process cost

effects have been the subject of extensive research for the past 40 years. The current status of this application is, however, extremely uncertain because of public distrust of any processes connected with nuclear energy.

In any discussion of radiation applications, it is necessary to consider the does level, or the total radiation delivered to the food. The dose level, measured in krad, may be of interest in providing a yardstick for the lethality of radiation doses. Bacterial spores are most resistant to this treatment, requiring 100 to 500 krad to reduce their number by a factor of 10. Sterilization normally requires that the number of spores be reduced by a factor of a hundred billion or more, and a sterilization dose ranges from 1,000 to 6,000 krad. In contrast, insects are much more radiation-sensitive, so that a dose of 10 to 20 krad results in effective sterilization. Humans are even more sensitive—a whole body irradiation with 1 krad would almost certainly be lethal. Of course, the radiation applied to foods is not transferred to the people who eat the food, any more than steam sterilization exposes people to overheating. Legitimate safety issues are, instead, the potential for the production of undesirable chemical compounds and concern about the safety of radioisotope installations in food factories. These matters have been addressed in a very extensive and responsible manner by various U.S. and international organizations.

From a *technical* point of view, the following applications seem to be feasible, cost-effective, and safe (Karel 1989):

- The use of low doses of radiation (up to 50 krad) to destroy insects in fruits and vegetables being shipped across state and national boundaries, and in international grain shipments.
- The pasteurization of poultry, fish, and feed stocks to eliminate the very serious danger of epidemics of disease due to *Salmonella, Yersinia, Campylobacter*, and related organisms. Doses of 150 to 500 krad would be quite effective in this respect.
- The sterilization of spices, which constitute a very small portion of the total diet but can carry some dangerous microorganisms.
- The elimination of sprouting in selected plants.

At the present time legal restrictions on the use of radiation are quite severe, with the worldwide applications limited primarily to some disinfestation work on grain (USSR), some pasteurization (Europe), and some potato sprouting inhibition (Japan).

Petitions currently are pending for permission to irradiate poultry with several hundred krad to eliminate *Salmonella, Yersinia*, and *Campylobacter*. This application is likely to be approved on technical grounds, but a fight may ensue on various nontechnical or pseudotechnical grounds, led by the antinuclear lobby.

If public concern can be overcome, irradiation is likely to be used in combination with other food processing methods for sterilization of spices, insect eradication, elimination of pathogens, and extension of shelf life of poultry and seafood in combination with refrigeration. Another potentially large application is the sterilization of containers in aseptic packing. Food plants may use electron machines or X-ray machines. The use of radioisotopes such sa Co-60 is likely to be extremely limited, done only in isolated locations for contract processing. In any case, the current public attitude is extremely hostile to any applications of food irradiation. Several states (including New Jersey, which was the location hosting the early commercial food irradiation) have banned food irradiation. The recently proposed use of irradiation to destroy insects in Florida citrus fruit has encountered substantial public opposition.

Other Electromagnetic Radiations

The innate desire of humans to overcome the limitations of nature is very strong, and has been instrumental in producing vast technological changes. Unfortunately, it can also lead researchers on a wild goose chase. This is true in many fields, as evidenced by the "cold fusion" controversy, by the famous artifact of "polywater," and, in my opinion at least, by the "megavitamin" proponents. Similarly, many allegedly miraculous food preservation methods have been cropping up periodically, including the use of laser processing, high magnetic fields, and other proposals. Unfortunately, the physical principles of food preservation remain limited: thermal, ionizing, or mechanical energy must be applied to destroy microorganisms, or the organisms must be physically removed from the food and separated from the edible food constituents. The last-mentioned possibility is one of the applications of membrane processing.

Membrane Processes

Membrane processes, which are quite common now, are mentioned among innovations because of a potential for new combinations of membrane processes that might produce novel products. All the membrane processes use the membrane pores for separation, driving components by pressure (reverse osmosis), electric charge (electrodialysis), concentration difference (dialysis), or combinations of these driving forces. The novelty lies in imaginative application of these processes for specific cost-effective uses. As an example, food liquids may be deacidified by electrodialysis and then concentrated by reverse osmosis.

Engineered Foods

Engineered foods are foods that have been modified or assembled in such a way as to achieve some functionality, that is, some key performance characteristic.

One of the major advantages of engineered foods, whether composed of semisynthetic or of natural components, is their flexible composition, which is very important in some market situations. In engineered food, it is possible to replace a coconut oil with other fats, if indeed that is desirable (as has been the case recently when "tropical oils" have been implicated in the popular press in having undesirable health effects). Similarly, one could replace corn if there were aflatoxin contamination in a corn-growing region. The flexibility of engineered foods allows a similar response to price changes, or to political crises.

Similarly, engineered foods offer flexibility with respect to functionality. Soft-center cookies may be produced by replacing part of a crystallizable component, sucrose, which is crisp, in the center portion with another sugar or starch that inhibits crystallinity, thus yielding a center that is "soft." In low-calorie foods, one can engineer the perception of fat by physical treatment of polymers or proteins and generate a market for fat substitutes other than triglyceride. Engineered foods also can have specific functionality in their method of use. For instance, one can build in suitability for microwave cooking, and already many products are being marketed that are specifically tailored for use in a microwave oven.

It should be noted that an engineered product may use no synthetic components whatsoever. Bread is an engineered product. It has built into it a certain number of air cells, a crust, a crumb, a certain mix of flavor compounds produced by yeast, and a caloric content. Engineering simply means taking components and developing them in a way that gives the desired functions. The flexibility of engineered food also gives the product development staff the ability to respond to changing consumer attitudes. It is possible to engineer bread, cookies, or even meat extenders using "desirable" fiber sources, such as oats or psyllium.

At the present time, the potential of engineered foods is limited primarily by nontechnical issues. One of them is the desire to maintain the "natural" image for both labeling and advertising purposes. As a result, there is a price advantage to using natural substances that are chemically identical with synthetic material.

A major area in which technical advances are likely is polymer engineering. Starting with materials such as polysaccharides and proteins, which are "natural" and acceptable polymers, one can build the desired functionality by producing derivatives that may act as sensors within the foods. These substances may impart taste, flavor, appearance, or nutritional value. Such measures as physical treatment of the polymers to produce aggregation or disaggregation, depolymerization and polymerization, or orientation and cross linking are all capable of producing ingredients with useful functionalities.

The engineering of lipids is another key area for present and future work because of consumer concern about calories, and the fact that fat is the most important carrier of calories. There has been ever-growing pressure to develop a fat substitute. Unfortunately, with some noncaloric lipids there is a catch-22: those lipids that are absorbed, even to a slight extent, require a determination of potential residues or effects on the liver or other organs; and if they are not absorbed, they present some problems of a gastrointestinal nature, such as diarrhea and "anal leakage."

An important aspect of engineered foods with an enormous potential is flavor engineering. Researchers have not yet been able to generate the kind of flavors that exist in nature, but this capability is going to come. Food engineers already have almost limitless analytical capabilities; what is needed in addition is knowledge about how a given composition affects the brain, how it interacts with the sensors in the nose and in the mouth, how that signal is translated. Once that knowledge is available, and artificial intelligence computers may be of help here, there will be a revolution in flavor engineering of the same order as the genetic engineering revolution.

Another important area is tailoring foods for specific groups. Some of the key applications are shown in List 17-3. They include tailoring of foods for specific health problems, whether inborn errors of metabolism, drug-induced problems, or the need for truly sterile food during cancer chemotherapy. This last area fortunately is still a very small market, but it is very difficult to provide people with sterile foods when their immune systems are out of commission. Unfortunately, there also is a very large group of people with impaired immune systems—AIDS-sufferers; and sterile foods may be one more part of their therapy. The society also has a continuing concern with atherosclerosis, as it is the major limiting factor in the average life span.

The area of food and flavor engineering will be advanced greatly by the next scientific revolution, which I think will occur in brain science. We are getting

---

List 17-3. Engineering foods for specific consumer groups.

1. Dietetic foods—weight control:
   - Sweeteners
   - Fat substitutes
   - High-fiber foods
2. Foods for people with problems due to food–drug interactions:
   - Mineral balance problems (Ca, K)
   - Amine intolerance for people using psychoactive drugs
   - Sterile foods for people during cancer chemotherapy
   - Formulations for specific disease states
3. Foods designed to reduce risk of atherosclerosis:
   - Fatty acid balance (saturated vs. unsaturated, omega 6 vs. omega 3, lauric vs. stearic acids)
   - Cholesterol content control
4. Foods for people with allergies
5. Foods targeted at specific age groups

closer to discovering a way to control appetite; there is considerable progress in understanding the impact of dietary components on moods and brain function. Researchers are still dealing with the very loose ends of a number of ideas. The current ideas probably are wrong in focusing simply on serotonin and amino acid transport, but a picture is beginning to emerge, and when it does, the opportunity for food engineering will be enormous.

Food preservation techniques of the next century will be modular, as shown in List 17-4.

ADVANCES IN PACKAGING

The same kind of tailoring that helps to control food composition is being used, and will be used on a much larger scale, with food packaging materials. Various combinations of polymers will be tried to achieve packaging functionality, of which the most important aspect is product protection. We can tailor atmospheres in the package to be compatible with the quality of the contents. This achievement will require appropriate sensors and the ability to control the process because the safety of the package contents depends on maintenance of the composition of the atmosphere, and of the temperature. Therefore, preservation achieved solely by packaging in a controlled atmosphere depends on the ability to have very rigorous control of the system.

Another important innovative area is that of "active packaging" (Labuza and Breene 1989). By this we mean using the surfaces or the accessible interiors of the packaging materials as reaction sites of some sort. Thus one can produce compositions that will absorb oxygen; compositions that will desiccate (remove

---

List 17-4.   Food preservation techniques of the year 2000: Characteristics.

1. Flexibility:
   • Modularity, adapted to characteristics of raw materials and desired products
2. Combination of different methods into single process:
   • Electron beam or X-ray equipment
   • Heat exchangers
   • Microwave equipment
   • Water activity control
   • Control of gas composition
   • Controlled release of preservatives
3. Computer-aided control:
   • Real-time response
   • Specific indicators for specific properties
   • Data acquisition and retrieval

water); and compositions that will absorb ethylene, so that ripening of fresh fruits and vegetables is delayed or controlled. One can build into the package devices for directing the microwave energy. One can now build enzymes into surfaces that can do certain things with any volatiles that contact them. Of course, all of this methodology requires good control methods.

In addition to absorbing or removing undesirable atmospheric components, it is possible to release or generate flavors, inhibitors, antioxidants, or other active atmospheric components from suitable systems incorporated into the package. A Japanese package system has a controlled release package containing absorbed ethanol, which is released slowly along with some vanilla flavor within packages of cookies or other baked goods. This maintains a sufficiently high concentration of ethanol on the surface of the cookie to prevent mold growth. One would not want to rely on this system to prevent botulism, but it is effective in preventing spot growth of molds, and the vanillin used prevents one from smelling raw ethanol.

Many other possibilities exist for package-incorporated active systems. For instance, they provide capabilities for "automatic switching." Assume, for example, that one is concerned with botulism. Assuming a refrigerated, low-pH product, one would be assured of the safety of the anaerobic condition as long as the pH was below 4.5. One could develop a device that would sense the pH, and when the pH was over 4.5, would generate oxygen or would puncture a hole in the package so it would admit air. This is a simple example, but other automatic switching capabilities exist, and many companies are looking at that kind of technology, which surely will become a reality in the near future.

Another area in which great advances will be made, beyond those already achieved, is shelf-life prediction. Developers at this time are focusing primarily on simple dating, either in code or in plain numerical code. This shows when things were produced or when the manufacturer recommends that product usage be discontinued. But in reality the life of a product is a function not simply of time but of conditions of storage. It is possible to build into the package, as is now being done in some products, a device that can be scanned automatically at the checkout counter, that can inform the consumer not only that a given product has been on the shelf n days, but that it has seen conditions that are equivalent, say, to $(n + 20)$ or $(n + y)$ standard days (referred to some reference temperature). One then can decide to accept or reject a product on the basis not only of age, but of age plus abuse. This might not be a particularly desirable device for the manufacturer, as it would result in increased rejections of products, but it might offer other advantages. The manufacturer could direct the distribution in such a way that the company would not necessarily ship first the material produced the longest time ago, but instead would ship products that had received the most abuse and would be likely to spoil sooner.

REFERENCES

Graham, J. D., Green, L.C., and Roberts, M. J. 1988. *In Search of Safety: Chemicals and Cancer Risk*. Cambridge, Mass.: Harvard University Press.

Hui, Y. H. 1979. *United States Food Laws, Regulations and Standards*. New York: Wiley-Interscience.

Karel, M. 1989. The future of irradiation applications on earth and in space. *Food Technol*. 43: 7, 95.

Labuza, T. P. and Breene, W. M. 1989. Applications of "active packaging" for improvement of shelf-life and nutritional quality of fresh and extended shelf life foods. *J. Food Process Preserv*. 13: 1–69.

McHugh, M. and Krukonis, V. 1986. *Supercritical Fluid Extraction, Principles and Practice*. Boston, Mass.: Butterworth Publ.

Seltzer, R. 1989. Alar on apples. *C&E News*, May 22, 1989, 4.

Sperber, R. M. 1989. New technologies for cholesterol reduction. *Food Processing*, Nov. 1989, 154.

Saguy, I., Levine, L., Symes, S. and Rotstein, E. 1990. Integration of computers in food processing. In: "Biotechnology and Food Process Engineering" (Schwartzberg, H. G. and Rao, M. A. eds.) chapt. 14. Marcel Dekker, NY.

Wells, J. H. and Singh, R. P. 1989. A quality based on inventory issue policy for perishable foods. *J. Food Process Preserv*. 12(4): 271–292.

Whitney, L. F. 1989. What expert systems can do for the food industry. *Food Technol*. 43(5): 120.

Chapter 18

Europe 1992: Constraints and Potentials for Food Manufacturing

Klaus Paulus and Susanne Langguth

INTRODUCTION

There has hardly ever been a political endeavor that has caused such a stir as the anticipated completion of the single market in 1992. Inside and outside the European Community (EC) the single market project has triggered a number of remarkable effects in advance of the event: national governments are beginning to see the acceleration of structural change as a key task of economic policy; a wave of company mergers is beginning to roll across Europe; U.S. observers criticize the European "fortress"; EFTA (European Free Trade Association) Member States are beginning to check their national legislation for compatibility with Community legislation. Clearly, what is behind all this is a general awareness that 1992 means a serious challenge and urgently calls for activities to help Member States remain competitive. There is a certain atmosphere of commencement, partly fueled by the "Cecchini-Report" (Cecchini 1988) itself and its prognoses, according to which the EC market will in the medium term increase its economic growth by 4.5% and create 1.8 million new jobs. But, there is also an undertone of skepticism from those who fear that the single market will curtail workers' rights, erode consumer protection, mean more problems for economically depressed geographic areas, and be a further burden on the environment. However, there is no time to be skeptical. The EC Commission as well as the EC Member States are trying to get as many draft directives adopted by 1992 as possible, in an effort to enhance integration by removing non-tariff barriers to trade.

THE SINGLE MARKET

The Cecchini Report was ordered by the Commission and contains relevant data concerning the European economy. The following facts and figures are taken from this report.

The EC is to change into a single economic space and to open up all internal borders by the end of 1992. For the time being, fragmentation still exists. There are different technical standards and regulations, different corporation laws and fiscal laws, and a large number of other trade barriers standing in the way of what is to be the Community's single market. For the time being, such barriers are causing major losses to Europe's business enterprises and, obviously, to its consumers.

Implementation of the single market represents a great challenge to political and business leaders. In accepting this challenge, they must set the scene for steady growth and international competitiveness. It can be expected that within a few years, given the inherent dynamics of a market integration process, Europe's gross national product (GNP) will grow by an additional 4 to 7%.

There are three types of trade barriers that must be removed to create a single European market:

- Material barriers, such as customs checks at internal borders, which cause delays and administrative costs.
- Technical barriers, such as national product regulations and technical regulations.
- Tax barriers, particularly with regard to different VAT (value added tax) rates and other consumption taxes.

A study involving 11,000 companies from a large variety of industries indicated that too much red tape and different national regulations are the two worst obstacles to trade in Europe. To the food industry and its companies, the large variety of technical regulations and standards in EC member countries is a continuous problem in trading across borders in Europe. The Cecchini Report states that contradictory regulations on ingredients and additives in only four products (chocolate, beer, ice cream, and pasta) cause an 80% cost increase over and above their total annual cost of one billion ECU (European Currency Unit). The European food industry, which is the EC's most important sector in terms of employment and value added, enters the competition of the 1990s well prepared. However, it must be noted that the ten most important producers in the world—with the exception of the two at the very top, Unilever and Nestlé—are U.S. companies. Non-tariff trade barriers not only restrict supply diversity but are costing the food industry between 500 million and 1 billion ECU every year (2 to 3% of value added).

For ten of the most important product groups (pastry, confectionery, ice cream, beer, mineral water, soft drinks, spirits, pasta, soups, and baby food) in the five EC Member States with the highest population, more than 200 non-tariff trade barriers were found, as shown in Table 18-1.

According to EC Commission studies, most European food producers are sticking to their old domestic markets. Only about every tenth company is so far represented in all five of the most populated EC countries, which means that a substantial portion of potential business is being left to competitors from third countries. On the whole, however, the production and marketing of foods constitute a very important business factor in the domestic market. The food sales

Table 18-1.   Non-tariff-barriers in foodstuffs.

	Identified	% of total
• Specific import restrictions	64	29.4
• Packaging/labeling laws	68	31.2
• Specific ingredient restrictions	33	15.1
• Content/labeling regulations	39	17.9
• Fiscal discrimination	14	6.4
	218*	100

*This is the aggregate number of barriers affecting the ten items studied in five countries concerned.

volume is about 400 billion ECU. So far only 6% of the European food market has been supplied by internal European imports, but the volume of this trade can be expected to increase soon.

The single market, once it exists, will be an entity of a respectable size. Its 325 million inhabitants created a 4.7-trillion-dollar GNP in 1988. This is about the same as that of the United States and about 70% more than that of Japan. The EC's trade volume with third countries in 1987 was 790 billion dollars, which makes it higher than that of the United States or of Japan.

CONSTRAINTS FOR THE FOOD INDUSTRY

It is extremely difficult to give a full, detailed account of all the constraints and conditions the food industry in Europe and non-European companies must struggle with when delivering products to the European market. Let us, then, narrow this analysis down to the three factors that most influence the situation.

The first important factor is legislation. The second important factor is the market situation, or, in the final analysis, the consumer. Even though we know that there never will be any such thing as the average European standard consumer, it is particularly important to scrutinize consumer structures and habits and their potential development between now and the year 2000. Finally, the last factor to be studied in this analysis is the possible impact of science and technology—that is, any scientific developments on the product side and any technological developments on the processing side.

These crucial elements, together with the food industry itself, determine the interplay of forces in the food market. Their interaction naturally is far more complex than can be shown here and needs to be carefully analyzed for every single concrete situation.

The Impact of Community Food Legislation

The producing and the marketing of food are important to the Community. Consequently, differences in foodstuffs regulations have a significant negative impact on the free flow of goods within the Community. More than 30 years after the foundation of what was then the European Economic Community (EEC), there still are a large number of such barriers along with many unsolved problems although the Community, soon after it began to exist, started making efforts to unify food regulations. The intent was to replace national provisions with European legislation, and what was achieved in those early efforts should not be overlooked. There is the EEC directive on labeling, and there are various directives on food additives, to name only a few prominent examples. However, the original attempt to harmonize rules about the composition and quality of foodstuffs, and, in the final analysis, the formulations of individual foods, largely failed. Moreover, there has been a general change in philosophy, brought about by some remarkable rulings by the European Court of Justice, based on Articles 30 and 36 of the Treaty of Rome—the principle that every product lawfully marketed in any of the EC Member States is marketable throughout the European Community. National regulations restricting the marketing of a specific item are only permissible where they can be demonstrated to be necessary in order to satisfy mandatory requirements such as public health, public safety, and consumer protection. Thus a food made and marketed in one Member State cannot be turned away at the border of another even if this product does not meet the legal requirements of the importing country.

In its "White Paper on Completion of the Internal Market," the Commission outlined its intended course of action to implement the Internal Market and get it to function properly by 1992. The Commission's strategy is basically to take the principle of mutual recognition of national regulations and norms as laid down in Articles 30 and 36 of the Treaty and combine it with a new attempt to make those laws conform that need to be in agreement.

The new unified accord concerning foods is outlined in the EC Commission's communication entitled "Completion of the Internal Market: Community Legislation on Foodstuffs."

The "White Paper" postulates, with regard to non-tariff trade barriers, that a product produced and put on the market lawfully in one Member State can be sold without any restrictions anywhere in the Community. The basis of this postulate is the assumption that "mandatory requirements in Member States regarding the protection of public health, safety and the environment are in essence equal."

Against this background and taking into consideration Court decisions based on Article 30 of the EEC Treaty, the adoption of conforming provisions is to be limited to those areas where the Court would otherwise rule national regulations to be permissible, even in cases where they might constitute a barrier to trade. It is mainly safety aspects that are affected.

The Commission does not intend to propose a unified agreement on the quality requirements of foods, so as not to introduce a vertical conformity that would lead to a Community-wide definition of formulations. It considers any food manufactured anywhere in the Community marketable everywhere, provided that it is offered under a label that gives the consumer sufficient information and is in no way misleading.

Here are two cases in point:

- Although it so far has been against the law in the Federal Republic of Germany to add vegetable protein to meat products, this provision will no longer apply because there are Member States that consider such products permissible.
- Although in the Federal Republic of Germany it has not yet been permissible to mix milk fat with vegetable fats, such products will in the future be allowed because other Member States have authorized them.

It is left to the individual Member State to say in each case whether the abolition of former bans is to apply only to imported foods from other Member States, or whether a liberalization should also apply to products manufactured in the country itself.

If in the future the exclusive principle will be that of mutual recognition, and there will be no Community provisions about the composition of foods, then labeling will begin to play a key role in ensuring the free movement of foodstuffs within the Community. The food name is particularly important; it fulfills the most important function of the product label in affecting the consumer's decision to purchase, in addition to other criteria. A number of difficult and still partly unanswered questions arise in this context: Whose food name is the correct one—the one used in the exporting country or the one used in the importing country? Can a Danish producer of marzipan, which is not marzipan under the German law because it is made of peach kernels instead of almonds, call his or her product marzipan in Germany, or, perhaps, Danish marzipan, or does the producer have to use a Danish word followed by explanations in German?

These questions appear rather trivial at first glance, but they are extremely important to the European food industry and to third-country suppliers, such as U.S. companies wishing to do business in the European market.

The EC Commission is seeking a symbiosis of several approaches to the removal of trade barriers, a combination of the basic jurisdiction by the European Court of Justice based on Articles 30 and 36 of the EEC Treaty and a blending of national provisions. The creation of Community legislation is reserved for those areas where the public well-being is concerned in the broadest sense.

It is the general perception of the Commission that especially food additives, packing materials coming in contact with food, dietetic foods, pesticide residues and environmental contaminants, veterinary drugs, specific manufacturing and treatment processes (food irradiation, deep freezing, certain methods of bio-technology), labeling provisions, and a Community system of food inspection should be included in Community provisions. This includes making those provisions conform that relate to sampling and analytical methods that will help official inspections.

In some of these areas, Community laws already exist; in other areas, legislation is in the process of being made. Unlike the principle of mutual recognition, the principle of this legislation is based on the assumption that the protection of public health is indivisible in the Community. This means that a provision, once it is adopted, must be applicable to all Member States, and no exceptions can be granted.

The EC Commission is—to give an important example—currently dealing very intensely with the regulations on food additives and their conditions of use in the individual Member States, to bring them into agreement. This can be done on the basis of a simple addition of all existing national provisions for a given substance provided that its ADI (acceptable daily intake) and maximum intake values permit this. In other cases, negotiations are required. It is the wish of all concerned to have health protection at the highest level possible. The work of the Codex Alimentarius Commission may also be of some significance in this context.

The EC Commission is supported in its activities by the Scientific Committee for Food (SCF), which operates like the Joint Expert Committee on Food Additives (JECFA) in that it assigns ADI values and performs other evaluations. Any Member State can designate its own scientists to advise the Commission.

The Commission has in all public statements emphasized the irrevocable character of the trend toward a Europe without any internal borders. The date when it is thought that the Internal Market will be a reality, December 31, 1992, is mainly a political date with no legal significance. Member States have set their own deadlines, and politicians have to discipline themselves to act accordingly. The deadline has no immediate legal consequences. There will be an Internal Market on January 1, 1993, only so far as provisions have been adopted by that time. It can be safely assumed that total harmony will not have been achieved by then, and not all trade barriers will have come down.

The Impact of the "Euro-Consumer"

To the food industry as well as to the individual food producer it is important to know the composition of a potential market. Thus certain market characteristics are of great importance to food producers in estimating future market potentials.

As shown in Figure 18-1, the European Internal Market will be the most densely populated market of the Western world (Heyder 1989). Its population distribution, both absolute and relative, is shown in Figure 18-2.

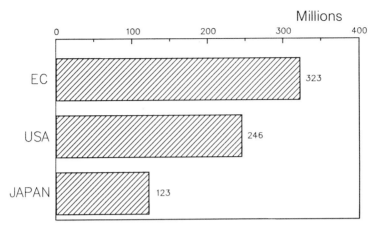

Figure 18-1. Comparison of the total population of three major consumer markets (Heyder 1989).

The Internal Market will be an attractive place for business not only with regard to its consumer potential but also in monetary terms. In 1988, people in the EEC spent 2,840 billion dollars on consumption, whereas people in the United States spent 3,140 dollars. In per capita terms, however, the EEC falls far below the levels of the United States and Japan. In 1988, the average annual spending levels for private household consumption per capita were at 5,613 ECU in the EC, 14,077 ECU in the United States, and 8,298 ECU in Japan. Between EC countries, there naturally are major differences in consumer spending (Figure 18-3). Germany is at the top of the list with its 8,336 ECU; Portugal is at the bottom with 1,654 ECU. This difference clearly reflects the difference in the distribution of wealth in Europe. Spending on food is the highest

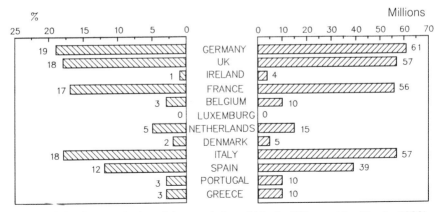

Figure 18-2. The distribution of the population within the EEC countries (Heyder 1989).

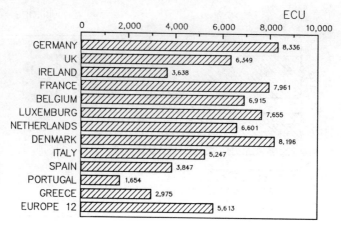

Figure 18-3. Per capita consumer spending of personal households in 1988 (ECU = European Currency Unit; Europe 12 = average of all 12 countries) (Heyder 1989).

in Denmark, where it amounts to about 1,961 ECU. Germany with its 1,443 ECU falls somewhere in the middle, together with Belgium, The Netherlands, and Italy. France (1,650 ECU) and Ireland (Eire) (1,623 ECU) are clearly above that level. In relative terms, Greece and Portugal also have a large percentage of total consumption spent on food (Figure 18-4).

These figures reflect different structures in consumer spending but also different market situations. A future leveling out of market differences is certain to bring about changes in consumer behavior, and, in the long run, it also will

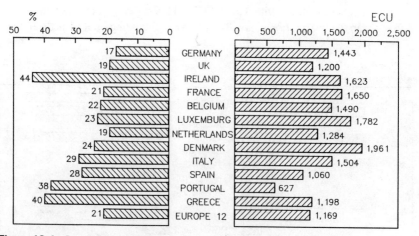

Figure 18-4. Per capita spending on food in 1988 (ECU = European Currency Unit; Europe 12 = average of all 12 countries) (Heyder 1989).

have consequences on the structure of consumer spending. Figure 18-5 shows the relative development of food spending in the EC. It appears from this graph that there will be an almost spending constant level in the next few years, especially because there will be hardly any additional population growth.

Another determinant of market opportunities in Europe is the European consumer's attitude vis-à-vis this large new marketplace. Consumer attitudes in the EC are mainly positive. With regard to food, a considerable portion of the European population considers it an advantage that attractive goods will be on sale in all EC countries. What consumers wish to see is a product range for sale in their own country that is equally available in other countries—that is, similar product diversity all over Europe.

Against this rather general background, we now address some specific points. These comments are related to some general changes affecting consumer habits. The Commission itself has ordered several studies to be made in this field, and some of their main results will be summarized.

In a study on technological change in agriculture and in the food industry and on policy changes with regard to food production, nutrition, and consumer health and safety, several factors were found that will be most relevant to future developments of the food system (Gormley, Downey, and O'Beirne 1986):

- The interaction between food, health, and the consumer will continue to constitute an important challenge for the food production and processing sectors.
- Consumer organizations will gain further influence in Europe and bring more pressure to bear in food-related problem areas.
- Consumers will continue to prefer foods that are valuable from a nutritional and physiological point of view as well as being attractive in appearance,

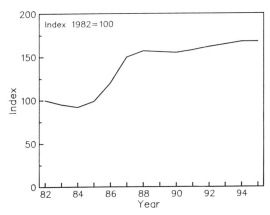

Figure 18-5. Annual spending on food in the EC (1982 = 100) (Heyder 1989).

fresh, and natural. Organic food will continue to be in fashion. On the other hand, there will be an increasing demand for convenience foods and ready-to-serve products with a healthful quality.

- There will be an increasing need for a European consensus in official recommendations on food intake, and this will have an effect on individual eating habits as well as on nutrition policies. Unfortunately, in EC Member States no full and comparable data are available on actual food intake. A study currently is under way in Germany on this subject, which will provide much more accurate information on actual food consumption and concomitant eating patterns than has so far been obtained from consumption statistics.

- It is essential that there be comprehensive nutrition education programs, which would be instrumental in stopping the kind of misconceptions that sometimes develop with too much information. A proper nutrition education is fundamental to a sound general attitude about health. Consumers are increasingly worried about hidden hazards in their daily diet. These worries can be remedied only if the consumers have adequate knowledge about nutrition and are well informed on the causes and the true extent of potential risks in food.

Another report looks at eating behavior in various industrialized countries (Wheelock et al. 1987). In these countries there is growing agreement on what constitutes desirable nutrition behavior; so recommendations can be kept to a few generally accepted essentials:

- There should be a balance between energy intake and energy consumption.
- Given today's living situation, it is recommended that consumption of fat be reduced, especially saturated fatty acids.
- Sugar consumption, too, generally is seen as unhealthy, not because sugar is harmful in itself but because a decrease in its consumption can have a favorable effect on reducing energy intake.
- The consumption of salt is largely viewed as too high although salt-related health problems generally affect only consumers with hypertension.
- An increased intake of dietary fiber generally is regarded as desirable.
- It is recommended that alcohol be consumed only in moderation.

These recommendations agree well with dietary recommendations in the United States. They have been endorsed and actively supported by some national governments, so that they do have an effect on people's eating behavior.

In nearly all EC countries the demand for milk has declined. The demand for certain dairy products, however, such as milk desserts, yogurts, and soft cheese, has increased enormously over the past 10 or 15 years. Moreover, there is beginning to be a decline in meat consumption, and there have been noticeable shifts in demand from some meat products to others. The increase in poultry consumption has been considerable. Despite a trend to more natural and fresh products, the demand for convenience products continues to increase in all types of food. The demand for fish, too, has been increasing in the past 10 years. Consumption of fruit and vegetables continues to rise, and in some areas, such as fruit juices, enormous rates of increase have occurred. Whole grain cereal products have doubled in quantity over the past decade. Sugar consumption has not continued to increase, but has declined somewhat. In fat products the balance between saturated and unsaturated fatty acids has changed favorably, with a decrease in the saturated variety.

On the whole, greater emphasis has been placed on vegetable products than on animal products. This has helped to increase the proportion of carbohydrates in the average diet, which, given present living conditions, has been found to be greatly desirable.

The Impact of Food Science and Technology

Food processing is a technology that must not be seen in isolation; it has many links to other disciplines. Historically, it usually has taken a long time before progress in other technological fields has eventually trickled down to the food processing sector, however. This is so partly because of the size and structure of the food industry. It is a leading industry in all EC countries in terms of sales, but its structure differs very much from that of other large industries, as it is dominated mainly by small and medium-sized companies.

Given the importance of the food industry, a number of surveys have been undertaken to determine where future developments will lead it and to characterize its most important parameters. Of special importance is whether and to what extent developments in food science and technology will have an impact on the EC food industry by the year 2000. In the context of these developments one can see the needs of the European food industry, as well as some important indicators for a European science and technology policy and other relevant EC policies. It is of particular value to try to estimate which of the new technologies and scientific developments will have the greatest impact on the future of the food industry.

In a survey involving 63 experts, an attempt was made to forecast developments until the year 2000 (Young 1987). In the 1990s food science and technology will have a great impact at the manufacturing, product, and consumer levels, resulting in more efficient production of foodstuffs and effecting improvements in both quality and "freshness." More efficient production will be achieved by a variety of techniques, with the most important contributions probably coming from increased levels of computerized automation and process control. Major improvements in process and equipment design and more efficient processing methods (e.g., microwave heating and aseptic processing) also will help to increase production efficiency. The possible impact of processing methods by the year 2000 is shown in Table 18-2. The rate of consumer response to the processes listed in Table 18-2 is expected to influence the intensity and the speed of development. (An example is food irradiation, with a quite variable legal status throughout the EC and differing attitudes about the method among consumers in different countries.)

The net consequence of these developments will be a predicted 25% decline in employment levels in the EC food industry by the year 2000. Although it is difficult to quantify their impact, developments in science and technology will contribute to a continuing decline in the usage of certain food additives, notably synthetic colors and flavors (excluding synthesized nature-identical materials) and preservatives. The probable reduction by the year 2000 is shown in Table 18-3. The bulk of food additives replacement will relate to synthetic colors and flavors, as listed in Table 18-4. The likely development of a new range of preservation techniques will fuel the reduction in the use of preservatives.

Despite the current uncertainty about irradiation, results from this study indicate that it will have a medium to major impact by the year 2000, particularly in the areas of microbiological control, sterilization of packaging material, increasing the shelf-life of fresh produce, and pest control in commodities and raw materials. If adopted on a widespread scale, irradiation could markedly reduce the incidence of food-poisoning outbreaks throughout the EC. With the bulk of food-poisoning outbreaks associated with the consumption of fresh/chilled foods, the predicted doubling in the consumption of such products over the next 15 years makes the widespread adoption of irradiation techniques even more desirable. Clearly, if irradiation is going to be in use in the year 2000, industry will have to exert a considerable effort to counter the ever-stronger voice of the antinuclear lobby.

The impact of biotechnology into the food industry will not be so great as in the agricultural sector although, clearly, some developments in the agricultural

Table 18-2. Impact of processing methods by the year 2000.

	None	Slight	Moderate	Major	Total replies
Aseptic processing	0	1	18	25	44
Irradiation	0	11	18	15	44
Gas/modified-atmosphere packaging	2	2	22	18	44
Microwave/RF heating	0	3	21	20	44
Ultrafiltration/reverse osmosis	0	10	17	17	44
Extrusion cooking	0	5	23	16	44

Table 18-3. Predicted % replacement of synthetic additives by
natural additives.

Year	Lower quartile	Median	Upper quartile	Total replies
1990	10.5	20.0	46.5	42
1995	24.0	37.0	59.5	42
2000	30.0	52.5	77.0	41

sector will indirectly benefit the food industry. For example, the use of cell culture techniques and cloning will cause an improvement in the quality of a number of primary raw materials used by the food industry. Cyclical shortages of some food ingredients, notably natural gums, also could become a thing of the past through the exploitation of genetically modified plant strains that are less susceptible to climatic change than strains today. Possibly the most important contribution of biotechnology to the food industry will come from its use to modify raw materials (e.g., fats and starches), imparting to them improved processing and sensory characteristics. One could envisage the modification of fats by enzymes or microorganisms so that they would be less harmful from a dietary standpoint.

Turning to traditional processing techniques, the growing importance of fresh/

Table 18-4. Predicted changes in the use of food additives in the
EEC food industry by the year 2000 (100 represents
no change; 200 represents a doubling).

	Lower quartile	Median	Upper quartile	Total replies
Natural colors, including synthesized, nature-identical colors	150	200	285	41
Synthetic colors, excluding synthesized nature-identical colors	25	40	80	41
Natural flavors, including synthesized, natural-identical flavors	135	185	273	42
Synthetic flavors, excluding synthesized, nature-identical flavors	30	80	85	42
Emulsifiers and stabilizers	90	104	130	42
Flavor enhancers	70	100	134	42
Natural sweeteners	80	100	135	42
Synthetic sweeteners	110	131	172.5	42
Preservatives	50	75	105	41
Antioxidants	62.5	92	115	41

chilled foods in the market has been demonstrated, with a doubling in consumption predicted by the year 2000. Over the same time period, the experts estimated the consumption of canned foods would decline 30%, a figure in line with the views of many research centers. For frozen foods they predicted an increase of 10% by 1990, but there was some uncertainty about subsequent consumption, as further development probably would be affected by the unpredictable contributions of novel food processing techniques. The average forecast was a cumulative increase in frozen food consumption of 25% by 1995 and of around 35% by 2000, but the variation in the estimates was from minus 3% to plus 88%.

As to the likelihood of scientific and technical innovations over the next 15 years, the inherent and predictable conservatism of the food industry will tend to be a limiting factor. Growing consumer awareness and concern about food processing practices (e.g., irradiation) also could limit innovation.

Although there is a continuing trend toward increased scientific and technical sophistication, there could well be a growing consumer demand for products manufactured by traditional methods. This in itself would create the need for a more skilled, knowledgeable, and versatile work force.

With the predicted increasing dominance of large and technically more sophisticated companies, attention also should be paid to small operations, which do not enjoy the same economies of scale. To this end, an increase in the number of regionally centralized facilities, offering the latest processing techniques and advice, should be encouraged.

At the production level, developments in the area of process control and more widespread use of mathematical modeling techniques will enable the food manufacturer to produce a more uniform product in terms of taste, texture, color, and so on.

New packaging materials and techniques will result in the appearance of more fresh, portion-controlled food products, catering not only to the consumer at large but specifically to the increasing number of elderly consumers. The prime aim will be to provide all consumers with increasing levels of convenience.

Thus, the general impact of science seems to be rather clear, but it could be useful for individual food manufacturers to recheck the situation as it affects them from time to time.

POTENTIALS FOR THE FOOD INDUSTRY

The various constraints and potentials cannot be readily separated from one another; so some of the food industry potentials were covered in the preceding section of this chapter.

The food industry is, in itself, part of the food system. Therefore, it is important first of all to take a look at the system as a whole in order to better describe the patterns of system interactions and how they impact on the food industry. Then we shall see how the European food industry thinks a joint EC policy conceivably might look. Finally, this section will show how an individual company will have to adjust to the situation if it wants to use the potential of the Internal Market well.

The Food System in Europe

The main elements of the food system can be characterized in a simple diagram (Figure 18-6), which also shows the interdependence of the individual elements (Dawson et al. 1986a). The food system in the EC accounts for 20% of the work force, or 24 million people employed. Of these, 10 million work in agriculture, 4 million are employed in food processing, and another 10 million work in the sectors of catering and distribution. The food system contributes 10% of the Community's GNP and accounts for about 10% of its imports and 8% of its exports. This makes it an important component in a growing world food market, from which it imports about 20% of its food and to which it exports 16% of its production (Commission of the European Communities 1988). Food processing comprises 2% of the GNP and employs 3% of the Community work force. What must be remembered with these figures is that there are differences between all levels of the system, as well as within and between individual Member States. Agricultural production units vary from a few acres up to several thousand acres, and the food processing sector ranges from family-operated cheese dairies to gigantic multinational corporations; and in distribution the

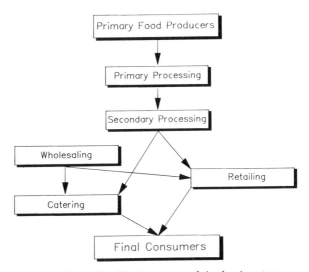

Figure 18-6. Simplified structure of the food system.

scope is from the independent local corner store to highly concentrated super-market chains. In catering, there are fast-food franchises on the one hand and exclusive restaurants on the other.

In Figure 18-6, a distinction is made between primary and secondary processing. Primary processing means agriculturally oriented companies that turn agricultural produce into a semifinished product for further processing, such as flour milling. Secondary processing includes companies that make products geared to consumer needs, mostly with a high degree of convenience level.

Various interactions among the components of the food system tend to indicate trends in the single market. Another recent survey (Dawson et al. 1986b) yielded the following predictions;

1. For the primary producer/processor interface:
   - The number of farms is expected to decrease.
   - The average size of the production unit in agriculture is expected to increase.
   - Food processing will be continuously concentrated in larger plants.
   - Larger firms are expected to become more important in food processing.
   - More vertical integration will take place between primary producers and food processors.
   - There will be an increase in agricultural cooperation.
   - Price support from the European Community for agricultural products is expected to decline.
   - Grants from the European Community for investment in food processing are unlikely to become more generous.
   - The involvement of multinational companies in food processing in the European Community is expected to increase.
2. For the processing/wholesaler/retailer interface:
   - Direct trading between retailers and food processors is expected to continue to increase.
   - Concentration in food retailing is expected to increase.
   - The number of product lines carried by food retailers is expected to increase.
   - The product ranges of food processing companies are expected to widen.
   - The number of food retail enterprises will decrease, indicating a concentration on this area as well.
   - The share of grocery sales taken by private label brands is expected to increase slightly.
   - More joint planning will take place between food retailers and food processors.

3. For the retail/consumer interface:
   - Price is currently the most important element for the consumer, but product quality is expected to grow in importance.
   - Increased awareness of food ingredients is likely to be an important element in food-buying decisions for one-third to two-thirds of consumers.
   - There will be some trend to the use of small shop formats in food retailing, but it will be of minor significance.
   - The increasing segmentation of consumer markets will encourage the development of specialized food retailers.
   - Extension of shopping hours is expected, particularly by 1995. This will mainly benefit large food retailers.
   - It is expected that at least 25% of supermarkets and hypermarkets will adopt laser scanning systems by 1990, and 50% will have adopted these systems by 1995.
   - Shopping by television is unlikely to have a major impact on consumer shopping behavior for food.

The Views of the European Food Industry

More than 30 years ago the various national organizations of the European food industry joined together to form today's Confederation of the Food and Drink Industries of the EEC (CIAA). Among other activities, the CIAA tries to monitor developments in the European domestic market that are relevant to its industries and to stimulate activity as needed, in addition to channeling industry concepts and requirements into relevant EEC processes in order to get the food industry directly or indirectly involved in decision making. In the past few years, the CIAA has made repeated significant contributions to developments at the EEC level, either by contributing its expertise in difficult technical matters or by providing its own general policy deliberations.

In a 1989 position paper, the elements of an EEC food industry policy were reevaluated (CIAA 1989). With regard to the four priority areas to be regulated at the EEC level, the CIAA took a clear position:

- *Protection of public health:* The food industry assigns top priority to this issue and thus has cooperated with all organizations that have made efforts in this field, and it will continue to support the Community as it has done in the past in every effort to promote a high level of public health. Some prominent areas of concern now and in the near future are food additives, packaging materials especially plastics, irradiation of foodstuffs, flavors, and organic products.

- *Consumer information and protection:* The CIAA welcomes the Commission's concept of ensuring the provision of adequate consumer information, mainly via labeling. Irrespective of this, however, it should be possible in specific cases to introduce product specifications in order to bring about a certain minimum quality standard.
- *Fair trade:* The principle of mutual recognition comprises not only consumer protection but also the protection of the producer against unfair competition. In the food industry context this would include the use of systems that verify specific claims concerning, say, quality, and that take charge of verification and certification processes.
- *Food control:* In order to handle the above concerns adequately, the firm regulation of food control is of paramount importance. The CIAA considers it absolutely essential to coordinate national regulations because differences of the type that do still exist between Member States must be seen as obstacles to the free exchange of food products in the Community. Moreover, the consumer must be able to rest assured that imported foods are safe to eat; otherwise, it will be impossible to develop free trade. The control necessarily must be carried out in the producer country, but the methods have to be identical everywhere. Food control institutions in each Member State have to operate according to the same concept, which obviously requires them to be at the same technical and information level.

The key policies of the EEC's food industry, roughly described above, show that there is considerable agreement between the concepts of political leaders and those of the food industry. It is the aim of the CIAA to find a viable and justifiable solution for the future of the common food market, to stand by that solution within the food industry, and to help implement it in practice. To achieve these goals, a framework is needed within which individual companies can operate under a given set of circumstances. Hence, major action is required at the company level to monitor developments of the single market and to evaluate and plan one's own potential development.

The Necessary Actions of Individual Food Manufacturers

A summary of developments over the past few years and of the forecasts for the next few years reveals a number of aspects that are of general importance to the future of the food industry in Europe. Figures 18-7 through 18-12 summarize these points (Paulus 1987). The illustrations first show the developments that led to the situation described, followed by the necessary actions of the food industry and finally the general problems that must be solved, particularly at the R&D level.

Figure 18-7 depicts the globalization of food sourcing on the European

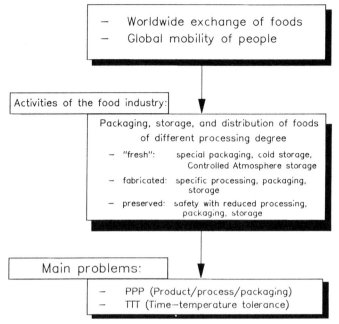

Figure 18-7. Aspects of the greater variety of foods with globalization.

market. This constitutes a challenge to the food industry in that the products vary in terms of degree of processing (value added), which calls for adjustments, particularly in terms of PPP (product, processing, packaging) and TTT (time–temperature tolerance).

The trend toward less intensely processed products and for more natural foods is considered in Figure 18-8. In this case, it is especially important to bear in mind the food system discussed above under ''The Food System in Europe.'' The main problems arise in the area of storage conditions for untreated and chilled foods, with regard to hygiene. Recent incidents involving *Listeria monocytogenes* have demonstrated that the situation is not quite as clear as it sometimes is assumed to be.

The situations documented in Figures 18-9 and 18-10 reflect the fact that despite a trend toward more natural foods there is a persistent interest in products with a long shelf life and a high level of convenience. However, consumers also are expected to develop a growing quality consciousness. There are still major activities required of the food industry, as outlined in the figures. The main difficulties listed in each case suggest that it will be necessary to take a much closer look at process optimization, with regard to both the kinetics of processes and process-induced changes in relevant ingredients and physical properties of the products concerned.

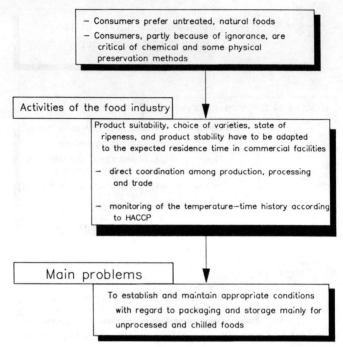

Figure 18-8. Aspects of producing a greater proportion of less intensely processed food products.

Figure 18-11 relates to the health food trend. This illustration covers products that rank among health foods because of their original composition, such as products with a high dietary fiber content or a high nutrient density, and products to which certain ingredients have been added.

Figure 18-12 is concerned with the need to close the gap that frequently exists between industrial production and kitchen use. In many fabricated foods, the chain of unit operations is interrupted at a certain point, leaving the remaining steps to be performed in the consumer's kitchen. The transition often is not a very smooth one, and industry should do something about it. The problem is of a technical nature, and persons addressing it should solicit the cooperation of manufacturers of household equipment.

From the information presented in Figures 18-7 through 18-12 we conclude that the food development of the 1990s most likely will be characterized by three key issues: safety, nutrition, and quality.

Although the food industry will have to take a more scientific approach to meet the challenges of the 1990s, its total R&D expenditure still is comparatively low. The R&D spending-to-output ratio was increased from 0.2 in 1970

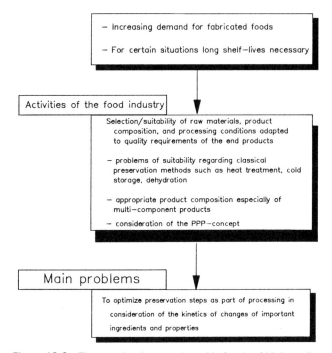

Figure 18-9. The growing interest in stable foods of high quality.

to 0.8 in 1980 (OECD 1986). This is a standard OECD measure regarding the level of technology in a given sector. According to this standard, the food industry has moved up from "low-tech" to "medium-tech." Despite this positive development, it must be said that the food industry is confronted with a large number of problems regarding innovation, and product innovation in particular. This makes it all the more important to select the right research activities today to lay the foundations for developments that may require another 10 or 20 years to be achieved.

Food-related research in the EEC in the past was limited to two COST (European Cooperation in the Field of Scientific and Technical Research) projects, one on the physical properties of foods and the other on quality changes in foods. Both projects drew worldwide attention despite their relatively low financial support. Meanwhile, there are two concrete programs in the field of agro-industrial research, FLAIR (food-linked agro-industrial research) and ECLAIR (European collaborative linkage of agriculture and industry through research). FLAIR is intended to increase the food industry's efficiency and competitiveness, especially in small and medium-sized enterprises, in order to improve the safety and the quality of foods for the benefit of the consumer, as well as to

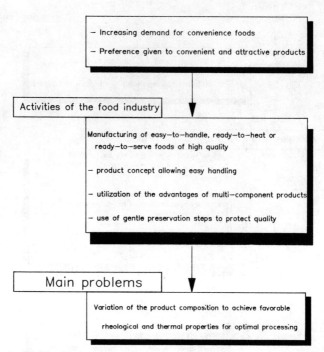

Figure 18-10. The growing interest in convenience foods of high quality.

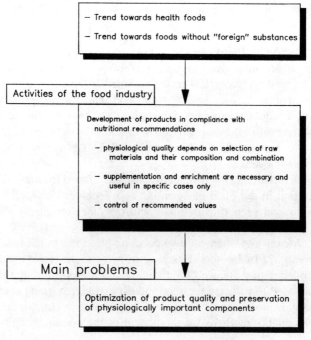

Figure 18-11. The development of health foods.

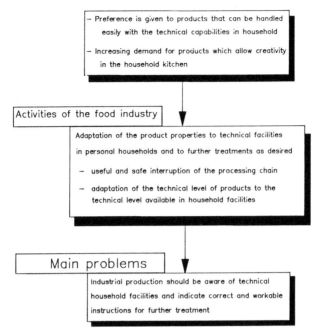

Figure 18-12. The development of products adapted to technical standards of household equipment.

enhance the sector's scientific and technological infrastructure and in that way help the European food industry.

The other long-term program, ECLAIR, aids the investigation, adaptation, and development of agricultural products for industrial use, in addition to investigating and promoting new industrial technologies for the processing and conversion of farm products, with the aim that marketable industrial products will be made under economically viable conditions.

Without doubt, the movement toward a single European market has significantly spurred research activities. Research constitutes an important link that will bind the elements of the European food industry even more closely together.

OUTLOOK

The question arises of how one company can possibly meet the challenge of the single market. The answer is that it can do so only with the necessary amount of quality assurance. The purpose of a quality assurance system will always be to secure the quality of products in the framework of company goals and company policy, to identify quality problems, and to plan, carry out, and monitor remedial action.

Quality assurance is a hierarchical structure consisting of quality policy, quality management, quality control, and quality documentation (Paulus 1989). Quality assurance is a far-reaching concept that needs to be fully supported by the whole company. It deals with all kinds of points, of both an individual and a collective nature, that may possibly have an effect on the specific product quality of a food. Quality has to be understood as the most comprehensive description of a product's relevant properties. The essential component that must be integrated into such a quality assurance system, and into a company's strategy, is the significant development of food legislation, as has been elaborately described in this chapter. Provided that the obstacles are duly considered in a forward-looking manner, a company operating in the single market will, despite certain constraints, find that the single market brings a tremendous opportunity for growth.

REFERENCES

Cecchini, P. 1988. *Cecchini Report. The Advantage of the Internal Market*. Baden-Baden: Numos Verlagsgesellschaft.

CIAA. 1989. *Elements of an EEC Food Industry Policy*. Brussels: Confederation of the Food and Drink Industries of the EEC.

Commission of the European Communities. 1988. *The FAST II Programme: Results and Recommendations*. Vol. 5: *The Future of the European Food System*. Brussels: Directorate-General Science, Research and Development.

Dawson, J. A., Shaw, S. H., Burt. S., and Rana, J. 1986a. *Structural Change and Public Policy in the European Food Industry, Part 1*. Brussels: Forecasting and Assessment in Science and Technology, Commission of the European Communities.

Dawson, J. A., Shaw, S. H., Burt, S., and Rana, J. 1986b. *Structural Change and Public Policy in the European Food Industry, Part 4*. Brussels: Forecasting and Assessment in Science and Technology, Commission of the European Communities.

Gormley, T. R., Downey, G., and O'Beirne, D. 1986. *Technological Change in Agriculture and the Food Industry, and Public Policy in Relation to Food Production, Nutrition and Consumer Safety*. Brussels: Forecasting and Assessment in Science and Technology, Commission of the European Communities.

Heyder, H. 1989. *1992 und der "Euro"-Verbraucher*. Bonn: Centrale Marketinggesellschaft der deutschen Agrarwirtschaft m.b.H.

OECD. 1986. *R and D, Invention and Competitiveness*. Paris: OECD Science and Technology Indicators.

Paulus, K. 1987. Can market and consumer trends as well as nutritional requirements be realised technologically? *Kemia. Kemi*. 14(10 B): 1049.

Paulus, K. 1989. Maintenance of food quality: more important than ever. *Food Marketing & Tech*. 3: 11–14.

Wheelock, J. V., Frank, J. D., Freckleton, A., and Hanson, L. 1987. *Food Consumption Patterns and Nutritional Labelling in Selected Developed Countries*. Brussels: Forecasting and Assessment in Science and Technology, Commission of the European Communities.

Young, J. N. 1987. *The Impact of Food Science and Technology on the EEC Food Industry in the Next 10–15 Years*. Brussels: Forecasting and Assessment in Science and Technology, Commission of the European Communities.

Chapter 19

Strategies for Global Product Development

Ray A. Goldberg

The purpose of this chapter is to outline trends affecting the global food system and the positioning of firms in it. As these firms develop strategies for global product development, they do so in the context of a restructuring of the value-added food chain from input supplier to ultimate consumer. To assess the impact of changes on the global food system, one must have a reference point against which to measure potential changes in the structure, linkages, functions, and kinds of participants in the food system. Table 19-1 shows the dollar changes in the major sectors of the food system over the last four decades with projections forward to the year 2028. Global farm supplies by 2028 will have had a 16-fold increase, from $44 billion in 1950 to an estimated $700 billion in 2028; farming a nearly 12-fold increase, from $125 billion in 1950 to $1,465 billion in 2028; and food processing and distribution a 32-fold increase, from $250 billion in 1950 to an estimated $8,000 billion in the year 2028. The $5\frac{1}{2}$-trillion-dollar agribusiness economy of the year 2000 will become a 10-trillion-dollar economy by 2028.

What have been the trends and private and public policies that have helped to shape the food system of the past, and what structure will emerge in the future? Historically, from the end of World War II to the early 1970s global grain surpluses in the United States acted as a shock absorber for the food system of the world. In many cases government programs determined price signals, and most food processors and retailers really did not believe that they were part of or needed to be part of a vertical value-added food chain from input supplier to ultimate consumer. Raw materials were freely available. The 1970s changed all of that, as suddenly the shock absorbers were no longer present. Processors and retailers became aware that a shift had occurred to a seller's market so that the quantity and quality of agricultural commodity products no longer were always assured. Food and energy prices fueled global inflation. In both developed and developing nations, the recognition of the importance of a global agribusiness that utilized half the world's assets and half the world's labor force, and provided half the world's consumer expenditures, made that business a political and economic priority for all nations. Food security, nutrition, resource management, food safety, efficiency, yield, and value-added became important

Table 19-1.   Global agribusiness estimates (billions of dollars).

	1950	1960	1970	1980	2000	2028
Farm Supplies	44	69	113	375	500	700
Farming	125	175	255	750	1115	1465
Processing and Distribution	250	380	600	2000	4000	8000

Source: Author's estimate based on discussions with USDA economists.

factors in evaluating food policy and the private–public policy changes of the food system.

The 1980s led to volatile changes in supplies, with gluts and shortages occurring throughout the decade. In the midst of the new awareness of a global food system, scientific breakthroughs in molecular biology provided new knowledge of the component parts of plants, animals, and humans that enabled scientists to make changes in the production process, nutritional components, and diagnostic procedures that improved the efficiency, quality, health aspects, and nutrition of the world's food supply. The advances in molecular biology also enabled land to become not just a food, feed, and fuel factory but a potential pharmaceutical factory as well. In essence, this new scientific tool enabled farmers for the first time to adjust to changes in climate and to provide alternative ways to improve traditional crops and animals while creating nontraditional products in a more environmentally sound manner. This freedom and flexibility at both the farm and the manufacturing levels made it possible for tailor-made foods, feeds, fuels, and pharmaceuticals to be produced on and off the land. It also provided means for closer collaboration of all the segments of agribusiness—farm suppliers, farmers, food processors, and distributors.

The 1990s are fast becoming the decade in which new uses of molecular biology actually will result in branded products with real differences in taste, appearance, nutritional values, and product safety. This value-added focus at every stage of the vertical food chain is occurring at the same time that dramatic shifts in population and age groups and attitudes toward health, safety, and nutrition are taking place. The "graying" of America and other developed countries has led to a new consumer group that requires special attention, in terms of product, packaging, and presentation. At the same time, political and social attitudes have changed to the point that many consumers want and expect to have a choice in selecting bodily and environmentally friendly products. All of these changes in product and population are part of an agribusiness revolution that is global in the sense of markets, sourcing, technology, and competition.

REVOLUTIONS

The revolutions that have occurred have been in the areas of biotechnology, packaging, organizational structure and demographics.

Biotechnology

Biotechnology makes it possible to produce noncaloric noncholesterol beverages and foods without adversely affecting the taste and texture of traditional foods. These foods can be tailored to meet specific nutritional, taste, and safety specifications. Specific seed companies already have been approached to develop a "seed brand" for a specific type of cereal in cooperation with major cereal companies. Such seed gene innovations are patentable under the plant variety protection laws. In such a case, the farmer is asked not only to share in the increased yield of his or her crop but also to share in the increased value-added of the crop. For the first time in history the farmer is able to brand his or her product and move away from the traditional commodity structure of the farm. Even the by-products of grain at the farm level such as corncobs and cornstarch enable environmentally sound products such as biodegradable plastic bags to be produced, which in turn provide additional outlets for farm production. Again, the by-products can be branded. Similarly, unique feeds have been produced that when fed to chickens lower the cholesterol content of eggs or help produce eggs that when consumed lower the cholesterol of the consumer. These new feeds exist in Europe and produce eggs that sell for twice the price of regular eggs. Similarly, nonresidue grapes sell for 20¢ a pound more in one supermarket chain. Farmers are producing not only food, feed, and fuel but pharmaceutical products as well. The farm is fast becoming a plant factory that is capable of producing brandable differentiated products and by-products. In addition, in animal agriculture, growth proteins not only increase livestock, poultry, and fish yields, but they do so in a way that increases the meat content and lowers the cholesterol levels of these foods.

Historically, the farm commodity surpluses of the past tended to rely on commodity processed private-label products to help get rid of unwanted surpluses. Most of the time these surpluses were pushed through farm cooperatives rather than being market-driven. Today members of the farm community are desirous of improving both yield and quality as well as adding unique attributes to their products. They have witnessed the success of the Ocean Spray Cooperative approach and want to use that type of product differentiation as their model.

The ability to control quality and value from farm inputs to final consumer products is creating new joint ventures between manufacturers, input suppliers, and farmers, as well as new joint ventures between retailers and farmer-owned manufacturing operations. In California alone, five regional chains own a common dairy and a common orange juice operation that, in turn, has contractual relationships with the farmers. These relationships also exist overseas. One supermarket chain provides orange trees and production boxes, and the Chinese, in turn, provide labor and land to produce mandarin oranges of a certain quality for that chain. Similarly the Eli Lilly Company and Amul Dairy of India recently signed a memorandum of understanding for the development and registration of a range of biotechnology products for use in dairy cattle and buffalo in India, including bovine somatotropin (BST) and other new agricultural products of biotechnology. The NutraSweet Division of Monsanto, having created a "brand" for a sweetener input, is working on other new ingredients and new foods for the twenty-first century such as Simplesse, which reduces cholesterol in ice cream and other dairy products. In essence the technological, legal, patentable nature of tailor-made seeds, animals, and major ingredients in the global food system has added a new and increasingly important brand partner in the value-added food chain. The willingness of the consumer to pay a premium for these quality, nutritional, and safety-oriented products is, of course, key to the ultimate funding of these new joint ventures and new companies.

Packaging

A second revolution is occurring in the packaging that maintains the quality of fruits, vegetables, and meats (as discussed at length in Chapter 5).

The aseptic package has had a major impact on shelf life and quality of a variety of products. For example, in New York City as this is being written (in 1990), Minute Maid is test-marketing a plastic aseptic package for its premium orange juice. I was told that researchers sampled the product after 120 days of storage and found its quality identical to that of the highest quality orange juice put into the package at the start of the packaging process.

There are firms such as the Don Watt Company Case that specialize in changing either the label or the package or both for a product. They can enable that product to move from a number 2 position in the world, not by changing the product but by changing the label and/or the package. These types of consulting firms work with both store-owned brand or manufacturer's brand operators. In essence, the package and the label have become as important as the product in communicating to consumers a genuine response to their taste, nutritional, health, and safety priorities. In addition, some stores have created a whole new brand, such as Loblaw's President's Choice and new Loblaw's President's Choice Green, that represents environmentally and bodily friendly products. These products include safer natural nontoxic nonresidue pesticides as well as organic vegetables and biodegradable plastic bags and containers.

Structural Change

The structural revolution is being fueled by new global competition, consolidation, and volatilities and a new market orientation among marketing boards, industry associations, and private–public cooperative national food policy institutions. In 1988 alone, U.S. acquisitions by overseas companies amounted to 33 billion dollars from the United Kingdom (such as Grand Met's acquisition of Pillsbury and Christian Brothers), as well as Canada's 10 billion dollars, Japan's 8 billion dollars, France's 7 billion dollars, and Australia's 4 billion dollars. Some 25% of all U.S. farm inputs are produced by non-U.S. firms, with some 1% of U.S. farmland and 20% of U.S. food manufacturing and retail distribution owned and operated by non-U.S. firms.

Consolidation is occurring at every level of the global value-added food chain, from input suppliers to distributors. Even at the farm level, of the 155 million farms in the world 133 million have less than 10 acres of land, and 1 million of them produce most of the commercial farm sales. In the United States, some 1 million farms out of 2 million receive 85% of their income from nonfarm sources. The top 200,000 super family farms produce most of the U.S. farm products. Not only are the functions in the food system being performed by fewer decision makers, but the logistic system is being shortened by the elimination of some of the traditional distributors and replaced by more direct sales, contracts, and/or even joint ventures.

While these consolidations are occurring, price volatilities in the basic commodities of the food system are increasing because of dramatic shifts in grain inventories (180 million tons in one year, with 130 million tons in the United States alone—along with genuine concerns about the greenhouse effect, water shortages, etc.), as well as the freeing-up of foreign exchange rates, interest rate changes, and a lowering of the level of government programs. These factors have all added new uncertainties to the food system. New risk management tools are being created to manage these new risks, together with futures markets, which exist 7 days a week, 24 hours a day to provide ways of minimizing the risks. These risk management tools are used by both buyer and seller and thus in many cases become another approach to utilize with buyers and sellers.

Not only is consolidation occurring on an individual firm base, but horizontal joint ventures are taking place as well, such as the recently announced joint venture of U.K., Holland, Italian, Swiss, and German supermarkets, providing a purchasing group with multi-billion-dollar purchasing power on a global market basis. In addition, vertical arrangements are being encouraged by firms that specialize in bringing buyers and sellers together in joint product promotion operations, even joint R&D product development. The learning curve advantage of these new experimental horizontal and vertical strategic alliances will permit those firms not to view each other in an adversarial buyer–seller position, but as partners trying to meet the consumer's new priorities in the global food system.

Many of these firms originated as quasi-governmental bodies and have become market-oriented to the point of creating their own global brands, such as the Dairy Cooperative and Marketing Board of New Zealand. Other countries try to develop a national awareness of their food products in national terms, such as the food processors and the government of the United Kingdom.

All of these new alliances indicate structural changes that encourage more direct relationships among the participants in the vertical value-added food system.

Demographics and Intelligence Networks

The most important trend, which drives all the other revolutions, is the change in global and domestic demographics. Globally the engine for change is Southeast Asia. In the next 40 years, the proportion of world income is expected to shift from its present 30% in Southeast Asia to over 60% in those countries. Thus countries such as Korea, Malaysia, Thailand, the Phillipines, and so on, will play a pivotal role in the changes affecting both commodity and value-added product markets.

Domestically, the consumer demand for quality, convenience, nutrition, health and safety, and products that are environmentally sound, and the system's ability to respond to these justifiable needs have led to minimarkets that are housed by super stores to provide responses to the various market segments. The information revolution, with the ability to know instantly what each consumer wants and when and how these wants can be translated into demand, has helped the retailer to play a more important role in creating brands that not only reflect the image of the store but also directly respond to the market segments to which the store wants to appeal.

ORANGE JUICE—A CASE IN POINT

Twenty years ago, as I did my original work in the orange juice industry, the concern was that the wholesale price differential could not be too high; otherwise, a firm would lose marketshare. The industry was dominated by private labels primarily owned by farm cooperatives. The wholesale price differential was at the 22% level for the leading brand, and 83% of the product was frozen, with chilled accounting for only 17%. By 1988, frozen orange concentrate had declined to 44% of the market. Three leading brands now exist rather than one, with the wholesale price differential for the three averaging over 40%. Selected premium chilled brands and freshly squeezed orange juice vary from promotional prices of chilled brands of $1.99 for 64 ounces plus general promotional allowances to a regular price of $2.39 for a 64-ounce package. Freshly squeezed orange juice varies from $2.99 for 64 ounces at Trader Joe's to $4.59 for that same 64-ounce package at selected gourmet supermarkets. Packaging, as noted above, now includes aseptic biodegradable plastic containers. Not only is there brand and product proliferation, but quality differentials have been improved by an upgrading of technology to get the highest recovery of orange essence and the lowest oil content. At the same time, one can buy Orange Light (with aspertame instead of fruit sugar), or one can purchase orange juice with calcium added. The nature of the whole industry has changed. The supply is now global, with Brazil and other importers smoothing out the U.S. supply and protecting the shelf space of the whole industry, as the commodity nature of private labels is reduced to only slightly more than a third of the market.

ALTERNATIVE STRATEGIES FOR THE 1990s

The following six approaches are examples of how individual firms or collections of firms are responding to these changing phenomena:

1. *Marks & Spencer and Loblaws:* Their approach is to be the leader of change and create unique brands, such as St. Michael's, President's Choice, and Nature's Choice, that provide premium brand leadership for the market.
2. *Unilever:* This company has acquired a major plant research biotechnology entity in the United Kingdom in an effort to relate R&D to the tailor-making of foods for its total organization.
3. *Pioneer Hi-Bred Seed Company:* This company is revising its R&D to help the farmer increase not only yield but also quality; and it is doing so with joint ventures in mind, in order to tailor foods for either the manufacturer or the retailer or both.
4. *ConAgra:* This company is the largest farm supply company in the United States with over a billion dollars in sales just at the farm level; and at the same time it is the second-largest poultry and the largest beef and flour miller and frozen dinner manufacturer in the country, providing value-added at each level of the vertical food chain. In addition, it is beginning to work on a collaborative basis with retailers developing potential joint market intelligence programs for their products. Moreover, the company understands that grain is at the heart of its vertical value-added food system, and it is an active participant in the international grain trade.
5. *Grand Met:* This company represents a new breed of global brand product leaders. Their publicly stated mission is to be global, to be low cost, to have brand leadership, and to develop new products. Grand Met's acquisition of Pillsbury in the United States has already led to a global emphasis on the unique products of this company.
6. *Consortiums:* Finally, we have the emergence of consortiums, such as that noted in the *Wall Street Journal* of Europe on May 19–20, 1989, in a story about the accord reached between Argyll Group PLC and two European food companies (see Figure 19-1), which offered opportunities for cooperation in the areas of "marketing, distribution, production, development and exploitation of store formulas," as well as management

THE WALL STREET JOURNAL/EUROPE FRIDAY - SATURDAY, MAY 19 - 20, 1989

EUROPEAN BUSINESS ROUNDUP

Argyll Studies Links With Ahold, Casino

LONDON – Argyll Group PLC said it signed accords with two European food companies that may lead to cooperation agreements.

Argyll, which trades as Safeway Stores in Europe and the U.S., said it will examine commercial opportunities with Koninklijke Ahold NV of the Netherlands and Etablissements Economiques du Casino Guichard Perrachon & Cie. of France.

Links among the three concerns could be made in marketing, distribution, production, development and exploitation of store formulas, Argyll said. The companies will also consider ties in management informations systems and other computer applications.

Ahold, a retail grocer that owns the Albert Heijn supermarket chain, had sales of 15.3 billion guilders ($7 billion) last year. The company owns substantial food-processing capacity and is an institutional catering supplier.

Casino is a food retailer that operates a variety of stores, from convenience outlets to hypermarkets. It also processes food and has commercial restaurant operations. Casino had sales of 51.4 billion French francs ($7.8 billion) last year.

In the U.S., Casino owns restaurants, retail stores and cash-and-carry warehouses. Ahold operates in the U.S. through Bi-Lo Stores, Giant Food Stores and First National Supermarkets. (AP-DJ)

Figure 19-1. Announcement of Argyll–Ahold–Casino accord. Source: *The Wall Street Journal/Europe*, May 19–20, 1989.

information systems and other computer applications (Anonymous 1989). From this article it is evident that these firms are already planning for a more unified Europe in 1992. They have already been joined by an Italian supermarket chain since the news release.

All of these strategies call for new working relationships with all segments of the vertical value-added food system and the ability to take each firm's strengths and figure out how to utilize the products of biotechnology, information, packaging, and structural revolution to meet the needs of an ever-changing global market. Those firms that can obtain a competitive advantage in anticipating change and wisely choose the appropriate partners to respond to that change will be the global leaders of the food system. Moreover, the aging of the population of the developed countries and the extreme youth of the developing world, with its anticipated population explosion of another billion people by the turn of the century, require the development of foods that meet the nutritional needs of all segments of society.

Throughout this book, the emphasis has been on food product development from concept to marketplace; but the ultimate driver of the system has been a market-oriented economy that recognizes the importance of food in providing for a healthy and productive society. Both public policy leaders and consumers are demanding better quality, nutrition, safety, packaging, efficiency, and information from the global food system. They recognize that over 50% of the increase in longevity in the United States alone over the last ten years has been due to a change in diet. The announcement in March of 1990 of proposed new labeling recommendations—to better inform consumers of the saturated fat, cholesterol, calorie, and fiber content and the serving size of the contents of food packages—is but a first step in improving the knowledge base of consumers so that they can make better-informed decisions on the new products that are being developed by the food system. The success of "Healthy Choice" products in the marketplace is but one indication of the fact that people do not look upon food simply as a means to enable them to improve their health; rather they want food to keep them healthy. At the same time, some consumer groups are concerned about new biotechnological breakthroughs, as they do not understand the scientific principles or the terminology involved. Creative communication is needed to educate consumers about the new products based on these breakthroughs, which are enabling the production of tailor-made differentiated products.

In summary, biotechnology and information breakthroughs are providing a new revolution in food product development. The ability of the food system to respond and develop new products that are more efficiently produced, that are packaged for a longer shelf life, that are environmentally friendly, that are nutritionally responsive to each of the emerging segments of society, and that meet maximum food safety requirements has never been greater. What is required in the transition is a management perspective that can provide leadership in this increasingly complex but most exciting industry. The competitive arena is global, and the market needs and expectations are enormous. The challenge invites our most creative solutions.

REFERENCE

Anonymous. 1989. Argyll studies links with Ahold, Casino. *The Wall Street Journal/Europe*, Friday–Saturday, May 19–20, 1989, European Business Roundup.

RECOMMENDED READING

Goldberg, R. A. 1988. Company strategies in a restructured global seed industry. In *Research in Domestic and International Agribusiness Management*, Vol. 8, ed. Ray A. Goldberg, pp. 265–289. Greenwich, Conn.: JAI Press.

Goldberg, R. A. 1988. A global agribusiness market revolution: The restructuring of agribusiness. In *Research in Domestic and International Agribusiness Management*, Vol. 9, ed. Ray A. Goldberg, pp. 145–154. Greenwich, Conn.: JAI Press.

Index